Tears, Liquids and Porous Bodies in Literature Across the Ages

Tears, Liquids and Porous Bodies in Literature Across the Ages

Niobe's Siblings

Norbert Lennartz

BLOOMSBURY ACADEMIC
LONDON • NEW YORK • OXFORD • NEW DELHI • SYDNEY

BLOOMSBURY ACADEMIC
Bloomsbury Publishing Plc
50 Bedford Square, London, WC1B 3DP, UK
1385 Broadway, New York, NY 10018, USA
29 Earlsfort Terrace, Dublin 2, Ireland

BLOOMSBURY, BLOOMSBURY ACADEMIC and the Diana logo are
trademarks of Bloomsbury Publishing Plc

First published in Great Britain 2022
This paperback edition published 2023

Copyright © Norbert Lennartz, 2022

Norbert Lennartz has asserted his right under the Copyright,
Designs and Patents Act, 1988, to be identified as Author of this work.

For legal purposes the Acknowledgements on pp. viii–x constitute
an extension of this copyright page.

Cover design by Eleanor Rose
Cover image: Auguste Dominique Ingres, La source (The source) (1856), Musée d'Orsay,
Paris. Courtesy Peter Willi / ARTOTHEK

All rights reserved. No part of this publication may be reproduced or transmitted
in any form or by any means, electronic or mechanical, including photocopying,
recording, or any information storage or retrieval system, without prior
permission in writing from the publishers.

Bloomsbury Publishing Plc does not have any control over, or responsibility for,
any third-party websites referred to or in this book. All internet addresses given
in this book were correct at the time of going to press. The author and publisher
regret any inconvenience caused if addresses have changed or sites have ceased
to exist, but can accept no responsibility for any such changes.

A catalogue record for this book is available from the British Library.

A catalog record for this book is available from the Library of Congress.

ISBN: HB: 978-1-3501-8696-5
       PB: 978-1-3501-8711-5
       ePDF: 978-1-3501-8697-2
       eBook: 978-1-3501-8698-9

Typeset by Integra Software Services Pvt. Ltd.

To find out more about our authors and books visit www.bloomsbury.com
and sign up for our newsletters.

Contents

List of figures	vii
Acknowledgements	viii
List of abbreviations	xi
Introduction	1

1 Porous bodies before (and after) the discovery of pores   19
   Ambivalent manly tears on the stage   19
   Niobean fountains   28
   Liquid masculinity: From dark Shakespeare to oozy Metaphysicals   35
   Utopian and dystopian floods – abdominal tears and drowning Quixotes   51
      Pornutopian halcyon days   51
      Drowning Don Juans – invitations to banquets of bulimia   57
      The Quixote's disgust at Pandora's box   65

2 Niobean bodies in the era of Romanticism   73
   Niobean sentimentalism   73
      Pamela's effusions in the closet   73
      Porous *Hommes* and *Femmes Machines*: *Fanny Hill*   81
      Porous Gothic porn: *The Monk*   86
   Stony poetics versus porous effusions: Wordsworth and Coleridge   93
      Wordsworth's anti-porous architecture   93
      Coleridge's riotous fountains   100
   Niobean snakes, giants and monsters in Keats and Byron   107
      Keats's alchemy of evaporation   107
      Tidal and porous 'affairs' in Byron's poetry   115

3 Far from the madding Romantic crowd: The anti-porous turn in the Victorian age   127
   From body to stone: The myth of Pygmalion reloaded in Victorian fiction   127
      The sister as Pygmalion: *Goblin Market*   127

Pygmalion and the genre of the *Bildungsroman*: *Jane Eyre* and *David Copperfield*	133
Marital mausoleums, sepulchral beds and tragic masks in damp times	143
The Gorgon in the Victorian marriage bed	143
The mad and porous woman in the tomb	148
The advent of the stony stoic	151
A stoic in distress: *Tess of the d'Urbervilles*	151
The failure of stoicism and dry Niobean convulsions: *Jude the Obscure*	156
Vampiric agents of porosity	161
The importance of being self-contained: Victorian dandies	171
4 (Re-)Liquefaction at the dawn of the twentieth century	**181**
Rebirth of carnivalism in James Joyce's *Ulysses*	181
Modernist language as a laxative	181
The descent into the porosity of death	188
'After us the savage god', or the explosion of the new porous women	193
Porousness unleashed: Unsexing Bloom	201
Re-enter Mrs Grundy: Lawrence's rekindled puritanism	209
Misogynist wrath	209
Therapeutic porosity in *Lady Chatterley's Lover*	216
Linguistic Pentecost or a new word-prudery?	224
5 Niobean reverberations in post-war literature	**231**
Bibliography	241
Index	260

Figures

1. Leonardo da Vinci, Drawing of the Female Sexual Organs (n.d.), Bibliothèque des Arts Decoratifs, Paris — 30

2. Alonso Cano, *San Bernardo y la Virgen* (Saint Bernard and the Virgin) (c. 1645–52), Prado, Madrid — 50

3. Thomas Rowlandson, *A Family on a Journey. Laying the Dust* (1800), London, British Museum — 69

4. Jean-Baptiste Greuze, *La cruche cassée* (The Broken Pitcher) (1771), Paris, Louvre — 75

5. Gustave Courbet, *L'origine du monde* (The Origin of the World) (1866), Paris, Musée d'Orsay — 122

6. Jean-Louis Gerôme, *Pygmalion et Galatée* (Pygmalion and Galatea) (1890), Metropolitan Museum of Art, New York — 128

7. Guido Reni, *San Sebastian* (Saint Sebastian) (1615), Genoa, Palazzo Rosso — 177

8. René Magritte, *Le Viol* (The Rape) (1934), Menil Collection, Houston — 183

Acknowledgements

Working on my previous monograph *'My Unwashed Muse': (De-) Constructions of Eroticism in 17th-Century Literature* (published in German with De Gruyter in 2009), I not only came across a huge number of unwashed, sleazy and frowsy Muses, but I was also confronted with a disquieting array of open bodies, among which featured most notably that of the flagellated and crucified Christ: bruised, oozing with sweat and blood, weeping and in an abject state of porousness. The curiosity with which incredulous St Thomas penetrates Christ's wound with his transgressively probing finger in Caravaggio's famous 1601 painting invited me to follow suit and, after indulging in the pageantries of blood that painters and poets created out of Christ's and his martyrs' bodies, I widened my focal lenses on secular bodies and, with Niobe as my mythological patient zero, became interested in the porous responses that humans of different epochs gave to grief, pain or sexual stimulation.

Endowed with a good amount of curiosity, I began probing my academic fingers into many wounds, eyes and other inexpressible cavities, so that friends and colleagues wavered between amusement, pity and embarrassment when I embarked on my adventurous journey from the unwashed Muses to their porous and oozing sisters (and brothers). The journey was an adventurous, exciting, but also happily circuitous one, at times making me understand what astonished Gulliver must have felt when he was faced with the Brobdingnagians' shockingly magnified pores. That the journey into the pores and deepest recesses of the body took a bit longer than I expected was, however, not only due to Gulliverian curiosity, but also due to my two-year spell as one of the vice-principals of my university, an important time which introduced me into the vexingly Celanesque 'Porenbau' of German academic life.

I am very grateful to many colleagues who invited me to their classes, symposiums and conferences and gave me a chance to come out of the academic closet and to present tentative and raw versions of later chapters of this book: Nicholas Roe and Jane Stabler who invited me to St Andrews to present a still fragmentary version of my later full-length chapter on Byron and the Romantics' fear of Niobean bodies, Holly Furneaux (then still in Leicester), Lilla Crisafulli and Keir Elam (both in Bologna), all of whom invited me to their Master's classes to discuss my ideas about Dickens and the subversiveness of male tears and Gerold Sedlmayr from Dortmund who gave me the chance to be part of his fabulous panel on bodies at the 2012 supernumerary NASSR conference in Neuchâtel and generously granted me the rights to re-use parts of my essay 'Who's Afraid of Niobe? Lord Byron and the Romantics' Scepticism about Porous Bodies' (*Romantic Bodyscapes: Embodied Selves, Embodies Spaces and Legible Bodies in the Romantic Age*, ed. Gerold Sedlmayr, Trier: WVT, 2015, 199–210) in this book. At the memorable 2016 Wordsworth Conference at Rydal Hall, I was not only furnished with invaluable advice on Wordsworth's 'stony poetics', but also acquainted with great and dedicated scholars who opened up new vistas for me and veritably oozed with brilliant ideas. In this context, I was happy to meet Denise Gigante from Stanford who was willing to share ideas with me – an invaluable experience that introduced me into and made me appreciate the wonderful Anglo-American culture of feedback.

Other people were repeatedly and mercilessly subjected to my embarrassingly porous effusions on tears, fluids and bodies, and they responded not only with unwavering stoicism, but also with interest, encouragement, help and intriguing comments, in particular in phases when torrents of ideas, hypotheses and (often weird) assumptions were on the point of inundating me. My special and heartfelt thanks go to Aaron Mitchell for invaluable linguistic help; to Margarete ('Maggie') Schmidt for listening to many (provisional and often boring) pages with an unflinchingly supportive smile; to Elke Kalbe for wonderfully constructive feedback and prodding me on to send a sample chapter to the publisher; to Shona M. Allan who not only provided me with an ever-accessible 'helpline', but was also ready to undertake the Herculean task of proofreading the manuscript; and finally to Ben Doyle at Bloomsbury who so readily expressed his interest in this quirky project.

I am very grateful to the University of Vechta for (partially) overcoming their disgust at the topic and granting me a sabbatical to finalize most of the chapters; to my wonderful team at the English Department, Michaela Hausmann, Dana Jahn, Swantje van Mark, Oliver Schmidt and Leonore Sell who proved to be wonderful researchers, interlocutors and indefatigable sleuths in search for bodily porosity, sometimes perilously on the point of catching the infection of seeing porosity everywhere; to Teresa Pham, my patient colleague from the Linguistics Department who was never safe from my porous shop-talking and courageously endured its most vigorous onsets; and finally to Susan Marsland for her refreshing impersonations of muse, femme fatale and chef during the last stages of the book.

But my last and most sincere thanks go to Norbert Lennartz senior, my dad and most dedicated collector of my books, and also to my esteemed supervisor Rolf Lessenich who since my first seminars that I attended as a student at my alma mater, the University of Bonn, had been a source of ever-flowing inspiration and knowledge for me. It was Rolf who introduced me into the world of literature and opened up magic casements into fields where, unimpressed by dry and repetitive theoretical phraseologies, critics still crushed the rare grapes of joy against their palates. That his untimely death in February 2019 prevented him from seeing the book's publication and receiving it as a gift for his eightieth birthday fills me with deepest regret and grief.

Norbert Lennartz
Vechta, in the summer of 2020

Abbreviations

BH	*Bleak House*
BLJ	*Byron's Letters and Journals*
CHP	*Childe Harold's Pilgrimage, CPW 2*
CPW	Byron's *Complete Poetical Works*
D	*Dracula*
DC	*David Copperfield*
DJ	*Don Juan, CPW 5*
DS	*Dombey and Son*
E	*The Excursion*
FH	*Memoirs of a Woman of Pleasure (Fanny Hill)*
FLW	*The French Lieutenant's Woman*
GM	*Goblin Market*
JE	*Jane Eyre*
Jn	Gospel St John, New Testament
JO	*Jude the Obscure*
LCL	*Lady Chatterley's Lover*
M	*The Monk*
P	*The Prelude*
PA	*Pamela*
PDG	*The Picture of Gorian Gray*
Ps	The Psalms, Old Testament

SL	*Sons and Lovers*
Song	*The Song of Solomon*, Old Testament
T	*Tess of the d'Urbervilles*
U	*Ulysses*

Abbreviations of Shakespeare's Works

AYL	*As You Like It*
Cor	*Coriolanus*
Cym	*Cymbeline*
Ham	*Hamlet*
H5	*King Henry 5*
JC	*Julius Caesar*
KL	*King Lear*
Mac	*Macbeth*
MV	*The Merchant of Venice*
Oth	*Othello*
R2	*Richard 2*
R3	*Richard 3*
RJ	*Romeo and Juliet*
Son	*The Sonnets*
TC	*Troilus and Cressida*
Tit	*Titus Andronicus*
TKN	*The Two Noble Kinsmen*
TS	*The Taming of the Shrew*
VA	*Venus and Adonis*
WT	*The Winter's Tale*

Introduction

But adieu; these foolish drops do something drown my manly spirit. Adieu!
– William Shakespeare, *The Merchant of Venice* (c. 1596)

We track all things that weep, and bleed, and live.
– Percy Bysshe Shelley, *Prometheus Unbound* (1820)

In his 1977 *A Lover's Discourse*, Roland Barthes lamented the non-existence of a cultural history of tears and bodily fluids and asked the pertinent question: 'Who will write the history of tears?'[1] In the intervening forty-odd years between 1977 and 2020, this gap seems to have been partially filled, since critics such as Tom Lutz (in *Crying*) and Thomas Dixon (in *Weeping Britannia*) have written extensively on periods of intense lachrymosity, on literary works drenched in tears, and in the special case of James Elkins, even on sentimental paintings eliciting a profusion of tears from their admirers.[2] While these scholars concentrate on tears as cultural markers, as indicators of particular 'wet decade[s]'[3] and their outlandish rituals of grief, they tend to disregard the fact that a study of tears is only partially about real teardrops. More often than not it is a story about metonymies, about tears standing vicariously for otherwise unspeakable and embarrassing porosity, and about the loss of restraint in the face of an ooziness and incontinence (sweat, menstrual blood, urine, semen) that for a long time could only be discussed in metaphorical detours.

In contrast to what Rose-Lynn Fisher suggests in her recent volume of photographs *The Topography of Tears* (2017) where tears are seen along the lines of a disembodied *art pour l'art*,[4] tears and fluids cannot be thought of without

---

[1] Barthes, *A Lover's Discourse*, 'In Praise of Tears,' 180–82.
[2] Elkins, *Pictures and Tears*.
[3] Dixon, *Weeping Britannia*, 39.
[4] Magnified under a microscope, Fisher's tears metamorphose into arabesques and fantastic topographies. *The Topography of Tears*.

reference to the bodies and the sexes that exude them; a study on tears and fluids thus inevitably adds another stor(e)y to the Babelian tower of books about bodies and anthropology, about the history of sentiments and passions, and provokes questions as to the existence of gendered tears and fluids: is there a difference between female and male tears, are certain bodies more prone than others to sweating, dripping and oozing, and, from a diachronic perspective, what did different cultures and epochs do to conceal or to highlight such manifestations of bodily porosity? Steering clear of such anthropological questions, Dixon aims to frame tearfulness solely in terms of nation-building and thus sets about painting a portrait of the British nation 'through a series of lachrymose miniatures – a string of twenty historical teardrops'.[5] This hypothesis is as compelling as it is problematic and myopic: believing that the British weep differently, have divergent attitudes towards tears and are unique in their struggle with their proverbial 'stiff upper lip', Dixon posits another Brexit, this time in the history of tears and emotions. As a riposte to this kind of emotional nationalism, this book argues that tears and other bodily fluids are not so much a matter of nationality, of Britishness, Germanness or Frenchness: they are deeply embedded in European narratives of gender, body and anthropology. Romeo's blubbering body is, thus, neither genuinely British nor Italian, but that of an adolescent man in Renaissance times, of an immature sixteenth-century *Jedermann* who, by losing control of his economy of bodily fluids, is in danger of forfeiting his God-given position in the universal Chain of Being. That his tears are culturally (but not chemically)[6] different from those of Werther can then be traced to the fact that, in the course of 200 years, tears undergo redefinitions and revalorizations that are, however, never confined to one country, but, as Richardson's Pamela, Radcliffe's Valancourt, Schiller's Karl Moor or even Gustave Flaubert[7] seem to confirm, spread all over the world and even cut across fuzzy boundaries of species.[8]

The (literal) fountainhead of such a study is thus neither Margery Kempe, a notably 'extreme weeper' and, according to Dixon, 'the *fons et origo* of English tears',[9] nor Sinon whose excessive 'weeping / Did scandal many a holy tear',[10]

---

[5] Dixon, *Weeping Britannia*, 10.
[6] That older men shed saltier tears is an unproven assumption *in Coriolanus* 'Thou old and true Menenius, / Thy tears are salter than a young man's / And venomous to thine eyes'. *Cor* 4.1.21–23.
[7] In his semi-fictional novel *Flaubert's Parrot*, Barnes claims that Flaubert was a 'great weeper'. *Flaubert's Parrot*, 189.
[8] In *The Expression of Emotions in Man and Animals* (1872), Charles Darwin assumes that there are also weeping animals. Cf. Neu, 'A Tear Is an Intellectual Thing', 36.
[9] Dixon, *Weeping Britannia*, 15.
[10] *Cym* 3.4.59–60.

but the mythological figure of Niobe, a European goddess that, both in the context of Greek and Roman mythology and in (Christian) literary history, tends to be neglected in favour of more glamorous, awe-inspiring and erotic heroines, such as Danaë, Philomela, Proserpine or Eve-like seductresses. The daughter of Tantalus and Dione, the sister of froth-generated and aquatic Venus, she is shown in Ovid's *Metamorphoses* as boasting to Latona of her fertility and abundance of children (seven sons and seven daughters), thereby incurring Apollo's and Diana's wrath for their mother's humiliation and inducing them to eradicate her entire family (which had already been weakened by the loss to suicide of Niobe's husband Amphion). Niobe's tragic life as a bereft mother and wife has not only been considered less flourishing and, for artists of all stripes, less attractive than that of other mythological beings;[11] the medieval tradition based on the fourteenth-century didactic poem *Ovide moralisé* even exhorted its readers to comprehend her story as an early illustration of the deadly sin of pride and overreaching; only Dante seems to have taken a more lenient approach to her fate when he refused to consign her to hell, but rather, by way of compromise, placed her into the liminal sphere of the first circle of Purgatory in his *Divina Commedia*.

Yet, as soon as one takes Dante's cue and shifts the focus from what was, in the Middle Ages, pilloried as offensive and monstrous haughtiness by a woman to a more sympathetic and feminist view of her unbearable grief, Niobe turns into a more enigmatic and intriguing figure than artists and writers were ready to admit. Devastated by her disproportionate punishment, Niobe returns to her native region of Lydia where she is transformed by pitiful Jupiter into the miracle of a stone which is anything but 'numb and incapable of further emotion',[12] but has rather been incessantly and copiously shedding tears ever since: 'et lacrimas etiam nunc marmora manant'.[13] This paradox, which reverberates through different ages and cultures, from the biblical Pentateuch to T. S. Eliot's manifesto of Niobean absence in *The Waste Land* (1922), also invites readings from a new angle of anthropology and gender studies, since the moment Jupiter transforms Niobe into a weeping stone, he not only makes her represent two conflicting and irreconcilable extremes, liquidity and petrification, but also invests her with conditions, qualities and bodily textures that, in the subsequent centuries, came to be hotly contested in texts exploring the blurry roles of women and men.

---

[11] There is a considerable number of images of the death of her children (the Niobides), but Niobe's fate seems to have inspired no major works of art.
[12] Bate, *How the Classics Made Shakespeare*, 43.
[13] Ovid, *Metamorphoses*, 6.312.

It is at this point that the narrative of porous bodies touches upon and intersects with the oft-cited and well-documented history of the body's imaginary streams. While, in this context, the focus lies on the mythic fluid of black bile whose preponderance determines the fine and indistinguishable Theophrastic line between pathology and ingenuity, porous bodies tend to be, within the speculative framework of the Galenic humoral system, phlegmatic bodies not only exuding huge quantities of slime, rheum and saliva, but also expelling, in an act of cathartic evacuation, excremental tears and sweat.[14] Tears, sweat and other slimy and watery substances are, in contrast to the two bilious fluids, humours that are liminal, defined by the fact that they are 'expressed' and ejaculated from the inside to the surface of the skin and, thus, unlike the invisible or interior fluids, are embarrassing manifestations of what Julia Kristeva sees jeopardized as 'the integrity of one's "own and clean self."'[15] While both sexes were said to be made up of certain quantities of bodily fluids (with the male body having a more natural inclination for the biles and blood and the female body being more swayed by the 'moist star,'[16] the moon, and thus prone to irrepressible and visible eruptions of the watery and phlegmatic humour), physiologists at that time also stuck to the legendary idea that masculinity was synonymous with stony inflexibility, that man's life was a perpetual quest for hardness, solidity and form, whereas women challenged the economy of humours not only by being perilously open, abject and prone to liquidity, but also by being obstinately bent on enticing men to join them in their realms of watery and wasteful disorder.

In her (involuntary) blurring of the boundaries between stone and water, between humanity and the semi-animate world of objects, weeping and stony Niobe stands for a type of equivocation that early modern man found unsettling and as indicative of hellish chaos as the bearded Weird Sisters in *Macbeth*, who were shown to be neither male nor female and ready to change from corporeality to insubstantial watery bubbles.[17] Dreading what later critics defined as the impending 'crisis of distinction,'[18] faced with a hierarchy of beings which, in contradiction to E. M. W. Tillyard's later myth of order and ontological accuracy, lacked precision, the story of Niobe, as it was transmitted by Ovid in Arthur

---

[14] See Bright, *Treatise on Melancholy*, esp. 135–48.
[15] Kristeva, *Powers of Horror*, 53.
[16] *Ham* 1.1.117. See also the moon as the 'the watery star' in *WT* 1.2.1.
[17] Cf. Banquo's speech: 'The earth hath bubbles, as the water has, / And these are of them'. *Mac* 1.3.79–80.
[18] See Pfister, 'Man's Distinctive Mark', 33. That Pfister's 'crisis of distinction' pinpoints the 'porous demarcation line between man and animal' has also been corroborated by Höfele, 'Bestiarum Humanum', 86.

Golding's 1565 translation, must have been more than just a simple allegory of female overreaching and excessive grief. It encapsulated in a stone (rather than in a nutshell) the disquietingly paradoxical blending of porous femininity and petrified masculinity which generations of writers following the Tudors tried to comprehend, but more often to separate, to renegotiate and to correct.

Over the centuries, Niobe proved to be vexingly protean and seemed to take on numerous different identities. As an incessant weeper, she came to be conflated with the (Catholic-biased) Mary Magdalene in the Baroque age or with the (Protestant) Ophelia whose full-body affinity with water fascinated the Romantics and the Pre-Raphaelites, inspiring them to imagine her in the liminal role of a nymph, a mermaid or undine. While there is undeniably a difference between Catholic and Protestant approaches to tears and grief, with the latter subjecting Catholic effusions of tears to 'uptight Protestant astringency',[19] there is certainly no difference between Catholic and Protestant female bodies: both were denigrated as being porous and 'messy',[20] the difference in this case being only that Mary Magdalene actively 'expresses' and elicits the streams of lachrymose fluids while Ophelia's porous body yieldingly seems to absorb the brook's impregnating water.

Although stoniness was hardly considered compatible with ideas of femininity and the female gender was defined exclusively in terms of liquidity and oozy openness, the original Niobean antithesis of water and stone was not entirely forgotten, as it came to be elaborated into the popular image of the female fountain (the more civilized and modern equivalent of the rough Niobean stone in Ovid's version). As fountains of tears, but also of various other bodily fluids (menstrual blood, milk and vaginal fluid), women and their oozy condition were thought to be in dire need of being translated into objects of sophistication and male artistry. Fountains of all descriptions sprang up in Renaissance gardens, but also in public squares such as in Bologna where, at the central Fontana di Nettuno, wide arches of water are squeezed out of women's breasts and female lactation becomes an element of aesthetic joy. All these fountains aptly illustrate the male artist's Jovian self-understanding as a tamer not so much of shrews as of women's anarchic flows of liquids, whose grotesque hyperbolism he is entitled

---

[19] Dixon, *Weeping Britannia*, 34.
[20] See Munich who in this context refers to another porous woman in ancient mythology, Andromeda, contrasting with 'the knight's metallic containment' in various nineteenth-century paintings. *Andromeda's Chains*, 13–16.

to regulate, mitigate or orchestrate into elliptical patterns.[21] That the humiliating process of the shrew's taming in Shakespeare's early comedy of humours *The Taming of the Shrew* (c. 1589) ends in the *exemplum horrendum* of the rebellious woman as a muddy, clogged and troubled fountain is only consistent with Niobean notions of women as sources, streams and rivulets. In Shakespeare's play, the process of taming is tantamount to an act of cleaning and sifting the fountain's dirty waters of grotesque medieval times; that women's ooziness cannot be stopped (as the biblical Song of Solomon makes its male readers believe), but can only ineffectually be manipulated proved to be a continuous source of male dissatisfaction, anxiety and disgust.

Considering the fact that Shakespeare sees Niobe in a traditionally negative light, either as the epitome of female dissimulation in *Hamlet* (1601) or as the personification of performative tearfulness attributed to women such as Hecuba,[22] and thus prefers to stick slavishly to the pre-modern heritage that cast a slur on Niobean grief and ooziness, the narrative of this book unpredictably starts with a man, with Macduff in *Macbeth* (c. 1606) who, at the moment of finding himself flung into the Niobean situation of bereavement, is on the verge of losing his stony masculinity and of being converted into a male weeper. Bereft of his wife and his children ('my pretty chickens, and their dam'),[23] Macduff is shown on the cusp of turning into what was seen as the disgrace of a male Niobe, when he is restored to his state of masculine petrification by a good example of early modern male bonding: Ross and Malcolm instantaneously remind him of his stony masculine duties, of his obligation to translate grief into revenge and not into torrents of emasculating tears.

While writing these lines as a plea for Renaissance masculinity, Shakespeare must have been alert to the fact that the story of Niobean porosity was concurrently gaining new momentum at the beginning of the Catholic-friendly Stuart age and with James I as a more effeminate patron of the arts. In the guise of what later came to be known as Metaphysical poetry, in John Donne's allegedly 'strong lines', a new rhetoric of amplified grief and a new incontinence of words and tears gain ground; and what is, in this context, even more momentous is that poets of the early seventeenth century give up their self-fashioning as slavish imitators of sculpture and start to concentrate on the human body with

---

[21] See Bakhtin's definition of the grotesque body in terms of 'hyperbolization' in *Rabelais and His World*, 317. The Niobean body is, by contrast, a body tampered with, the product of embarrassment and Gulliverian shock at the gigantic dimensions of its apertures.

[22] See *Ham* 2.2.450–56 and also *TC* 5.11.18–19: 'There is a word will Priam turn to stone, / Make wells and Niobes of the maids and wives'.

[23] *Mac* 4.3.221.

the scrutinizing gaze of a medic or scientist. Still indebted to the Simonidian tradition of *ut pictura ut poesis*, Shakespeare, in the role of an 'iconic poet',[24] keeps on seeing human skin in terms of stony materiality, as marble, alabaster or bronze and stalwartly ignores what medical discourses in the wake of Thomas Elyot's *Castle of Helth* (1534) had insistently propounded: that man's body is not a slab of stone, but, to many people's dismay, an 'expressive screen',[25] covered by a membrane that is riddled with holes or pores, thus making him and her the epitome of frightful and unmanageable porosity.

With these insights seeping into the poets' store of knowledge, porosity, by the end of the seventeenth century, acquires a disquietingly new quality, in particular when, in the poetry of the Earl of Rochester, Niobean tears are marginalized and reinterpreted as seminal liquids that, at the moment of the speaker's premature ejaculation, ooze from every pore and threaten his masculine identity with the horror of total dissolution. While the Niobean body of weeping stone in Ovid is exempt from erosion and, irrespective of rules of economic calculation, knows no humoral exhaustion, the poet's sudden awareness of his oozing pores brings about the mortifying *anagnorisis* that the myth of the impervious male body is about to collapse under the piercing gaze of Enlightenment criticism. Macduff's unwavering grip on the masculinity of his stony body has, by the end of the seventeenth century and the dawn of modernity, been washed away and supplanted by what had hitherto been considered a monstrosity: the advent of porous Niobean man.

With the discovery of pores in literature, the history of the open body becomes confusingly multi-focal. While women and young porous men in Shakespeare's plays (such as Romeo, Laertes or Lucius giving a didactic lesson to his son in *Titus Andronicus*[26]) were still mono- or at least bifocal in the sense of being scandalously open either from their eyes or genitals (as Macduff had to learn in his burlesque conversation with his porous alter ego, the Falstaffian Porter), men in Rochester's Restoration circles were suddenly alerted to the shocking presence of innumerable cavities and orifices which defied all efforts at cerebral control. With the transference of the porous body into the modern age, the idea of the Niobean body becomes poly-focal, increasingly gender-neutral and all-inclusive, since the fluids that the porous bodies of both sexes exude are no longer emissions that can be confined to one or two manageable sources. The broadening of the concept of the Niobean body, the displacement of its tears by

---

[24] See Hagstrum, *The Sister Arts*, 73.
[25] Connor, *The Book of Skin*, 21.
[26] 'Come hither, boy, come, come and learn of us / To melt in showers'. *Tit* 5.3.159–60.

other bodily fluids (best exemplified by the 'perineal tear')[27] is, from different perspectives, supported by both Dixon and Lutz. While the former refers to a poem attributed to Alexander Pope that scathingly describes a (female) reader's response to Joseph Addison's play *Cato: A Tragedy* (1713) – 'But while her Pride forbids her Tears to flow / The gushing Waters find a Vent below'[28] (thus, marking the foray into grotesque openness as a faux pas) – the latter intriguingly suggests that the biochemical contents of tears can also be found in other bodily fluids and that, according to this scientific approach, the hyperbolism of tears, as it is found in the morally restrictive period of sentimentalism, is also a code for the emission of repressed and linguistically deflected genital fluids. Prior to Peter Carey's recent novel suggestively entitled *The Chemistry of Tears* (2013), people started to think about the components of tears and became aware that, alongside 'water, mucin, and oils', tears contained prolactin, a hormone that is also 'responsible for milk production'.[29] This milky ingredient can also be found in other chemical substances such as lactic acid which circulates through the whole body and is, in different degrees, discharged in sweat, urine and vaginal fluids. Thus, at the threshold of the modern age, the Niobean body is no longer that of an excessive weeper, and no longer is it confined to the British as 'a nation of proficient, sometimes virtuosic weepers';[30] it rather denotes bodies of both sexes and all nations that weep in a broader sense and from a variety of porous 'eyes', that uncontrollably break into perspiration, discharge urine or burst into exhaustive fits of bleeding which, at least since the disconcerting emergence of the Bleeding Nun in Matthew Gregory Lewis's Gothic novel *The Monk* (1796), had been understood as traumatic signs of 'menstrual excesses'.[31]

Despite the light of reason infiltrating into the seventeenth and eighteenth centuries, the body and its porous parts remain a dark territory. Even the language dedicated to bodily functions, to its oozings and hidden cavities is still replete with obscurities and mannerisms, as not only Samuel Pepys's diary and his macaronic confessions to extramarital porous skirmishes disclose. In this context, the eighteenth-century preoccupation with weeping, sweating or bleeding bodies turns into a lingua franca for the unspeakable sexual act, for the

---

[27] For this gynaecological aspect of an unsutured genital wound, see Bourke, 'Sexual Violence, Marital Guidance, and Victorian Bodies', 422.
[28] [Alexander Pope], 'On a Lady who P—st at the Tragedy of Cato: Occasion'd by an Epigram on a Lady Who Wept at it' (1713), quoted in Dixon, *Weeping Britannia*, 5.
[29] Lutz, *Crying*, 106.
[30] Dixon, *Weeping Britannia*, 5
[31] For these tokens of the 'horrifying disruptiveness of female materiality', see Mulvey-Roberts, *Dangerous Bodies*, 40.

odium of masturbation, or, if indulged in jointly, for the mingling of sexualized fluids (the prime example for Barthes and Lutz being Goethe's *Sorrows of Young Werther*).[32] The more the pores are opened and bodily fluids are discharged in moments of excessive sentimentality, the more the necessity of exercising what Eve Kosofsky Sedgwick circumscribes as the 'sphincter' of the will, of imposing a rigorous muscle-like form of (self-)censorship becomes prevalent.[33] While Victorian women revert to anorectical castigations as a way of censoring their unruly open bodies, the shell-like harnesses, the corsets and the carapaces of crinoline are definitely male inventions and responses to the unmanageably female genital fountains, strategies to incarcerate the threateningly porous body of the 'other' sex into sarcophagi of wire, whalebone and cloth (as if it emitted miasmatic fumes or radioactivity).

Representatives of the patriarchal Establishment, however, waged their war in the cause of restraint not only against women, but also against various tempters and emissaries of porous misrule sent into the world in the shape of monsters, beast-like imps and vampires to inveigle women into slackening their volitional sphincters and into escaping the mausoleums of Victorian decency. In particular, vampire literature – ostensibly so out of tune with Victorian sober-mindedness and Positivism – must be reread in the context of the persistent threat of Niobean porosity, but also of the putative infiltration of the membranes of non-resilient effeminized bodies by Oriental microbes.[34] The various metamorphoses that vampires such as the Transylvanian Dracula adopt are pernicious ruses to gain access to clean and aseptic Victorian women (and via their bodies also to men) and to reveal that, behind the facades of the disembodied angels in the house, the throbbingly luscious bodies were waiting to be tapped, to be set flowing, but also to be impregnated by all sorts of destabilizing germs of dissipation and disease which destroyed the strict regimen of marital chastity.

While the Victorians embarked upon all sorts of ideas and projects to shield women from discovering and indulging in their Niobean qualities and, as a precaution, relegated Niobe to the status of a museal curio and innocuous artefact, it was Lord Byron who previously introduced Niobe into his poetry in an astonishingly new light which, however, failed to invite critics to reassess discourses on the Romantic body. In Canto IV of his famous, meandering poem

---

[32] Barthes, *A Lover's Discourse*, 180 and Lutz, *Crying*, 39. Werther sharing tears with Lotte during a thunderstorm is a good example of the new, but embarrassingly circumlocutory 'culture of feeling'. Dixon, *Weeping Britannia*, 69.
[33] Sedgwick, 'Jane Austen and the Masturbating Girl', 831.
[34] Cf. Otis, *Membranes*, 151.

Childe Harold's Pilgrimage (1812–18), Byron has his autobiographical speaker connect the ruinous city of Rome with Niobe. Thwarting readers' expectations of seeing the speaker's melancholy reflected in the dilapidated city and his tears echoed in the rushing of the Tiber, Byron shows Rome, his 'Niobe of nations',[35] as being empty, dry and drained of tears.

Challenging the Romantics' inclination for following in Goethe's italophile footsteps and contributing to the apotheosis of Rome, Byron is attracted to his 'city of the soul', because, as the '[l]one mother of dead empires',[36] she seems to be responsive to the speaker's weltschmerz and his feeling of irremediable dislocation. In contradistinction to the Victorians' image of Niobean women as suspicious fountains whose spouts had to be hidden, draped, immured and rigorously monitored, Byron ushers in a new reading of the Niobean body, emphasizing her unflinching stoicism and her stony pertinacity. Deserted by her dead children and her inhabitants, bereft of her traditions and history, she is the epitome of stony deprivation (childless, crownless, voiceless), refusing to be compared to all concurrent or preceding representatives of inconsolable grief ranging from Ophelia and Mary Magdalene to Macduff and Manfred.[37]

Not only does Byron's re-contextualization of Niobe surprisingly repudiate the weeping and porous body (eventually culminating in Clara Talboys's stoic 'Niobe's face, sublimated by sorrow' in Mary Elizabeth Braddon's sensational novel *Lady Audley's Secret* (1861–62)),[38] texts by William Wordsworth and John Keats also prove that the Romantics were more partial to stones, petrification and architecture than stereotypical views of Romanticism seem to suggest. The Niobean body whose original equilibrium between stone and water had, in the wake of eighteenth-century sentimentalism, been ostensibly tilted in favour of tears and fluids, seems, with the advent of Romanticism, to be taking a turn towards stoniness. Although Keats is indissolubly linked to the epitaph that he wished Joseph Severn to paradoxically inscribe on his gravestone in the Roman cemetery for the Protestants – 'Here Lies One Whose Name Was Writ In Water'[39] – in his poetry, he seems to be more fascinated by stones, by Grecian urns and Elgin marbles, which, in the bitter competition with the bloody porousness of

---

[35] *CHP* IV, 703–06.
[36] Ibid., IV, 694/696.
[37] For the broader context of Romantic grief, see also Sandy, *Romanticism, Memory and Mourning*, in particular, 79–95.
[38] Braddon, *Lady Audley's Secret*, 200. Clara Talboys's Niobean face is cast in marble rigidity. In this respect, she is more in line with Byron's Niobe than with the myriads of swooning and tearful angels in the Victorian house.
[39] Cf. Roe, *John Keats*, 394.

his illness, promise longevity and the frozenness of the fleeting and flowing moment. The same holds true for Wordsworth: while there is admittedly, in Jonathan Bate's words, a 'constant under-presence'[40] of water to his life and an abundance of rivers, springs and lakes in his poetic works, there is also a striking tendency to keep the aquatic element in check, to revert to the stoniest subgenre of poetry, the epitaph, and to portray himself as a medieval builder of Gothic cathedrals.

Seen from this perspective, the Romantics were not only inordinately suspicious of corrosive water, tears, oozing and porous bodies, in their sympathy with dry, dehydrated and stoic Niobes, leech-gatherers or stony pipers, but they also presage late Victorian stoics and impervious heroes, the most notable of which is the dandy, the descendant of the Byronic Beau Brummell of the Regency period whose refined manners, impeccable dress and wordy cascades were supposed to be gem-like shields protecting him from the ooziness of the human condition. That Oscar Wilde, in his pose as an aestheticist and dandy, apostrophizes Niobe in his mythology-laden poem 'The Burden of Itys' (1882) is extremely intriguing: with an oblique intertextual reference to Keats's 'Ode on a Grecian Urn' – 'Sing on! sing on! O feathered Niobe, / Thou canst make sorrow beautiful'[41] – he turns Niobe into a Philomela-like emblem of beautiful sorrow which, in the subsequent stanza, is then pitted against the bleeding body of Christ which, as the emblem of abjection, falls short of the beauty of the ancient representatives of sorrow. Wilde even suggests a kind of hierarchization of grief, allotting Niobe – here devoid of all indications of bodily openness – the top position, followed by Philomela (vexing the 'sylvan quiet' with the acoustic porousness of her 'wild impassioned song'),[42] and then by Christ's sculptured, but repellent medieval body, wrecked as it is with porousness and pain: weeping and bleeding. As a bird-like chimera in Wilde's poem, nineteenth-century Niobe has undergone an astonishing range of metamorphoses from a ruinous city to a feathered evocation of the Romantics' nightingales and provided insights into the ways late Romantics and Victorians activated their volitional sphincters to respond to all onsets of porous grief.

Byron's and Wilde's array of personifications of porosity and suffering makes it clear that a study of Niobean bodies not only daringly straddles cultures and epochs, but that it is also a story of conflations, of analogies and appropriations which challenges and rewrites the givens of mythological tradition. When poets

---

[40] Bate, *Radical Wordsworth*, 18.
[41] Wilde, 'The Burden of Itys', 241–42. *Complete Poetry*, 48.
[42] Ibid., 258.

such as Byron reconstruct their Niobes according to their tastes or prejudices, and when Victorian writers disembody the female sex to create the illusion of turning the early modern phenomenon of the Bakhtinian 'leaky vessel'[43] into an angelic and decorative statue, the myth of Niobe suddenly and unexpectedly touches upon and overlaps with the myth of Pygmalion, the sculptor who, while chiselling a female figure out of a marble (or ivory) block, falls in love with it and entreats Venus to have it animated. In particular, the nineteenth century saw many resuscitations of the myth of Pygmalion, but what is strikingly new in the context of the Niobean body is not only that the Galateas refuse to meet the expectations of their creators,[44] but also that nineteenth-century men readily turn into anti-Pygmalions who are less interested in seeing their Galateas transformed into pulsatingly vivid and porous womanhood than in reconverting them into lifeless slabs of stone, ice or wax. Upending the love story between Pygmalion and Galatea and turning it into a narrative of power and subjection, of bodily enfranchisement and entombment, the narrative of porous bodies is also one of sexual antagonisms, clashes and battles which men wage to keep their own bodies immune from female porosity and from the corroding influences of emasculation. In this respect, there is a long and painful tradition that unexpectedly links Laertes in *Hamlet* with Jonathan Harker in *Dracula*, or Rochester's premature ejaculator in 'The Imperfect Enjoyment' with Leopold Bloom in *Ulysses*, the latter two in particular prove to be sexual failures and, instead of being able to objectify their female counterparts and turn them into marble objects, suddenly burst into floods of porosity that leave them annihilated, defeated or the abject and oozy butt of ridicule and stigmatization.

While the role of the anti-Pygmalion denotes activity, dynamism and the indomitable will to exercise the volitional sphincter, to incarcerate, to seal and to petrify their own and the female body, other men prefer the passively self-referential Narcissus as their role model and reduce Niobean women not so much to statues as to the dwindling voices of a repetitive echo. The dandies' narcissism (which, as Wilde illustrated, readily turns Niobe into a singing voice), their self-centred love and their obsession with parading their sartorial facade in front of mirrors is one of the most radical and defensive responses to the porosity of the democratized body politic, to the revolting seepage of the modern, effeminized metropolis, and as such a misogynist reaction to female ooziness which layers of cloth, paint and jewellery were unable to absorb. In Wilde's *The Picture of*

---

[43] See for the term, Paster, 'Leaky Vessels: The Incontinent Women of City Comedy', 43–65 and later her full-length study *The Body Embarrassed*, 23ff.

[44] Danahay, 'Mirrors of Masculine Desire', 49.

Dorian Gray (1891), there are, apart from Lady Narborough, only two women, Lord Henry's subsidiary wife, Victoria, an awe-stricken Wagnerite, a pithless creature 'leaving faint odour of frangipanni,'[45] and Sibyl Vane, a shell-like suicidal actress; both women flit through the novel as disembodied voices and echoes of their narcissistic lords and masters. While other harbingers of porosity, such as the vampire, are even deprived of narcissistic mirror reflections and need other porous bodies to attach themselves to, the dandy as the epitome of stoicism is not only a self-sufficient, inveterate hater of food and flesh, but he also minimizes the female porous body into nothingness so that the fetishization of his mirrored existence is never intruded upon by dreaded intimations of (female) corporeality.

It is certainly one of history's quaint (but also logical) choreographies that the dandy's narcissistic pageantry of bodily control is eventually succeeded by the incisive, but also interludic chapter of the roaring and porous 1920s when, after the transient period of post–First World War, men and women intermittently forgot their ingrained loathing of their bodies, felt, like Ralph Denham in Virginia Woolf's early novel *Night and Day* (1918), the rare 'pleasure of owning a body'[46] and began to rediscover the carnivalesque potential that lay dormant in their bodies. In this respect, the two aesthetically divergent novels *Ulysses* (1922) and *Lady Chatterley's Lover* (1928) prove to be pivotal texts, hallmarks in the history of gender studies and body. Showing women divesting themselves of their effacing sartorial sarcophagi they also give credit to men's porosity and to a fluidity which not only in Dickens's time, but also, according to early twentieth-century newspaper advice columns, should only be indulged in furtively and in rooms of utmost seclusion.[47] It is to Joyce's and Lawrence's merit that they, for at least a short time, release men (and women) from their narrow closets of bodily invisibility and encourage them to rejoice openly in their porous carnivalism. The fact that this enfranchisement of the body – this celebratory rewriting of the body's cavities and its various secretions – is not unconnected to derogatory comments on twentieth-century man's emasculation, becomes apparent when one notices that it is Lawrence himself who aligns the softening of twentieth-century man's body with a perverse 'hen-sureness' which he, in line with Nietzsche's legacy of the superman, not only harshly castigates, but

---

[45] *The Picture of Dorian Gray*, 38.
[46] Woolf, *Night and Day*, 192.
[47] Dixon quotes the editorial of the 1908 *Daily Mirror* advising weepers to close their doors, to 'lock them, and weep in private'. *Weeping Britannia*, 222. Examples of the 'wonderful, secret, and motionless gymnastics to restrain [one's] tears' are legion around the turn of the century. See Wells, *Ann Veronica*, 23.

also contrasts with the monstrosity of the ascendant female 'cock-sureness'.[48] For Lawrence, porousness is clearly a woman's affair which man is advised to espouse condescendingly, but which, in the interest of his masculinity, should never agree with.

The question that Barthes wants to see addressed – '[i]n which societies, in which periods, have we wept,' since when and why have people stopped weeping and what is the reason for such a ban on male tears?[49] – must, in this context, be widened and ramified into the discussion of how and why and in what situations people weep, how they suppress their tears and to what extent they make use of tears to conceal other indecorous porousness. It is also pertinent to follow up these sundry questions with the overwhelming (albeit less Prufrockian) question of what makes them stop weeping, repudiate their fluids and conceal all orifices that might betray a disorderly ooziness. In this context, approaches by cultural historians such as Peter Gay are thought-provoking: Gay suggests expanding the Victorian age geographically, consequently writes about French, German and Italian Victorians,[50] and positions himself against all those writers who myopically seem to argue that the long Victorian age neatly terminates with the First World War; my (admittedly daring) hypothesis is more in line with Gay, but even tends to out-Gay Gay when, in its plea for a chronological expansion, it is premised on the idea that the Victorian age has never ended and was, if at all, only in abeyance during the raucous 1960s. This provocative hypothesis, which, in a dizzying sweep of remapping ossified periods, conflates post–Second World War postmodernism with the Victorian age and posits a protracted Neo-Victorianism, is not so much moored in the existence of a plethora of historical (and metafictional) novels and films as in the upsurge of a Grundyism and hostility to bodily fluids which, in certain phases, even outdoes the Victorians' body phobia. Thus, Laura Otis is certainly right when she says that '[o]ur fears of "leakage" and desires for containment, today centered around HIV, are a continuation of nineteenth-century terrors that our membranes – and with them, our identities – will be ruptured'.[51] While the Victorian obsession with closure was increasingly challenged by a proliferation of meandering cliffhanger novels, this striking imbalance between form and content, between the formal templates and the bodies that are expected to be regulated and closed in them,

---

[48] Lawrence, 'Cocksure Women and Hen-Sure Men', 123–27.
[49] Barthes, *A Lover's Discourse*, 180.
[50] Gay, *Schnitzler's Century*, Preface, xxv.
[51] Otis, *Membranes*, 7.

is later reversed, leaving the reader with the insight that there is often a vexingly dissonant relationship between the sexual bodies and their textual corpora.

The concept of porousness itself has an interesting (albeit fitful and short) history and can be found in different contexts and discourses: in the realm of socio-theology, critics highlight that weddings and funerals are 'emblematic' of a striking modern 'porousness of family life, bringing together geographically far-flung relatives, spouses and ex-spouses, siblings and stepsiblings'.[52] While porousness is here equated with disintegration and the loss of social adhesives, scholars from a cultural or aesthetic background define porousness as a necessary component of textual communication: 'reading', Barbara Hochmann asserts, 'depends on the porousness of boundaries between reader and text'.[53] For one area of academic discourse, porousness is a symptom of decadence and social disintegration, an attack on the traditional notion of a tightly knit family, whereas for the Humanities it seems to be a prerequisite for engaging with literature, for making the act of reading an osmotic experience of culture, without which author and reader would be stuck in antagonistic non-communication. And yet, it will be evident in this book that texts themselves have different degrees and strategies of porousness: while some texts seem to display their openness, and by apostrophes and personal addresses try to absorb their readers into their tear-soaked pages, other texts (predominantly poems indebted to seventeenth-century Metaphysical poetry or nineteenth-century Symbolism) seem to be clothed in impervious membranes of concetti, tropes and arcane metaphors, so that textual porousness in terms of a sensual encounter between reader and text is more often than not forestalled.

One of these inaccessible, closed texts, a specimen of the *poésie pure* as practised by Stéphane Mallarmé, is Paul Celan's hermetic and cerebral poem 'Engführung' ('Stretto', 1957/58),[54] which, despite its forbidding darkness and repellent endgame atmosphere, has come to be well known and anthologized on account of its perplexingly neologistic use of the concept of porousness. Evoking a textual landscape of destruction, perdition and death, in this poem, Celan seems to imply that the poet's toilsome post-war reconstruction of the world is preceded by various intermediate stages, one of which is that of a porous building or quarry, 'ein Porenbau'. While linguistic architects of previous ages such as Shakespeare or Wordsworth (especially the latter as the imaginary builder of his ecclesiastical *Recluse*) insisted on the solidity of their 'stanzaic'

---

[52] Wuthnow, 'Reassembling the Civic Church', 167.
[53] Hochmann, *Getting at the Author*, 19.
[54] Celan, *Speech-Grille and Selected Poems*, 154–67.

rooms, post–Second World War (and post-Holocaust) poets had to come to terms with the traumatic insight that the Sisyphean project of reintegrating the 'par-/ticle flurries' ('Par-/tikelgestöber') into a stone, into the precious solidity of 'a myriad crystal' ('Tausendkristall', 124) was taxing. What is intriguing in this context is that the Sisyphean labour, the (re-)construction of the textual world into verbal transcendencies, is, for Celan, undertaken with 'dry eyes' (111), without bodily fluids, sweat, tears or blood. Struggling with the atomized debris of his language (shown in split and broken words such as 'par-/ticle flurries' or 'Ho, ho-/sanna'), the speaker in Celan's poem sees the porousness of the textual edifice as a transitional process which links the successive vegetative and organic states (the 'stalked' and the 'renal' parts) with the 'last membrane' that finally encompasses the crystal world – a world which, like its text, is imagined as being solid, petrified and inaccessible. Apart from this act of demiurgical creation, of converting porosity into crystal solidity, Celan typically takes no interest in the bodiliness of porosity, and in this respect, he is unexpectedly close to Isaac Newton's atomistic idea of creation in his *Opticks* (1718), where 'porous Bodies' are only a residual product of solid matter.[55] Even newly coined references to kidneys ('nierig') which Joyce would have taken up eagerly and interwoven into Bloom's urine-centred interior monologue remain an incoherent non sequitur in the ontological debris of this recondite, hermeneutically anti-porous poem.

Celan's concept of porosity could not be more remote from what Gavin Hopps defines as the 'porous worlds' in Byron's epic poems.[56] Using the word 'porous' in a strictly theological sense, but without the gloomy prophecy of the 'increasing porousness of American society',[57] Hopps detects a leakiness in Byron's poems which opens the traditional (more often than not fossilized) stanzaic forms to amazing ways of 'showing forth or participating in the being of God'.[58] According to this innovative understanding of the word porosity, 'porous' is here synonymous with epiphanic, with the sudden moments that pierce the humdrum reality of life and, for a short time, show the Byronic protagonists, in the guise of a Caspar Friedrichian spectator, in divine communion with the supernatural. Porousness in the manner of a 'penetration into the horizontal of a "spiritual verticality"',[59] another intriguing way of defining the experience of religious ecstasy, certainly underlies staple parts of Canto III of Byron's *Childe*

---

[55] Quoted in Greenblatt, *The Swerve*, 261.
[56] Hopps, 'Porous Worlds', 109–20.
[57] Wuthnow, 'Reassembling the Civic Church', 166.
[58] Hopps, 'Porous Worlds', 109.
[59] Ibid., 115.

Harold's Pilgrimage, the Canto which was evidently written under the influence of cloying Wordsworth physic. What, however, weakens Hopps's argument is that after quickly weaning himself off this hallucinogenic Wordsworthian drug, Byron no longer shows a similar epiphanic leakiness in his down-to-earth *Don Juan*. Although there are a few instances of the speaker's apostrophizing higher entities, a blurring between earthly and heavenly spheres is rare, formulaic and often parodic.

As will become evident, Byron's porousness is anything but ecstatic; it is not so much about the tenuous and diaphanous demarcation lines between metaphysics and the realm of squalid carnality as about the constant infiltration of bodily ooziness into the high-flown concepts of Shelleyean intellectual beauty. The 'very buttons' that Byron undoes – to take up a Hopkins quote that Hopps cites[60] – are thus less those of our being than those of his characters' trousers, shirts and dresses laying obscenely bare the hitherto hidden pores, cavities and orifices of sweating, bleeding and genitally discharging bodies. Although Hopps's theologization of the term 'porousness' seems to be compelling and well argued, Byron, the self-styled 'bad metaphysician',[61] is doubtless in league with many other poets who are shown favouring a much more corporeal definition of porousness.

In this book, porosity is, thus, to be understood as being osmotic: on the one hand, men are depicted as being threatened by an uncontrollable expenditure of fluids, about to be drained and shrivelled in acts of sentimental or sexual overindulgence, whereas, on the other, women are imagined as liminal, Ophelian creatures discharging and absorbing water, oozing fluids in such gigantic and carnivalesque quantities that men, despite their rockiness, are left haunted by fears of being drowned, washed away or eroded to nothingness. If there is, in the context of this definition of porosity, an epiphany, it is only an epiphany in a strictly Joycean sense, an epiphanic or anti-ecstatic feeling of diminution, of failure and loss of control.

Narratives such as this (selective) study of tears, liquids and the porous bodies are, by definition, porous structures themselves and good examples of Celan's transitional 'Porenbau'. A survey of porous bodies, of the suppression and liberation of bodily fluids (and their existence in relation to imaginary, public and pathogenic fluids) is not only by necessity open-ended, it is also one full of gaps and holes, concentrating on certain epochs, authors and literatures

---

[60] Hopkins's letter to A.W.M. Baillie, 22 May 1880, quoted by Hopps, 'Porous Worlds', 118.
[61] Letter from Byron to Lady Melbourne of 1813, quoted in Marchand, *Byron: A Portrait*, 153.

while omitting others ostensibly more prone to porosity and fluidity. With a new awareness of political correctness rapidly gaining ground in the twenty-first century and iconographies of porosity being eclipsed by persistent ideologies of bodily hygiene and artificiality, this book (and its against-the-grain close rereadings of texts) wants to invite a new flow of criticism, a new critical porosity which not only goes beyond the ossified and stony templates of theories, but is also ready to drill new holes into the corpora of various canonical texts, there to tap new streams of academic debate.

1

Porous bodies before (and after) the discovery of pores

Ambivalent manly tears on the stage

In Act IV, Scene 3 of Shakespeare's dark tragedy *Macbeth* (c. 1606), Macduff, the powerful and soldierly Thane of Fife, suddenly finds himself flung into an unexpected Niobean situation: courageously demanding the truth from his bush-beating friends – 'Be not niggard of your speech. How goes't?' (*Mac* 4.3.181) – he learns the horrifying fact that Macbeth has not only slaughtered his family, but also extirpated his entire household in a fit of barbarian revenge: 'Wife, children, servants, all that could be found' (*Mac* 4.3.213). That the vent for Macduff's grief is a strikingly different one from that of Niobe or even men of the Romantic age is immediately made clear. Instead of drowning his sorrow in a gushing flood of tears, Macduff is reminded of his duties of masculinity and expected to '[d]ispute it like a man' (*Mac* 4.3.223). Although concepts of masculinity were anything but fixed and tended to show degrees of diversification, there was universal agreement that it was mandatory for men to aspire to the ideal of the *cortegiano*, to a type of man who, according to Baldassare Castiglione's widely read manual and its 1561 translation by Sir Thomas Hoby, *The Courtyer*, should refrain from appearing 'soft and womanish'[1] and fashion himself as a stoic who is at pains to seal his body from any onset of dissolution and what David B. Goldstein calls 'a problematic liquidity'.[2] The narration of the Porter's losing battle against the urge to urinate, which Macduff had banteringly provoked in Act II, Scene 3, is only a burlesque reflection of early modern man's dread of bodily openness and, in

---

[1] Castiglione, *The Book of the Courtier*, 39. Castiglione's book serves as a kind of homosocial varnish and gloss in which, next to porous gender erosions, 'social frictions, sexual combat, and power are all carefully masked by the fiction of an elegant *otium*'. Greenblatt, *Renaissance Self-Fashioning*, 162.
[2] Goldstein, 'Liquid *Macbeth*', 165.

contrast to the courtier and soldier, shows the clown (like children or women) at the mercy of his intractable abdominal regions.[3]

Passages like these and admonishings in conduct books like *The Courtyer* stress that manliness was only loosely defined and that Italianate courtiers were constantly in danger of losing 'the hardness and stability of male perfection and melt[ing] into unstable but protean imperfection'.[4] Averse to relapsing into medieval habits of carnivalesque openness (which were related to certain classes and confined to certain 'popular-festive' seasons of revelry),[5] Renaissance man saw himself indebted to a new ideal of restraint and obliged to channel the rush of overpowering feelings into ducts of rational enunciation:

> Give sorrow words. The grief that does not speak
> Whispers the o'erfraught heart and bids it break. (*Mac* 4.3.210–11)

Malcolm's, the future king's, advice to translate sorrow into words and later into stony redemptive revenge – 'Be this the whetstone of your sword' (*Mac* 4.3.231) – is clearly based on early modern man's fear of effeminization, on the dissatisfaction that people evinced at the idea of 'one elastic sex'[6] that oscillated between dry and solid manliness and a phlegmatic and tearful melancholy, which, in the context of Galenic pathology, was seen as a token of perilous degeneration into coldish, watery and oozy femininity. While yellow bile, black bile and even blood were hidden fluids and could only be made partially visible by conscious (and male) acts of blood-letting, tears, sweat and other phlegmatic exudations (sometimes seen as 'lubricant[s] and coolant[s]',[7] sometimes as 'excrementitious humours'[8]) were not only embarrassing evidence of a lack of masculine control, but also testimony to a deceptiveness and dishonesty that, due to common misogynist parlance, was attributed to scheming women. The 'gradual emergence of men of feeling in sixteenth- and seventeenth-century literary texts', as Jennifer C. Vaught argues,[9] is thus a daringly compelling hypothesis which, however, most of the texts included here do not support.

---

[3] Another example of this clownish porosity is the 'young German, the Duke of Saxony's nephew' in *The Merchant of Venice*. Portia is repelled by the fact that he is not only on a par with a beast, but also that as a heavy drinker of 'Rhenish wine', he has reduced his body to little more than 'a sponge.' *MV* 1.2.91/94.

[4] Laqueur, *Making Sex*, 125.

[5] Bakhtin, *Rabelais and His World*, 228.

[6] Laqueur, *Making Sex*, 125.

[7] Porter, *Blood and Guts*, 26.

[8] Burton, *The Anatomy of Melancholy*, quoted in Dixon, *Weeping Britannia*, 43. The idea of tears as 'excrementitious humiditie of the brayne' is also prominent in Bright, *Treatise on Melancholy*, 144 and thus common knowledge.

[9] Vaught, *Masculinity and Emotion*, 2.

Even a self-proclaimed villain such as Richard III finds himself in tune with early modern customs and practices, when, in the presence of Anne, he boasts of the fact that the account of his father's death did not elicit a single tear from his eyes: 'in that sad time / My manly eyes did scorn an humbler tear' (*R3* 1.2.166f.). The negative connotation of tears as 'childish drops' (*R3* 1.2.157) shows that Richard fully subscribes to the ideal of masculine dryness, and thus it comes as a surprise when Richard finally avows that his eyes have been made 'blind with weeping' (*R3* 1.2.169). This psychological inconsistency within a few lines not only reveals that Richard is an inconstant and psychologically liminal character, it also underlines the fact that Richard must be classed among a group of fitful and uninhibited weepers in Shakespeare's plays who, by the hyperbolism of their gender-incompatible 'emotional expressiveness',[10] are suddenly unmasked as dissemblers, actors and Machiavellian schemers. One of these dissemblers is one-handed Titus in Shakespeare's early and derivative tragedy *Titus Andronicus* (c. 1594) who rantingly casts himself as a drunkard vomiting tears;[11] another is Gertrude in *Hamlet*, who is less hyperbolic, but more calculating and reported to have shed excessive and false Niobean tears over her dead husband's corpse and in the presence of her next (incestuous) husband.[12]

While Barthes eulogizes tears as the 'truest of messages', as the purest and most sincere of signs in a semiotics of bodily language,[13] Shakespeare and his contemporaries seem to argue for the opposite, for the prevalence of tears as instruments of treachery and falsehood. Not only does *Hamlet* make a strong case for tears as excremental humoral fluids that easily lend themselves to (female) manipulation, their inherent staginess and histrionic quality also proved to be the appropriate and fashionable subject matter for several cynically misogynist plays on women's, and in particular widows', duplicity.[14] While, as a widower, Macduff knows how to suppress these tokens of treachery and uses them to fuel his fiery-mettled revenge, widows in lurid Jacobean tragedies are shown as being on a par with Gertrude, exhibiting 'short liu'd Widowes' teares' only to conceal the fact that, rejoicing in their new sexual freedom, they were 'laughing vnder a Maske'.[15] As if to live up to the ominous liminality to which widows were

---

[10] Ibid., 4.
[11] *Tit* 3.1.232.
[12] 'Like Niobe, all tears'. *Ham* 1.2.149.
[13] See Lutz, *Crying*, 52.
[14] The histrionic quality of tears, however, stands in ironic contrast to the 'verisimilitude of feeling [that] was requisite in Elizabethan acting' and that the audience wished their actors to weep authentically, see Cohen, 'Tears (and Acting) in Shakespeare', 23.
[15] *The Widow's Tears* 1.1.125–26. *The Plays of George Chapman: The Comedies*, 483.

relegated, one of them, Gratiana in Chapman's *The Revenger's Tragedy*, fashions herself as a cunning launderer of tears (and other juices) and thus as the glaring opposite of a man stoically coming to terms with his grief:

> I'll rinse it [= her guilt] in seven waters of mine eyes.
> Make my tears salt enough to taste of grace;
> To weep is to our sex naturally given,
> But to weep truly, that's a gift from heaven.[16]

With their alchemist-like power to brew, adulterate and distil their tears 'in seven waters' of their eyes, women seem to have mastered their bodily fluids more than men were ready to admit. The image of the female sex as being hopelessly at the mercy of their riotous fluids, as creatures desperately unable to police their bodily orifices was a myth that men preferred to cherish in order to cement the idea of women's liminality and to confirm their inferiority in the one-sex-based Chain of Being.[17] That this simplified binary structure was jeopardized not only by manipulative widows' alchemist adeptness at distilling their bodily fluids, but also by male adolescents' proneness to tears is paradigmatically shown in *Hamlet* and *Romeo and Juliet*.

Young, immature and characterized by a disturbingly fluid masculinity, Laertes and Romeo trespass upon dangerous territory when they yield to their effeminizing tears in a flamboyancy which is rebelliously innovative, theatrical and dangerously hybrid. Both have lost (or are on the point of losing) a beloved companion; but although their responses to these challenges of fate are dissimilar, both characters are stuck in an impasse where bookish concepts of culture and masculinity have ceased to function. Having consented to become involved in a black plot against Hamlet, Laertes is suddenly thrown off his balance when he learns (from deviously aquatic Gertrude) about his sister's suicidal madness and her dehumanizing death in the swampy ooziness of nature:

> Her clothes spread wide
> And mermaid-like awhile they bore her up,
> Which time she chanted snatches of old lauds
> As one incapable of her own distress,
> Or like a creature native and endued
> Unto that element. But long it could not be
> Till that her garments, heavy with their drink,

---

[16] *The Revenger's Tragedy* 4.4.53–56. *Three Jacobean Tragedies*, 119.
[17] Laqueur, *Making Sex*, 125.

Pulled the poor wretch from her melodious lay
To muddy death. (*Ham* 4.7.173–81)

More than other female characters in Shakespeare's plays, tongue-tied Ophelia is a liminal creature par excellence (evidenced by her marginal position at court and in the play), so that in her death she seems to return to a sphere where the neat categories of the Chain of Being are blurred and invalid. In his study on the *Gender of Death* (1999), Karl S. Guthke refers to and concentrates too exclusively on the terrifying representations of early modern death as a skeleton, as a male fiddler in the garish dances of death or as an apocalyptic horseman.[18] As Ophelia's self-inflicted death, however, shows, death could, at that time, also be imagined in more feminine terms, as a slow thalassian transition and metamorphosis from corporeality to a mermaid-like and watery liminality. Like mermaids, sirens or other chimerical creatures, Ophelia is 'native and endued' to water and thus absorbed by a 'body of fluid' that, according to Kaara L. Peterson, together with the various flowers denotes menstrual fluid and the *furor uterinus* that is raging within her.[19] The phrase 'heavy with their drink' seems to corroborate this and underlines the fact that (female) death is only an osmotic process, a kind of drinking and being drowned by a festering 'stew-like stagnation of liquids',[20] and thus in line with the medieval conviction that women belonged to the element of water and were consequently cold, moist and a strange mixture of disgustingly phlegmatic juices: tears, milk, 'flowers' (= menses) and slimy vaginal lubricants.

Ophelia's watery death instantaneously causes Laertes to put a censorial ban on his fluid grief: 'Too much of water hast thou, poor Ophelia, / And therefore I forbid my tears' (*Ham* 4.7.183–84). This imbalance makes him tragically akin to Hamlet who constantly oscillates between Herculean hardness and the lure to let his 'too solid flesh … / Thaw, and resolve itself into a dew' (*Ham* 1.2.129–30).[21] Unable to restrain his tears and forced, at this moment of intense distress, to let porous female nature hold sway over him ('nature her custom holds'), he fallaciously believes that with these irrepressible tears the last vestiges of a lurking femininity in him will be exorcized: 'When these are gone / The woman will be out' (*Ham* 4.7.186–87).[22] In contrast to Macduff, who immediately transforms

---

[18] Guthke, *The Gender of Death*, 82ff.
[19] Peterson, 'Fluid Economies', 47.
[20] Ibid., 48.
[21] Peyré, 'Niobe and the Nemean Lion', 129.
[22] In her essay, 'Representing Ophelia', Showalter argues that 'Ophelia's story [is] the female subtext of the tragedy, the repressed story' both of Hamlet and Laertes. Their 'disgust at the feminine passivity' is translated into the horror of female ooziness (79).

his grief into the rhetoric of a stony revenge, young Laertes, like Hamlet or the Duke of Exeter in *Henry 5*,[23] finds himself momentarily overwhelmed by a female, maternal and watery 'folly' which shamefully deprives him of a male 'speech of fire' (*Ham* 4.7.188–89). At a loss to reconcile these onsets of softness with a world of armatorial competition,[24] Laertes overcompensates for his temporary loss of masculinity with hyperbolic and declamatory language that is not only alarmingly replete with images of petrification, but also underlines the tension that, like a leitmotif, runs between solidity and fluidity throughout the entire play:[25]

> Now pile your dust upon the quick and dead
> Till of this flat a mountain you have made
> T'o' ertop old Pelion or the skyish head
> Of blue Olympus. (*Ham* 5.1.240–43)

While Laertes puts up a fierce (and almost histrionic) resistance against all feminine tendencies that might adulterate or wash away the foundation of his belligerent manliness, Romeo is so inundated and frenzied by his excessive sorrow and melancholy that he is on the point of forfeiting not only his masculinity, but also his anthropological dignity. Given that Shakespeare shows a heightened interest in the fuzziness of the Chain of Being, in the transitional creatures in which two links of the chain often overlap, the reader must make allowance for the fact that Romeo, Shakespeare's youngest tragic hero and pubescent teenager, is still precariously poised between femininity and uncompleted manhood.[26] In this respect, Romeo is one of the most hybrid and Niobean of Shakespeare's male characters, like Laertes still an embryonic man and killed off before reaching the top of the Macduffian scale of hardness and non-porous perfection.

After subscribing to the dull theoretical love for the Petrarchan nonentity Rosaline at the beginning of the play, Romeo suddenly ignores all regulations and shows a deep contempt for moral, political and even sexual boundaries. Triggered by his rapturous infatuation with Juliet, an almost fourteen-year-old girl, whom Shakespeare even insists on making younger than she was in

---

[23] 'And all my mother came into mine eyes / And gave me up to tears'. *H5* 4.6.32–33.
[24] Shakespeare's contemporaries might later see what happens to a man whose eyes are made 'to sweat compassion'. *Cor* 5.3.196. The metonymy shows the extent to which references to male tears were anathematized.
[25] Cf. Peyré, 'Niobe and the Nemean Lion', 129.
[26] In his chapter on 'Sex and Love in *Romeo and Juliet*,' Wells only stresses Juliet's 'liminality' and tends to underestimate Romeo's wavering position between girlishness and aggressive manhood. *Shakespeare, Sex, and Love*, 154.

Arthur Brooke's poem,[27] and whose closeness to her former wet nurse, a leaky, and otherwise nameless woman, foregrounds her unfledged youth, Romeo is suddenly swayed by outbreaks of violent sexual rebellion which perilously tear off his trappings of Renaissance self-fashioning. Switching from being a voluble imitator of Petrarch's de-profundis lover to an anarchic transgressor of 'stony limits' (*RJ* 2.2.67), Romeo is eager to demolish all cultural constructions which had been erected to keep young women's and men's temperamentally volatile and porous bodies in check. His sophistical idea of observing conventions and objectifying Juliet into a 'holy shrine' (*RJ* 1.5.93) is immediately called into question, when Romeo refuses to heed the sanctity of his imagined shrine and endeavours to kiss her.

Romeo's shrine is a fleeting adolescent's fantasy: immured in the stanzaic construction of the sonnet, his shrine doubly immobilizes his beloved and, despite their 'holy palmers' kisses', keeps her body locked and petrified. Rebelling against his own pseudo-male aspirations to petrify and immobilize the female body (as Leontes later does with Hermione's body in *The Winter's Tale*), he hurriedly leaps over the walls of the orchard, the symbol-laden and gendered *hortus conclusus*, and overthrows all ossified principles of the courtly *ars amandi* so that even Juliet is startled at this precipitation and longs for some ceremony: 'Fain I would dwell on form' (*RJ* 2.2.88). Seen from this perspective, *Romeo and Juliet* can be read as a play revolving around the conflict between time-honoured form and the adolescent negation of form, between fossilized notions of sexual politics and the younger generation's anarchic, but abortive dissolution of bodies (private and politic), which in the long run was to destroy the revered and God-given Chain of Being.

Appalled by the fact that Romeo killed her kinsman Tybalt, Juliet begins to understand that all inherited ideas of form and epistemological traditions are inventions that scarcely stand the test of reality. In a string of clipped antitheses, Juliet gives temporary expression to her anxiety about the fact that she is witnessing the collapse of order and form and that Romeo, her icon of masculinity, is made up of equivocations which prove the deceptive foulness of fair appearances. It takes only one more scene, and the Chain of Being, the scale of upward masculine perfection, seems to have dissolved with Romeo discrediting his 'noble shape' of manliness and turning out to be a melting 'form of wax' (*RJ* 3.3.125) which lacks contours and digresses from the image of the transgressive amorous overreacher to a lachrymose and hysterical parody of a

---

[27] Ibid., 152.

human being. To what extent this 'digress[ion]' (*RJ* 3.3.126)²⁸ from (masculine) normativity is an assault on ontological categories is evident when Friar Laurence rebukes Romeo not so much for his breach of the well-established order as for his excessive, emasculating indulgence of inebriating tears: 'with his own tears made drunk' (*RJ* 3.3.83). Imitating a girl like Juliet who is melting in tears – 'Blubbering and weeping, weeping and blubbering' (*RJ* 3.3.87) – Romeo is suddenly on a dangerous downward spiral and on the point of deconstructing ideals of upright and phallocentric chivalry (as the Nurse inadvertently indicates: 'Stand, and you be a man' *RJ* 3.3.88). As Edward Topsell's later pseudo-scientific classification of animals, *The History of Four-Footed Beasts* (1607), highlights, the categories and degrees of the Chain of Being were vexingly open and constantly in danger of producing hybrid and fuzzy forms such as sphinxes, man-apes or satyrs.²⁹ A tear-drunken man was, thus, not simply seen as a sentimental fool and a laughing stock, but as a blasphemous and morbid transgressor of God-given demarcation lines in the divine pattern of creation. In this context, Friar Laurence's harangue against Romeo's formlessness and the boy's Niobean porousness (which refuses the translation of grief into rational discourse) is highly fraught with theological implications:

> Art thou a man? Thy form cries out thou art.
> Thy tears are womanish, thy wild acts denote
> The unreasonable fury of a beast.
> Unseemly woman in a seeming man,
> And ill-beseeming beast in seeming both! (*RJ* 3.3.108–12)

Leaning on a canon of consolatory literature with Plutarch's letter to Apollonius and Boethius's *De Consolatione Philosophiae* as the *loci classici*,³⁰ the clergyman leaves his audience in no doubt that 'tears are womanish' and will corrode the Renaissance anthropological axioms, as they had been formulated in countless treatises from Pico della Mirandola to John Lyly or Roger Ascham.³¹ What is considered even more alarming, as Enobarbus in *Antony and Cleopatra* underscores, is that a weeping man is not only highly and shockingly effeminate, but that he also runs the whole gamut of degeneration and eventually ends up not so much as an 'onion-eyed' idiot or 'ass',³² but as a nondescript beast in

---

[28] See *OED* 'digress' 3b trans. 'to transgress'.
[29] Topsell, *The History of Foure-Footed Beasts*, 16–19.
[30] Tromly, 'Grief, Authority and the Resistance to Consolation in Shakespeare', 25.
[31] For the wider context, see also Pincombe, *Elizabethan Humanism*.
[32] *AC* 4.2.36.

deceptively human form.³³ While Niobe was still seen as an example of proud overreaching and was even given the epithet 'procax' (= impudent) in emblems and edifying literature of the time,³⁴ Romeo must, in this context, be understood as the crass opposite, as an 'underreacher' when he behaves as unreasonably as a beast and, after literally descending (and upending) the Platonic ladder of love,³⁵ in a fit of inverted hyperbolism, envies carrion flies their position in the obsolete Chain of Being:

> More validity,
> More honourable state, more courtship lives
> In carrion flies than Romeo. They may seize
> On the white wonder of dear Juliet's hand
> And steal immortal blessing from her lips[.] (*RJ* 3.3.33–37)

The image of carrion flies crawling over Juliet's hand and stealing 'immortal blessing from her lips' is reminiscent of countless early modern vanitas paintings and, thus, full of tragic irony. What is pertinent here, however, is that Romeo is extreme and tragically lacking the virtue of moderation. In his grief, he becomes alarmingly liminal, wavering between the bestial and the hermaphroditic, assuming a female leakiness that, as Lady Capulet indicates, was only tolerated in banterings with girls: 'How now, a conduit, girl?' (*RJ* 3.5.129). Beside himself with fury, Romeo adopts a role of perverted masculinity that is not only more bestial, but also more transgressive than ever before. As if acting upon his own puerile porousness, he appears with a mattock and a crowbar in the graveyard and is resolved to desecrate (and make porous) the Capulets' sanctified tomb just as he had opened the shrine of Juliet's body before.

The contrast between Romeo and Paris could not be greater and more ironic: while the latter is shown in the process of observing a feminized ritual of mourning and watering Juliet's sepulchre with an alchemical (but far from schemingly widow-like) distillation of his tears – 'thy canopy is dust and stones / Which with sweet water nightly I will dew, / Or wanting that, with tears distill'd by moans' (*RJ* 5.3.13–15) – Romeo, the adolescent, has grown so savagely desperate that he is ready to massacre not only any opponent, but also himself. Yet, even at the moment of his self-inflicted and debased death, the hybridly feminine element of water seems to haunt and engross him: apostrophizing

---

[33] See also Capp, 'Masculinity and Emotion', 75–108.
[34] *Emblemata*, 1656.
[35] For the translation of the Platonic ladder of love into bodily reality, see also Targoff, *Posthumous Love*, 116.

death as a 'bitter conduct' and a 'desperate pilot', he visualizes his end as a shipwreck with his body as a 'seasick weary bark' (*RJ* 5.3.116–18) dashed on the rocks of his fateful life. That the tragedy ends with the Montagues' and the Capulets' mutual pledge to erect a golden monument to the sad memory of their children ironically takes up Romeo's former idea of enshrining Juliet; but what is now meant to be a hopeful sign that the streams of 'civil blood' will be staunched and the two families' 'grudge' finally ended (*RJ* Prologue, 3/4) also becomes the sadly parodic emblem of the restoration and eulogy of the impervious body. The young generation's fluid (and sexual) subversion of the fossilized body politic is hereby not only nullified, but their monument will also be the triumph of the domesticated and impervious body in which all suspicious cavities and phallic attributes (daggers and sheaths) are smoothened and the young rebels are recast into golden and anti-porous immobility.

Niobean fountains

There was a general agreement that visible fluids oozing from the body were an embarrassment and a dangerous sign of a loss of (masculine) control. Differences between tears, sweat, saliva or nasal mucus were tenuous and conjectural:[36] some natural philosophers and physicians indiscriminately lumped them together as forms of thin excremental waste,[37] whereas others preferred to give tears a more exclusive, cerebral meaning, but what was uncontested was the fact that, in certain quantities, tears were a sign of histrionic imposture that had to be combatted in the same way as their treacherous producers. In line with masculine ideals of non-wateriness, it was tacitly assumed (and condoned) that children's and women's bodies were prone to shedding tears and to being embarrassingly porous in general. In his 1586 *Treatise of Melancholy*, addressed to a 'melancholicke friend', Timothy Bright, endowed with the authority of a scientist and empiricist, gives the Galenic humoral pathology, and in particular the watery and melancholic temperament, a clearly gendered underpinning. It is, thus, undoubtedly non-sexed children and oversexed women who have an innate inclination to weep and, by analogy, to fail to keep their bladders tightly shut, 'the one having by youth the body moist, rare & soft, and the other by sex'.[38] To cast pubertal and liminal Romeo and Juliet as two excessive weepers shows

[36] Lange, *Telling Tears in the English Renaissance*, 28.
[37] Bright, *Treatise on Melancholy*, 145.
[38] Ibid., 144.

that Shakespeare was aware of the gaps and blurry inconsistencies of the medical knowledge of his time, but, by showing Macduff struggling for self-containment, he knew that he was perfectly in line with common medical lore and the belief that men were 'drier by nature, and more compact, and the[ir] passages and poores [were] close'.[39]

This biased and speculative idea that women not only are made up of watery, thin and almost excremental substances, but also outrageously lack (or pretend to lack) the capacity to keep 'the passages and poores close' coincides with a spectacular absence of knowledge about female anatomy. The assumption that the female genitals corresponded to the man's penis and scrotum and solely differed in the fact that, on account of cold and watery bodily fluids, they were retained within the women's bodies is evidence of early modern man's complete ignorance of women's physiology. Andreas Vesalius's depiction of the vagina as an interior penis[40] is as expressive of glaringly anatomical non-education as Leonardo da Vinci's illustration of the female genitals as a menacingly gaping hole, a gigantic pore that Shakespeare and his contemporaries used to verbalize as an 'O' or just as 'nothing' (as the absence or castrated remainder of the phallic 'thing')[41] on the stage (Figure 1). Intrigued and challenged by this genital 'O', early modern writers were inventive in visualizing this blank spot on the anatomical map which was persistently explored by anatomists who, such as the Padua physician Gabriele Fallopio, arrogated their Adamitic right of giving names (such as the Fallopian tubes) to this disquieting terra incognita. One of these visualizations turns out to be particularly pertinent to and illustrative of the idea and insistent dread of female porousness: imagined as a 'large-mouthed bottle hanging from a woman',[42] the vaginal region – in addition to the prevalent idea of a nondescript hole – came to be seen in the wider context of a receptacle that was turned upside down, but whose contents were – as menstrual blood and other emissions disquietingly proved – constantly replenished, like an unstoppered vessel incessantly dripping, pouring and spending.

Pseudoscientific learning or mythologizing about female genitals as bottles, vessels, itinerant uteruses and the like coalesced with the 'knowledge' or weird 'alternative facts' derived from the realms of myth, folklore and the Bible. The

---

[39] Ibid. This is one of the earliest incidences of the word 'pore' ('poore') in Shakespeare's time.
[40] Cf. Laqueur, *Making Sex*, 82.
[41] See the entries 'nothing' and 'O' in Williams, *A Glossary of Shakespeare's Sexual Language*, 219 and 221. Shildrick intriguingly uses the term of women as 'castrated men'. *Leaky Bodies and Boundaries*, 43.
[42] The French surgeon Jacques Duval quoted in Laqueur, *Making Sex*, 93f.

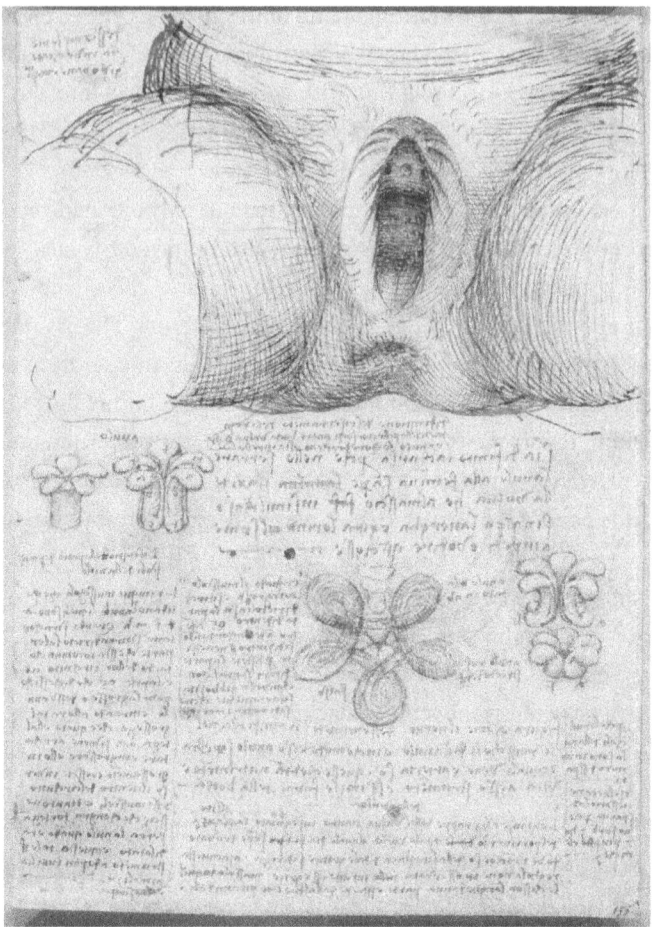

Figure 1 Leonardo da Vinci, Drawing of the Female Sexual Organs (n.d.), Bibliothèque des Arts Decoratifs, Paris. Courtesy Keith Corrigan/Alamy Stock Foto.

result was that the ominous 'O' was given new, but more often than not more sophisticated shapes and objectifications. In the wake of the iconographically seminal Song of Solomon in the Old Testament, women had always been visualized as enclosed gardens who offered their lovers not only the exclusive privilege to enjoy the exotic spices and fragrances of their bodies, but also the cooling refreshments of their highly elaborate vaginal fountains. Enumerating his addressee's bodily attractions in the manner of a *blason*, the speaker of the Song of Solomon, a strikingly erotic panegyrist, praises and elevates the female body but leaves his readers in no doubt that this fascinating territory conceals dangers that need to be confronted. Thus, a woman's body is, on the one hand, revealed as a Niobean producer of incessant streams of water – 'A fountain of gardens, a well of living waters, and streams from Lebanon' (Song 4.15)[43] – but, on the other, the speaker is adamant that Sulamith's bodily fluids must be subjected to strictly astringent measures, to keep her elemental and anarchic flow permanently checked and domesticated by man-made devices and arts:

> A garden inclosed is my sister, my spouse; a spring *shut up*, a fountain *sealed*. (Song 4.12, my italics)

The horticultural imagery of this biblical passage spawned not only numerous poems and references to women as gardens (even corroborated by Bright when he refers to the 'foutain [sic] of teares'),[44] but also the tradition of conceptualizing gardens as female bodies with the fountain as their most private and sexualized element. Countless early modern pleasure gardens with undulating hills (or *montes Veneris*), with bowers hidden and overgrown by (pubic) hair-like intricacies of plants and fountains refreshing the luscious vegetation with sprinkles of moisture were created all over Europe. In an unprecedented instance of a cross-fertilization between horticulture and literature, these feminized gardens inspired numerous literary works by men in which horticultural women were imagined encouraging coy young men to enjoy their bodies as parks, as sexual playgrounds where they could plunge from hilly elevations into moist genital depths, 'where the pleasant fountains lie'.[45]

While in *Venus and Adonis* Shakespeare's Venus not only advertises her genital fountains, but also refers to the 'ivory pale' (*VA*, 230) which hems in her bodily territory, the complex relationship between water and stone in female bodies is pinpointed again and, from the speaker's male perspective, interpreted along patriarchal lines. Despite the fact that Shakespeare's Venus exhibiting her vaginal fountains and openly inviting Adonis to a round of cunnilingus[46] verge on the parodic and hardly tally with what women were supposed to be, the image of Venus's genitalia as a fountain, which is locked in the seclusion of an ivory boundary, reflects the strategy that men insistently used to channel women's intractable floods of bodily juices. The terrifying circumstance that Shakespeare's dark lady in the Sonnets refuses to comply with these horticultural traditions of the Renaissance and, instead of being a fenced-in 'several plot', prefers to be both the 'wide world's common place' and 'the bay where all men

---

[43] Song 4.15. *The Bible*, OT, 762.
[44] Bright, *Treatise on Melancholy*, 144.
[45] *VA*, 234.
[46] See Fisher, 'Cunnilingus in *Venus and Adonis* and in English Culture', 333–46.

ride',[47] makes the enormous changes that men's concepts of femininity in the seventeenth century were to undergo absolutely clear. Not only the degrading image of the body as a 'common place', but also that of the spacious bay questions early modern man's project of controlling, artificializing or petrifying women's leaky bodies and conjures up the first glimpses of a nightmarish Byronic vision of man being dwarfed and engulfed in the wide watery regions of female bodies.

Shakespeare's tendency to portray women in terms of a schematic dualism also brings the reader face to face with two contradictory types of women: those who comply (or are forced to comply) with the expectation of being a beautiful and richly ornamented fountain and those who flatly refuse to succumb to early modern man's horticultural visions of the female body. It is to the former type that Katherine in *The Taming of the Shrew* (c. 1589), the aggressive amazon turned into an obedient wife, belongs. Having undergone an ordeal of painful correction, which entails not only the loss of her unbridled and masculine language, but also the blocking and warping of her feminine perception, Katherine delivers her final monologue in which she not only accords her husband the position of an absolutist king in the family ('thy lord, thy king, thy governour'; *TS* 5.2.144), but also *ex negativo* compares the ideal woman and wife to a refreshing fountain. Katherine's forty-three-line plea for a female porosity channelled into rigid structures is the longest and most programmatic speech in the play partially based on scriptural authorities that Shakespeare uses as guarantors:

> A woman moved is like a fountain troubled,
> Muddy, ill-seeming, thick, bereft of beauty
> And while it is so, none so dry or thirsty
> Will deign to sip or touch one drop of it. (*TS* 5.2.148–51)

As can be concluded from depictions of intricate Renaissance gardens,[48] a 'fountain troubled' did not fit into the well-patterned structure of the Renaissance *jardin d'amour*. The unruliness of its dirty streams would have outbalanced principles of aesthetics which, in early modern times, were firmly moored in rules of proportion and God-given ideas of order. Translated into gender discourses of Shakespeare's times, the passage insinuates that rebellious and intractable women are blots on prevalent concepts of beauty and that, even in times of erotic privation and drought, their unmanageable genital refreshments will be despised. It is only a clear and well-groomed fountain that epitomizes the

---

[47] *Son* 137, 9, 10 and 6. For the meaning of 'several' etymologically derived from Latin 'separalis' (= separate and distinct), see *OED*, 'several', 1–3.

[48] Cf. Strong, *The Renaissance Garden in England*, 17–18.

ideal of patriarchal order in which the husband saw himself entitled to regulate his wife's economy of fluids and to hedge her malleable body, 'soft, and weak, and smooth' (*TS* 5.2.171), with the insurmountable walls of gardens, houses and exclusive rooms.

A 'fountain troubled' of the perverse sort and, as such, a truly tragic reversal of the biblical image of woman as a revitalizing fountain is Lady Macbeth. Scorning the gushes of the 'milk of human kindness' (*Mac* 1.5.17) in her effeminate husband, in her first soliloquy, she clearly reveals herself as a liminal creature that – like the three hermaphroditic Witches before – crosses the gender boundaries and defines her role less as a nurturing fountain than as a cauldron of poisonous fluids. Soliciting demonic spirits, she scandalously desires to be 'unsexed' and to be filled 'from the crown to the toe, top-full / Of direst cruelty' (*Mac* 1.5.42–43). Her abhorrence of traditional porous femininity could hardly be more emphatic when, instead of overflowing and being refreshing for others, she desires to be on the receiving end of the filling process, and, in what looks like a grim parody of a prayer, begs to have all orifices and passages of her porous body blocked, so that the milk in her breasts ferments and is turned into venomous gall:

> Come to my woman's breasts,
> And take my milk for gall, you murdering ministers,
> Wherever, in your sightless substances,
> You wait on nature's mischief! (*Mac* 5.2.47–50)

Conjuring up the image of a Medean mother who, in the very act of breastfeeding her infant, commits the horrible crime of infanticide, Lady Macbeth not only turns seventeenth-century concepts of maternity[49] into a monstrosity, but she also seems to fulfil the function of being a counter-figure to the multitudinous images of the lactating Virgin Mary in Continental Baroque paintings. Without assuming that Shakespeare was familiar with the spate of paintings that flaunted full-breasted Madonnas feeding their chubby baby Jesus, one must see it as an intriguing cultural coincidence that, on the critical fringes of the European Baroque, Shakespeare created the counter-image of a malicious and poison-instilling demon-Madonna (which only bears comparison with the anti-Christological 'pelican daughters' Regan and Goneril in *King Lear*).[50] In the upside-down world of *Macbeth*, it is thus the men – milky Macbeth, bleeding Duncan or the urinating Porter – who are the leaky bodies, the manipulated

---

[49] For the 'cultural belief in the morally constitutive powers of breast milk' in the early modern period, see Sachdev, 'Of Paps and Dugs', 49.
[50] *KL* 3.4.74.

Niobean fountains; and it is only at the end of the play, with Lady Macbeth mentally deteriorating, believing herself to be drowning in floods of Duncan's blood ('Yet who would have thought the old man to have had so much blood in him?' *Mac* 5.1.39–40) and Macbeth calling for his impervious armour, that the traditional hierarchy of genders, the old gender-related allocation of fluidity and steeliness, seems to resurface.

Despite its porosity, its fountains of blood and urine (which, in his feverish imagination, Macbeth also sees gushing from Scotland's diseased body politic), Shakespeare's *Macbeth* is conspicuously lacking in tears. In the mad world presided over by bearded hags and women fashioning themselves as pots of poison, all passages to cathartic weeping seem to be blocked and or translated into a new carnivalism which, in its squirts of odious juices, erodes the old Tudor concepts of the body. This contradiction which lies between the characters' stoic tearlessness and their need to live in a world soaked with blood, urine and women's uterine juices (with the cauldron that issues the regal offspring turning into the witches' womb) is as unresolvable as the psychological inconsistencies in other characters in Shakespeare's dark Jacobean tragedies. Outwardly sharing Macduff's stoniness, Othello and King Lear profess to be 'unused to the melting mood',[51] but, within a few lines of their speeches, they go back on their words and show themselves susceptible to uncontrollable fits of passion in which, not unlike the histrionic Richard III, they exude fluids, 'as fast as the Arabian trees / Their medicinable gum'.[52]

These paradoxes are further proof of a world in transition in which cherished patterns of women as sumptuous fountains and men as their cool operators became increasingly obsolete. Despite his conservatism and lack of iconoclasm, Shakespeare seems to sense the concussions of an impending cultural earthquake, when in his poetry and plays he anticipates the harbingers of a new age in which 'sexually sophisticated'[53] dark ladies openly defy Petrarchism and men no longer aspire to the objectification of women into statues or shrines. Instead, a new species of 'liquid' men readily succumbs to fits of lachrimosity, and a new phalanx of writers of allegedly 'strong' and masculine lines rivals Shakespeare's works by ventriloquizing female martyrs and inundating seventeenth-century poetry with creamy tears, gushing wounds[54] and other pungent fluids. In the

---

[51] *Oth* 5.2.347. See also King Lear on the heath who struggles against 'women's weapons, water-drops': 'You think I'll weep, / No, I'll not weep'. *KL* 2.2.466, 471–72.
[52] *Oth* 5.2.348–49.
[53] Greenblatt, *Will in the World*, 143.
[54] Cf. Covington, *Wounds, Flesh, and Metaphor*, 35–42.

chequered history of the body, the advent of oozing Metaphysical poetry thus proved to be as revolutionary and cataclysmal as the new philosophy which was about to replace the fossilized Ptolemaic world system.

Liquid masculinity: From dark Shakespeare to oozy Metaphysicals

In marked contrast to François Rabelais who from 1532 to 1564 zestfully subscribed to the medieval concept of the grotesque body and concentrated on what Bakhtin highlights as the entrances and gates to the body as an 'entire cosmos' (including the abyss of libidinal hell),[55] Shakespeare seems to be idiosyncratically reluctant to dwell upon his characters' gapingly porous cavities. Apart from the clownish Porter in *Macbeth* and Falstaff in *The Merry Wives of Windsor*, both of whom may be understood as Rabelaisian concessions to early modern pop culture, Shakespeare was inclined to associate porousness and uncontrollable ooziness with hideous forms of degeneration and symptoms of disease. As the Porter's flippant remarks about excessive indulgence in alcohol underline, it is not so much the equivocal responses from his penis (wavering between erection and detumescence) as the loss of control of his bladder that makes the fool the target of laughter; and, by the end of the play, the fool's carnivalesque porousness is turned into the tragically disgusting image of the body politic drowning in fluids and having its discharge examined by helpless doctors.

In the dark Jacobean decade of his output, we see Shakespeare stemming himself against a new wave of porosity, a surge of tears and bodily fluids which, devoid of Rabelaisian connotations of fertility, was about to wash away the cherished principles of the *cortegiano*. This shift of paradigm was expressed not only in the transition from intricate Renaissance fountains to Baroque cataracts of fluids, but also in the chasm that divides Shakespeare's early sonnets about the self-contained love for the young and androgynous man[56] from the 'dark lady' sonnets, the most savage of which, Sonnet 129, pinpoints the atrocious consequences of what happens when – due to the porous love for an untamed

---

[55] Bakhtin, *Rabelais and His World*, 318.
[56] The 'young man' sonnets have various Renaissance images and similes which denote closure and (to a certain degree, claustrophobic) containment such as the 'up-locked treasure' (*Son* 52), the sculptural power of rhymes that exceeds marble or 'the gilded monuments / Of princes' (*Son* 55) or the young man's entombment in men's eyes (*Son* 81).

and incontinent woman – the (male) economy of the bodily fluids is severely jeopardized. Premised on the lore that a man's vital spirits were 'contained in his semen' and that it was of 'finite quantity',⁵⁷ every loss of fluids, either in the act of weeping, sweating, masturbating or in the perilous act of heterosexual love, was a foolhardy 'expense', a suicidal waste that could never be recompensed and was likely to reduce passionate men (Othello, Antony or the foolish 'taker' of the bait) to the position of madmen. This painful trajectory that leads mad men from visions of the hygienic heaven of the aseptic *amour courtois* to the nightmare of the real hell of the dark lady's vagina was, around that time, translated by the old and misanthropic King Lear into the image of a centaur: while up to the girdle women were deceptively theomorphic and clean, from the waist down they were thought to be made up of a 'sulphurous pit' oozing with liquids and teeming with a whole stock of porous venereal diseases.⁵⁸

Dipping into the turbulent seventeenth century, Shakespeare ostensibly seems to lose touch with the heavenly regions of the centaurs and to focus more on the unfathomable O of the swampy female body, on unleashed torrents of fluids that not only aggravated men's horror of porosity, but more often than not also threatened to fling them into what Jonathan Bate sees as a parodic and pathologized travesty of 'the mythological image of Cupid's fountain:'⁵⁹ the sweating-tub. While the open pores were here meant to 'absorb the quicksilver',⁶⁰ the sweating-tub also served as an apt symbol of the festering genital cesspool that Shakespeare associated with liquidity, with the nether regions of the female body and saw spreading into all spheres of life.

A sweating-tub, or a swamp of political dimensions, is the royal bed of Denmark, which, after old Hamlet's death, degenerates into a scenario of uninhibited seepage. While the rightful king in Shakespeare's times was required to embody the paradox of fertility and temperance,⁶¹ Claudius, the villainous king, is characterized by a long list of transgressions, among the most outrageous of which is, next to (or triggered by) his incestuous relationship with his former sister-in-law, his sexual porosity and his perfidious strategy of making the old monarchy corrosive and open to penetration. While Metaphysicals such as John Donne saw the female body in terms of a topography that needed digging and drilling holes into,⁶² Shakespeare saw the state (of Denmark) transformed into

---

⁵⁷ Bate, *Soul of the Age*, 185.
⁵⁸ *KL* 4.6.124.
⁵⁹ Bate, *Soul of the Age*, 188.
⁶⁰ Ibid., 188f.
⁶¹ Temperance is one of the 'king-becoming graces' that Malcolm enumerates. *Mac* 4.3.91–92.
⁶² Donne, 'Elegie XIX', 29: 'My Myne of precious stones […]'. *Poetical Works*, 107.

an effeminized body politic in which corrosive, pungent and poisonous fluids were instilled into the king's vulnerable body via his receptive and almost womb-like ear.[63] In this context, the Machiavellian Claudius is in line with Iago and Lady Macbeth, both of whom indulge in fantasies of kinky and power-crazed sex when they imagine pouring their venomous and quasi-seminal fluids into their victims' ears.[64] In contrast to the lawful king's, Malcolm's, virginity and bodily closure in *Macbeth* ('I am yet / Unknown to woman'),[65] seventeenth-century despots, 'unsexed' overreachers and erotic colonizers of Donne's calibre are shown not only as being sexually active, but also as sexual spendthrifts deeply immersed in and attracted by bodily juices.

Thus, it is not only Hamlet's overheated imagination, but also Shakespeare's darkening mind that depicts Claudius's (and Gertrude's) nauseating and porous activities in the royal bedchamber as grim testimony to the patriarchal court in a state of transition from a place of (moderate) husbandry to a 'moor' (*Ham* 3.4.65)[66] of unfathomable porousness and kinky obscenity. The additional repulsive image of 'the rank sweat of an enseamèd bed / Stewed in corruption' (*Ham* 3.4.90–91)[67] is Shakespeare's most graphic and dystopian depiction of the body politic's porosity, darkly insinuating that the incisive deaths of old and soldierly Hamlet, Duncan or Henry V paved the way not only for uncontrollable Niobean tearfulness, but also for an emasculating leakiness which, by the end of the seventeenth century, was to become institutionalized at Charles II's frivolous Restoration court.

Shakespeare's dislike of leaky and expending bodies, his deep loathing of 'the sordidity of the mouth and the belly' (as Septimus Warren Smith in Virginia Woolf's *Mrs Dalloway* aptly puts it)[68] is indebted to an old world view of economic austerity which increasingly elicited contradiction in the literature, music and painting of the early seventeenth century where it was challenged by a new ideology of prodigality and waste. With the advent of the writers of Metaphysical, Mannerist or Baroque poetry (whose euphuistic style Shakespeare had ridiculed more than once as linguistic porousness), the idea of the grotesquely overflowing body eventually finds its belated way into British culture. While urine, sweat,

---

[63] See Folkerth, *The Sound of Shakespeare*, 72ff.
[64] Cleopatra is most obscenely aware of the vaginal function of her ear when she desires 'fruitful tidings' to be 'ram[med]' into her ears. *AC* 2.5.24.
[65] *Mac* 4.3.125–26.
[66] See *OED* 'moor' 2 † a marsh.
[67] The word 'stewed' is also reminiscent of another connection between sex and sweaty porousness: the brothels which were called 'stews' on account of their former euphemistic connection with humid and steamy bathrooms, bagnios, places of (pathogenic) bodily porosity.
[68] Woolf, *Mrs Dalloway*, 75.

saliva, menstrual blood and semen (the 'sex water' believed to be exuded by both men and women)[69] belong to the medieval heritage of the grotesque body and were accounted for in terms of a necessary 'periodic discharge' in medical discourses,[70] seventeenth-century poets and artists were no longer reluctant to open the sluices of sweat, blood and tears[71] and – and this was the novelty – to define these fluids in terms of gifts, privileges and signs of election.

In this respect, even the Lord Protector Oliver Cromwell freely accepted the *donum lachrimarum*[72] and unwittingly followed the lead of the Counter-Reformation writers who emulated and overshot the mark set by Christ's contagious tears. The fact that 'Jesus wept' in Jn 11.35[73] confirmed seventeenth-century writers in their pursuit of a new, liquid and even 'alternative' masculinity.[74] Convinced that they had left behind a period of 'rigorism' and bodily closure, Metaphysicals were enthusiastic about following in Christ's footsteps and about rethinking the body's exudations.[75] The hyperbolism of passions and tears to which they now so readily reverted, at first glance, seems to be a relapse into Petrarch's fourteenth-century tempests of sighs and emotional turmoil. Yet, while the Petrarchists all over Europe (best epitomized by Shakespeare's languishing and sonneteering Romeo) were shown pubescently wallowing in their excessive grief, besotted with their own tears, the Metaphysicals tried to reclaim the (male) body's disquieting liquidity in a manner that was as un-Petrarchan as it was un-Shakespearean. In their criticism of Petrarch's formulaic grief, they certainly shared Shakespeare's conservative restrictions about spectacular mourning, but, in their revalorization of all sorts of bodily fluids, they specialized in juicy poems which make it abundantly clear that Shakespeare's poetics of astringency had been supplanted by a new aesthetics of ooziness, by the dedication to bodies that were no longer sealed, marmoreal and subjected to an economy of non-expenditure.[76]

---

[69] Laqueur, *Making Sex*, 68.
[70] Porter, *Flesh in the Age of Reason*, 50.
[71] The medieval heritage of the grotesque body is also evident in Donne's 'Satyres', which are clearly indebted to Juvenal and Martial. Cf. Mills, 'John Donne, Bodily Fluids and the Metaphysical Abject', 183–99.
[72] For Cromwell's 'ostentatious blubbering', see Dixon, *Weeping Britannia*, 65.
[73] *The Bible*, NT, 132.
[74] Capp, 'Masculinity and Emotion', 97.
[75] Pigman, *Grief and English Renaissance Elegy*, 28–29, and in Parrish, 'Moderate Sorrow and Immoderate Tears', 217.
[76] Cf. Vaught who, instead of differentiating between Shakespeare's Renaissance culture of moderation and Donne's Baroque exuberance, problematically lumps them together and, in her vertiginous list, even includes Ben Jonson, Izaak Walton and David Garrick, *Masculinity and Emotion*, 8.

A good example of the Metaphysicals' reframing of the bodily fluids, and in particular, of tears, is Donne's poem 'A Valediction: Forbidding Mourning', a Niobean response to Shakespeare's critical approach to tearful grief in *Romeo and Juliet* and to all those blubbering, lachrymose protagonists who, in their indulgence in self-consuming grief, are unwilling to refrain from shedding more than a 'holy and obsequious tear'.[77] At first glance, Donne's ideal of expressing one's grief and emotional turmoil seems to be that of silence and private communication. It is only '[d]ull sublunary lovers['] love'[78] that compels young couples to lament their physical separation in a special rhetoric of mourning including 'teare-floods' and 'sigh-tempests' (6). Averse to this pageantry of unbridled emotions, Donne's speaker prefers to elevate his relationship with his lover to the level of an elitist priesthood that is shielded from the 'layetie' (8) and invulnerable to the 'prophanation' (7) of debasing tears which only the vulgar and uninitiated are used to shedding in their unprivileged position outside the hallowed love temple (*pro fano*).

This un-Petrarchan renunciation of tears is, at first sight, suggestive of Laertes's exorcism of effeminizing tears, but what is noticeable is that it is preceded by a line that tallies neither with Shakespeare's nor with early Neo-Classicists' ideas of masculine solidity. The second stanza begins with the speaker inviting his female addressee to join him in abandoning his human morphism: 'So let us melt, and make no noise' (5). This unobtrusive phrase quietly ushers in a new preference for gender blurring and gender osmosis, which for Shakespeare was tantamount to perversion. In spite of using a plethora of personae and poetic masks which, in his œuvre, range from those of hard-boiled seducers of women to those of religious Ganymedes and catamites imploring to be raped by God ('Holy Sonnet' XIV), in this poem, Donne also foregrounds (and ventriloquizes) a new species of man that readily dispenses with his stoic stoniness and longs for a female dissolution into watery formlessness. That this idea of melting is later corrected by the famously Mannerist *concetto* of the lovers as a pair of 'stiffe twin compasses' (26) is explicable by the Metaphysicals' quirky delight in the illogical and absurd; but the image of a man joining his wife or beloved in a process of melting, thawing and liquefying is new and the first beacon of a radically different concept of masculinity. Thus, it is no longer astounding that the speaker in Holy Sonnet

---

[77] In Shakespeare's philosophy of mourning, a 'holy and obsequious tear' seems to be a limit that should not be exceeded. *Son* 31.5.
[78] 'A Valediction: Forbidding Mourning', 13. *Poetical Works*, 45.

XVII is not ashamed about melting in a 'holy thirsty dropsy',[79] while another (or a different facet of the same) speaker reveals himself as an uninhibited weeper causing the world to drown in a deluge of tears.

It is in the poems 'Twickenham Garden' and 'A Valediction: Of Weeping'[80] that Donne finally leaves the closet and, as a Metaphysical poet with Baroque proclivities, openly partakes of the new culture of weeping and melting. In 'Twickenham Garden', Donne's speaker casts himself as an inveterate love melancholic, '[b]lasted with sighs, and surrounded with teares' (1), who seeks refuge in a paradise which he, 'selfe traytor' (5), has poisoned and wrecked with the intrusion of evil: his 'spider love', which, in a perverted Eucharist, 'transubstantiates all' (6) and turns manna to gall, has unleashed the serpent and thus turned the paradisiacal garden into a terrarium of poison. Wishing to be inanimate and objectified – '[s]ome senslesse peece of this place' (16) – the speaker reverts to an image which encapsulates his new desire for a gender-crossing Niobean existence: 'Make me a mandrake [...] / Or a stone fountaine weeping out my yeare' (17–18). In popular lore, mandrakes were the result of sexual porousness, plants etiologically sprung from the sperm of hanged people, whereas the 'stone fountaine' stood for the liquidity which denoted both female tears and, by extension, the vexing incontinence of the female body. That his ambiguous exudations should be collected in 'christall vyals' (19) and tasted as 'loves wine' (20) reminds readers of the existence and use of lacrimatories, '[s]acred vials fill'd with tears,'[81] in which people of the Baroque age used to store the fetish of their precious tears.

What makes the whole image problematic and obscene is that here the idea of tasting tears (later to be expatiated upon in a different context by Richard Crashaw) is clothed in an invitation for a homoerotic exchange of tears and bodily fluids: the speaker's tears that the other disgruntled male lovers are encouraged to take and to fill their phials with are meant to be compared unfavourably with their 'mistresse Teares at home' (21). The message of this quirkily syllogistic poem is provocative: reverting to the old topos of women's tears as being 'false' (22), the speaker assumes the role of a Niobean fountain which, however, offers not so much excessively self-referential grief as an oral-erotic degustation and refreshment for its male users; and while the fountains in the wake of Shakespeare's shrew stay muddy and 'troubled', Donne's homosocial fountain promises to meet male needs: lachrimal wine and misogynist assistance.

---

[79] Holy Sonnets XVII, 8. *Poetical Works*, 301.
[80] *Poetical Works*, 26 and 34.
[81] *TNK* 1.5.5.

Although written in the first decades of the seventeenth century, 'Twickenham Garden' is infinitely remote from Shakespeare's austere Renaissance economy of fluids; and so is Donne's 'Valediction: Of Weeping', which is, as the title suggests, programmatically in accordance with the hyperbolism of all-gender weeping in Counter-Reformation literatures.[82] Yet, in contrast to the then-mushrooming poems revolving around and celebrating penitential tears, swamping the literary market with Ignatian meditations on tearful remorse, Donne, in this poem, astounds his readership with his overbold mannerisms and with an overtly heterosexual charging of his imagery of tears. Like an ejaculation, Donne's speaker pours forth a shower of tears before (or rather into) his lover's face, the effect being that each tear is given the impression of her features and is thus made 'pregnant' and full of her:

> Let me powre forth
> My teares before thy face, whil'st I stay here,
> For thy face coines them, and thy stampe they beare,
> And by this Mintage they are something worth,
> For thus they bee
> Pregnant of thee[.][83]

For the very first time, tears are not just juices of superfluous phlegmatic femininity or telltale signs of degeneration, they are now matrixes in a twofold sense: material stamped and impregnated by the beloved's face and little bubbly wombs filled with her body, foreshadowing Joyce's image of the 'liquid of womb of woman eyeball' in *Ulysses*.[84] Unlike Niobe's incessant and sterile stream of tears producing never-ending waste, Donne's weeper weeps fruitful tears, emphasizing that these '[f]ruits of much griefe' (7) are little uterine microcosms which contain his lover as a *homunculus*. Elaborating on the paradox of gigantic littleness, the poet argues that the little tears shed by him turn into 'globe[s]' (16), which, mixed with her tears, grow into a deluge of biblical dimensions. With the female contribution to this flood, her 'waters', all masculine frames are eventually eroded and yield to total liquefaction, a vision that Shakespeare would have recoiled from:

> Till thy teares mixt with mine doe overflow
> This world, by waters sent from thee, my heaven dissolved so. (17–18)

---

[82] The Counter-Reformation spilled into Protestant England in the poetry of the Jesuit Robert Southwell, whose best-known poem is 'Mary Magdalen's Funerall Teares'. Yet, even after his death in 1595, Counter-Reformation ideas and images still imperceptibly continued to seep into England. See also Sweeney, *Robert Southwell*.
[83] 'A Valediction: Of Weeping', 1–6. *Poetical Works*, 34–35.
[84] *Ulysses*, 274.

With this image of the dissolution of the speaker's cosmos paramount at the end of stanza 2, the poem eventually shows the speaker entreating his powerful lunar lover ('O more then Moone', 19) to refrain from resorting to the utmost: from drawing up the seas to drown him and to weep him dead. Although courting a masochistic death in the female element, the speaker – as if falling back on Laertes's and Macduff's virtues – still retains the hope that he might not be completely drawn into the vortex of his lover's fluid chaos. Although writing his poetry in the key of the new culture of liquidity, Donne every now and then reveals himself to be a contemporary of Shakespeare's and Jonson's and finds himself interlacing his oozing Baroque poetry with insistent reminders of and unexpected relapses into Renaissance moderation: 'forbeare / To teach the sea, what it may doe too soone' (21f.). Shakespeare's awareness of the danger of lavish expenditure for both man's and the world's economy (and even ecology) of fluids resonates through Donne's poetry and alerts him to the fact that an excess of passion is liable to 'do me more harme, then it purposeth' (25).

This random oscillation between two modes and cultures might be an explanation for the fact that, next to the diluvian cascades of tears, there is a fascination for apocalyptic images of the world running dry in Donne's poetry. The reservoir of life's juices, visualized as a womb-like 'limbecke' (21) in the gloomy poem 'A Nocturnall upon S. Lucies Day, Being the Shortest Day',[85] seems to have been completely drained. With the world's 'sap' being 'sunke' (5), the poem's two lovers, by analogy, have over-spent themselves in excessive floods of tears and are now shrivelled to 'carcasses' (27). This situation of negation, death and ontological drought is aptly expressed by the two uncommon metaphors which identify the speaker as being both the world's 'Epitaph' (9) and the 'Elixer' (29) distilled out of nothingness. A similar dryness is also the condition of the dying world in 'An Anatomy of the World. The First Anniversary': 'in a common bath of teares it bled, / Which drew the strongest vitall spirits out'.[86] Having squandered its energy and health in prodigal quantities of tears, the world is now depicted as being sick, feverish and in a state of mortal consumption. Faced with a new zeitgeist in which old notions of economy are discarded in favour of exuberance and cornucopian plenty, Donne seems to be both attracted and repelled by the Baroque concepts of openness and, in his poems, thus, provides the missing link between lingering ideas of Renaissance containment and the new semantics of Baroque fluidity. Yet, in spite of his evasiveness and in-between

---

[85] *Poetical Works*, 39–41.
[86] 'An Anatomy of the World: The First Anniversary', 12–13. *Poetical Works*, 208.

position in seventeenth-century culture, Donne has moved a considerable way from Macduff's or Laertes's self-imposed ban on tears and, by casting himself into the role of a Niobean fountain, he underlines his avant-gardist position in the hitherto unwritten history of tears, porous bodies and gender diffusion.

While Donne is still apprehensive of completely severing his umbilical cord with Renaissance ideology, it is intriguing to see that, at one point, even Shakespeare goes Metaphysical and ventures to trespass upon the territory that he perceived with great misgivings. It is certainly daring, but not completely far-fetched to suggest the hypothesis that Richard Crashaw's imagery of bleeding tears and weeping or sweating blood is not only rooted in Continental traditions of Counter-Reformation poetry (which Crashaw imbibed to satiety in his Italian exile, in Loreto), but also in a hitherto neglected tributary of English Baroque iconography that was fed by Shakespeare's erotic and satirical verse narrative *Venus and Adonis*.

Off the beaten track, suffering from the closure of the theatres due to the plague epidemic of 1592, Shakespeare surprises his readers not only with an overtly erotic verse tale (whose function twenty-first-century critics see along the trivializing lines of early modern Viagra, 'prescribed as treatment for erectile disfunction [sic]'),[87] but also with a theme that Baroque culture readily embraced on account of its porousness, fleshiness and hagio-pornographic potential. Typological congruences between Adonis and Christ or between Venus and Mary Magdalene lead critics such as Gary Kuchar to subscribe to the belief that there are strong intertextual links between Shakespeare and Robert Southwell's Catholic aesthetics of blood and tears,[88] thus consolidating the theory that Shakespeare must have spent his seven 'lost' years in the milieu of the Jesuits; what is, however, more plausible is the assumption that Shakespeare, in his protean versatility and his unerring instinct for the demands of the literary market, indiscriminately absorbed the new trends of his age and enjoyed experimenting with and ironizing them in his works. In this context, *Venus and Adonis* ought to be read as an exercise in the Baroque mode of writing, but also as strong evidence of the fact that Shakespeare was responsive to, albeit highly sceptical of, the new 'grammar of tears',[89] the public performances of weeping which revert to medieval mysticism and consequently seriously challenge his concept of soldierly masculinity.[90]

---

[87] Stanton, *Shakespeare's 'Whores'*, 135.
[88] Kuchar, *The Poetry of Religious Sorrow*, 31–76.
[89] Ibid., 2.
[90] See here Bale, 'Where Did Margery Kempe Cry?', 15–30.

Having before dealt with the transition from the phallocentric *ars bellandi* to the epicene *ars lachrimandi* from the perspective of a writer of tragedies, Shakespeare now assumes the position of a parodist when he has a vigorous and butch Venus harass a boyish Adonis and vainly coax him into making love to her.[91] As a persistent and almost pestering Venus Genetrix (the earthly sister of the twin Venuses),[92] she runs the whole gamut from being a persuasive 'lovesick queen'[93] (oozing sweat and other amorous juices),[94] to a female rapist who 'glutton-like' (*VA*, 548) feeds on Adonis's mouth and intends to 'draw his lips' rich treasure dry' (*VA*, 552). Adonis's prim refusal to enjoy the goddess's sexual porousness echoes and reverses Aristophanes's *Lysistrata*.[95] But the crucial moment of the poetic sex comedy comes when Venus learns that her brittle (and one-sided) relationship with Adonis is intruded upon not so much by a rival poet (as in the later Sonnets) as by a monstrous boar which, to cap the parodic drift of the narrative poem, is unmistakably invested with the attributes of a destructive homoerotic lover who/which grotesquely rings the changes on the motif of the (female) beauty and the (male) beast. Her impending defeat and the boar's sexual ferocity dawn upon her when she sees the beast's 'frothy mouth, bepainted all with red, / Like milk and blood being mingled both together' (*VA*, 901f.). Bewailing the loss of her wayward lover by opening the 'floodgates' (*VA*, 959) of her eyes and letting the 'silver rain' (*VA*, 959) flow without inhibition, Venus is compelled to see that the boar is not only a victorious rival, but also much more effective in demolishing the boy's facade of amorous indifference and in tapping his feminized body's fluids.

Identifying Venus's eyes with 'floodgates' or 'sluices' (*VA*, 956) proves Shakespeare's familiarity with hyperbolisms, burlesque metaphors, but also with the 'deeper connection' that Shakespeare is supposed to see 'between human ontology and seawater'.[96] But what must have fascinated and teased readers even more (making it Shakespeare's most successful publication in his lifetime) is that the burlesque not only assumes monstrous qualities, but that it also provides an underpinning of the entire 'erotic epyllion' and shows Shakespeare surprisingly

---

[91] Staub refers to her as being a 'troubling maternal figure', thus giving their unequal relationship a ring of incestuousness. 'Shakespeare's Venus', 21.

[92] See Stanton, *Shakespeare's 'Whores'*, 138 who also refers to the Renaissance phenomenon of the Geminae Veneres.

[93] *Venus and Adonis*, 175. *Shakespeare's Poems*, 148. Venus's sweat is here the pathological result of her perverted love and completely different from the 'fast balm' that cements the lovers' hands in Donne's 'The Extasie', 6. *Poetical Works*, 46.

[94] See also Langley, *Narcissism and Suicide in Shakespeare*, 77.

[95] See also Wells, *Shakespeare, Sex, and Love* who discusses the 'sex strike' of the Greek comedy with reference to *TS*, 99.

[96] Brayton, *Shakespeare's Ocean*, 92.

enmeshed in a delicately woven net of gay pornography, eroticized theology and frivolous typology. Hence, Venus's tear-veiled eyes are immediately and jealously drawn to a gaping and flowing genital gash which, in its semantic embroidery ('purple tears', weeping wound), is shockingly out of tune with the phallus-driven monstrous boar and which seems to give Shakespeare a welcome opportunity to reduce the Baroque fetishization of the stigmata, tears and blood to complete absurdity. What beneath the Ovidian tale of abortive eroticism vibrates is a coup of witticism and anti-Baroque satire: the Baroque discourse of saints being martyred, flamboyantly receiving wounds, or Christ's body being wounded by (phallic) nails and arrows, is here naughtily overlaid by the preposterous story of a young man who is harassed by a brawny 'tidal' woman,[97] raped by a monstrous beast and eventually reclaimed by feminine liquidity:

> The wide wound that the boar had trenched
> In his soft flank, whose wonted lily white
> With purple tears, that his wound wept, was drenched:
> No flower was nigh, no grass, herb, leaf or weed
> But stole his blood and seemed with him to bleed. (*VA*, 1052–56)

In this grotesque love triangle of boy-woman-beast, Venus is defeated by a roving boar that, by perforating the boy's body ('his soft flank'), conflates discourses of transgressive homoeroticism with iconographical conventions used in myriads of depictions of Christ's Crucifixion. Seen from this perspective, Shakespeare's parodic foray into the Baroque mode is daringly blasphemous, recasting the 'purple tears' of Adonis's blood into the feminized (and Niobean) fountain of blood that Christ profusely sheds in numerous sixteenth- and seventeenth-century representations of the Passion.[98] In the new role of a scoffer at Baroque porousness, Shakespeare even outstrips Metaphysical conventions when he has nature join in this blood-drenching and sodomitical spectacle: every flower, every blade of grass and herb seems to be eager to participate in this bloody mash-up and, like true Niobean dissemblers, borrow some of Adonis's blood and falsely join him in the expenditure of bodily fluids.

The poem, betraying the dramatist by its abundance of direct speech and interactivity, is thus an exceptional poem in Shakespeare's œuvre eclipsing the subsequent *Rape of Lucrece* in its facetiousness and iconoclasm and proving to be more than a mere stopgap financially tiding him over the precarious

---

[97] Ibid., 98.
[98] For the broader context, see Lennartz, '*My unwasht Muse*', 81–104.

time of the plague. *Venus and Adonis* is a manifesto pinpointing Shakespeare's attitude towards Baroque ooziness, hagioporn, the erosion of traditional gender constellations and the advent of liquid masculinity. To mitigate the impact of this story, Kuchar invites us not only to read Shakespeare's Venus as 'another demonic parody of Magdalene's compassionate weeping over the body of Christ',[99] but also to understand the whole story as the warped and diseased perception of a Venus/ Mary Magdalene whose mind is comparable to the distortions of anamorphic paintings, at that time *en vogue* in European Mannerism.[100] Since Shakespeare chooses to have the farcical tale transmitted through Venus's unreliable and mad eyes – 'Her eyes are mad that they have wept till now' (*VA*, 1062) – it is then open to conjecture to what extent the scandalously zoophilic and pornographic end, the cross-species intercourse between a boy and a boar ('nuzzling in his flank, the loving swine / Sheathed unaware the tusk in his soft groin'; *VA*, 1115–16), is also the result of a 'sick-thoughted' and overheated female imagination. Leaving Venus wallowing in dead Adonis's 'congealed blood' (*VA*, 1122) and thus bringing the narrative to an 'unsavoury end' (*VA*, 1138), Shakespeare finishes his digression into an proto-expressionist *ésthetique du mal avant la lettre* and almost does in this poem what he was about to do with the Petrarchan sonnet tradition and what his contemporary Cervantes was planning to do with the romances in his *Don Quixote*: to make a satirical butchery of the time-honoured tradition, and here to expose the gender-warped bleeding and oozing bodies to ridicule, to turn Baroque iconography into an absurd heap of porous, gashed and ravished bodies and to facetiously blur the line of distinction between woman, boy and boar.

In the same way as Adonis's body is suddenly 'melted like a vapour' from Venus's sight (*VA*, 1166) leaving his blood to be metamorphosed into an anemone (that was finally crushed and 'wither[ed]' between Venus's breasts, *VA*, 1182), Renaissance concepts of Mars-like masculinity were rapidly being eclipsed by exotic, burlesque or monstrous harbingers of gender-erasing porosity. John Dowland's popular song 'Flow, my teares' (1600), later expanded into the seven-part pavane *Lachrymae*, aptly gives expression to a culture in which artists became obsessed with the depiction of tears and poets openly questioned the once irrefutable fact that only women were versed in the fraudulent alchemy of tears, the 'siren tears / Distilled from limbecks foul as hell within'.[101]

---

[99] Kuchar, *Poetry of Religious Sorrow*, 102.

[100] To what extent tears distort the perception in the manner of an anamorphic painting, see *Richard 2*: "Sorrow's eyes, glazed with blinding tears, / Divides one thing entire to many objects, / Like perspectives, which, rightly gazed upon, / Show nothing but confusion[.]" *R2* 2.2.16–19. See also Kuchar, 'Andrew Marvell's Anamorphic Tears', 345–81.

[101] *Son* 119, 1–2.

In the context of this controversial culture of Baroque porosity which was also fuelled by the popular revenge tragedies ludicrously steeped in blood, tears and other fluids, Richard Crashaw finally emerges as a writer of unprecedented fluid-soaked poetry that has not only provoked strident criticism and allegations of bad taste,[102] but also divided generations of readers on account of its depictions of grotesque porousness, excruciatingly masochistic pain and eroticized mourning. With regard to all these components, Shakespeare's *Venus and Adonis* must have proved to be a useful manual. With notions of gender dualism evaporating and the dominance of male voices in Renaissance poetry on the wane, Crashaw is one of the first male poets to adopt female identities and, as a ventriloquist of female voices, he clearly suppresses his masculinity in order to contribute to a rapid 'feminisation of grief' in the arts.[103] While Donne could not resist crossing gender boundaries once in a while, especially when in Holy Sonnet XIV he visualizes himself as a besieged female city married to the devil and secretly 'labour[ing] to admit' God with all the connotations of being inseminated and suffering pangs of birth,[104] Crashaw's consistency in impersonating female saints and martyrs is conspicuous and a further indication of the growing confusion of genders leading up to the end of the old *cortegiano* ideal. The fact that in 1645 Crashaw leaves England for France and Italy is not only a reaction to the raging Puritanism of his age, but also a consequence of England's inability to engage with poems that celebrated female ooziness and championed a one-sex model that was now a thoroughly feminine one.

Having imbibed the influences of Giambattista Marino's sensual poetry, Crashaw writes his famous and controversial poem 'The Weeper' in his Italian Counter-Reformation exile. Incorporated into the 1646 collection of religious poems called *Steps to the Temple*, the poem is, like all the other poems, a tribute to and, to a certain degree, a rewriting of George Herbert's *The Temple* (1633), notwithstanding the fact that Herbert advocated a poetry of moderation and seemed to subject the flamboyance of the Continental literature of tears to parodic castigation.[105] Worlds apart from Herbert's Calvinistic poetics and his concept of man in persistent search for a *dieu caché*, Crashaw's weeping Mary Magdalene never doubts God's sensual presence, when she sheds a profusion of tears that provides a liquid bridge between this world of deprivation and the

---

[102] An early example of this allegation is provided by Adams, 'Bad Taste in Metaphysical Poetry', 271.
[103] For a strong tendency of feminization in early modern arts since the Middle Ages, see (apart from Vaught, *Masculinity and Emotion*) Bynum, *Jesus as Mother*.
[104] Holy Sonnet XIV, 6 *Poetical Works*, 299.
[105] Martz, 'The Action of Grief in Herbert's "The Church"', 132f. See also Kuchar, *Poetry of Religious Sorrow*, 77.

otherworldly realm of God's oozy richness. If there is a Christian equivalent to Niobe it is Crashaw's Mary Magdalene who, as a weeper of a profusion of tears, is worshipped as a penitent in myriads of paintings in which she is not only increasingly divested of her tormenting hairy shirt, but also denuded and, like bathing Susannah, exposed to the penetrating male gaze.

From the very first line, Mary Magdalene's Niobean affiliations become evident, when she is introduced into the poem as a human fountain with her eyes producing 'sister springs' (1).[106] But while Niobe and her Niobean sisters from the Antiquity to Shakespeare's plays produce streams of self-referential or histrionically deceptive tears that flow nowhere and effect nothing, Mary Magdalene's incessant expenditure of tears – 'Still spending, neuer spent' (5) – is so productive, precious and even nourishing that each tear is invested with mystical and supernatural qualities. Weeping eyes are thus no longer signs of female weakness, but agents of a cosmological harvest:

'Tis seed-time still with thee
And starres thou sow'st, whose haruest dares
Promise the earth to counter shine
Whateuer makes heaun's forhead fine. (9–12)

Mary Magdalene's proliferation of tears corresponds to the poem's structure as a string of bead-like stanzas in which each tear drop is shown in a process of permanent metamorphosis. Thus, the image of sowing and reaping stars is immediately modified ('But we are deceiued all'; 13), changed and augmented by prism-like new facets such as the component of tears as mystical food, reminiscent of Donne's 'Twickenham Garden', where, in the image of tears as restorative wine, he had betrayed his submerged Catholic sympathies. While Donne's reference is only isolated, Crashaw belabours and develops images into clusters of absurdity. Setting aside all criteria of logic and gravitation, the reader is invited to see Mary Magdalene's eyes in terms of an overflowing Baroque cornucopia which produces liquid stars that, in subsequent stanzas, turn into milk, flow beyond the Milky Way and, in their galactic process of refinement (embedding both the Greek and Latin words for milk: *gala* and *lac*), are eventually whipped into a most exquisite cream.

Vpwards thou dost weep.
Heauen's bosome drinks the gentle stream.

---

[106] *The Poems, English, Latin and Greek of Richard Crashaw*, 308–14.

Where th'milky riuers creep,
Thine floates aboue, & is the cream. (19–22)

By miraculously flowing upwards and turning from salty water into sweet cream, Mary Magdalene's tears come from lactating eyes that, in a moment of mystical transformation, themselves turn into breasts and feed '[h]eauen's bosome', thereby mystically underlining what later physiologists discovered as a semblance of chemical substances between tears and milk. Living in a cultural climate that was more syncretistic than scientific, Crashaw took less interest in (and was blissfully unaware of) chemical analogies and rather preferred to pinpoint mythological and Christian parallels, so that his Niobean weeper with lacrymose breasts or lactating eyes conjures up other legends of porosity in Baroque readers. While some readers might have felt reminded of the Virgin Mary who, as in Alonso Cano's mystical painting *San Bernardo y la Virgen* (Figure 2), feeds Saint Bernard of Clairvaux in a marvellous arc of breast milk, others saw Crashaw's Mary Magdalene in a superior position to Juno who, by taking Hercules off her gushing breasts, was said to have created the Milky Way, devoid of any refining cream. In contrast to Juno's senseless and random spillage of milk, Mary Magdalene's milky tears are teleological, rarefied and nutritious, inducing the poet to have the image culminate in the weird idea of a 'brisk Cherub' (26) sipping them as his daily matinal repast.

From the brief description of this angelic, oral-erotic 'Breakfast' (30) the reader is immediately led on to stanzas where Mary Magdalene's tears are suddenly hardened into 'proudest pearles' (42) or into the paradox of '[w]arm syluer shoures' of coins (126). Constantly switching from images of liquidity to ones of hardness and deliberately reversing all notions of logic, Crashaw's poem eventually neutralizes the last vestiges of Renaissance moderation by juxtaposing them with (proto-) modern notions of vastness. In stanza XV, the 'wit of loue' (89) still enables the poet (and the reader) to see the structure of a well-ordered garden, a limited *jardin d'amour* in Mary Magdalene's face – 'Fountain & Garden in one face' (90) – but it then takes only twenty lines for the eyes' 'faithfull fountaines' to exceed their boundaries and to swell from two 'walking baths' (112) into the surreal notion of '[p]ortable, & compendious oceans' (113/14). The poem ends on a phantasmagorical note, when, as Kuchar writes, 'metrical foot becomes flesh'[107] and the tears are eventually given voices in order to declare, in a key of humility, that their up-flowing streams and showers are only invested

---

[107] Kuchar, *Poetry of Religious Sorrow*, 89. Kuchar also refers to the fact that Crashaw literalizes Southwell's image of tears as 'mighty orators' in *Marie Magdalenes Funeral Teares* (87).

Figure 2 Alonso Cano, *San Bernardo y la Virgen* (Saint Bernard and the Virgin) (c. 1645–52), Prado, Madrid. Courtesy The Picture Art Collection/Alamy Stock Foto.

with meaning when they are finally diverted and channelled onto the lowest parts of Christ's bleedingly abject body, 'our lord's FEET' (186).

Outside the territorial and ideological boundaries of Britain, Crashaw reinterprets the figure of Mary Magdalene as a larger-than-life phenomenon of porosity and abjection wallowing in milky or menstrual ooze;[108] he, thus, familiarizes his readership with concepts of a pervasive femininity that, more

---

[108] Cf. Sabine, 'Crashaw and Abjection', 423–43.

than a generation after Shakespeare and his tentative attempts at penitent weepers,[109] refuse to be reconciled to traditional images of women as neatly trimmed gardens (with male-operated fountains). Exceeding the narrow boundaries imposed on them by the old garden imagery, oozy women celebrating the Kristevan 'erotic cult of the abject'[110] in Crashaw's ventriloquizing poems are no longer to be dovetailed into well-cherished illusions of women's bodies as little 'several plots' (and their husbands as their would-be Priapistic guardians); torrential floods of tears, streams of blood and milky juices are, in the first decades of the seventeenth century, the new markers of a rapid feminization of culture which, inspired by Christ's tears in St John's Gospel, subjects all male domains to unwonted intrusions of Niobean liquidity.

Utopian and dystopian floods – abdominal tears and drowning Quixotes

Pornutopian halcyon days

The seventeenth century is a porous age par excellence: while mythologies and Christian narratives are rewritten along the lines of porous bodies (leaving some of them as drained as Niobe in Donne's *Epigrams*: 'By childrens births, and death, I am become / So dry, that I am now mine owne sad tombe'),[111] astronomers become alert to the existence of a porous cosmos. Questioning the Ptolemaic geocentric world view and drilling enlightened holes into their well-cherished myths of the impervious firmament or God's 'marble mansion',[112] they are faced with a similar porosity as are the physicians who, by exploring and scrutinizing the human body, see that its microcosm has also become porous, a topography riddled with holes, craters and cavities. As a refusenik or occasional parodist of both forms of porousness, Shakespeare inveterately sticks to the old finite cosmography and, via Lorenzo in Act V of *The Merchant of Venice*, extols to his audience the inexpressible beauty of the thickly inlaid firmament. In the same way he refuses to budge from the belief in the integrity of the human microcosm and subscribes to the myth of man's skin as an impervious slab of blue-veined marble or a similar stony substance (excluding the word 'pore' categorically

---

[109] Cf. Antigonus's speech in *WT* 3.3.25: 'her eyes / Became two spouts'.
[110] Kristeva, *Powers of Horror*, 55. See also Sabine, 'Crashaw and Abjection', 426.
[111] Epigrams, 'Niobe'. *Poetical Works*, 67.
[112] *Cym* 5.2.60.

from his dramatic and poetic œuvre). Regardless of Shakespeare's cultural conservatism, people were increasingly coming to terms with the sobering fact that their macro- and microcosmological notions of firmness, economy and containment were fables of the past. Holes in the macrocosm, visions of a galactically leaky universe started to jostle people out of their certainty of anti-porous anthropocentricity in the same way as microscope-based facts did when revealing bodies honeycombed with pores. Supported by instruments of relentless empiricism, the telescope and the microscope, the unsettling knowledge of porousness inevitably seeped into seventeenth-century people's minds and elicited various responses from medical, literary and (pseudo-) philosophical discourses.

A cursory glance at early modern medical manuals makes it astoundingly clear that, for Shakespeare's contemporaries, pores were not new, but almost threateningly omnipresent. In the context of medicine, the skin was always a prominent site of liminality where the interior and the exterior met and where the surface of the body suddenly transmutes into a perilous 'place of permeability and mysterious metamorphoses'.[113] For physicians who were not only cosmographers of the human body, but also physiological economists, the idea that the skin was to be conceived of as a place of irrepressible seepage where countless odiferous drops could enter or rivulets of sweat and other exudations could render the body bankrupt and humorally insolvent had always been a matter of serious concern. In his anatomical compendium, *Microcosmographia* (1615), Helkiah Crooke challenged the poets' idea of a marmoreal skin by visualizing the skin as an 'unseamed garment' that is broken by an infinite number of 'breaches' and pores which 'serue either receyuing or letting out'.[114] The opinion that the abundance of 'pin-hoales' dotting the skin was an important instrument of regulating the economy of bodily fluids and of giving sweat, the alchemical 'excrements of the third concoction',[115] a natural outlet was common knowledge among early modern physicians which, however, clashed with the writers' obstinate view of the body from a sculptor's perspective.

It is certainly an oversimplification to interpret the early modern writers' inclination to freeze women's bodies into statues or 'virtuous monument[s]'[116] as a complete disregard for medical or anatomical truths. With the chasm dividing science from poetry, poets, however, continued to ignore what sixteenth-century

---

[113] Benthien, *Skin*, 39.
[114] Crooke, *Microcosmographia*, 72.
[115] Ibid., 73.
[116] *Luc*, 391.

physicians such as Thomas Moulton (*This Is the Myrrour or Glasse of Helth*, 1545) and Sir Thomas Elyot (*The Castle of Helth*, 1534) had been propagating for quite a while: the concept of dermatological openness. The treatise *Haven of Health*, which was written in 1584 by the Oriel fellow Thomas Cogan, 'Chiefly Gathered for the Comfort of Students', even stressed the importance of the pores and the skin's openness and strongly argued for the purifying effect of sex, the (male and female) seminal discharge functioning as a life-preserving and cathartic ejection of stale bodily fluids. Medical manuals like those aforementioned ostensibly undercut early modern man's self-fashioning as a stoic Macduff and thus touched upon the Renaissance taboo of man and woman's equality in porousness. If the knowledge of pores and the body's porousness did feed into literary discourse, then it did so as an annoying female intrusion into the male sphere: in his satire *The Poetaster* (1601), Jonson has the female personification of Envy precede the Prologue proper and speak of 'a freezing sweate [that] / Flowes forth at all my pores'.[117] Along the same lines, it is considered to be the effusion of women's irrational and ill-boding dreams when statues or heroes' monuments suddenly start to become porous: 'She [= Calphurnia] dreamt tonight she saw my statue, / Which, like a fountain with an hundred spouts, / Did run pure blood',[118] so says Shakespeare's Caesar condescendingly, and thus dismisses this nightmare of Niobean porosity into the category of 'foolish' female fear-mongering.[119] And although Calphurnia's divinatory dream proves to be well grounded, the porosity of a man's stony or marble body continues to be a taboo in the same way as the idea that men were imperceptibly losing control of their humoral economy.

The extent to which the skin became an unignorably critical place, a threshold where, according to Bakhtin, 'acts of the bodily drama' were hourly being staged[120] was to make itself felt in post-Shakespearean times. But before Restoration writers such as the Earl of Rochester became witnesses to the advent of the modern body as a dermatological catastrophe and saw their skins turned into intractable 'spouts', a coterie of Neo-Classicist poets, the so-called Cavaliers, nostalgically looked back to an age when porosity was not only a female affair, but also a relic of the delectable ooziness in the utopian land of Cockaigne.

At about the same time as Crashaw was writing his poetry as a liquid-saturated response to the Puritan fundamentalists (whose self-incurred hardness was

---

[117] *The Poetaster, or His Arraignment*, Prologue, 31–32. *Ben Jonson*, vol. 4:204.
[118] *JC* 2.2.76–78.
[119] Ibid., 2.2.105.
[120] Bakhtin, *Rabelais and His World*, 317.

proverbial and even Shylockian),[121] the Cavaliers indulged in a short intermezzo of Anacreontic porousness. Repelled by the inflationary representations of Christ as a gushing blood fountain (with sometimes more than four or five spouts), by Saint Thomas's finger inquisitively probing Christ's wound and by Mary Magdalene's abjectly fetishistic relish for blood-stained feet, the Cavaliers set out in their quest for hedonistic (and misogynist) banquets of tasty female bodies. For a short time, for the span of halcyon days (a term that the Cavaliers used to refer to their brief enjoyment of utopian hedonism), porousness was invested with positive and epicurean delights, devoid of indications of grief, pain or imminent humoral bankruptcy. When, in one of his escapist country-house poems, in 'To my Friend G.N. from Wrest', Thomas Carew explicitly mentions pores, as in 'porous bosom',[122] he uses them to denote a counter-world of Arcadian fertility which the Puritans either suppressed or denounced as decadent and incompatible with Christ's soteriological porousness. In their epicurean constructions of the past, of the mythic Golden Age as found in Torquato Tasso's *Aminta* (1580),[123] poets such as Richard Lovelace in 'Love Made in the First Age: To Chloris' (c. 1650) nostalgically wallowed in dreams of a pre-Christian and pre-Attic porousness which was supposed to be free of both the odium of pain and Niobean mourning. No longer restricted to Christ's excruciating martyrdom or to Niobe's irredeemable punishment, Cavalier ideas of porousness are utopian male fantasies in which passive women are shown as contributing to and partaking of a universal porousness with the entirety of their deliciously leaky bodies.

Wedged between the Metaphysicals' discovery of men's liquidity and the Puritans' hostility to bodily openness, the Cavaliers imaginatively transported themselves into a secular paradise in which tears of mourning and remorse were believed to be non-existent – 'there was no tear'[124] – and female bodies were redefined as juicy titbits, exuding appetizing sexual fluids at every pore for the free degustation of the male lover. Eclipsing the popular weepers of the seventeenth century and denying concepts of male liquidity, the Cavaliers preferred to conflate the myth of the permissive Golden Age with the story of Don Juan, which, since its emergence on the Spanish stage around 1613, had intriguingly juxtaposed sexual incontinence with male control and stoniness (as

---

[121] See Gratiano's rhetorical question and response in *MV*: '[…] which what's harder – / His [= Shylock's] Jewish heart!' (4.1.78–79). Greenblatt's contrary argument that Jews were accused of unnatural porousness and that Jewish men were even believed to menstruate is evidence of the contradictoriness in the representation of 'the other'. Greenblatt, *Will in the World*, 259.

[122] 'To my Friend G.N. from Wrest', 12. *The Poems of Thomas Carew*, 86–89.

[123] Cf. El-Gabalawy, 'The Trend of Naturalism in Libertine Poetry', 35–44.

[124] Lovelace, 'Love Made in the First Age. To Chloris', 37. *Ben Jonson and the Cavalier Poets*, 320–22.

epitomized by the stony Commendatore at the end). In default of stony guardians or avengers of morality and without presentiments of the libertine's descent into harrowing hell, the Cavaliers' donjuanesque paradise is a juicy place where the taking of a girl's virginity, defloration, is on the same level as the indiscriminate plucking of flowers (*flores*):

> [...] lads indifferently did crop
> A flower and a maidenhead. (17–18)

In the same way as promiscuous sex is dissociated from sin and equated with the innocent act of collecting a bunch of flowers, bodily liquids are no longer part of a semiotics of penitence, but rather streams, rivulets or brooks in a (porn) utopian nature where the female body is as available as that of a milk-yielding cow, and where the bucolic tradition blurs into a bizarre form of pornographic lactation:

> Then unconfined each did tipple
> Wine from the bunch, milk from the nipple,
> Paps tractable as udders were[.] (19–21)

While images of female fountains were linked to the imposition of an artificial structure and order upon the anarchic flow of female juices, and depictions of lactating women were restricted to the Virgin Mary (or women closely related to Christ), the Cavaliers' vision of a sexualized land of Cockaigne, brimful of sap and milk, is the thirsting libertine's wishful thinking of a secular, guiltless and exploitative Arcady. Ostensibly drawing on the iconography of a Rubens-like Roman charity suckling an old, decrepit man at her full breasts, Lovelace quickly perverts the idea of female fertility and charity into the image of women as stupid, but sexy cattle proffering their udder-like breasts for the immediate comfort of hedonistic man. In his description of the eccentric Venus in *Venus and Adonis*, even Shakespeare had already reverted to the bucolic image of a woman as a 'milch doe whose swelling dugs do ache' (*VA*, 875). While Shakespeare's bovine goddess of love belongs to the category of parody, Lovelace's evocations of milk-oozing women are part of a donjuanesque concept of an eroticized countryside in which agricultural ideas of femininity spawn further misogynist images: on a par with olives dripping with 'wholesome jellies' (22) and defined by juices which the amorous gourmet squeezes out of women's 'bellies' (23), the female sex is nothing more than an appetizing orchard which the speaker ambles through in pursuit of free and exquisite sexual cuisine.

That the gourmandizing foray into the female body is a rake's *reverie* is made clear by the end of the poem. Awakening to drab reality and finishing the poem on a masturbatory note – 'Enjoying of myself I lie' (60) – the speaker insinuates that his idea of a strict division of mankind into porous cattle-like women and men as active erotic harvesters and connoisseurs of women's free-flowing genital fluids is not only a utopian construction of Tasso's or even Aretino's spirit,[125] but also a witty code of Royalist male bonding which the Puritans anathematized. Similarly, the idea of assuming the role of a roving, 'empty Bee' on his mistress's labyrinthine body gives the Cavalier libertine in Carew's poem 'A Rapture'[126] the illusion of still being in control of his libertine's paradise, of exploiting and manipulating the juices that an imaginary porous female body offers up to him; even when confronted with the female body as the wide expanse of 'a sea of milke' (81), the rakish Cavalier leaves his aristocratic circles in no doubt that he never loses his sense of navigation and that it is he who eventually has the power to ruffle the smooth surface of the (female) ocean with a seminal tempest which, in libertinistic circles, was reminiscent of the genital shower of gold that Jove bestowed upon Danaë. Carew's reference to the myth of Danaë is intriguing here, since it shows that even the highest and most masculine god is capable of revealing himself as being liquid. But what makes this myth so convenient for the Cavaliers is the fact that Jove's liquefaction is a deliberate act and a feat of deceptive and economic ingenuity (that the shower was made up of golden coins must have reassured the Cavaliers and alerted them to the attractive link between sex, fluidity and cash).

Beset on all sides with religious fundamentalism, moral austerity and the prospect of a Puritan coup d'état, the Cavaliers nostalgically adopt the role of the jovial courtier who either subjects the woman's body to his random inseminations or, in the guise of a predatory animal (or insect), feasts on its lavish juices. As a sign of rakish generosity, he is even ready to temporarily entrust his rudder (= penis) to his lady's 'bold hand' (87), thereby, in an erotic and reckless dalliance with the Chain of Being, to promote her to the position of a 'skilfull Pilot' (88) who in the act of 'guide[ing/His] Bark into Love's channell' bathes him in a 'juyce of kisses' (93). That this image of female sexual empowerment is meant to be a hoax, a short spell of carnivalesque liberty, is underlined by the reference to the 'halcyon days', to the 'Halcion calmnesse' (97), indicating

---

[125] El-Gabalawy sees Carew's poems in the tradition of Aretino's libertinism, 'The Trend of Naturalism in Libertine Poetry', 42.
[126] 'A Rapture', 55. *The Poems of Thomas Carew*, 49–53.

that the Cavaliers were disturbingly aware of living (and loving) in a period of precarious poise and saw that a change for the worse was looming large.

Behind the Cavalier's generous renunciation of the captain's role on the ocean of the female body the reader notices an attitude of condescension, a play with donjuanesque masks and roles which ultimately turn out to be part of a libertinistic choreography that forces women into sexual intercourse. The peremptory tone of the poems clearly underlines the Cavaliers' self-fashioning as rapists, predators and robbers of any 'virgin-treasure' (32), staving off the sad truth that the rake's utopia is on the point of being overshadowed by a dystopia of rigorism. Carew's 'A Rapture' thus follows the structure of a risky game: masculine control is playfully forfeited, the position of the love boat's pilot is ceded to the mistress in an act of daring gender swapping – right to the very moment when the Cavalier resumes his authority and reinstalls himself in the position of an active connoisseur who, after dallying with ideas of female sexual empowerment, translates and objectifies his mistress's porous body into Classicist concepts of sculptural beauty. When he eventually imagines his 'enfranchized hand' touching and taking possession of his mistress's 'naked polish'd ivory' (29/30), he confidently banishes the threat of the porous female body into the realm of art and seems to hold all those men in contempt who, like Shakespeare's Antony, see their '[a]uthority melt'[127] and, instead of dictating the rules of the amorous game, tend to be engulfed and nullified in the 'sea[s] of milke' or other pools of female liquidity.

Drowning Don Juans – invitations to banquets of bulimia

The halcyon days of the libertine's erotic mise en scène ended in 1642; the Cavaliers' dreams of a Golden Age of sexual carnivalism, of playing naughty games and banqueting on female porosity, turned into a nightmare of religious fundamentalism (in which oozing bodies were signs of sinfulness and disgrace). The eighteen-year Interregnum is thus a watershed of many sorts, and even though the Restoration aimed to reinstitute the divine and patriarchal monarchy, it no longer supplied strategies to prevent the history of masculinity from turning into a shatteringly modern narrative of man's 'melting of authority'. In this context, the Cavaliers' habit of praising the leaky female body and pushing it into the centre of male pornographic desire was a short-lived fantasy, a feeble

---

[127] *AC* 3.13.95.

threshold that was unable to keep the flood of unleashed and self-destructive libertinism in check.[128]

Even if Virginia Woolf's image of the seventeenth-century Great Frost followed by a diluvian thaw in *Orlando* (1928) is fictitious and hyperbolic, it is a good metaphor to illustrate the enormity of what happens in Restoration literature which is still inadequately discussed in terms of flippancy, frivolity and erotic provocation. The river 'strewn with icebergs', the smashing of stones and iceblocks 'against the piers and pillars'[129] and the ensuing chaos fittingly captures the impact of John Wilmot's, the Earl of Rochester's, poetry. While pre-Interregnum poets still desired solidification, bodies whose ooziness could easily be converted into stones, marble, ice or gems, Rochester inaugurates the thaw, the liquefaction and the opening of the pores that henceforth turn Don Juans into terrifying, gushing Niobean streams.

Habitually neglected or disparaged as the excrescences of a pornographic and insane mind, Rochester's poems are ground-breakingly pivotal, since they record the moment when the male protagonist loses his footing in the battle of the sexes, and when the porousness of the female body – erstwhile nonchalantly enjoyed and manipulated – turns into a real nightmare threatening the male speaker with total nullification. In this respect, the poem 'The Imperfect Enjoyment' (1680) is an intriguing piece of cultural history or even 'a living laboratory',[130] recording the memorable transition from Cavalier ludic libertinism to the devastating insight into man as the helpless victim of his unmanageable pores. Trivialized by critics due to references to the long burlesque tradition of *ejaculatio praecox*-poems which ranges from Ovid's *Amores* to poems by Etherege, Congreve and even Aphra Behn,[131] the poem is usually considered to be a literary extravagance, an early modern dramatic monologue intended to amuse the Restoration court (and to jostle the courtiers out of the lingering torpor of leaden Puritanism). Before the backdrop of the chequered survey of the porous body, the poem is saturated with meaning, since it represents the swansong of the early modern concept of stony masculinity and the advent of the new *cortegiano* of Charles II's calibre who, in alarming emulation of his king, proves to be not only supremely profligate, but also at the mercy of his emasculating porousness.

---

[128] In this context, Turner uses the apt term 'masculine extremism'. *Schooling Sex*, 272.
[129] Woolf, *Orlando*, 44.
[130] Vanhaesebrouck and Dehert, 'Introduction', 4.
[131] Ellis claims that a poem on a 'premature ejaculation mishap was almost an obligatory exercise for the Restoration poet'. *The Complete Works*, 325. For the genealogy of the 'imperfect-enjoyment poems', see also Thormählen, *Rochester: The Poems in Context*, 85–86.

Drawing upon the literary scene before the Interregnum, Rochester freely plagiarizes the Metaphysicals' vocabulary in his poem. But what at first looks like an obscene rewriting of Metaphysical love mysticism unexpectedly turns into an almost prophetic and nightmarish vision of what was soon to be hailed as the age of porosity-ridden sentimentality. What is striking and alarming is that, right from the beginning of the poem, the female part in the sexual performance is an unusually active one – 'She clips me to her breast and sucks me to her face'.[132] When the speaker continues to stick to the conviction that, in this sexual contest, he is still in full command of his role as an amorous Jove and that he is able to release his phallic 'all-dissolving thunder-bolt' (10) at his own discretion, he unwittingly ironizes himself and betrays the distance that separates him from the Cavaliers. While underestimating the power of his lover's tongue – '(Love's lesser lightning)' patronizingly put into parenthesis – the poem's rake is suddenly flung into a state of ecstasy which emphatically underlines the difference to what Donne had described in the martial image of a parley between two souls, between 'two equal Armies' in his 1633 poem 'The Extasie'.[133] While Donne's souls 'negotiate' on equal terms and leave their bodies in a condition of death-like liminality ('like sepulchrall statues'),[134] Rochester never reaches beyond his wayward flesh and finds himself locked in a battle in which the transgressive Don Juan encounters a new race of women: oversexed, coolly calculating and now no longer willing to relinquish the pilot's position that women had temporarily been given in Cavalier poetry.

With his 'fluttering soul' (11) hanging 'hovering o' er her balmy brinks of bliss' (12), Rochester's speaker is on the verge of a crisis that goes beyond the *malheur* of a premature ejaculation. The alliterative 'balmy brinks of bliss' have ceased to be pleasant and nourishing fountains in a beautiful bodily *locus amoenus*; the 'brinks' have now become slippery and treacherous vaginal precipices in which hopes of erotic bliss are turned into dystopias of bodily disintegration. The liminal experience of orgasm, the crisis of the 'little death', so far a *res tacenda* in literature,[135] is here condensed into an irregular two-line iambic pentameter which encapsulates a radically new and deconstructive view of masculinity. The donjuanesque image of man as a sexual warrior, a rover and a colonizer of the passive female body is, within the space of ten metrical feet, not only

---

[132] 'The Imperfect Enjoyment', 6. *Complete Works*, 28–29.
[133] 'The Extasie', 13. *Poetical Works*, 46.
[134] Ibid., 17 and 18.
[135] See Shakespeare's description of a mutual orgasm in Juliet's speech: 'Give me my Romeo, and when I shall die / Take him and cut him out in little stars'. *RJ* 3.2.21–22.

reversed, but also replaced by a new narrative of man's effeminizing liquidity, by the Restoration courtier who, in a few seconds of porous (anti-) climax, finds himself transformed into an oozing cipher and into what the later Victorians dreaded as 'spermatorrhea':[136]

> In liquid raptures I dissolve all o'er,
> Melt into sperm and spend at every pore. (15–16)

Approximately seventy years after Shakespeare's pejorative sonnet on the orgasm as a pointless moment of expenditure and economic waste (in which the word 'bliss' is clearly aligned with 'woe'),[137] Rochester lets his cluster of onomatopoeic words revolving around man's unprecedented metamorphosis into an uncontrollable Niobean fountain terminate in the word 'pore'. While the 'liquid raptures' still echo the Cavaliers' key of erotic bravado, the rapid succession of the words 'dissolve', '[m]elt' and 'spend' culminating in the shattering rhyme 'all o'er/pore' aptly summarizes man's tragic undoing and the end of early modern male self-fashioning. With their 'all-dissolving thunderbolt[s]' rebounding on themselves and finding their bodies riddled with holes which previous writers had studiously ignored, the Restoration courtier is quickly identified as a *miles gloriosus*, as a braggart who boasts of being a Jovian predator and who ends up whining, vociferating and oozing from myriads of unstoppable holes. That this trajectory from a Jovian thunderer (*Jupiter tonans*) to a porous nonentity falls short of the eighteenth-century category of the mock-heroic becomes clear when critics stop reading Rochester as a riotous enfant terrible and rather see him as a sensitive reflector of a new understanding of masculinity.

Exposed to the vindictive irony of his female partner, who not only 'from her body wipes the clammy joys' (20), but also – quite in anti-Cavalier fashion – taunts him by coquettishly asking the nullifying question 'Is there then no more?' (22), the rake, now squeezed dry, sexually insolvent and precariously open, rapidly dwindles into a dehydrated nonentity ('despairing, limber, dry / A wishing, weak, unmoving lump I lie'; 35–36). Left to vent his impotent rage on his shrivelled penis, the swashbuckling libertine is completely dismantled and ridiculed, in particular when his poor performance is contrasted to the donjuanesque 'cock' and bull story spreading the rumour that his penis was the random perforator of thousands of women and boys.

---

[136] 'In spermatorrhea, the body becomes a sieve, losing vitality from every orifice'. Roseman, *Unauthorized Pleasures*, 24.
[137] *Son* 129, 11.

While Rochester's traumatic description of his male porous condition is clearly confined to this poem (marking the poet's career from 'a youthful, erotic perspective to the ironic and satiric purview of his maturity'),[138] various other poems in his slim œuvre show man in a similarly debasing situation: shockingly exposed to and on the point of being sucked into the miry and infectious openness of the female body. As if taking their cue from old misogynist King Lear voicing his hatred of vaginal sulphurous pits, the speakers depict porosity as being invariably repulsive; in blatant contrast to the appetizing banquets which were provided by the female genitals in the Cavaliers' poems, Rochester, via his speakers, looks into odious cesspools in which corrupting and disease-spreading liquids are mixed into a poisonous brew. Adopting the role of a voyeuristic flâneur, the speaker of what critics, for want of a better generic term, have labelled a pasquinade, a lampoon or a travesty,[139] 'A Ramble in St James's Parke' (c. 1671), leaves the tavern to take a stroll to the park with the express intention to 'see / Drunkenness relieved by lechery' (5f.). What fits into the satirical pattern of Rochester's poems is that, as in 'The Imperfect Enjoyment', he responds to a pretext, in this case to the encomiastical and unctuously deferential poem 'On St James's Park, As Lately Improved by His Majesty' (1661) written by Edmund Waller whose sweetness and classical suavity Rochester came to disapprove. In this respect, courtly readers, habitually in a 'satirical relationship between Court and town',[140] were meant to derive superficial fun from the comparison of the two texts, but, what goes beyond Rochester's jaundiced rewriting of Waller's ingratiating text is that, from the outset, he unmasks himself as a moralist who not only dwells on the tittle-tattle of 'who fucks who and who does worse' (2), but also goes deeper and takes a subcutaneous view of a society in which porousness and erosion have become paramount on all levels.

In 'this all-sin-sheltering grove' (25), he witnesses not only the most atrocious and unnatural forms of sexuality, 'buggeries, rapes, and incests' (24), but also the most dramatic blurring and melting of authorities, the erosion of what the Tudors had venerated as the God-given Chain of Being. In Rochester's poem, porosity thus unfolds a wide spectrum of meaning, covering female bodily ooziness, but also including the leakiness and suppuration of the ailing body politic and the crumbling of the order-sustaining symbol of the chain.[141] Whores of all kinds, chambermaids, heiresses, even 'divines, great lords' and an

---

[138] Johnson, *A Profane Wit*, 126.
[139] Ibid., 152. See also Turner, *Schooling Sex*, 268.
[140] Stallybrass and White, *The Politics and Poetics of Transgression*, 101–02.
[141] For this imagery of 'revolting sexual liquefaction', see Turner, *Schooling Sex*, 272.

alliterative string of 'Prentices, pimps, [and] poets' (30) mingle here and share their promiscuous desire for uninhibited bestial sex. The flâneur's unruffled complacency is disturbed for the very first time when he sees that his lover Corinna belies the pastoral associations of her name and lets herself be toadied to by three animalized fops with 'wriggling tails' (44). The fact that these three young court blades have been metamorphosed into a pack of dogs, 'humble curs' (84), picking up the scent of her 'salt-swol'n cunt' (86) is certainly scandalous, but what aggravates the scandal and reveals the flâneur's detachment as feigned is his (rather snobbish) assertion that female genitals no longer respond to a hierarchy of quality, but, instead, espouse a 'sexual democracy'[142] and assume the function of being 'passive pot[s] for fools to spend in' (102).

The idea of the genitals as 'passive pot[s]' is in line with early modern lore and reminiscent of the various pots, cups, jugs or well-like 'O's which writers reverted to in order to speak about female leakiness, menstruation and conception. While these receptacles were always suspected of a certain porosity (thus accounting for women's illimitable sexual craving), Rochester's grotesque image of Corinna as 'a sexual glutton'[143] and her vagina as a gargantuan receptacle in which 'the seed of half the town' (114) has been stored, mixed and left festering is monstrous and menacing. Even the last vestige of sexual civilization, the genital fountain (as a sexualization of the Niobean fountain of tears), has now been abandoned; and while the Cavaliers glossed over ideas of leakiness with references to eating and banqueting (thus making genital leakiness palatable to the Don Juan as a gourmet), female porosity is, in Rochester's poem, equated with an iconography of bulimic disorder: As early as in Shakespeare's *Othello*, Emilia had linked sex with bulimia, comparing men to overstuffed stomachs and women to the food that is finally thrown up ('when they are full / They belch us');[144] but while in this image of bulimic porosity men were still in control of their erotic food, in Rochester's poem the tables seem to have been literally turned: female Don Juans and Lear's centaurs gorge their nether parts with all sorts of fluids and slimy substances which they sickeningly discharge afterwards: 'your lewd cunt came spewing home [...] / Full gorgèd at another time / With a vast meal of nasty slime' (113/117–18). The classical, albeit troubled, female fountain of Elizabethan times (with its muddiness caused by disobedience) has, in Rochester's imagination, undergone a transformation into a grotesque gullet that, according to Stallybrass and White, has, after a

---

[142] Zwicker, 'Lord Rochester: A Life in Gossip', 89.
[143] Cherniak, *Sexual Freedom*, 77.
[144] *Oth* 3.4.106–07.

spell of absence, been 're-territorialized'[145] and filled to the brim with a long-abandoned load of seminal dirt and genital vomit.

With the female genitals as absorbing gravitational centres of a rout of bestialized men and the porous female body reduced to a 'devouring cunt' (119), a gigantic and ravenous pore, the speaker contends that a perilous disintegration of the *homo rationalis* has already set in: 'reason lay dissolved in love' (132). It is striking that Rochester uses the word 'to dissolve' (and also 'love', which is definitely a misnomer) again, here to convey the idea that (male) rational solidity has been superseded by the imperative of the abdomen, and that the discourse of stony reason (enjoined upon Macduff by Malcolm) has been corroded by vast bulimic vaginas, by oozing genital pots and men ejaculating from every pore. What in this context is so alarming is that even the moralist's most poignant weapon, his reason, dissolves, because his 'revenge' (153, anything but a teleological whetstone) vents itself in a more than thirty-line execration which not only lacks the level-headed coolness of a courtier, but also impressively stresses that he is intricately involved in the seeping canine sex that he pretends to despise so ostentatiously. By the end of this scandalous poem, it is not only the foundations of politics (the king as the self-contained head of the body politic), religion (the Chain of Being) and masculinity (defined as the rational corrective to the leaky female body) that have been completely destroyed; it is also the story of Niobe's tearful porosity that has, in Rochester's poetry, been rewritten along the lines of Pandora's myth of the leaky vaginal box, the discovery (and uncovering) of which symbolically ushered in the evaporation of man's rationality.

While late seventeenth-century people celebrated the restoration of the monarchy in 1660 as the dawn of belated Enlightenment and lauded Charles II as the embodiment of the *Astraea redux* (so the title of Dryden's turncoat panegyric on the Stuart King), Rochester became the spearhead of a counter-discourse of doubt and disillusion. Next to the smutty and quasi-pornographic texts nowadays ascribed to him, such as the farcical *Sodom*, 'Signor Dildoe' and 'Tunbridge Wells', Rochester gave expression to a serious criticism of the Enlightenment myth of man's Cartesian supremacy of the mind. In the long, deconstructivist poem, 'Satyr against Mankind' (c. 1675), Rochester ransacks ideas in texts from Juvenal to Montaigne and Hobbes to cement his argument against the widespread belief that man is in rational control of the lower oozing parts of his centaur existence. Surprisingly meeting with more ferocious

---

[145] Stallybrass and White, *Politics and Poetics of Transgression*, 102.

resistance than his downright obscene poems did,[146] Rochester seems to have touched on one of his contemporaries' raw nerves, when he, more persistently than the Restoration dramatists, unmasks man's self-fashioning as a *homo rationalis* as a great swindle. In his subversive, trend-bucking wish to be

> [a] dog, a monkey, or a bear,
> Or anything but that vain animal
> Who is so proud of being rational. (5–7)

he not only turns the last vestiges of the Chain of Being upside down, but also decries man as a creature that is morally inferior to the animals (particularly dogs and monkeys) which, in the long tradition of animal symbolism, had always been regarded as devilish, moist and grovellingly obsequious. The reader is instantaneously reminded of whining Romeo who found carrion flies running over Juliet's hand superior to himself, or of the self-loathing image of humanity as zombies, 'carrion men, groaning for burial', in Antony's speech[147] to form an idea of the persistent undercurrent of anti-rationalism in English literature. Yet, while Tudor and early Stuart writers were never in doubt that these onsets of irrationality occurred in the presence of God, a Herbertian *deus absconditus*, for Rochester, writing in the wake of Hobbes, God is dead and reason, God's former 'viceroy' (Donne), has failed to take his place. Considering that reason is 'an *ignis fatuus*' (12) in man's mind and that in his erroneous pursuit of illusions he is more often than not obstructed by '[m]ountains of whimseys heaped in his own brain' (17), man is in a deplorable state of delusion and obfuscation. What is more, the image of man that the speaker of this misanthropical poem imparts to his readers seems to have undergone a tremendous change: rid of the role as a bestial hunter of leaky female genitals and as an animalized Don Juan, Rochester's anti-rationalist man – wading through 'error's fenny bogs' and '[t]umbling from thought to thought' (15/18) – now closely resembles a quixotic fool, a dunce who, in his meandering walks through the thicket of fatuous thoughts, suddenly falls headlong down

> Into doubt's boundless sea, where, like to drown,
> Books bear him up awhile and make him try
> To swim with bladders of philosophy. (18–21)

---

[146] See Johnson, *Profane Wit*, 201.
[147] JC 3.1.275.

Rochester's image of quixotic man clutching at 'bladders of philosophy' in the vastness of doubt's sea is the traumatic reaction to several cultural changes and inglorious revolutions in the face of looming modernity at the end of the seventeenth century. While 'philosophy' is disseminated in 'reverend bedlams, colleges and schools' (83), and 'cloistered coxcombs' (92) arrogate the position of instructors, Rochester, via his reviling speaker, cannot help giving his argument a circuitous drift. As Johnson convincingly shows, it is a 'theriophilic eulogy of beasts [that] begins and ends the "Satyr"'[148] and insinuates that Rochester intentionally conflates the genre of satire with the liminal and beast-like figure of the satyr.

Rochester's poems – written from the satiric underground[149] – leave the reader faced with a strange imbalance: on the one hand, there is the vast number of bestialized people cutting across all early modern stratifications of society, dog-like creatures, human curs, bitches and even hybridized hogs, all of them revoltingly porous, dripping and exuding slimy substances, while on the other, there is the dwindling group of moralists and philosophers (represented by the speaker) who constantly forfeit their rational distance by either being drawn into the abdominal depths of the human zoo or drowning in the floods of scepticism and nothingness. Rochester's concept of the modern courtier as a mixture between angry young rebel, whistle-blower and foolish Quixote completely unhinges Restoration optimism, the zeitgeist of frivolity and rationalism, and instead of catering to the people's predilection for lascivious comedy and utopian eroticism, he viciously confronts the court rakes with the unnervingly acrimonious image of the donjuanesque hero as a drowning, porous and disintegrating fool, hopelessly at odds with life, women and his recalcitrant penis.

The Quixote's disgust at Pandora's box

Deconstructivist und underground poems of Rochester's calibre are rare, out of tune with the (official) merriment of the age in which characters such as Horner in William Wycherley's *The Country Wife* (1675) or Dorimant in George Etherege's *The Man of Mode* (1676) cemented the idea of the Restoration hero as a man fully in control of his transgressive wit, his masculinity and his bodily pores. Quixotic fools, by contrast, were alarmingly porous, gullible and

---

[148] Johnson, *Profane Wit*, 205.
[149] von Maltzahn, 'Rochester and the Satiric Underground', 99–120.

generically subsumed under the derogatory terms of fops, blades and coxcombs. The end of the Restoration period and the enthronement of the Protestant William of Orange in 1689 brought an end both to the licentious court culture of the Catholic Stuarts and to the subversive underground poetry of Rochesterian inflection. Given the fact that the reigns of the last (Protestant) Stuart Queen Anne and the Hanoverians were less flamboyant, and comparable satirists and harsh moralists did not appear for the next few decades to come, the character of the quixotic fool, the gull and the nerd was still to survive in a number of Jonathan Swift's poems of the 1730s. Without imputing the fact that Swift as an Irish clergyman was familiar with Rochester's salacious texts (even though the assumption of the moral superiority of animals and the veneration of horses in *Gulliver's Travels* suggest as much), there is no denying that Swift's poems congenially translate Rochester's negative anthropology, his moralist fury at the Yahoo-like beastliness of man and his dystopian nightmares of open bodies, of cavernous pores into the early eighteenth century. Forging a bridge from the Cavaliers to Swift might, at first glance, look rather audacious, but Swift's literary works encourage this approach, since most of them benefit from being read as literary rejoinders to the Cavaliers' bodily utopianism, as amplifiers of Rochester's pessimism written on the premise that the Age of Reason, the Augustan version of the *siècle des lumières*, was nothing more than wishful thinking and a hoax.

As the destroyer of the myth of rationalism and of the idea of the female body as a land of Cockaigne, Strephon, the Quixote in Swift's poem 'The Lady's Dressing Room', is a case in point: brought up on the erroneous idea that women, the dramatis personae of a universal theatrical pageantry, '[a]rrayed in lace, brocade and tissues',[150] are far beyond the pale of the human condition, Strephon turns into the quixotic explorer of Celia's boudoir that, in the typical manner of Juvenal's caustic satires, 'offers a check on lust' and makes him realize that Celia's body is the scandalous epitome of down-the-girdle porousness.[151] In his exploration of her dressing room, he comes upon various 'gallipots', 'vials' (33) and 'filthy basin[s]' (37) that give him a vague idea not only of the cosmetical tricks Celia relies upon, but also of the liquids that she herself, as a harsh parody of the Niobean fountain, constantly produces:

A nasty compound of all hues,
For here she spits, and here she spews. (41–42)

---

[150] 'The Lady's Dressing Room', 4. *The Complete Poems*, 448–52.
[151] Nussbaum, *The Brink of All We Hate*, 112.

The dirty towels that he finds scattered about also contribute to the destruction of his belief in the immaculate and disembodied existence of women, which not only sonneteers in the wake of Petrarch had disseminated, but was also propagated by the burgeoning movement of the sentimental comedy. Rummaging through an array of negative fetishes, among them the towels which are '[b]egummed, bemattered, and beslimed' (45–46), Strephon descends more and more into the dark and disillusioning hells of the female body, 'the secrets of the hoary deep' (98), only to find there as the nadir of female porousness – Celia's private toilet. The mock-heroic simile that compares Strephon to Epimetheus opening Pandora's box is not only witty, but it also aptly captures the idea of quixotic man now having to grapple with the fact that women's bodies materially differ from those of 'goddesses' and that, as the epitome of porousness, weeping Niobe has been rudely displaced by Pandora and her box of 'dissociative' and repulsively excremental dirt.[152] The Cavaliers' Anacreontic banquet of the female porous body is thus not only spoiled, but also invested with a despicable dirtiness which early modern writers seem to have had in mind when they conflated the female genitalia with the anal regions and maliciously resorted to the Tertullian topos that women were a *templum aedificatum super cloacam*.[153]

Driven by Augustan disgust (and rabid fear of insidious infection)[154] and endorsing ideas of femininity which are shaped by classical sculpture that glosses over all embarrassing apertures ('the true *skandalon* of both "classical" aesthetics and politics of the body'),[155] Swift's protagonist finds himself in the awkward position of being neither a savourer nor a tamer of the female porous body. While Shakespeare, in his squeamishness about corporeality, managed to devise strategies (taming, suicide or petrification) to avert the most terrifying consequences that might arise from female porousness, Swift, himself 'manically hygienic',[156] shows his Quixote completely discomfited and nauseated by the overwhelming evidence of female genital openness. Shocked at his contemporaries' reticence about the necessity of daily ablutions to keep the dangers of the Pandora's box at bay as much as possible, Swift seems to take sides with Rochester who, as a reaction to the Pandoran filth around him, had embarked on a Neo-Classicist campaign for bodily hygiene. Like Swift, Rochester clearly sensed that the Cavaliers' feasts of the dripping female bodies had been

---

[152] Stallybrass and White, *Politics and Poetics of Transgression*, 109.
[153] Lennartz, '*My Unwasht Muse*', 277.
[154] Mann, *Reading Contagion*, 37–43.
[155] See Menninghaus, *Disgust*, 56 and also Miller, *The Anatomy of Disgust*, 70.
[156] Stubbs, *Swift, the Reluctant Rebel*, 583.

celebrated in reckless oblivion of the dangers that accompanied unhygienic (female) porousness.[157]

Substituting sordid reality for mythological utopias, Rochester pioneered in his complaints about women's gross negligence of hygienic standards, especially when they expected to have sex either at intense moments of porousness, during their periods of menstrual bleeding, 'in time of flowers', or 'when the smock's beshit'.[158] As an early advocate of 'cleanly sinning' (14), he advises his addressee, Phillis, to make use of the hygienic practices of the dawning Age of the Enlightenment, paper for the bottom and 'sponges for before' (8), and thus to give him the short-lived illusion of women as being sterile, self-contained and in full control of their otherwise anarchic orifices. Swift seems to follow suit, when in his poem 'Strephon and Chloe', the speaker takes up Rochester's cue and gives the reader a deep insight into the Enlightenment poet's obsession with modern forms of cleanliness, especially when he – in marked contrast to previous visions of leaky, lactating or jelly-exuding women – depicts his Chloe as the Classicist ideal of bodily immaculateness:

> Such cleanliness from head to heel:
> No humours gross, or frowzy steams,
> No noisome whiffs, or sweaty streams,
> Before, behind, above, below,
> Could from her taintless body flow. (10–14)

In contrast to Lovelace's excessively leaky female bodies in a vague mythological golden age, Chloe's rigorous regimen of bodily suppression is the new Augustan projection of female corporeality, the Pygmalion dream of a 'taintless body' that is not subject to the human condition and, like an artefact, exempt from the 'necessities of nature' (20). Problems are bound to arise when 'goddess[es]' (85) such as Chloe are forced to live up to twofold expectations and try to combine the role of a deity ('Venus-like, her fragrant skin / Exhaled ambrosia from within', 87f.) with that of a wife on a wedding-night. Managing to resist and ward off Strephon's sexual advances for a moment, Chloe is eventually forced to yield to human nature and – due to the twelve cups of tea that she had drunk – to prepare herself for a complete demystification:

> Twelve cups of tea, (with grief I speak)
> Had now constrained the nymph to leak. (163–64)

---

[157] 'The unlikeness between prudish, careful, insecure Swift and the extrovert Rochester', which Stubbs posits, deserves a re-consideration. Ibid., 95.

[158] 'Song' 'By all love's soft yet mighty powers …', 3–4. *Complete Works*, 200.

While the paradoxical condition of her hands between ivory hardness and waxen softness ('Like ivory dry, and soft as wax', 26) does not provoke any persistent questions, she knows that, as a bride, a Niobean reconciliation between leakiness and hardness, a compromise between nature and idealization is not possible. Furtively trying to slip the chamber pot into the bed, she hopes to delude her quixotic bridegroom and to relieve herself without attracting his notice (and keeping her facade as a self-contained nymph untarnished):

> [She] Steals out her hand by nature led,
> And brings a vessel into bed:
> Fair utensil, as smooth and white
> As Chloe's skin, almost as bright. (171–74)

As the similes make it palpably clear, the male speaker of the poem wants to highlight the symbiotic, but also problematic connection between the two vessels in the bed: between the chamber pot which, in its porcelain beauty, closely resembles Chloe's 'smooth and white' skin, and Chloe, who, in her genital openness, is nothing more than a receptacle absorbing and yielding fluids. In anticipation of Thomas Rowlandson's hilarious illustration of contagious and collective porousness, *A Family on a Journey. Laying the Dust* (1800) (Figure

Figure 3 Thomas Rowlandson, *A Family on a Journey. Laying the Dust* (1800), London, British Museum. Courtesy The Picture Art Collection/Alamy Stock Foto.

3), the wedding night ends in an open challenge or parody of what Norbert Elias later identifies as the concept of the process of civilization, when the couple, like Rowlandson's family, decides to transgress the allegedly raised or expanded 'threshold of repugnance', to urinate in unison[159] and freely to abandon all remnants of socially induced bodily restraints: 'And as he filled the reeking vase / Let fly a rouser in her face' (191–92). While critics such as John Stubbs detect a 'lurking coprophilia' in the poem and espouse the theory that Swift surreptitiously indulged in indecencies,[160] the poem can also be read as the clergyman's (and scholar's) horror at the matrimonial loss of shame and the couple's *anagnorisis* of being Yahoos.

Swift's poem, centred around the quixotic loss of illusions, doubly terminates what the Cavaliers had briefly resuscitated and used as an escapism in a world of fundamentalist astringency: the myth that, under the guise of pastoral costumes, men and women could coquettishly enjoy an erotically porous repast is as rigorously denied by Swift as the myth of women's bodily purity which fools in the wake of Renaissance sonneteers doggedly stuck to. With the departure of the Cupids and other epithalamic personnel that used to hover around matrimonial scenes in the same way as they did in concurrent or belated Rococo paintings by Antoine Watteau and François Boucher, Swift's poem pronounces the end of utopian or *l'âge d'or* ideas of the body and brings its readers back to the crude and repellent realities of the body's prosaic abdominal demands:

> Adieu to ravishing delights,
> High raptures, and romantic flights;
> To goddesses so heavenly sweet,
> Expiring shepherds at their feet;
> To silver meads, and shady bowers,
> Dressed up with amaranthine flowers. (197–202)

High and 'romantic flights' induced by the worship of the female sex belong as much to the past as the swooning and crooning shepherds in theatrical de-profundis positions on the one hand, and the rovers of passive and paradisiacal female bodies on the other. Close to Rochester's poems in their harsh misanthropy, Swift's poems, however, differ from Rochester's by the fact that Swift's quixotic and gullible male characters undergo their trying processes of disillusion without suffering complete bodily disintegration or liquefaction.

---

[159] Elias, *The Civilising Process*, 71.
[160] Stubbs, *Swift, the Reluctant Rebel*, 585.

While depictions of Niobean grief are turned into ruthless explorations of the excremental and (diuretic) horrors of Pandora's genital box, the myth of man's integrity is never as radically called into question as it was in Rochester's blunt attacks on man's bestial atavism. The fact that man's 'goddess [is] grown a filthy mate' (244) sums up the Rochesterian lesson which, after a fitful history of repressed and unleashed porosity, can be extracted both from Swift's poems and from his *Gulliver's Travels* (1726), especially when in the satirical novel, dwarfish Gulliver, sitting astride a sixteen-year-old girl's gigantic nipple,[161] is traumatized by seeing the porousness and revolting dirt of the Brobdingnagians' female breasts. In terms of male porousness, Swift, however, refuses to cross the threshold of shame and, apart from the odd Rabelaisian description of (profuse) urination in *Gulliver's Travels*, he is reluctant to follow in Rochester's footsteps and to see his fools and Quixotes melt into dismal nonentities. The complete metamorphosis of man into a drowning, cursing and leaky vessel seems to be too dystopian a vision for eighteenth-century Tory circles and clubs to connive at; Rochester's radicalism is thus temporarily held at bay, waiting to be revitalized in the eighteenth-century garb of sentimentalism.

---

[161] The pores and their coarse skins elicit as much 'Horror and Disgust' as the quantity of urine which the Brobdingnagian girls freely discharge in front of him, 'the Quantity of at least two Hogsheads'. *Gulliver's Travels*, 108.

2

Niobean bodies in the era of Romanticism

Niobean sentimentalism

Pamela's effusions in the closet

It looks like an instance of cultural irony that the Enlightenment project of draining man's swampy body in the eighteenth century concurs with the sentimental rediscovery of tears.[1] While the constantly reiterated image of man as a producer of faeces, copious rivers of urine, slime and phlegmatic juices used to be linked to the prevalent genres of Menippean satire and sarcastic Restoration comedy, the emergent novel gives rise to a new concept of man, to the closeted individual who, in a response to the Augustans' bodily disgust, seems to be eager to seal their nether regions and to divert the intractable streams of juices into new Niobean floods of tears. Pandora's miasmatic and excremental box in Rochester's and Swift's poems is now, after a spell of Enlightenment reservation (best captured by Samuel Pepys's obsession with constipation and anti-porous blockage),[2] retransformed into Niobe's lachrymose and sentimental springs. With reference to Barthes, Lutz, however, makes it amply clear that the copious tears that the sentimentalists shed are never without genital connotations and that Werther's disposition to melt into tears must also be understood as 'a patently sexual act'.[3] While the language of sentimental literature seems to have been cleansed both of dirty abdominal allusions and of Baroque religious fanaticism, there is the intriguing assumption that mutual tears between lovers in sentimental novels (between Werther and Lotte, or between Emily St Aubert and Valancourt in Ann Radcliffe's *The Mysteries of Udolpho*[4]), in paintings or on

---

[1] See Wahrman, *The Making of Modern Self*, 38 and Koschorke, 'Physiological Self-Regulation', 472–74.
[2] See Pepys's diary entries for 7 and 13 October 1663. *The Shorter Pepys*, 312.
[3] Lutz, *Crying*, 39.
[4] '[T]hey wept together in silence, till Emily […] summoned all her fortitude to utter a last farewell'. *The Mysteries of Udolpho*, 155.

the stage signify more and function as the clean surrogate for sexual intercourse and its taboo exchanges of sordid bodily fluids.[5] Thus, it is advisable to read the eighteenth-century showers of tears not only as showy expressions of melancholy, as tokens of a pervasive weltschmerz, but also as repressed codes for sexual needs that, after the demise of Restoration libertinism, were increasingly banned, silenced and translated into a new bourgeois idiom.

Read before this backdrop, Samuel Richardson's epistolary novel *Pamela, or Virtue Rewarded* (1740) is an incisive break and a pioneeringly new work in which the last vestiges of Restoration profligacy are pitted against a new bourgeois ethic of virtue, privacy and tearful sentimentality. After Desdemona's 'willow song' (as it appears for the first time in the 1623 First Folio) – in which she interestingly weeps by proxy, by quoting a song about Barbary, whose 'salt tears fell from her and softened the stones'[6] – weeping and wailing women (with the odd exception of Mary Magdalene) had, for more than a century, become a rarity in cultural history. A new sentimental demand now seems to be met by Pamela, who, in the company of Jean-Baptiste Greuze's countless languishing girls in French Rococo art (Figure 4), freely indulges in her tears. Forced to discard her identity and to assimilate herself to her husband's soldierly and male world, Desdemona had been forbidden to feel more than itching eyes – 'Mine eyes do itch, / Doth that bode weeping?'[7] – Pamela, by contrast, is now constantly overwhelmed by her tears and so extremely swayed by her Niobean feelings that she is compelled to break off writing her letters more than once: 'O how my Eyes run! – Don't wonder to see the Paper so blotted!' (*PA*, 11).

Resorting to unreliable narration (which elides the male stentorian voice of omniscient narration from the novel) *Pamela* becomes a succès de scandale through its omissions and ambiguities, but most of all through the scandalous fact that a sentimental female protagonist releases floods of (eroticized) Niobean tears which she then channels into torrents of words hastily scribbled onto myriads of tear-stained pages. Pamela's provocative confession that she loves writing ('for I love Writing, and shall tire you', *PA*, 17), thus making her divert her bodily juices into streams of ink, was an open challenge and an instance of female trespassing upon the male territory of the *logos*. The first female writer to be blamed for arrogating this male privilege was Aphra Behn. As savage onslaughts of criticism by her male enemies show, her texts were never seen in terms of a new, feminine perspective of Restoration culture, but rather as obscene evidence of a dangerous

---

[5] Lutz, *Crying*, 40.
[6] *Oth* 4.3.45.
[7] Ibid. 4.3.57f.

Figure 4 Jean-Baptiste Greuze, *La cruche cassée* (The Broken Pitcher) (1771), Paris, Louvre. Courtesy Peter Willi/ARTOTHEK.

porosity, a sublimated form of genital incontinence. While, in the context of late seventeenth- and early eighteenth-century literature, writing became strikingly synonymous with emotional effusions and leakage, it was particularly female authors who were suspected of an ominous porousness which was liable to have serious intellectual, moral and sexual implications. Vilified as a leaky whore who allegedly produced her texts with her vaginal discharge,[8] Behn, as one of the first professional writers, resisted being thus stoppered in male-dominated

---

[8] See also Todd, *The Critical Fortunes of Aphra Behn*, 3–18.

Restoration times and continued to produce libertinistic texts in all genres.[9] Others withdrew into privacy and not unlike Pamela produced texts as secret messages, while the majority of women was intimidated into muteness and chose intellectual self-containment.

For Mr B, one of the last descendants of misogynist Restoration culture, innocent Pamela personifies a vexing paradox: while Pamela is excessively leaky and open with respect both to her tears ('blubbering', *PA*, 24) and the profusion of words that she writes ('always scribbling', *PA*, 26), when it comes to her sexuality, he perceives her as being as sealed and locked as the various letters and rooms that she seeks physical and psychological refuge in. Preferring the phallic pen to the traditional female needle (with the eye of the needle as a hackneyed allusion to the vaginal orifice),[10] Pamela quickly exposes herself to accusations of perverse, liminal sexuality and unwittingly gives rise to a spate of 'anti-*Pamelas*':[11] 'I believe this little Slut has the Power of Witchcraft, if there ever was a Witch' (*PA*, 49). The tear-drenched textual intercourse of the sentimental age, which replaces (or more precisely, modifies) the predatory sexual intercourse of the Restoration libertines, aims to redefine linguistic openness and volubility.

It is certainly one of the commonplaces of literary history that sentimental writers concentrate on the heart and conceive of it as a vessel under pressure that can only be kept from bursting by a sympathetic flow of words and tears. All persistent attempts to de-eroticize these sentimental effluvia are, however, fallacious and spawn misconceptions of what critics have, for want of more precise terminology, misleadingly tagged as the priggish age of sentiment or *Empfindsamkeit*. What becomes clear is that eighteenth-century sentimentalism was never one-dimensional, drooling and virtue-ridden, but most of all, due to subtle strategies of titillation, complex and highly charged with sexual meaning. While Richardson and Fielding are stereotypically seen in terms of an ideological antagonism, a dichotomy which is commonly simplified into a battle between the Augustan Age and the burgeoning Romantic period, it might prove to be more rewarding to read their novels as being complementary and as parts of a complicated and deeply interwoven cultural tapestry. Seen from this angle, Restoration libertinism and sentimentalism do not so much oppose as interact with each other, producing a new (aristocratic) hedonism that is given a special momentum when brought into contact with the bourgeois love of virtue.

---

[9] Stapleton, 'Aphra Behn, Libertine', 75–97.
[10] Cf. the entries 'eye' and 'needle' in Williams, *A Glossary of Shakespeare's Sexual Language*, 118 and 214.
[11] Mudge, *The Whore's Story*, 199.

Mr B's multifarious and futile efforts to intrude upon Pamela's privacy were not only read by Fielding as stimulating preliminaries that were meant to shatter her facade of virtue; the fact that this constellation provided the pattern for later pseudo-pornographic Gothic novels and was the prototype for countless literary rapists waiting to break open the rooms and bodies of their sentimental female antagonists shows that the relationship between Mr B and Pamela was, from the very beginning, highly fraught with sexual potential.

More than once Pamela mentions in her letters that Mr B manages to put 'his Hand in my Bosom' (*PA*, 32). To clarify this point, Anne Hollander refers to various eighteenth-century illustrations of *Pamela* and *Clarissa* (1748) that frivolously dallied with the indistinct demarcation lines that existed between veiling and nakedness, between imperviousness and allusions to porousness. The dislodged neckerchief was an important visual element in women's fashion in the 1740s and even '[n]ipples peeping out of gauzy stuff, as if accidentally, became a standard device, probably in actual life as well as in art'.[12] What Hollander nonchalantly circumscribes as 'corsage carelessness'[13] is also (even if implicitly) prevalent in Richardson's novel and shows that the new discourse of Evangelical modesty is always contradicted by the odd seductive element. Fleeing from Mr B, who, in these erotic pursuits, is more and more portrayed as an Ovidian satyr, Pamela even loses part of her dress: 'he follow'd me so close, he got hold of my Gown, and tore a piece off, which hung without the Door' (*PA*, 32). What certainly fits into and intensifies this erotic undercurrent of the novel is, in Letter XVI, Pamela's metonymic use of eyes and crying: 'my Eyes were swell'd with crying' (*PA*, 33). Barthes's essay 'La métaphore de l'œil' (The Metaphor of the Eye) inspired by Georges Batailles's pornographic novel *L'histoire de l'œil* (1928) is not the first text to note that there has always been a symbolic proximity between eyes and genitals, and that tears and genital fluids have always been conflated.[14] It is intriguing (albeit conjectural) to read Pamela's lament about her swollen and moist eyes as a codified reference both to her sentimental tearfulness and her forbidden physical lust, which is duly reified in the monstrous and faun-like figure of the lascivious Mr B.

Richardson even gives the eroticism of his novel a (calculated?) boost, when he lets his readers intrude not only upon what Pamela's pen oozingly traces on the paper, but also upon her private rooms in which she, in the company of her chaperon Mrs Jervis, undresses: 'I pulled off my Stays, and my Stockens, and

---

[12] Hollander, *Seeing Through Clothes*, 211.
[13] Ibid.
[14] Barthes, 'The Metaphor of the Eye', *Critical Essays*, 239–47.

my Gown, all to an Under-Petticoat' (*PA*, 63). By awkwardly placing not only Pamela's parents, but also all her readers at the keyhole of her bedroom and giving them a free view of her corsetless and almost naked body, Richardson inadvertently treats his readership to a pornographic effect:[15] turning them into accomplices and idle onlookers he puts them into the position of the old men in the apocryphal Biblical story of Susannah and the Elders who are now watching the titillating scene of Pamela undressing and Mr B rushing out of a closet with the intent to rape her. That he again seizes the opportunity of groping her almost naked breasts is scarcely astonishing, but the ambiguous piece of information that Pamela was 'in a cold, clammy Sweat' (*PA*, 63) shows that her body involuntarily responds to Mr B's sexual attacks and that the sweaty moisture could, at least in early modern parlance, easily be translated into a reaction ranging from female hysterics to pent-up sexual lust. What the novel's subtext, as it was unearthed by Fielding and other male readers, seems to insinuate is that the sternness of the Evangelical policing of the female body's orifices often provokes a corresponding rise of drippingly carnal desire, which duly camouflaged and censored as crudely barbarian violence seems to provide a reliable stimulation for eighteenth-century readers.

The traditional Restoration clash of the sexes is, however, given a different direction when, in Letter XXVIII, the reader gets a first glimpse of how sentimental porousness not only affects women, but also starts the halting process of a redefinition of the male gender. In spite of the fact that, in a conversation with Mr Longman, Mr B sticks to his position of being the petrified and hardhearted master of the house and shows himself impervious to his interlocutor's entreaties not to send Pamela away, there is a sudden moment of relenting in Mr B which proves that he is gradually losing control of the aristocratic solidity of his body. In what turns out to be a most paradoxical situation, old Mr Longman has no scruples about revealing himself as the representative of the new (and effeminizing) mode of sentimentality – 'I am quite melted' (*PA*, 74) – whereas young Mr B persistently abides by his role as an ossified Restoration tyrant. Yet, all of a sudden, the rake cannot help disclosing that the impervious facade of the libertine has got fissures (be they ever so lacy and invisible) and that for a brief moment he is on the brink of turning into what he later no longer resists becoming: a porous man of feeling.

What makes this novel so pivotal in cultural history is that Pamela manages to instil her ambiguous ideas of bourgeois virtue into Mr B and to make him

---

[15] Gwilliam, 'Pamela and the Duplicitous Body', 121.

eventually buy into what Ildiko Csengei calls 'an institutionalised culture of tears and compassion', eventually culminating in Henry Mackenzie's *The Man of Feeling* (1771).[16] Having defected to the camp that he used to vituperate as the 'romantick Idiot[s]' (*PA*, 163), Mr B is, by the end, ready to renounce his ideology of hard and aggressive libertinism and to show himself susceptible to a new discourse of sentimental liquidity, which, behind its cant and Evangelical appropriation, seems to retain a wider scope for frivolousness than most of the 'romantick Idiot[s]' and graveyard haunters of the melancholy 1740s were prepared to admit. The (putative) antagonism between 'Lambkin' and wolf (*PA*, 195), between rakishly hard cynicism and porous sentimentality, is thus eventually resolved in the concept of a marriage in which the libertine and Don Juan of bygone times is absorbed into the new ethics of the bourgeoisie, which, due to the rising influence of Wesleyan Methodism,[17] is characterized by a conspicuous lack of emotional self-containment on the side of Pamela's father: 'my dear Father, not able to contain himself, nor yet to stir from the Place, gush'd out into a Flood of Tears, which he, good Soul! had been struggling with' (*PA*, 294).

What symbolically underlines the intermingling of hitherto contradictory discourses is the bizarre fact that Pamela's father is not only eventually reconciled with Mr B, but that, in spite of Pamela's reservations, he is even dressed in the reformed rake's clothes: 'as I saw afterwards, they fitted him very well' (*PA*, 312). Given the fact that a very distinct sartorial symbolism, a stigmatizing 'power of dress',[18] pervaded the cultural periods right up to the Victorian Age, it is of vital significance that, while his aristocratic son-in-law turns into an exemplary bourgeois, Mr Andrewes is suddenly changed into 'a great Beau' (*PA*, 313); and, as if to cap the whole process, his metamorphosis does not even stop short at the suit, but goes so far as to encompass his most private garments such as his stockings, linen and shoes. While his daughter more than once whetted Mr B's appetite by undressing and unwittingly displaying her (semi-)nudity, Mr Andrewes eventually pleases Mr B by slipping into the libertine's clothes and turning into his alter ego; a circumstance that Mr Andrewes comments on by giving free rein to uncontrollable and polyvalent tears: '[he] could not refrain Tears' (*PA*, 313).

---

[16] Csengei, *Sympathy, Sensibility and the Literature of Feeling*, 126.
[17] For the sentimental effusiveness and porousness of Methodism, see Dixon who sees their open-air preaching as 'one of the ancestors of modern mass tearful responses to both sporting events and pop music'. *Weeping Britannia*, 71.
[18] Cf. Dickens, *Oliver Twist*, 5.

At the end of this dodgy class and culture swapping, it is not only Pamela's father who has changed his identity, but also Mr B who benefits from 'a kind of amnesiac reading'[19] of his Restoration misogyny and ultimately finds his place in the new bourgeois circle of Evangelical austerity and Niobean tearfulness. This is impressively made clear when, as a sign of his new role, he alternates with Mr Williams, the vicar, in the recital of the tearful Psalm 137 ('By the rivers of Babylon … ')[20] and reads the sentimentalized version of that psalm which Pamela wrote in one of her desperate attempts at conflating ink and tears.

Richardson's *Pamela* is at the beginning of the new 'sensibility wave' which left eighteenth-century readers not only embarrassingly lost in the overwhelmingly intimate details of private fiction,[21] but it also showered them with enticing and scabrous iconographies of bursting or broken vessels, flooded mines and oozing Muses, covering the body's porousness with alibi fig-leaves of figurative language. While some writers cleaved to the image of the eighteenth-century universe (and its inhabitants) as wrought-iron clockwork machinery and saw not only man, but also God as a 'Great Oeconomist'[22] who takes every precaution to avoid waste and overspilling, it was the sentimentalists (so at least the legend goes) who were resolved to oppose all ideas of rationality, mechanism and normative hardness with images of reckless expenditure, liquidity and porousness. Taking their cue from Richardson and from Jean-Jacques Rousseau's *Nouvelle Héloïse* (1761) alike, they not only subverted the prevalent philosophy of cool and self-contained Enlightenment with their naiveté, they also seemed to be eager to wash away the errors of the *siècle des lumières* and its Restoration prelude with their refreshing and abundant tears. Yet, as the italicized word '*Oeconomy*' (*PA*, 502) in the epilogue of *Pamela* suggests, the word could be appropriated by different cultural movements and obviously carried different associations. For the Augustans, it meant a rigorous policing of riotous bodily fluids, for the sentimentalists in the wake of *Pamela*, it signified marital bliss seasoned with sympathetic and allusive tears.

---

[19] Gwilliams, 'Pamela and the Duplicitous Body', 122.
[20] In contrast to the version of Ps 137 used in the *King James Bible* (OT, 716), Williams uses the 1562 metrical Old Version of the psalm by Thomas Sternhold and John Hopkins which, instead of the mere reference to weeping ('yea, we wept'), puts more emphasis on the sentimental and eruptive tearfulness of the exiles: 'The Tears for Grief burst out' (317).
[21] Porter, *Flesh in the Age of Reason*, 281.
[22] See Young's *Night Thoughts*, 1089. By the end of the monumental poem, he refers to the human body as a 'nice Machine' (2188) which death as a breakdown eventually brings to a standstill.

Porous *Hommes* and *Femmes Machines*: *Fanny Hill*

In John Cleland's *Memoirs of a Woman of Pleasure* (1748), one of the most notorious spin-offs of *Pamela* and universally known as *Fanny Hill*, sentimental readers became shockingly aware of the fact that the 'female activity' of weeping (so at least Richard Steele was convinced in *The Tatler*)[23] was neither economized nor confined to the eyes and that the sentimental protagonists' rooms (like their bodies) were made accessible to various men of feeling, who, unlike frustrated and later reformed Mr B, experienced their formative years in porous prostitutes' boudoirs. While Sarah Toulalan claims that 'modern pornography does not widely employ comedy as part of its erotic repertoire',[24] the long and complex eighteenth century provides ample evidence of the fact that flights of oozing sentimentality could as easily be accommodated to frivolous comedy, satire and the burlesque, and that a special form of facetious pornography could be elicited from the saucy confessions of Fanny Hill and her friends, thus turning the word '[m]elting' into an iridescent synonym for (auto-induced) orgasm, laughter and various other manifestations of pleasant incontinence.[25]

The witty parody of the fashionable sentimental epistolary novel *à la* Richardson is, on closer inspection, not only a confession of an erotic sinner; it is chiefly an ambitious project that aims to reconcile the concept of the female leaky vessel with La Mettrie's *homme machine* in a new form of burlesque sentimentality. While Pamela tries to confine her ambiguous leakiness to the upper Cartesian regions of her eyes and to the torrents of words that she pens in spontaneous overflows of panic-stricken emotion, Fanny Hill (via her telling name) immediately directs the reader's attention to her porous nether parts, the *mons Veneris* and her voracious mouth-like vagina. From the very first moment of her sexual initiation as a prostitute, Fanny Hill acquiesces in (and does not object to) the fact that every relationship between man and woman is that of a ruthless battle of the sexes, of a clash between woman's liquid nature and man's steely machinery. This idea of heterosexual antagonism, which Richardson's Pamela is so terrified of, is here not only mitigated by interspersed scenes of comedy, but it has also induced critics such as Donald H. Mengay to subject the novel to a conjectural homosexual rereading and to interpret the autodiegetic protagonist in terms of a drag queen focused on anal penetration.[26]

---

[23] Carter, 'Tears and the Man', 158.
[24] Toulalan, *Imagining Sex*, 195.
[25] Ibid., 201. What Toulalan confines to the seventeenth century, to the Restoration period, finds its repercussions in eighteenth-century epistolary novels and the various smutty epics in prose.
[26] Mengay, 'The Sodomitical Muse', 185–98.

Starting her career as a prostitute from the position of a voyeur, Fanny (and the reader as her accomplice) watches the sexual intercourse between Phoebe and one of her clients, a horse-grenadier. This episode sets the pattern for the entire book: the woman is passive, porous, but also a perilous geographical spot, a 'greasy landskip' divided by 'a wide open-mouth'd gap' and treacherously 'overshaded with a grizzly bush' (*FH*, 24). Reverting to the time-honoured imagery of the female body as a topography, Cleland is in line with poets and dramatists from Shakespeare to the Restoration period, all of whom preferred to see women in terms of territories, slippery, wet, oozing and broken by insidiously hidden gaps, holes and chasms. As if to defy eighteenth-century conventions of taste and to disavow what Winfried Mennighaus identifies as the pervading tradition of the classical smooth belly, 'its flat-out negation',[27] Cleland almost seems to revel in his anachronistic descriptions of women's bodies as exotic, uncultivated, cave-like and porous terrains.

Only at first glance is Cleland's novel characterized by an appallingly simplified libertinistic conservatism, reinforcing early modern gender constellations in which young men seem to be the reverse of sentimental travellers, remote from the embryonic men of feeling (St Preux, Harley and Werther) and rather grotesque and belligerent hybrids between animals and machines. Phoebe's lover is, thus, described as a 'sturdy stallion' that, to her mixed feelings of dismay and lust, produces a penis in the form of a 'wonderful machine' (*FH*, 25). As if this hybridization of the male lover (animal-machine) was not sufficient, the semantic field of machinery and burgeoning industrialization is then further extended to that of warfare, in which the phallic machines and priapic tools metamorphose into lacerating weapons. Sexual attacks like these invariably leave the girls' genital regions devastated and looted, wounded, perforated, dripping with blood or seminal fluids – 'her thighs open, between which I could observe a kind of white liquid, like froth, hanging about the outward lips of that recent opened wound' (*FH*, 31) – and providing illuminating material for what Elizabeth Kubek sees as 'a complexity of attitude toward sexuality, in which the main secondary affect is one of horror, at times shaded with grotesque humor'.[28]

While Pamela evoked the idea of being a (charming) fortress unsuccessfully beleaguered by Mr B and frustrating all ruses at forcing entry into her bodily fortifications, Cleland makes lavish use of lexical fields such as wounds, lesions and blood which are ostensibly meant to convey that the bourgeois idea of the

[27] Menninghaus, *Disgust*, 71.
[28] Kubek, 'The Man Machine: Horror and the Phallus', 174.

unconquerable female body is short-lived and that the re-localization of female porousness is always linked with (voluptuous) pain. As if foreshadowing the later Marquis de Sade's chambers of sexual torture in *Justine, ou les malheurs de la vertu* (MS 1787), one of the most radical rewritings of Richardson's sentimental novel, Cleland even goes so far as to show sexual intercourse as a moment of extreme martyrdom, when Polly, in a suicidal fit of sexual longing, runs upon 'the flaming point of this [= the young man's] weapon of pleasure, which she stak'd herself upon, up-pierc'd, and infix'd to the extremest hair-breadth of it' (*FH*, 33). The oxymoronic idea of 'sweet violence' (*FH*, 33), which is at the core of the sexual warfare in Cleland's novel, is based on the Baroque convention that women court their martyrdom and that they are vessels or territories that are made to be tapped, invaded and ripped open. While, however, the numerous ravaged Baroque bodies were supposed to shed their copious blood in the imitation of Christ's crucified body, the wounds of the women's bodies in Cleland's erotic novel aim to revitalize the muddy and hitherto disused genital fountains.

Yet, despite the martial cruelty of this pornographic forerunner of de Sade's novels and despite the uncanniness of its depictions of the mechanical sex,[29] Cleland's narrative of painful sexual intercourse, however, is ample evidence of the fact that – in contrast to Rochester's obsession with dysfunctional bodies and repulsive sex – the sexes and their organs in *Fanny Hill* complement each other, that the combatants are attracted by each other so that, as a nuance of the utopian concept of the flourishing pornographic literature of the eighteenth century,[30] they eventually show 'signs of a close conspiring extasy' (*FH*, 33). As if anticipating Keats's later ode 'To Autumn' (1819), where there is an amorous conspiracy between the sun and the autumn, there is a strange, 'conspiring' correspondence between the machines and the female genital *loci amoeni*, between the (male) swords and the (female) sheaths. In order to convey this idea of matching and fitting and to convince his new generation of sentimental pornographers of the fact that female bodies gravitate towards the harmonious union with their phallic instruments of torture, Cleland, via his female narrator, regards it as no contradiction that, in the course of Fanny's Hogarthian progress as a whore, the industrial engines and weapons suddenly undergo a quick metamorphosis into musical instruments which, resonant with Hamletian implications, wait for 'the country / [cuntry]-dances' (*FH*, 112) to begin.[31]

---

[29] Ibid., 179.
[30] For the proliferations of pornography in London, 'the sex capital of Europe', see Peakman, *Lascivious Bodies*, 1.
[31] See Hamlet's allusion to 'country matters' (*Ham* 3.2.110) in the play-acting scene.

Susan Morgan is certainly right when she maintains that 'eighteenth-century novels constantly invoke the dynamic of male sexual aggression and female sexual powerlessness',[32] but Cleland invites us to read (passages of) his novel in an unexpectedly different light. So it is in hidden passages like those quoted above that Cleland disavows his early modern (and archaic) affiliations and shows that, in the narrow confines of pornographic fiction, he is prepared to leave the well-trodden misogynist paths to subject the deeply entrenched eighteenth-century gender roles to a subtle sentimentalized revision. This is best evidenced by the fact that the daunting phallic machines and instruments of 'the boudoir sublime'[33] are – on closer inspection – of an unsettlingly antithetical quality: fiercely transgressive, while at the same time liable to spend soothing juices and ready to subvert all calculations in the masculine economy of humours. Yet what is an even more unmistakable indication of the extent to which the novel is deeply moored in Richardson's sentimentalism is that all the sexual battles in Cleland's novel end up not only in the expected female porous surrender, but also – and this was outrageous and astonishing for the consumers of pornographic fiction – in male porousness. While the image of the male ejaculation as a 'titillating inspersion of balsamic sweets' (*FH*, 42) still fits into the pornographic discourse of male lovers generously filling their partners' leaky vaginal cavity, it is images of stalwart youths with 'over-siz'd machines' and penises in the prodigious shape of a maypole dying away in Fanny's arms, 'melting in a flood' (*FH*, 75), which subvert traditionally dichotomous gender roles and show that the ideology of sentimentalism clearly left its imprint on the phallocentric genre of post-Restoration pornography.

Compared to the Earl of Rochester's traumatic image of a man losing self-control at the moment of premature ejaculation and finding his self-fashioning as an aggressive libertine dissolved into nothingness, Cleland seems to be eager to reconcile traditional images of militant manliness with a new pre-Romantic approach, which gives men the chance to turn into a Niobe after exhausting themselves in debilitating Dionysian performances (the hypothesis being still prevalent that one ejaculation equalled forty blood-lettings).[34] It is this idea of a sentimental reconcilement of the sexes in 'simultaneous orgasmic finales',[35] fuelled by the eighteenth-century notion of mutual ejaculation,[36] which

---

[32] Morgan, *Sisters in Time*, 29.
[33] Folkenflik, 'Memoirs of a Woman of Pleasure and the Culture of Pornography', 118. See also Blackwell, 'Sublime Masculinity and the Aesthetics of Disproportion', 39–63.
[34] Stone, *Family, Sex and Marriage*, 311.
[35] Kubek, 'The Man Machine: Horror and the Phallus', 186.
[36] For this wide-spread belief in female ejaculation, see Laqueur, *Making Sex*, 182.

underlines the fact that *The Memoirs of the Woman of Pleasure* is not only a crude parody and travesty, but also a further development of the sentimental novel. The idea of melting and merging in orgasmic ecstasy which Donne had cast in his convoluted and Platonized images of twisted 'eye-beams' and sweaty 'intergraft[ed]' hands[37] is now translated not only into a more bodily idiom, but also into an imagery that shows the eighteenth-century *homme machine* helplessly and sometimes ridiculously at the mercy of his own body's porosity.

As has to be expected of an eighteenth-century text, Cleland's rehabilitation of both sexes' leaky bodies and of their overall porosity is not without its satirical lunges – further substantial proof that Toulalan's hypothesis of the incompatibility of pornography and comedy is scarcely tenable. Thus, one butt of embarrassing facetiousness is a certain Mr Norbert, a man with a 'taste of maiden-hunting' (*FH*, 129), who, as a sexual Quixote, mistakes a scheming prostitute for a virgin, and who, as an *homme machine* programmed incorrectly, is – despite various incentives – only able to have short-lived erections which make him, a truly Rochesterian descendant, melt away 'in a washy sweat, or a premature abortive effusion' (*FH*, 139). The homosexual couple which the narrator – in a moment of intertextual libelling – dismisses as 'these unsex'd male-misses' (*FH*, 160) is another target for abrasively sarcastic criticism, since the conjunction of sword and sheath in one and the same body is an intolerable monstrosity that has to be castigated; and eventually there is the episode about the country bumpkin, tellingly nicknamed 'Good-natur'd Dick' (*FH*, 160), who, utterly out of proportion with his lack of intelligence, is equipped with such a monstrous 'man-machine' (*FH*, 163) so that, for Louisa, a friend of Fanny's, sexual intercourse increasingly takes the shape of a round of bear-baiting: 'so that she was tied to the stake, and oblig'd to fight the match out, if she died for it' (*FH*, 164). This episode in the course of which the girl is totally devastated – 'torn, split, wounded' (*FH*, 164) – ends on a note that takes a rather taunting look at the axioms of Rousseauistic sentimentalism and its ideal of the noble savage: the good-natured country man is unmasked as a 'young savage' that subjects his amorous prey to 'worryings' and ferocious bites (*FH*, 164), while the girl herself is gradually transformed into 'a machine' (*FH*, 165), a lifeless automaton of her uncontrollable lust that, by the end of the annihilating struggle, is left in a state of overflowing openness and out of touch with the old

[37] Donne, 'The Extasie', 7 and 9.

'plumber's view of the body', according to which 'a nice balance between the production and discharge of fluids' was deemed essential.[38]

In a survey of porous and dissolving bodies, Cleland's novel is a solitary landmark, undermining the Puritan foundation that is at the core of Richardson's allegedly strait-laced sentimentalism and translating the French tradition of the frivolous *fêtes galantes* into British literary history. Taking his cue from Richardson's fast-selling epistolary novel, Cleland quickly departs from Pamela's panic-stricken coyness when he records the rapid process in which his protagonist is familiarized with and becomes appreciative of her own bodily apertures and fluids which no longer issue from her eyes, but lubricate all the parts of the body that sentimental literature took great pains to ignore. The novelty of this novel, thus, lies not so much in the fact that the reiterative accounts of bodily pain are so deeply interlaced with pleasure and laughter as in the astounding fact that the porousness of the entire human body is so exuberantly and freely celebrated. Casting the body's genital openness into a profusion of metaphors and puns, Cleland seems to take up the loose ends that the Cavaliers left behind at the inception of the Puritan tyranny, but also paves the way for another form of sentimental porosity: the girl-in-distress motif in Matthew Gregory Lewis's Gothic porn novel *The Monk* (1796).

Porous Gothic porn: *The Monk*

Turn-of-the-century pornography in the guise of the Gothic seems to turn the clock back and to divest the porous body of the essential components which readers of Cleland's novel enjoyed by the end of the allegedly melancholy 1740s: delight, laughter and ideas of a carnal banqueting – elements which were neatly tied up in the predominant image of sexuality as a dripping feast, as the sharing of juicy meat with the prospect of 'an after-course of pleasure' (*FH*, 76). With the bodily orifices and pores tightly shut again and the watering female 'neither-mouth[s] [sic!]' (*FH*, 82) suddenly deprived of their phallic morsels by a new religious (Catholic) fundamentalism (often represented by the Spanish Inquisition), sentimentality, in Lewis's novel, is prima facie reinterpreted along Richardsonian lines foregrounding harassed, coy maidens persecuted by transgressive, but also frustrated men. Yet, while in both Richardson's prototypical novel and in Cleland's spin-off the attribution of porousness and petrification was always on the point of being renegotiated within the tight

[38] Stone, *Family, Sex and Marriage*, 312.

traditional framework of genders (with Mr Longman and Pamela's father playing pioneeringly subversive roles), *The Monk* seems to start from the vexing premise that Gothicized pornography follows the traditional categories of gender and that men triumph over female porous abjection. The astounding falsification of this premise is what attracts readers to this 'crucial experiment in the history of the "pornographic" imagination'.[39]

One of the leitmotifs of the novel, which has intriguingly been designated as a 'Gothic *bildungsroman*',[40] is the theological, but also psychological concept of revelation, of 'unveiling', which resonates with a forbidden sense of eroticism, kinky voyeurism and hidden scandalous nakedness. Right from the beginning of the novel, the theme of concealed, masked and veiled bodies is prevalent, when people flock into the cathedral in order to listen to Ambrosio, the abbot of the Capuchins, and hide their identities behind quantities of gauzily pellucid cloth. What is, on the very first pages, teasingly revealed behind Antonia's 'thick veil' is a neck 'which for symmetry and beauty might have vied with the Medicean Venus' (*M*, 9). The reader is, thus, made aware of a secluded ecclesiastical world which is highly artificialized and in which female bodies are expected to imitate the statuesque qualities of ancient art. The 'new frankness' of the eighteenth century which Faramerz Dabhoiwala posits seems to have been repealed in the monastic atmosphere of Gothic novels.[41]

Before Ambrosio's self-fashioning as a saint and Mosaic foundling is shattered by an outrageous and, up to then unrivalled, instance of cross-dressing, he is shown as having manipulative and revelatory powers. He not only enchants and spellbinds his audience like a hypnotizer, but he is also endowed with eyes whose glances are 'fiery and penetrating' (*M*, 18). While for writers from the early modern period to Richardson, eyes (due to their almond-shaped form and moistness) were charged with receptive and vaginal meanings, Gothic novelists, and in particular Lewis, gave eyes a new connotation and preferred to see the *oculi foedi* of their villains in terms of penetrative and almost phallic instruments.[42] In this respect, Ambrosio seems to be related to the monks in Radcliffe's novel *The Italian* (1796), and here especially to the brooding confessor Schedoni or the Inquisitor, the latter of whom is not only clad in forbidding black, but is also characterized by his 'piercing eye' and 'the natural ferocity of his visage'.[43]

---

[39] Mudge, 'How to Do the History of Pornography', 18.
[40] Lutz, *The Dangerous Lover*, 31.
[41] Dabhoiwala, *The Origins of Sex*, 343.
[42] Lennartz, 'Porous Bodies in Romantic Literature', 55–67.
[43] *The Italian*, 233.

Although, like Ambrosio, they are driven by ambition and fashion themselves as 'prodig[ies] for self-denial and severe discipline',[44] Radcliffe's monks are almost exclusively propelled by envy, revenge and jealousy; repressed sexuality and an inclination for sadism are, by contrast, paramount features of male Gothicism in which elements of female sentimentality tend to be either eclipsed or usurped by the male (Catholic) 'Other'.[45]

Ambrosio's facade of immaculate and ostentatious piety is consequently only kept intact for so long as Rosario, a novice and the monk's confidant, shrouds his identity in mystery and keeps his body concealed in his cowl. That the moment of Rosario's unveiling and the ocular penetration of the alleged boy's disguise takes place in the garden of the abbey is particularly significant in the way that the 'Fountains, springing from basons of white Marble' and cooling the air 'with perpetual showers' (*M*, 50) recapture the old idea of Niobean porousness arrested and channelled into masculine marble constructions. Apart from other features of artificialized porousness such as a 'rustic Grotto' (*M*, 50), there are alarming hints that the paradisiacal abbey garden is not so much a place of contemplation as one of latent sexual antagonism: thus, it is not accidental that the narrator refers to a porous nightingale which vocally '*poured* forth her melodious murmur from the shelter of an artificial wilderness' (*M*, 50, my italics) and thus inevitably reminds the reader of Ovid's *Metamorphoses* and the account of Tereus penetrating and maiming of Philomela's delicate body. It is before this symbol-laden backdrop that Rosario unveils his ambiguous identity and sobbingly reveals himself as the attractive woman Matilda. It is her unexpected presence in the monastic seclusion of the abbey garden that suddenly causes a shattering of certitudes and epistemological habits so that the typical sentimental constellation of male aggressor and female victim becomes questionable.

With neat gender roles in a state of bewildering flux, Ambrosio undergoes a critical moment of sexual epiphany when he sees the 'dazzling whiteness' of Matilda's beautiful, but also captivating breasts (*M*, 65). Breasts have always elicited conflicting responses in literature. While, on the one hand, they used to be the focus of male aggression (as in the case of St Agatha's severed breasts presented on numerous Baroque platters), breasts were, on the other, represented as porous fountains of nourishment and delight, conflating the 'erotic, the maternal, and a sacred orality'.[46] After the fetishization of breasts in

[44] Ibid., 263.
[45] For the 'linkage between misogyny and the feminine, Catholic "Other" in eighteenth-century Protestant discourse', see Blakemore, 'Matthew Lewis's Black Mass', 522.
[46] Richter, *Missing the Breast*, 23.

the early modern period – culminating not only in *blason* poems on beautiful and ugly breasts, but also in an unparalleled mammocentrism – Lewis's *The Monk* epitomizes the dark sides of Romanticism in which breasts are turned into gloomy or witch-like[47] signifiers and are thus given the negative connotations of being seductive instruments or frustrating Sodom's apples. When Matilda spectacularly threatens to stab herself and points a dagger at her enticingly bared breast (a form of blackmail that shames Lucrece's proverbial demonstrations of virtue), the narrator makes it unmistakably clear that the tables have now been turned on the ocular penetrator and that, in the imagination of the Gothic pornographer, Matilda's partially naked body has become the sadistic agent, the 'Lovelace-like seducer',[48] in the grim battle of the sexes. With Matilda's (milkless) breasts having been turned into weapons, 'the beauteous Orb[s]' prove(s) to be lethal when they radiate danger and death and send forth '[a] raging fire' (*M*, 65) through Ambrosio's limbs.

To what extent the monk's body has already been perforated and made accessible to the influences of the female sex and its poisonous liquids is underscored in the subsequent episode in which Ambrosio is stung by a serpent that is concealed among the roses, showing too little awareness of the fact that Matilda, as the true descendant of Lady Macbeth, looks like a flower and is the venomous serpent under it. Critics have commented on the heavy-handedness of this in-yer-face allegory,[49] but what the episode shows is the alarming vulnerability of the male body and the rapidity with which man's self-fashioning as a phallic transgressor and *homme machine* has come to an abrupt end. Thus, in the very first two chapters, Ambrosio's heavily veiled body is exposed to a severe process of deconstruction and perforation: Matilda, via the snake, succeeds in instilling her poison into him. That the bush of roses, to which she draws Ambrosio's attention, is planted right 'at the door of the Grotto' (*M*, 71) is a blatant hint that she manoeuvres the clergyman into the perilous vicinity of women's grotto-like vaginal regions. The snake's bite is a symbolic reference both to the venomous impact of female sexuality and to the 'new "manliness"'[50] which Matilda is about to reveal. When Father Pablos, the abbey's surgeon, unavailingly probes Ambrosio's wound with 'his Lancet' (*M*, 72) and Matilda (after letting a tear drop on his face) finally sets about 'kiss[ing] the wound and [drawing] out

---

[47] For the effect of the witch's breasts in 'Christabel', see also DeLong, *Mesmerism, Medusa and the Muse*, 59.
[48] Blakemore, 'Matthew Lewis's Black Mass', 524. For the Marquis de Sade's influence on Lewis, see also Wright, 'European Disruptions of the Idealized Woman', 39–54.
[49] Bruhn, *Gothic Bodies*, 130.
[50] Rummel, *'Delusive Beauty'*, 52.

the poison' with her lips (*M*, 88), Ambrosio is initiated into the realm of female porosity and involuntarily subjected to a process of effeminizing cunnilingus in which he is unable to resist having a porous, vaginal wound inflicted on his hitherto unsullied body.

Refusing to come to terms with his own sexual instability and never realizing that his illness was the crisis attendant upon his feminized defloration (the plucking of the rose!), he is more and more dismayed about the transformations that Matilda's ambiguous sex seems to be undergoing. From her performance as the hooded and devout Rosario, she shifts her identity to the voluptuous reincarnation of the Madonna in the picture and eventually turns into the disconcerting example of an unsexed Amazonian virago. Disgusted and concerned about Matilda being increasingly masculine or even 'supracorporeal',[51] Ambrosio focuses his evil designs on Antonia, a late descendant of Pamela's, whose sealed body he hopes to open not so much by burlesque attacks (in the manner of Mr B waiting in the wardrobe) as by the machinations of magic and black art. The 'constellated Myrtle' (*M*, 278), which Ambrosio is given at the end of an invocation of the naked devil, is meant to be an illusory phallic key both to the chamber and to Antonia's virginal body. Yet, if one considers that the myrtle is related to a fable according to which adulterous Phaedra beguiles the time by piercing myrtle leaves with a hairpin,[52] one cannot help recognizing that this plant is anything but phallic and that Ambrosio stubbornly misreads the submerged and enigmatic hints that the treacherous devil deigns to give: having once been given a vaginal wound, Ambrosio's sinful and effeminized body is now about to be prepared for further phases of tormenting porousness.

Having been given a spurious keyhole view of Antonia's Venus-like body by Matilda's magical mirror ('She was undressing to bathe herself', *M*, 271) and then subsequently hoodwinked by the devil into believing that he can be restored to the position of the male penetrator of a female body, Ambrosio is thwarted in his intention to rape Antonia's statuesque body and instead (in a moment of unintentional hilarity) finds himself and Elvira, her mother, petrified by their mutual Gorgon-like gaze. Even the next insidious plan to penetrate Antonia's body in the Piranesian vaults of the monastic cemetery fails, when the narrator depicts Ambrosio as a grotesque imitation of Shakespeare's Romeo, who, accompanied by 'the melancholy shriek of the screech-Owl', intrudes upon the nocturnal graveyard, descends into the terrifying depths of the 'private Vault'

---

[51] Mudge, *The Whore's Story*, 222.
[52] See the entry for 'Myrtle' in *Brewer's Dictionary of Phrase and Fable*, 804.

(*M*, 378), there to enjoy perverse sex with Antonia, whose beauty is, like that of Juliet, thrown into relief by the putrefying corpses around her. As a bad and almost ludicrous copy of Shakespeare's frantic teenager, Ambrosio unwittingly parodies the lovesick Montague, when he equips himself with an 'iron crow and a pick-axe' (*M*, 378) to gain phallic access to Antonia's body which Matilda, as a Mephisphelean and female reincarnation of Friar Laurence, had drugged into a forty-eight-hour sleep.[53]

Transferred from the bourgeois smugness of Mr B's manor into the uncanny vaults of Gothic architecture, Ambrosio plagiarizes not only Shakespeare's frantic lovers, but also most of the Jacobean tragedies where he conflates death and sexuality (the typical *Liebestod*) and is about to celebrate a necrophilic orgy which marks the beginning of dark Romanticism and supplies the various literatures of European decadence with a pattern of rampant perversion:[54] 'This Sepulchre seems to me Love's bower' (*M*, 381). The fact that Ambrosio now relies on Satan's assistance proves his apostasy both from God and from Mr B, appropriated as he was by Pamela's Psalm-singing Puritan family. Having accomplished his evil designs and gratified his perverse lust on Antonia's bruised body in the subterranean corridors of the graveyard (and of his subconsciousness), Ambrosio is overwhelmed by self-loathing and eventually kills Antonia in what looks like a final surrogate act of rape: 'Without allowing himself a moment's reflection, He raised it [= Matilda's dagger], and plunged it twice in the bosom of Antonia!' (*M*, 391). The intriguing fact that it is Matilda's phallic dagger which he thrusts into Antonia's bosom insinuates that, even in his final penetrative act, he is a puppet of Matilda, and that his masculinity has completely been usurped by a woman who, as Rosario with seductive breasts, is threateningly hermaphroditic and eventually sent to him as a sexually volatile demon.[55]

In the last chapter, it is scarcely surprising to find that Matilda is the abettor of a penetrative Lucifer, who, similar to the devil in Goethe's *Faust*, is shown proselytizing his victims and inveigling them into the forfeiture of their souls. Imposed upon, cajoled and tyrannized by Matilda, Ambrosio eventually faces a Lucifer who, like an impostor, no longer appears in seraphic (and homoerotic) nudity, but as a gigantic monster more suggestive of a Medusa-like chimera ('living snakes, which twined themselves round his brows with frightful hissings',

---

[53] The parallels between Shakespeare's love tragedy and *The Monk* are striking, only the sleep induced by Friar Laurence is six hours shorter.
[54] See Praz, *The Romantic Agony*, 202–03.
[55] The performativity of gender is also elucidated in Brewer, 'Transgendering in Matthew Lewis's *The Monk*', 192–207.

M, 433) than of Milton's Satan as the sublime fallen angel. Yielding to Lucifer's temptations and harrowing descriptions of death, Ambrosio is subjected to another perfidious penetration, when he has his skin perforated with an iron, blood-sucking pen. This new wound leaves the monk bleeding (analogous to the Bleeding Nun), and what is worse, in a state of emasculated porousness. The contract which Ambrosio signs at the very last moment corroborates the complete reversal of gender relations in this novel of sexual ambiguity: in the abject position of a sentimental girl in distress, the abbot vows eternal loyalty to the devil in terms which sound like a sentimental and queer love confession: "'I am yours for ever and irrevocably!'" (*M*, 437).

The end of the novel not only turns the expected conciliatory conclusion of both the sentimental and the female Gothic novel upside down, it also terminates the novel with a climax of perversion and a triumph of porous pornography. In a final tableau, which rather than fuelling Baudelaire's aesthetics of the disgusting proves why the Surrealists saw Lewis as one of their precursors,[56] Ambrosio dies an unprecedented death which is reminiscent not only of the punctured myrtle leaf, but also of the device of the *contrappasso* which, since Dante's 'Inferno', had subjected villains to a death that in its horror was similar to that which they had inflicted on their victims. While in the early modern period, the *contrappasso* was the ultimate expression of an existent metaphysical justice, in *The Monk*, it seems to be the apt instrument of a punishment in a world in which the devil reigns supreme and the 'Creator' is only a phantasm of anguish. With his identity revealed and arraigned by the devil as the rapist of his sister Antonia and the murderer of his mother Elvira – 'Inhuman Parricide! Incestuous Ravisher!' (*M*, 440) – Ambrosio has to undergo the sexualized and excessively multiplied agonies of the rapist raped: dropped by Lucifer from inconceivably Icarian heights, Ambrosio is impaled by the 'sharp point of a rock' and helplessly rolls 'from precipice to precipice' (*M*, 441) before swarms of insects vampirically drink the blood that oozes from his countless wounds and subject his formerly immaculate body to myriads of penetrations, to the surreal horrors of an entomic gang bang: '[the insects] darted their stings into his body, covered him with their multitudes, and inflicted on him tortures *the most exquisite* and insupportable' (*M*, 442, my italics).

---

[56] Antonin Artaud's and Luis Buñuel's collaboration on a script for a film version never materialized. See McEvoy, 'Introduction' to *The Monk*, xxx; for the extent to which a connection is established between Surrealism and the Gothic, see also Marwood, 'Imaginary Dimensions: Women, Surrealism and the Gothic', 42.

That Ambrosio not only survives the draining of his blood by these insects, but also temporarily sustains his life despite incredible injuries and lacerations inflicted on his body by rapacious eagles is another surreal or Promethean implausibility of the novel, which is meant to aggravate the superhuman torments which the monk has to endure in a world turned into a pandemonium. It is finally on the seventh day – in a scenario of apocalyptic chaos – that Ambrosio perishes and that his corpse is washed into the river. After the loss of his masculinity, 'continually transvestized',[57] tortured and having his hooded body transformed into that of a permeable epicene and devil's catamite, the monk is eventually conveyed into that element which, since Ophelia's suicide, had been associated with female death as a form of sentimental osmotic absorption.

Stony poetics versus porous effusions: Wordsworth and Coleridge

Wordsworth's anti-porous architecture

There is no record of what Wordsworth thought about Lewis's novel and Ambrosio's terrifying, but also feminized death; that Wordsworth must have read this scandalous book becomes at least plausible from Stephen Gill's assumption that friends such as Azariah Pinney might have passed on a copy of *The Monk* to him in the autumn of 1797.[58] The fact that a man's body ends in a state of abject porosity might, however, have elicited his disapproval in the same way as he saw Romantic literature challenging the attainments of the Enlightenment with the riotous resuscitation of mermaids, *Undinen* and other Ophelian figures, all of them precariously oscillating between humanity and the aquatic element.[59] He might even have frowned at the fact that a Classicist such as Auguste Dominique Ingres, the rival of the Romantic and Anglophile Eugène Delacroix, was unwilling to conceal his fascination for concepts of aquatic femininity when he repeatedly depicted lascivious women in the humid atmosphere of Turkish baths or allegorized them as sources, as origins of streams and rivulets. And even if one leaves Ambrosio as a negative (and Catholic) example of luciferic gender-crossing apart, Wordsworth must have felt concerned about the sentimental heritage that left the Romantic age curiously divided: on the one hand, with

---

[57] Blakemore, 'Matthew Lewis's Black Mass', 527.
[58] Gill, *William Wordsworth: A Life*, 107.
[59] Ophelia and the watery death of women is one of the motifs that brackets the Romantic and the Victorian ages. Cf. Alexander, 'Drowned Woman in Literature and Art', 67–85.

poems, novels and paintings showing women in conditions of alarmingly osmotic diffusion, absorbing water and exuding liquids such as tears, milk or blood, and, on the other hand, with men either threatened by this intractable flood of sentimentality or utterly at a loss how to cope with what the eighteenth century had benignantly circumscribed as 'tender tears'.[60]

As if stemming himself against a wave of sentimental novels culminating in Radcliffe's *The Mysteries of Udolpho* (1794) and Lewis's *The Monk*, William Wordsworth seriously engages with the model of the porous man, when in his 1798 radical poem 'The Last of the Flock', he depicts a young man in dire need of emotional correction and shockingly unable to repress his tears. The speaker, ostensibly a widely travelled man, seems to be ill at ease when he is suddenly confronted with '[a] healthy man, a man full grown' who weeps 'in the public roads, alone'.[61] He is even more dismayed by the fact that, despite the 'hasty retreat of the moist-eyed man of feeling' by the end of the eighteenth century,[62] he meets such a specimen of the sentimental man 'on English ground' (5), and not on gloomy French soil that was about to produce Senancour's *Obermann* (1804) or in the Germany of Werther mania. As if foreshadowing Goethe's later differentiation between Romanticism as sick and Classicism as healthy, Wordsworth's speaker seems to juxtapose the young man's health, sturdiness and adulthood with the embarrassingly sick fact that on the open road he is overpowered by his Romantic sentimentality and that '[h]is cheeks with tears were wet' (8). Painfully aware of the fact that his unmanly tears shed in public might be considered a scandal, the young man clearly sees the necessity to counteract his Werther-like gender ambiguity and endeavours to make both himself and his tears invisible:

> He saw me, and he turned aside,
> As if he wished himself to hide:
> And with his coat did then essay
> To wipe those briny tears away. (11–14)

Unable to evade the narrator's inquisitive questions, he gives a long account of his economic and moral deterioration ('To wicked deeds I was inclined', 71), which takes up eight out of ten stanzas and gives the poem a political slant. Despite its political agenda, the poem also addresses questions of sexual politics

---

[60] James Fordyce, a Scottish Presbyterian minister, quoted in Carter, 'Tears and the Man', 159.
[61] Wordsworth, *Poems Founded on the Affections*, 'The Last of the Flock', 1–2. *Poetical Works*, 90–91.
[62] Wahrman, *The Making of the Modern Self*, 39.

and shows the extent to which a healthy man publicly crying is a serious attack on conservative ideas of gender roles.

Subscribing to an ideal of masculinity which adumbrates the works of Carlyle and Browning, Wordsworth henceforth defines his task as a poet as quintessentially masculine and patriotic:[63] as a form of writing for men in the language of men and defending the realm of literature from 'frantic novels, sickly and stupid German Tragedies, and deluges of idle and extravagant stories in verse'.[64] It is striking that Wordsworth, on the one hand, uses the semantic field of porousness and liquidity to describe the overabundance of trashy literary works that threatened to inundate British culture from the outside; and that, on the other, he hopes to stem and stave off these sentimental 'deluges' by the Deucalion's stones of his clear masculine language, his strong lines and the rocky characters of his monumental poems.[65] One figurehead of Wordsworth's campaign against porous sentimentality is the mystical leech-gatherer in the poem 'Resolution and Independence'. In spite of his role as a purveyor of medicinable porosity, he is compared to a 'huge stone' that lies '[c]ouched on the bald spot of an eminence'.[66] With stony perseverance, the old pilgrim probes the depths of a muddy pond with his staff and gazes at the dim water '[a]s if he had been reading in a book' (81). The idea of water troped as a book, as an objectified container of letters, is here fundamentally opposed to the sentimental concept of the text as a stream of words which is meant to elicit uncontrollable floods of tears. For Wordsworth's 'stony' pilgrim in the wake of Macduff (like him bereft of his family), the aquatic element is a reservoir of signs whose semiotics need to be translated into meaningful words so that man can benefit from their healing powers. Sudden gushes of melancholy feelings and immersions into the biographies of suicidal or self-consuming writers such as Chatterton and Burns are ultimately revealed as being foolish, when the speaker juxtaposes the Romantics' frenzied onsets of porous dejection with the leech-gatherer's firm stoicism: 'I could have laughed myself to scorn to find / In that decrepit Man so firm a mind' (137–38).

---

[63] For Coleridge's famous characterization of Wordsworth in his *Table Talk* as the masculine poet par excellence, 'He is *all* man', see Wilson, *The Romantic Dream*, 85. Judith W. Page pinpoints Wordsworth's early reception as a '"namby-pamby" poet' wasting his genius on 'unworthy (i.e. feminized) topics: daisies, daffodils, mad women, and such'. 'Wordsworth on Gender and Sexuality', 649.

[64] 'Preface' to *The Lyrical Ballads. Wordsworth's Poetry and Prose*, 81.

[65] In his *Lecture on English Poets*, Hazlitt astutely saw Wordsworth's (and even Coleridge's) role as 'Deucalions', quoted in Bate, *Radical Wordsworth*, 203.

[66] *Poems of the Imagination*, 'Resolution and Independence', 57f. *Poetical Works*, 156.

Satirized and sneered at by Hazlitt as a quixotic man,[67] Wordsworth was certainly fighting against windmills when he positioned himself against the clichéd concept of the Romantic age as fluid, watery and blurry.[68] As his vested interest in Gothic architecture shows, Wordsworth's self-understanding as a poet is less that of a seaman, a Schillerian diver or a purveyor of drivellingly Gothic horror than that of a builder who not only envisions bodies as stones, but also defines his poetic œuvre in terms of the 'body' of a Gothic cathedral, with *The Prelude* as its antechapel and the minor pieces as 'the little cells, oratories, and sepulchral recesses'.[69] Wordsworth's preoccupation with the idea of (textual) corpora as stones, his concept of minor poems as 'sepulchral recesses' provide the key to Wordsworth's espousal of a genre which other Romantics showed no particular interest in: the epitaph. Inscribed in stone (and not 'writ in water'), epitaphs epitomize the symbiotic combination of words, stones and bodies, since, for Wordsworth, it is this genre of liminality that transcends literature by 'personat[ing] the Deceased, and represent[ing] him as speaking from his own Tomb-stone'.[70] Set down as 'tender fiction', epitaphs miraculously 'unite the two worlds of the Living and the Dead'[71] and, thus, stand for a new quality of Niobean grief, since these speaking tombstones or stony bodies reach beyond tears and are expressive of a petrified form of mourning whose words also lie 'too deep for tears'.[72]

Read before the backdrop of Wordsworth's interest in epitaphs and in petrified bodies, the 1805 poem 'Elegiac Verses. In Memory of My Brother, John Wordsworth' is a prime example of how an excess of grievous tears about someone who drowned is channelled into the metrical grid of an epitaphic and stony poem. While, in the fourth stanza of the poem, the speaker freely yields to his tears – 'Full soon in sorrow did I weep' (31) – and analogously finds his syntax dissolving into incoherent words and dashes – 'Sea – Ship – drowned – Shipwreck – so it came' (37) – the very next stanza shows him recollected and with his equilibrium regained: 'Glad am I, glad that it is past' (42). In what vaguely resembles Laertes's dire need to repress his grief, Wordsworth's speaker not so much vociferously calls for the exorcism of the feminine in his own body as for his duty as an architect to erect 'a monumental Stone' in verse (63), to

---

[67] Quoted in Wu, *William Hazlitt*, 11.
[68] See Casaliggi and Fermanis, *Romanticism*, 47.
[69] 'Preface' to *The Excursion, Being a Portion of The Recluse, A Poem* in *Wordsworth's Poetry and Prose*, 444.
[70] 'Essay upon Epitaphs' in *Wordsworth's Poetry and Prose*, 496–506; 505.
[71] Ibid.
[72] 'Ode. Intimations of Immortality from Recollections of Early Childhood', 207. *Poetical Works*, 462.

write an epitaph that has the quality of a 'Shrine' (64). This is a recurrent pattern of Wordsworth's stony poetics which he also uses in later years, when after the death of many of his children, friends and fellow poets, he always reverts to his mission as a builder of stanzas, erecting poetic stones to their memory. In this sense, Hazlitt was a good observer when he noticed that nobody had before written so intensely about stones the way Wordsworth did.[73]

Corrosives of Wordsworth's stony poetics, however, came not only from biographical strokes of fate, they also poured in from cultures that Wordsworth, despite personal entanglements, had strong reservations about. Wordsworth detects an abundance of over-sentimental tears not only in Germany, but chiefly in French art galleries, and here especially in Baroque works of art, as for instance in Charles Le Brun's interpretation of Mary Magdalene's penitence: 'with hair / Dishevelled, gleaming eyes, and rueful cheek / Pale and bedropped with everflowing tears'.[74] Although Wordsworth is remarkably taciturn about the painting itself and even appreciates Mary Magdalene as a 'beauty exquisitely wrought' (*P*, IX, 78), one can assume that Wordsworth in his Henry Tilney-like patriotism did not have too much sympathy with Catholic effusions of grief and the staging of ambiguous tears in the context of a Counter-Reformation *theatrum sacrum*. Baroque tears like all other ostentatious displays of bodily fluids are associated with cultures that lack restraint and indulge in porousness and hyperbolic pageantries of corporeality. As an eyewitness of the French Revolution at the height of its Terror,[75] Wordsworth had been increasingly repulsed by the unleashed forms of Jacobin violence which elicited 'river[s] of blood' (*P*, X, 584) from the aristocracy and absorbed the old body politic in a 'recent deluge' (*P*, XI, 36) of gore. While William Blake chose to channel the torrents of blood into the quasi-Baroque image of the human 'winepresses'[76] and saw the torments of the French during the Revolution within the wider framework of Christological redemption, Wordsworth, from the perspective of a later conservative, dreaded the eroding floods of tears and blood in cultures outside Britain.

There is only one place in Britain that exposes Wordsworth's ideal of stony tranquillity to a severe threat: porous and flowing London, the 'monstrous ant-hill' (*P*, VII, 149), whose chaotic and ever-bustling movement is troped as an 'endless stream of men and moving things' (*P*, VII, 151). There is an allegedly

---

[73] Quoted in Bate, *Radical Wordsworth*, 386.
[74] *The Prelude* IX, 78ff. *Poetical Works*, 494–588; 556.
[75] See Gill, *Wordsworth: A Life*, 77.
[76] *Milton* (1804), First Book, 30–31. *The Complete Poems*, 533.

conspicuous difference between the London of the *Prelude* and the London that Wordsworth described in his famous sonnet 'Composed upon Westminster Bridge, 3 September 1803'.[77] London is here shown wearing a garment of matinal beauty; the distinctive features of the expanding metropolis – 'towers, domes, theatres, and temples' (6) – seem to merge with nature and the all-engulfing sky. Glittering brightness is paramount in the poem, but the reference to the 'smokeless air' (8) is a clear indication of the fact that Wordsworth is aware of increasing ecological issues in London and that the matinal absence of smoke is only a coded reference to the asphyxiating masses of soot and fumes later in the day. The representation of London as a sleeping city, robed in splendour is an amazing illusion that through the crevices of the tight framework of the sonnet gives the reader a few telling glimpses of what happens when the metropolis, at that time a gravitating place of about one million inhabitants,[78] awakes and casts off its beautiful clothes.

It is this repellent and almost obscene moment of divestment that is then shown in *The Prelude*, where Book VII reflects Wordsworth's sojourn in London in the autumn of 1802 and his visit to Bartholomew Fair in the company of Charles Lamb. While Lamb seemed to enjoy the teeming life of the capital and was even induced to 'shed tears in the motley Strand from fullness of joy at so much Life',[79] Wordsworth responded to this centre of modern porous conurbation with loathing and strident criticism. In order to convey the dizzying idea of London as an 'endless stream' of men and things, Wordsworth not only reverts to the technique of the vertiginous list, he also alarmingly equates men and things and shows to what extent the modern metropolis is a leveller both of social and ontological categories. Here a 'thickening hubbub' (*P*, VII, 211), a Babelian mixture of tongues, jarring voices, strange sights and sounds converge into such a 'mighty concourse' (*P*, VII, 219) of phenomena that faces, shop windows, advertisements and 'pantomimic scenes' (*P*, VII, 262) are no longer distinguishable. In this maelstrom of things and human beings, Bartholomew Fair is the inner centre of chaotic porousness in which a cascade of all sorts of elements of modern pop culture liquefies and dissolves the achievements of civilization and turns them into vast pools of monstrosity. Among the welter of abominations which threatens to drown the speaker's

---

[77] While Sélincourt still sticks to 1802, Halmi in his recent Norton Critical Edition gives the annotation that Wordsworth corrected the year into 1803 as late as in 1838 (402).
[78] The monstrosity 'Babylondon' originates around that time. See Ackroyd, *London: The Biography*, 573–81.
[79] Letter from Charles Lamb to Wordsworth, 30 January 1801, quoted in Gill, *Wordsworth: A Life*, 210.

reason, Wordsworth also mentions a 'Stone-eater' (*P*, VII, 709), a grotesque opponent of all architectural effort, who not only adds up to the Bosch-like 'Parliament of Monsters' (*P*, VII, 718), but is also part of the 'one vast mill' which ravenously devours and, in a cascade of disgusting carnivalism, throws up its population: 'vomiting, receiving on all sides, / Men, Women, three-years' Children, Babes in arms' (*P*, VII, 720–21).

Having perceived the city's stark nakedness, replete with obscenely blurry, infernal and distorted shapes, and taken more than a voyeuristic glimpse of what Donna J. Haraway, in a different context, calls 'multispecies knots',[80] Wordsworth is far from taking Ben Jonson's carnivalesque point of view in *Bartholomew Fair* (c. 1614), when the latter, in a Rabelaisian celebration of porousness, captures Ursula, the pig woman, or Madame Overdo not only in the act of oozing fat and sweat, but also in that of throwing up and cleansing their bodies by the end of the play. Assuming the position of a sternly self-contained moralist and critic of modern urban life, Wordsworth is shocked at the sight of the metropolis as a gigantic leaky vessel, as a melting pot where solid hierarchies such as the outdated Chain of Being become porous and, in what could be compared to a perpetual churning process, melt and reduce everything to one unrecognizable lump: 'melted and reduced / To one identity, by differences / That have no law, no meaning, and no end' (*P*, VII, 726–28).

It is these forms of porousness and erosion that Wordsworth's poetry is composed to counter. The poet's 'plastic power' and 'forming hand' (*P*, II, 362/363) are constantly involved in channelling the incessant flux of sentimental, carnivalesque or obscene things into concrete structures, eventually culminating in the late church sonnets whose thematic petrification Tim Fulford finds reflected in the strict form of the poem.[81] In this context, 'The Ruined Cottage', the story about Margaret's grief embedded into *The Excursion* (1814), is interesting because this story about excessive grief and suffering takes as its objective correlative a building that is architecturally dysfunctional and lacks a good builder.

Although Margaret enlists readers' sympathy, her emotional excessiveness and hyperbolism of tears are reminiscent of Wertherian sentimentalism and scarcely tally with the tragic fact that her husband left her to join a troop of soldiers: 'I have slept / weeping, and weeping have I waked' (*E*, I, 769–70). Margaret's emotional porosity is not only shown in the conspicuous disregard

---

[80] Haraway, *When Species Meet*, 35.
[81] Fulford, *Wordsworth's Poetry 1815–1845*, 226. Fulford, however, makes it clear that the 'chapel is a porous form, and the sonnet composed in it is porous too' (227).

of her quotidian duties (her 'sleepy hand of negligence' (*E*, I, 822) being a crass indicator of female misdemeanour in Regency times); it is also visualized by the disorganization in which her little garden seems to be left. Reverting to the garden as the well-known symbol of order and containment, Wordsworth shows the extent of her (mental and bodily) disarray: the 'trim border-lines' of the flower-beds are broken, creepers such as 'the cumbrous bind-weed[s]' (*E*, I, 722/728) deprive the crop plants of their light and energy, but what is worse is that the sheep from the common break into her enclosed garden and destroy the bark of a young apple tree: 'The bark was nibbled round by truant sheep' (*E*, I, 842).

While William Holman Hunt (in *The Hireling Shepherd*, 1851) and Thomas Hardy (in *Far from the Madding Crowd*, 1874) use the motif of the straying sheep in order to alert their spectators and readers, respectively, to their Victorian ideas of moral disintegration, Wordsworth seems to upbraid not so much the careless shepherds as the wailing owner of the garden, who, in steeping herself in distress and melancholy, opens the microcosm of her body to all sorts of onsets and thus fails to reinforce the protective bark, skin and wall which Wordsworth uses as images of moral health. In the same way as the straw ceases to protect the tree, the bands of straw sealing up the thatched roof become permeable and expose the inhabitant to the dangers of frost, thaw and rain. To what extent the permeability of the garden and the house is transferred onto the protagonist's body, so that a perilous chain of porousness (house-garden-body) becomes visible, is made saliently clear when, in the last part of the inserted narrative poem, the depiction of the porous house is closely associated with references to Margaret's 'tattered clothes' (*E*, I, 909) and the resultant exposure of her breast to 'the nightly damps' (*E*, I, 908). Sentimental porousness, which started with Pamela and via Rousseau and Goethe became endemic in Europe, finds in Margaret a belated *exemplum horrendum*, a pitiable creature that has forgotten her life-sustaining duty to combat porosity and to staunch the bleeding wound of her sad life.

Coleridge's riotous fountains

Considering the fact that 'The Ruined Cottage' dates back to Wordsworth's Racedown years of 1797 and that it was finally included into the Book I of *The Excursion* in 1814, only after substantial revisions, the reader has every reason to believe that the addressee of the fictional conversation between the Pedlar and the speaker is gloomy Samuel Taylor Coleridge, whom Wordsworth had not only harshly criticized in letters, but also dismissed as a hopeless case.⁸² There is no gainsaying that a strong undercurrent of Wordsworth's poetry is Niobean grief (not only after the loss of his children Catherine and Thomas), but, while Coleridge and many splenetic Romantics steeped themselves in oozy dejection, Wordsworth had the gift of learning lessons from hardship and of integrating them into the overall concept of his work's Gothic architecture.

Coleridge's 'feeding on disquiet', his Keatsian 'glut[ting]' on dejection,⁸³ is incompatible with what Wordsworth's poetry gravitates towards: the growth, the maturing and the disembodiment of 'the philosophic mind'.⁸⁴ Denise Gigante intriguingly argues that Wordsworth's ideal of the 'mighty mind' is also that of a feeding one and that, at least in the 1850 version of *The Prelude*, it 'bears relation to Milton's God who digests – and excretes – the cosmos into order'.⁸⁵ Although inspired by Milton's alimentary cosmography, Wordsworth's philosophic mind, 'feed[ing] upon infinity' (*P*, XIII, 70), shuns all allusions to the inevitable outcome of the feeding process: the excrements and their orifices. When Wordsworth's concept of the philosophical mind occasionally allows for porosity and even induces him to visualize it as feeding or 'drink[ing] at every pore', there is scarcely any doubt that, for him, its bonds with the body are severed. It is not only a belated and striking example of T. S. Eliot's 'dissociation of sensibility', but also, as Anne K. Mellor aptly suggests, an expression of 'masculinist' and transgressive thinking.⁸⁶

Having conquered the leaking female world and replaced the porous feminine element with clean, aseptic and stony productions of his masculine mind,⁸⁷ Wordsworth is the provocative opposite of Coleridge who, deeply steeped in his 'drug-fuelled psychodrama',⁸⁸ lacked the capacity for philosophical self-containment. While Wordsworth 'preached his own bracing morality of self-contained self-control',⁸⁹ Coleridge ran the whole gamut of self-indictment and emotional porosity, thus emulating characters such as Margaret in their lack of physiological and psychological restraint. In the first book of his two-volume biography of Coleridge, Richard Holmes explained the difference between Wordsworth and Coleridge as an intriguing pair of metaphors, which could not

---

[82] Gill, *Wordsworth: A Life*, 133.
[83] Keats, 'Ode on Melancholy', 15. *The Complete Poems*, 348–49.
[84] 'Ode. Intimations of Immortality from Recollections of Early Childhood', 190. *Poetical Works*, 460.
[85] Gigante, *Taste*, 71.
[86] Mellor, *Romanticism and Gender*, 19.
[87] Ibid., 20.
[88] Wu, *Hazlitt*, 97.
[89] Byatt, *Unruly Times*, 49.

fit better into the overall pattern of this book: 'Intellectually, Coleridge was a huge river; while Wordsworth was a mighty rock.'[90]

As if to challenge Wordsworth's idea of the poet as a builder, architect or even geologist,[91] Coleridge fashions himself as a voyager, 'afloat on the wide sea unpiloted & and unprovisioned', as a passenger on a *bateau ivre*, exposed to the element of water, sometimes assuming the shape of a cormorant and diving into libraries in order to produce the radical opposite of the epitaph, a genre which he calls 'effusions'. Defined by Douglas J. Kneale as the poetic equivalent of the pouring forth of liquids, such as blood and tears,[92] Coleridgean 'effusions' differ fundamentally from the Wordsworthian epitaphic expression, which, Bruce Haley aptly formulates, was 'less an outpouring than a making'.[93] Associated with porousness, with the idea of a sudden and uncontrollable opening of the poet's body, Coleridge's effusions are best characterized as textual ejaculations, as an orgasmic or painful overflow from a body that is beyond tranquillity and recollection. In a letter to Robert Southey, Coleridge leaves his friend in no doubt that even as a philosopher (and plagiarist) he is painfully aware of the fact that thinking cannot be separated from corporeality, that thought is yoked to the body and that poetry is not so much an Icarian[94] flight into Shelleyan realms of 'unbodied joy' as the result of a corporeal ordeal making him ejaculate and exude a text that 'sweats beneath a heavy burthen of Ideas and Imagery'.[95]

The 'sweat' and the almost physiological porousness of his thoughts are evident in most of his poems, but all the more so in his Notebooks, where a more private and introspective Coleridge openly seems to challenge Wordsworth's concept of the dissociated philosophical mind and makes an undisguised display of the 'bodiliness' of his intellectual disintegration. Given to severe bouts of self-interrogation and repeatedly reverting to the semantic field of dissection,[96] Coleridge more often than not tries to probe the skin of his own body, to analyse the 'Cutaneous Complaints', which turned out to be the 'Terra[e] Incognita[e]' not only of nineteenth-century medicine,[97] but also of Romantic poetry and life-writing. While Wordsworth carefully consigns to paper what is stanzaic in an architectural sense, Coleridge has recourse to the textual medium of a

---

[90] Holmes, *Coleridge: Early Visions*, 151.
[91] See Heringman who calls Wordsworth the 'most geological of the Romantics'. 'Stones so wondrous Cheap', 51.
[92] Kneale, *Romantic Aversions*, 33.
[93] Haley, *Living Forms*, 130.
[94] 'To a Skylark', 15. *Poetical Works*, 602.
[95] Letter to Robert Southey, 11 December 1794. *Collected Letters*, 1:137.
[96] Holmes, *Darker Reflections*, 249.
[97] January 1804. *The Notebooks*, 1 (1794–1804), 1826/16. 209.

series of Notebooks which elusively hover between the privacy of diaries, the transitoriness of journalism and the emergence of the new impressionist and introspective genre of the autobiographical sketch which came to be associated less with Coleridge than with Baudelaire's posthumous publication of *Mon cœur mis à nu* (1887). In seventy-two notebooks, which are considered to be Coleridge's 'silent night-voice' soliloquizing for a period of almost forty years (1794–1834), he not only lays his heart bare, but also dissects the most intimate parts of his ailing body, revealing it as a naked, vulnerable and abjectly porous thing which obstinately opposes all endeavours to attain the maturity and aplomb of a philosophic mind. In a bluntness that goes back to Pepys's anatomies of his bodily functions in his diaries, Coleridge gives the prurient reader insights into the economy of his bodily fluids that is completely out of control.

Coleridge's susceptibility to his body's lack of containment is intriguingly captured by the use that he makes of water imagery and the symbol of the fountain. In a Notebook entry written when he was in Malta, he reminisces about the joy in his life which, due to his unrequited love for Sara Hutchinson, deserted him: 'I have forgotten what the Joy is of which the Heart is full as of a deep & quiet fountain overflowing insensibly; or the gladness of Joy, when the fountain overflows ebullient.'[98] The traditional image of the fountain is not only deployed twice, it is also used in a manner which clearly shows that the fountain in Coleridge's mind differs tremendously from that which Shakespeare envisioned in early modern drama. The fountain that used to be related to the female sex in a gendered garden and served as a symbol of how to channel, subdue and manipulate the unruly female element of water is here employed not only in a masculine context, but emphatically in a sense of transgressive immoderation and 'overflowing'. Coleridge's fascination for images of uninhibited porousness (at one point inducing him to enlarge on 'the whole system of Pores'[99]), his love of fountains overflowing and exceeding boundaries (of decorum, drug consumption and language) shapes his life, so that not least on account of his uncontrollable verbal and tearful outpourings of 'sensibility' and his anti-masculine proximity to the aquatic element, Holmes justifiably calls him an 'amphibious poet'.[100]

The more Wordsworth saw the process of writing poetry in terms of congealing porous feelings into the hard structures of his poetry, often using

---

[98] Malta, 23 November 1804, quoted in Holmes, *Darker Reflections*, 33.
[99] March 1820. *The Notebooks*, 4 (1819–26), 4646/28.5.f8.
[100] Holmes, *Darker Reflections*, 532.

the 'orbicular form' of the sonnet as an equivalent of stone circles,[101] the more Coleridge becomes aware of a porousness that affects his writing, his reception and his ailing body, leaving him often depleted and in the desolate state of having lost control over the precarious economy of his fluids. The leitmotif of his poetry is thus, in contrast to Wordsworth's architectural and rectilinear imagery, the self-consuming fountain that is fed by tributaries of suppressed energies and always on the verge of erupting into explosive and damaging porosity. In 'Dejection: An Ode', published on the occasion of Wordsworth's marriage to Mary, Coleridge still manages to adhere to a kind of public mode of self-containment, but makes it unmistakably clear that gushes of strong sentiment are welling up in hidden reservoirs, in fountains that 'are within', and which might explode into passionate porousness at any time. Suffering from leaden melancholy and wracked by frantic jealousy (hallucinating about Wordsworth and Sara Hutchinson having sexual intercourse), the speaker is dragged down by a 'stifled, drowsy, unimpassioned grief' which as yet finds no expression and relief in 'word, or sigh, or tear'.[102] Within the public space of the poem, the speaker is, thus, worlds apart from Shakespeare's Niobean Macduff who translated his grief into rational discourse. With his feelings bottled up and his emotional pain repressed ('stifled') the speaker reacts in a way that is fully expected of a man on the brink of the straitlaced Victorian age. The metaphor of the 'smothering weight' (41) that presses on the poet's breast is reminiscent not only of Henry Fuseli's oppressive nightmare that, in the famous 1790 painting, literally squats on the sleeper's breast, but also of the various gender-related and ideological fetters that hinder men in the Romantic age from publicly releasing their long pent-up torrents of tears. Even though the poet produces a long (albeit erratic) ode and thus channels his festering emotions into creative expression, it is evident that the 'viper thoughts' (94) that strangle the poet's mind are only partially allayed and always ready to produce new venom.

Considering the fact that Coleridge's poetry abounds in images of oppression and stagnation (frost, frozen or congealed water, inward fountains) the reader is justified in interpreting the obscure poem 'Kubla Khan' in terms of a codified description of emotional and sexual porousness. In this respect, the poem is so radically new and alarmingly off the beaten poetic track that Coleridge felt obliged to account for the poem as an opium-induced dream in the wake of reading *Purchas His Pilgrimage* (1613), the transcription of which was discontinued

---

[101] Fulford, *Wordsworth's Poetry 1815–1845*, 231.
[102] 'Dejection: An Ode', 22/24. *The Complete Poems*, 308.

due to the arrival of a mysterious, gender-neutral 'person on business from Porlock'.[103] These explanations added by Coleridge in the self-effacing third-person narrative in 1816, nineteen years after the poem's composition, serve as ways to gloss over semantic fields that could easily be read as images of eruptive sexual porousness.

What in the very first lines looks like a translation of an Arcadian place of fertility and plenty into an exotic ambience suddenly turns into a scene of terrifying Romantic sublimity. At first glance concealed by the 'stately pleasure-dome' (2), there is a 'deep romantic chasm' (12), an abyss or volcanic crater which is on the point of ejecting what was crusted, frozen and hidden beneath thick veneers of tradition, gender bias and taboo. There is unanimous agreement in literary criticism that the depiction of the eruption of the volcanic chasm reveals Coleridge's deep existential anxieties,[104] but it also shows that these apocalyptical visions are interwoven with traumatic images of ejaculation, tense moments of radical and irrepressible porousness. As in his Notebooks, Coleridge is no longer able to control the 'ceaseless turmoil' that is 'seething' (17) behind the facade of literary decorum; hence, he sexualizes the earth, when he describes it emitting voluptuous groans ('in fast thick pants [...] breathing', 18) and being on the point of a cathartic orgasm. The result of this violent climax is the emergence of a 'mighty fountain' (19) which differs enormously from other decorative fountains by its sheer eruptive power and the '[h]uge fragments' that, 'like rebounding hail, / Or chaffy grain beneath the thresher's flail' (21–22), it hurls through the air.

What makes 'Kubla Khan' such a vexing poem and a precursor of twentieth-century Surrealism is the simple fact that it baffles all entrenched concepts of gender and all conventions of writing about man's body and its sexuality. Well-wrought as its structure is, squeezing the volcanic content into stanzas of eleven, thirteen and twelve lines (and in Part II into a similar regularity of five, six and seven lines),[105] the poem reflects the inner conflict, a psychomachia, that seems to be going on in the poet. Penetrating even further into the taboo-ridden realm of bodily desires, Coleridge marshals geological images of a seethingly hot und tumultuous earth into a cluster of metaphors that, in the allegedly liminal state

---

[103] See Coleridge, 'Kubla Khan: Or, a Vision in a Dream. A Fragment', *Complete Poems*, 250. For the mystery that invests the anonymous person, see also White, 'The Person from Porlock in "Kubla Khan"', 172–93 and Wu, *30 Great Myths*, 108–14, who defines the person as an intruder 'from the Heraclitean flux of the quotidian' upon the poet's world of creativity (110).
[104] Wallbank, 'Coleridge's "Deep Romantic Chasm"', 13.
[105] For this hint I am indebted to Fred Burwick, who in January 2016 did an excellent close reading of 'Kubla Khan' at the University of Vechta.

between waking and sleeping, circumscribes the moment of eruptive male masturbatory relief: 'It flung up momently the sacred river' (24).

In the context of literature, this is one of the first explicit representations of masturbation after Lovelace's Anacreontic autoeroticism and prior to Christina Rossetti's warped allegorization of female masturbation in her mid-Victorian poem *Goblin Market*. Deeply moored in the eighteenth-century politico-economic discourse against masturbation, which was seen as a porousness that subverted not only the individual economy of bodily fluids, but also the public monitoring of privately insurgent lust,[106] Coleridge seems to be aware of the dilemma that, by freely yielding to his repressed onanistic desires, a reconstruction of the 'symphony and song' (43) of the Abyssinian maid has become as impossible as his reintroduction into the society of those who, like Wordsworth, aspired to the purity of the disembodied philosophical mind. The poem even adumbrates the medieval ostracism that the Establishment has in store for its transgressors of anti-porous decorum, pronouncing a spell over the polluter:

> And all should cry, Beware! Beware!
> His flashing eyes, his floating hair!
> *Weave a circle round him thrice*,
> And close your eyes with holy dread,
> For he on honey-dew hath fed,
> And drunk the milk of Paradise. (49–54; my italics)

It is open to conjecture how the poem would have ended if the mysterious person from Porlock had not intervened. Yet, since surmises like this are hardly tenable, we should be ready to understand the nondescript person from Porlock as a genderless personification of (self-)censorship which Coleridge seems to use as a protection after revealing too much of the sexual turmoil that was raging within him. Similar to, but also different from, Ernest Dowson's obtrusively censorious figure Cynara, who mars the speaker's forays into (porous) excess, into 'madder music and stronger wine',[107] the person from Porlock functions as a Freudian superego which bans emission and enjoins the poet to conceal his rebellious sexual fountains behind stony facades. The fragment as it is identifies Coleridge as a poet who not only crossed borders of masculine deportment, but (especially as a Unitarian preacher) felt himself under the surveillance of a moral regime which was fanatically determined to oppose all onsets of

---

[106] Cf. Schulkins, *Keats, Modesty and Masturbation*, 4f.
[107] Dowson, 'Non sum qualis eram bonae sub regno Cynarae', 19. *The Poems of Ernest Dowson*, 58.

corporeal, emotional and poetic openness. The circle woven three times around the transgressive masturbator is thus like an immobilizing curse on an outsider who audaciously imbibed the 'honey-dew' and the narcotic 'milk of Paradise' and, by setting in motion the intractable fountains of masturbatory delights, jeopardized the stony poetics of the Lakists.

Niobean snakes, giants and monsters in Keats and Byron

Keats's alchemy of evaporation

Situating the Romantic body at the interface between new medical science and literary tradition, Alan Richardson suggests that the younger generation of Romantics was – due to their increasing immersion in medical knowledge – no longer willing to uphold transcendentalist notions in their concepts of the body.[108] The more they, in the role of modern Fausts, looked into the 'filthy workshop of creation',[109] into the monstrous, the ugly and the blunt biochemical data, the more they found it difficult to believe either in philosophical minds dissociated from bodies or in the immaculate type of body propagated by Winckelmann.

That the loathing of the body is deeply ingrained in the Romantic age becomes recognizable in Keats's poetry. Weighed down by the burden of his disintegrating body, exhausted by the 'weariness, the fever, and the fret',[110] the speaker of 'Ode to a Nightingale' (1819) wishes to nullify his body to such a radical degree that he voices his (almost suicidal) desire to 'leave the world unseen' (19), to fade away with the bird and to 'dissolve' into nothingness (21). The speaker's sensation of bodily dissolution is reflected in a letter that consumptive Keats writes on 13 October 1819: 'I have a sensation at the present moment as though I was dissolving.'[111] What at first looks like a kind of 'liquefaction' which Gigante also sees 'poignantly registered in the bitter words of his own epitaph'[112] is, however, not so easy to pin down. While in his letters Keats is shockingly explicit about his uncontrollable bodily ooziness ('a violent rush of blood came to my Lungs that I felt nearly suffocated'),[113] in his poetry, he seems to be intent on dematerializing the idea of 'dissolving' and to transport its connotations of fluidity into a different aggregate state: into that of bodiless air, into evaporating nothingness.

---

[108] Richardson, 'Romanticism and the Body', 5 and 9.
[109] Shelley, *Frankenstein*, 55.
[110] 'Ode to a Nightingale', 23. *Complete Poems*, 346.
[111] Letter to Fanny Brawne, 13 October 1819. *Letters*, 2:223.
[112] Gigante, *Taste*, 157.
[113] Letter to Fanny Brawne, 10 (?) February 1820. *Letters*, 2.254.

Suffering from and being acutely aware of his sick body's uncontrollable porousness in his letters, Keats opens the 'magic casements' of his poetry and yearns for the body's dissolution into air or into the vapours of fantasy. The twofold interpretation of the word 'to dissolve' (to melt and to evaporate) can certainly be understood as a reaction to what Gigante identifies as the poet's deep-seated 'existentialist nausea', as a response to 'the material obtuseness of existence' which Keats, prior to Jean-Paul Sartre, felt overpowered by.[114] Hoping to accelerate the dissolution of his obtusely ponderous body by the physical act of drinking from 'the blushful Hippocrene' (16), the poet paradoxically reverts to the materiality of the written poem to voice his ardent wish for the total annihilation of his body into airiness, gearing his verses to the crucial moment when the invisible bird translates the act of physical pouring into a non-aquatic and spiritual effusion: 'While thou art *pouring forth thy soul* abroad / In such an ecstasy!' (56–57, my italics).

Following the typically Romantic trajectory from the Icarian heights of the 'viewless wings of Poesy' (33) to being an insensible and monosyllabic 'sod' (60),[115] Roe reads the entire poem alongside Coleridge's 'Kubla Khan' and De Quincey's *Confessions of an English Opium-Eater* 'as one of the greatest re-creations of a drug-inspired dream-vision in English literature'.[116] The calculated pattern of the eight ten-line stanzas and the tight syntactical control that the speaker exercises over the poem's body, however, show that Keats is different from Coleridge and not in need of Porlockian interventions to keep his textual and physical bodies from erupting into violent ejaculations. In marked contrast to Coleridge, Keats even seems to be overeager to keep the human bodies in his poetry in a state of Shakespearean ignorance of pores and, to a considerable degree, hygienically drained of the repellent ooze which he must have repeatedly come across in the anatomy theatre.

In this context, the 'happy melodist' in the 'Ode on a Grecian Urn' is to be envied, because he is, like the other figures carved into anti-porous stone, a participant of a '[c]old Pastoral' (45) that can never be eroded by water, Niobean tears and other oozing fluids (from which even 'ooze-born Goddess[es]' such as Venus are not completely exempt[117]). The idea of an entire civilization (including rivers and seas) congealed into marble henceforth seems to be the epitome of an aestheticism which, *avant la lettre* and a century prior to Yeats's wish to be absorbed into 'the

---

[114] Gigante, *Taste*, 152 and 156.
[115] Lennartz, 'Icarian Romanticism', 213–24.
[116] Roe, *John Keats*, 324.
[117] *Endymion* III, 893. *Complete Poems*, 185.

artifice of eternity',[118] negates the body and completely obliterates it from the poem. Relegated to the position of a Swiftian byword for disease, decrepitude and filth, the body with its nauseating fluids and orifices is, in Keats's poetry, increasingly anathematized and shown, then, as a memento mori object embarrassingly out of tune with visions of a Wordsworthian 'fellowship with essence', of life as an immaterial radiation and 'shin[ing] / Full and free of space'.[119]

In a deleted passage, which Roe unearths in his recent biography, the phrase of the 'fellowship with essence' was originally preceded by the pseudoscientific image of 'the richest Alchymy [sic]'.[120] It is this idea of a gradual refinement, of a purification and discharging of bodily dross that is at the core of Keats's alchemical poetology and which clearly reverberates through the multifaceted poem 'Lamia' (1819) – a poem arguably inspired by Keats's encounter with the sexually exacting Jane Cox. Translated into the concept of a complex metamorphosis, 'the richest Alchymy' involves the Romantic subject in a painful process of concoction: starting as a monstrous reptile, then reaching the paradox of living as a disembodied human being, the female protagonist, by the end, undergoes a transmutation into ethereal nothingness (only leaving the sartorial husks of her cast-off skin behind). As a snake at the beginning, Lamia is endowed with grotesque attributes of stereotypical female porosity: her eyes cannot help weeping 'that they were born so fair' (I, 62), and from her mouth the words dribble like 'bubbling honey' (I, 65); on the next rung of the alchemical ladder, she is then painfully turned into a woman whose body is characterized by secretions of fluids, by the exudation of juices that antithetically oscillate between dewy refreshment and venom: 'Her mouth foamed, and the grass, therewith besprent, / Withered at dew so sweet and virulent' (I, 148–49). The more her transformation from snake to woman progresses, the more her (sexual) porousness seems to decrease and the liquidity of her eyes (metonymically: her vagina) is dried up by heat and petrification:

Her eyes in torture fixed, and anguish drear,
Hot, glazed, and wide, with eye-lashes all sear,
Flashed phosphor and sharp sparks, without one cooling tear.
(I, 150–52)

---

[118] Yeats, 'Sailing to Byzantium' 24. *Yeats's Poems*, 301.
[119] *Endymion* I, 779.
[120] Quoted in Roe, *John Keats*, 174. According to Miriam Allott, this line belongs to a fair copy that was cancelled: 'And that delight is the most treasurable / That makes richest Alchymy'. *The Poems of John Keats*, 154. Barnard uses the variant: 'till we shine, / Full alchemized, and free of space', 779–80. *Complete Poems*, 127–28.

The fixation and paralysis ('fixed', 'glazed') of her eyes is an apt metaphor for the way she is progressively squeezed into the mould of proto-Victorian gender templates. This process of immobilization is further intensified by the fact that Lamia's gradual anthropomorphization is compared to a stream of lava which ruthlessly encroaches upon and encrusts the last vestiges of feminine vegetation. Unlike Coleridge's sexualized imagery of volcanic eruption, the lava here seems to visualize that Lamia's humanization is related not only to convulsive pain and to a rapid loss of beauty ('Nothing but pain and ugliness were left', I, 164), but also to a progressive drying up and petrifying of her bodily fluids, which in the end do not amount to so much as 'one cooling tear'.

While the 1819 odes tend to abbreviate the alchemical process of poetry and quickly open its magical casements, 'Lamia' lays bare the painful ordeal that underlies this ideal of refinement. Lycius, Lamia's young and sentimental paramour, does not realize that, after her dolorous transformation and domestication into a 'full-born beauty' (I, 172), Lamia becomes a bloodless illusion, a limp bodiless dream, which parodies his Pygmalion fantasy of having wrought a perfect woman out of a lifeless block of stone. Beguiled into the erroneous belief that he has found (or produced) a real, luscious woman in Lamia, Lycius acts up to what is expected of him in patriarchal circles: he increasingly objectifies her and, by treating her as an overflowing vessel created for his sensual satisfaction – '[l]eaving no drop in his bewildering cup' (I, 252) –he finally deprives her of her original serpent-like sexual identity. Accepting his 'secluded bubble',[121] his masculinist fallacy that she is a woman 'without / Any more subtle fluid in her veins / Than throbbing blood' (I, 306–08), Lamia decides to abandon her former role as a goddess and mythological creature and to fascinate Lycius in a new role, 'by playing woman's part' (I, 337).

As Schulkins convincingly argues, Lamia's adoption of the role of a nineteenth-century woman is tantamount to the abdication of her sexuality and her body's porousness.[122] By the end of the first part of the poem, Lamia has been unveiled not so much as a highly protean and theatrical femme fatale, but rather, tragically, as the epitome of feminine sensuality forced to hide her liminal body in the manner of a disembodied, fairy-like impostor, trying to live up to the expectation of a 'virgin purest lipp'd' (I, 189). That in Lamia's case the alchemical process is relentlessly attuned to patriarchal axioms is shown by the constant pressure that is exercised on Lamia and that induces her to camouflage

---

[121] Schulkins, *Keats, Modesty, and Masturbation*, 127.
[122] Ibid.

her female sexuality and to dovetail it into ready-made ideologies of femininity as they were, at that time, defined by male authorities. Turned into a target of 'hostile male pronouncement'[123] and finding that her compulsive dissembling will not stand the test of Apollonius's penetrative and 'sharp eyes' (I, 364), Lamia eventually cannot help surrendering to misogynist fanaticism as it comes disguised and 'robed in philosophic gown' (I, 365).

Sharing with Lewis's monk, Ambrosio, the piercing 'demon eyes' (II, 289), Apollonius turns out to be a rabid persecutor of Romantic chimeras and, like a true proselyte of Blake's Newton-like Urizen, tries to strengthen the tyranny of reason. In the same way as the terrorism of Newtonian 'cold philosophy' (II, 230) was said to have deconstructed the rainbow and all the mysteries of the Romantic age, Apollonius rivets his ruthless gaze on Lamia in order to expose her vexingly hybrid and illusive identity. Apollonius's deconstructivist gaze, however, has a twofold abortive effect:[124] using his eye '[l]ike a sharp spear' (II, 300) and thus perforating Lamia's body in the same manner as St George impales the dragon, Apollonius is neither able to 'unweave' her like the rainbow and to retrace the stages of her alchemical transformation from reptile to human being, nor is he able to preserve the intellectual and bodily sanity of his disciple Lycius, who was about to marry this phantasmagorical woman. When both Lamia and Lycius die, they elude the clutches of philosophy and the demands of social asceticism, the former evaporating in a truly Keatsian fashion – 'with a frightful scream she vanished' (II, 306) – and the latter being relieved of his 'heavy body' (II, 311) in the marriage robe now turned into winding sheets. It is intriguing and highly pertinent that Keats deflects from his source text, from the story of Lycius in Robert Burton's *The Anatomy of Melancholy* (1620), where Lamia weeps when 'she saw her selfe descried'.[125] In Keats's romanticized version of the story, Lamia reverts to a kind of dumb show, '[m]otion[ing] him to be silent; vainly so' (II, 303), and, in accordance with Keats's anti-porous creed, refrains from shedding a single tear.

That it is eventually the hostile gaze of bigoted 'cold philosophy' that brings about the ultimate, wished-for step, the vanishing of the body's materiality,[126] is an ironic twist of the poem. Concluding on the tableau of the dead Lycius attired in his (or Lamia's) 'marriage robe' (II, 311), the poem has a truly Shakespearean

---

[123] Narayan, *Real and Imagined Women*, 126.
[124] For Endo, Apollonius is even 'a more effective romancer than Lamia'. 'Seeing Romantically in *Lamia*', 122.
[125] Burton, *The Anatomy of Melancholy*, 3, 46.
[126] Keats disemburdens Lamia from the clutter of domestic life which Burton emphasized: 'she, Plate, Home, and all that was in it, vanished in an instant', ibid.

feel and as such pinpoints the fact that death, the body's dissolution and annihilation, is the only effective remedy to put an end to the body's fever, fret and abject ooziness. Lamia's 'explosion of the narrative frame and her departure from view'[127] has provoked various critical responses, the most prominent of which is Susan J. Wolfson's compelling hypothesis that Keats was trying to come to terms with his own 'gender crisis', by drawing on 'established gender capital' and showing men 'pumped up with power' over nullified women.[128] It is, however, open to speculation whether Keats was truly compensating for his 'gender diminution' and reasserting his masculinity by reducing women to ciphers or by effacing them from both his poetry and mind (although the evidence that Wolfson cites is overwhelming).[129] While, on the one hand, longing for lubricated female bodies, 'moistened and bedewed with Pleasures',[130] Keats was, on the other, eager to exorcize the corporeal from his poetry, because, in its persistent ooziness, it was not only a constant reminder of his repressed feminine side and, so Wolfson, of his dreaded state of being 'unsexed',[131] but also the admonishing emblem of his short life as – in McEwan's words – 'a slippery, porous slate', disintegrating ab ovo.[132]

Read from Keats's angle of the scepticism of the (female) body, it is no longer a paradox that Keats is at his most corporeal (and porous) in a poem that is radically devoid of human beings: 'To Autumn' (1819). Without visible trace of a speaker, Keats has his readers watch an autumnal spectacle in which the whole cycle of death-bound life is condensed into three stanzas. While Keats was watching his body deteriorate and show early symptoms of what eventually culminated in the consumptive porousness of haemorrhages, he surprises his readers by depicting autumn as a time of procreative activity and sexual scheming. Yet, even in his fear of being 'unsexed', writing a poem devoid of metamorphosing women, Keats cannot help realizing that ooziness is ubiquitous and that female carnality is firmly inscribed into nature. In glaring contrast to the traditional and Arcimboldian association of autumn with a season of harvest and bulbous-nosed senility, the autumn of the first stanza, in the guise of a collusive and oversexed nymph, openly defies sentimental concepts of femininity when

[127] Narayan, *Real and Imagined Women*, 126.
[128] Wolfson, *Borderlines*, 207–08.
[129] Ibid., 208. Wolfson also refers to one of Keats's earliest poems in which he utilizes a quote from Terence to the effect, '[f]rom this moment I efface from my mind all women' (210).
[130] Letter to Fanny Brawne, 8 July 1819, *Letters*, 2:356.
[131] Wolfson, *Borderlines*, 214. The misogynist atmosphere in which Keats was raised and wrote is best captured by Richard Polwhele's 1798 polemical poem *The Unsex'd Females, A Poem*.
[132] McEwan, *Nutshell*, 2. It is hardly surprising that, next to Shakespeare's *Hamlet*, Keats is referred to as a poet of nutshells and 'sweet kernel[s]' (14).

she is shown as being on a par with her '[c]lose bosom friend', the sun, and frivolously 'conspir[es] with him' (2–3) about how to impregnate nature and make it fruitfully porous. The word 'conspiring', another pivotal word which in this poem ingeniously conflates the etymological idea of breathing together in a kiss (*con-spirare*) with the modern meaning of a conspiracy,[133] an amorous plot, triggers a long syntactical chain which shows to what extent autumn, in the role of an efficient procuress, provides the sexualized sun with willing recipients and myriads of vegetative Danaës for his fruitful rays:

> [to] fill all fruit with ripeness to the core;
> To swell the gourd, and plump the hazel shells
> With a sweet kernel[.] (6–8)

Having successfully effaced women from his poem, but clearly not from his mind, Keats has his anthropomorphized nature not only assume human roles, but also revert to so pervasive a femininity that all natural phenomena seem to be part of one gigantic and receptive female belly. The 'swelling' and 'plumping' of the fruit are unmistakable indications of nature's pregnancy and of a porousness which underlines not only the illimitable fertility of nature's body, but also its shocking promiscuity. Unflinchingly pursuing their plan to inseminate and impregnate all kinds of fruit, the conspirative Jovian sun and autumn even go so far as to beguile the fauna and to make insects, in particular the bees in their 'clammy cells' (11), believe that this pageantry of plenty and uterine porousness will never end.

The second stanza of what Hagstrum erroneously calls Keats's 'chastest of his odes'[134] comes as a shock, as a song of sobering experience, not so much for the bees as for all delusional beings (including the poet in his autumnal *annus mirabilis*) who are scarcely aware of the abruptness with which sensual and manipulative autumn is turned into a female embodiment of death and eschatological judgement. No longer the companion of the libertinistic sun, autumn has now – in the manner of Lewis's Matilda – dropped its veil and revealed itself as a harbinger of death which might at first be mistaken for the moment of post-coital exhaustion, the aftermath of the orgasmic little death: 'on a half-reaped furrow sound asleep, / Drowsed with the fume of poppies' (16–17). The last image of the second stanza clearly underlines the fact that the porousness of nature's female body has an equivocal quality: while in the first

---

[133] *OED*, 'conspire', v. 6.
[134] Hagstrum, *The Romantic Body*, 67.

stanza the porousness is of a receptive and procreative kind, in the second stanza it is a death-bound leakiness from which, as in a liquid hour glass, the last drops of life's juices exude: 'by a cider-press, with patient look, / Thou watchest the last oozings hours by hours' (20–21).

The poem ends on (disembodied) references to autumn's elegiac music. After the 'frantic gape of lonely Niobe'[135] in *Endymion* and *Lamia*'s evaporation under the piercing philosophical gaze, Keats eventually tries to eliminate (female) corporeality into the Echo-like audibility of ephemeral animals chanting a polyphonous requiem. The dialectical goal of resolving life in bodiless and sexless autumnal music is finally Keats's escape route from the leakiness of the human condition and from the ooziness of the enticing female sex.

Keats's aesthetic escapism, his imaginative flight from man's (and female nature's) corporeality into music or hackneyed Platonic truisms elicited different reactions from his contemporaries, the most lacerating of which was the ferocious attack by John Gibson Lockhart, who ambushed Keats from behind the ominous pseudonym 'Z' and assaulted him for being one of the Cockneys intent on 'lisp[ing] sedition'.[136] Hardly less straightforward, Lord Byron criticized Keats's poetry not so much along political or moral lines as for what it unavailingly tried to combat: its alleged porosity, its infantile incontinence ('Johnny Keats's *p-ss a bed* poetry'[137]). By bringing Keats's poetry close to the taboo of masturbation – 'the Onanism of Poetry'[138] – Byron maliciously goes so far as to diagnose Keats's work as a sexual aberration that seems to be as detrimental and dysfunctional as the extreme opposite, the intellectual and sexual dryness of Robert Southey, the 'dry Bob' of the 'Dedication' to *Don Juan* (1818–24).[139]

In *Adonais* (1821), Percy Bysshe Shelley bewails Keats's death in the uncommon role of a male Niobe, mourning the young Cockney poet's death as both a feminized martyrdom and an erotic liquefaction,[140] whereas Byron uses Keats as a counterfoil to his ideal of the poet as a superhuman rebel, impervious and akin to Prometheus, who, as a sign of his anti-porous masculine hardness, was chained to a rock.

---

[135] *Endymion* I, 338.
[136] Quoted in Roe, *John Keats*, 265.
[137] Letter to John Murray, 8 October 1820, *BLJ*, 7:217.
[138] Letter to John Murray, 9 October 1820, *BLJ*, 7:217.
[139] 'Dedication', 24. *DJ*, *CPW*, 5.
[140] Keats's persistent reputation of being delicate and effeminized is also referred to in Thomson, 'Fanny Brawne and Other Women', 38.

Tidal and porous 'affairs' in Byron's poetry

From this perspective, it might, at first glance, appear like a contradiction that Byron's most famous and monumental poems *Childe Harold's Pilgrimage* and *Don Juan* are awash with bodily fluids, but while in the former poem Byron still struggles with the sentimental heritage, in the latter he is well settled in the new acrimonious position of a scoffer who enjoys holding up the mirror to his audience and confronting them with the sordidness of the oozy human condition. Opting for an anthropological realism that no longer hides behind turgid Shelleyan citations from ancient elegies or Keatsian risqué metaphors of post-coital oozings of hourglasses and swelling gourds, Byron moves from Promethean stoicism to carnivalism, providing his readers with a choice of imagery that precariously tiptoes on the verge of pornography and pathology and reverts to the Augustans' misanthropic satire. By the time of his *Don Juan*, Byron proves to be closer to Swift's and Rochester's dystopian images of dripping female genitals than to the school of Wertherian sentimentalism.

His sustained interest in Niobe and her excess of tears bears testimony to the way Byron readily engages with questions of bodily openness. While in his late poem 'The Age of Bronze' (1823), Byron briefly returns to the myth of Niobe, and by doing so, uses the reference to ancient mythology as an eclectic way of puffing up his criticism of the Church's capitalism – 'Mother Church [...] / Like Niobe, weeps o'er her offspring, Tithes'[141] – it is in his epic poem *Childe Harold's Pilgrimage*, unanimously seen as the foundation for his fame as a Romantic pop star and enfant terrible, that Byron succeeds in innovatively interweaving the myth of Niobe with his new, transgendered concept of the Promethean Byronic hero. Propelled by unmeasurable grief, Byron's weltschmerz-stricken hero Harold is a conglomeration of a dandy, flâneur and Niobe, hopelessly rent between his urge to weep at what he sees in his perambulations and the firm determination to give his emotional pressure no vent. A 'Kubla Khan'-like eruption of pent-up emotions bursting into a fountain of uncontrollable liquids was unthinkable for the Byronic hero who preferred to fashion himself as a stoic *ennuyé*. The striking fact that, at the very outset of the poem, a lingering sign of Niobean porousness, a 'sullen tear' (*CHP* I, 48), is still visible on Harold's face can only be interpreted as a belated tribute to or a relapse into sentimentality, which, in the subsequent line, is, however, duly arrested and transformed into a hardened, beady or glassy substance by the agency of Byronic pride: 'But Pride congeal'd the drop within his ee' (*CHP* I, 49).

[141] 'The Age of Bronze' (1823), 644–45. *CPW*, 7, 21.

In this respect, Harold is as remote from Werther as he can be and more akin to Byronic heroes such as the bastard Hugo and his relentless father Prince Azo in the neglected poem *Parisina* (1816),[142] both of whom, in their bitter conflict, ruthlessly refrain from shedding emasculating tears. In both *Childe Harold* and in *Parisina*, Byron evinces deep psychological intuition when he (apparently unaware of Friedrich August Carus's *History of Psychology* in 1808) visualizes and verbalizes the far-reaching effects that the repression of tears has on man's psychological make-up. While the Harold of Canto I avoids probing the depths that his freezing pride and ennui cover and eventually embarks on a journey which, in the course of the following Cantos, turns out to be a grand tour of disillusion, Azo cannot help feeling that the 'deepest ice which ever froze / Can only o'er the surface close' (*Parisina* 553–54). Nowhere is Byron more explicit about what happens psychologically behind the flawless epidermal facade of the ostentatiously unperturbed Byronic hero. While critics in the wake of Peter Thorslev's 1962 pioneering study on the Byronic hero formulaically emphasize the figure's ancestry in Milton's Satan and the *Sturm-und-Drang* rebels,[143] Byron rather seems to dissociate his protagonists from these early templates and to show that they are renegades of sentimentalism forcing back their torrents of tears to their 'fountain head', there to ferment in the remotest regions of the body, '[u]nseen, unwept, but uncongeal'd, / And cherish'd most where least reveal'd' (*Parisina*, 564/567). Since the composition of *Parisina* coincides with the publication of the early Cantos of *Childe Harold's Pilgrimage*, it is revealing to see to what extent its ideas about (female) porosity feed into the longer epic poem, how the Byronic hero actually overlaps with Niobe and how censoriously the speaker deals with Laertian relapses into a male loss of control. Having abjured the 'laughing dames in whom he did delight' (*CHP* I, 92) and given up his rakish pursuits as early as in Canto I, Harold is faced with a world in which the death of culture is ubiquitous and in which the absence of emotional and physiological porosity is compensated for by a keen sympathy with animals (the bleeding bull in the Spanish arena) or with dry and derelict objects such as the 'marble wilderness' of depopulated Rome (*CHP* IV, 710). The fact that Rome is personified as the 'Niobe of nations' (*CHP* IV, 703) is strikingly new and testifies not so much to Harold's frustrated longing for women as to an intriguing redefinition of Niobe in terms of a deserted city in which tears have evaporated and dust as a visual sign of bodily non-existence has become triumphant.

---

[142] For this invaluable hint I am indebted to Bernard Beatty who drew my attention to *Parisina* at the IABS conference in Gdansk in 2015. *CPW*, 3.
[143] Thorslev, *The Byronic Hero*, 74.

Whether Byron's interest in the myth of Niobe was kindled in Florence, where in the Sala della Niobe of the Uffizi Gallery he must have come across the seventeen statues focusing on Niobe's grief, remains a matter of conjecture; but the irony that the anonymous sculptor carved the bereaved mother into dry and polished marble even before her metamorphosis into a stony fountain and thus cast her into a situation of double petrification must have appealed to Byron who had been at odds not only with his, but also with women's intractable bodies since his formative years at Southwell.[144]

In this context, Byron's identification of Rome with Niobe is iconoclastic and in blatant contrast to the platitudinous images (or mirages) of Rome in Romantic literature and painting. Associating Rome with the myth of Niobe, who in the shape of a woman seems to have outgrown her tears and Romantic corporeality, Byron visualizes the Eternal City as a Byronic heroine who differs enormously from other feminine cities such as meritorious Venice, which, in radical contradistinction to Niobean sorrow, is related to icons of fertility and sexual openness, to the multi-breasted Cybele and the offensively impregnable Danaë ('the exhaustless East / Pour'd in her lap all gems in sparkling showers'; *CHP* IV, 15f.). Challenging iconographical traditions, Byron disembodies his Roman Niobe and turns her into a symbol of dryness, absence and emptiness – 'An empty urn within her withered hands, / Whose holy dust was scatter'd long ago' (*CHP* IV, 705–06). Having her refrain from tears (and other bodily fluids), Byron's speaker makes Rome not only the early figurehead of a century in which physiological dehydration is to be paramount, but also a symbol of repressive stoicism which Byronic heroes revered and considered to be a role model. While Wolfson maintains that the feminization of the Byronic hero starts with Donna Julia in *Don Juan*,[145] it is more convincing to argue that the feminization of the Byronic hero begins with the apostrophe to Niobean Rome as the paragon of stoic, Byronic suffering, as a mythic and liminal creature suckled by a 'She-wolf' (*CHP* IV, 784).

In marked contrast to Rome's Niobean desolation, Harold, by the end of the poem, metamorphoses into a 'drop of rain' (*CHP* IV, 1617), a particle passing, as later in Shelley's 'The Cloud' (1820), 'through the pores of the ocean and shores'.[146] As a radical sign of his final state of total and diminutive porousness, drop-like man eventually sinks into and merges with the unfathomable depths of the ocean, '[w]ithout a grave, unknell'd, uncoffin'd, and unknown'

---

[144] Cf. MacCarthy, *Byron, Life and Legend*, 53.
[145] Wolfson, *Borderlines*, 180.
[146] 'The Cloud', 75. *Poetical Works*, 602.

(*CHP* IV, 1609–11). While it is tempting to read the concluding stanzas of Canto IV as the ultimate bursting of the reservoir of 'unwept' and 'uncongealed' tears, as an image of emotional turmoil and eruption that refuses to be squeezed into the rationalized grid of the Spenserian stanzas, the transition from the Byronic hero as a tearless Niobe to man as a drop-like nonentity also serves Byron as an allegorization of his farewell to the ideal of the self-contained Classicist body epitomized in Antonio Canova's sculpture. Shelley's idealization of Keats's death as a 'liquid rest' is here given a flamboyant refutation.[147]

In *Don Juan* (1818–24), his most porous, incontinent and digressive poem, Byron intensifies the imagery of leakiness and the aquatic to such an extent that all concepts of the heroic are washed away right from the start. With the loss of heroism (which even drop-like Harold retained), the element of water also loses its sublimity and turns – as will become apparent later – into the exudations of colossal and monstrous bodies. The trajectory of the sublime to the ridiculous as it is described by Hazlitt[148] is, in Byron's *Don Juan*, extended to the obscene, monstrous and genitally porous. This is also corroborated by Byron's shift from the epitaphic Spenserian stanza in *Childe Harold's Pilgrimage* to the more vitriolic tone of the Italianate *ottava rima*. As in the earlier poem, man's 'nautical existence' (*DJ* II, 96) involves him in a perpetual battle against the erosions of water, but while the Byronic hero managed to suppress and to form a buttress against all forms of physical and emotional inundation for the most part of the four long cantos, the new epicene protagonist of *Don Juan* easily succumbs not only to all sorts of 'gender-play',[149] but also to onsets of porosity which clearly disqualify him for the role of the Byronic hero and mark him as a precariously feminized anti-hero. Pungent, salty and acrid liquids not only attack him from the outside and inside, but they now also eat through ships, institutions, edifices (the Trinidada as the nave of the Church) and obliterate hitherto sacred concepts of masculinity and patriarchal order.

The paradigm shift which separates the extremely different *Childe Harold's Pilgrimage* and *Don Juan* is best illustrated by the attitude that the narrators adopt towards their (anti-)heroes. While in the earlier epic poem the narrator and Childe Harold became more and more symbiotic in their flawed superhuman aspiration of forming a (ruinous) buttress against all kinds of ontological inundation, in *Don Juan*, the protagonist and his narrator are strikingly opposed in a relationship of ironic contrast. Thus, while, at the beginning of his voyage,

---

[147] *Adonais*, 63.
[148] Hazlitt, 'Lord Byron', *The Spirit of the Age*, 161.
[149] Wolfson, *Borderlines*, 169.

young Juan is in line with the numerous men of feeling of the Romantic age and freely gives vent to his torrential tears, when he takes an emotional farewell of his native country ('Juan wept, as wept the captive Jews / By Babel's waters, still remembering Sion'; *DJ* II, 121–22), the narrator makes it unmistakably clear that he fails to sympathize with Juan's outrageous lack of self-containedness and that, despite the poem's prevailing liquidity, his Muse 'is not a weeping Muse' (*DJ* II, 123). Transforming the outdated weeping Muse (Melpomene) into a modern Muse – bulimic, vomiting and genitally oozing – and acting on the forced, but programmatic rhyme of 'pathetic/emetic' (*DJ* II, 167/168), Byron challenges established ideas of (porous) sentimentality and shocks his Romantic contemporaries into the revolting insight that pathos in the original sense has been supplanted by pathology, which, in its nauseating leakiness, calls for unsentimental re-evaluations both of the body and of the poem as a textual body.

Addressing his beloved, Donna Julia, in the pathetic mode of the past and perusing her farewell note on board the (porous) Trinidada in Canto II, Don Juan undergoes his first painful moment of 'de-Romanticization' when he is suddenly made to realize that the Romantic programme of high-flown sentimentality cannot be sustained in the face of the peremptory demands of the belly: '"Beloved Julia, hear me still beseeching!" / (Here he grew inarticulate with retching)' (*DJ* II, 159–60). Underlined by the incongruence of the rhyme 'beseeching/retching', the triumph of the emetic and the porous over the pathetic is complete, and the man of feeling has to be re-conceptualized in terms of a leaky vessel, hopelessly at the mercy of his digestive system, of his gullet and other excretory tubes. If the rare (male) tears shed in the poem are the last remnants of what Wolfson calls the 'agon',[150] an ordeal and 'torture' (*DJ* II, 118), the hideously digestive porousness taking possession of Don Juan is an utter defeat, a prostration and an unepic loss of heroism and humanity. Given the fact that *Hamlet* also had a profound impact on *Childe Harold's Pilgrimage*, in particular in the 'opening Yorick-like stanzas to Canto II',[151] in *Don Juan*, the reader is even invited to read Byron's new concept of man's body through Hamlet's lenses: having gone through the egalitarian food chain and followed Polonius's body through the guts of a beggar, man's body is eventually reduced to a heap of 'noble dust' which, so gloomy Hamlet, can at least be used to stop a barrel's bunghole.[152] Byron's caustic misanthropy goes even further than that when he, by contrast, seems to be arguing that man is not so much the 'noble dust' as the rotten 'beer-barrel' whose myriads of 'bung-

---

[150] Wolfson, *Borderlines*, 176.
[151] McColl, *Stirring Age*, 42.
[152] *Ham* 5.1.193f.

hole[s]', orifices and pores can no longer be filled with the concepts (or cant) of idealized Romanticism. Hallowed ideas (and misconceptions) of self-contained and disembodied Byronic heroism prevalent in *Childe Harold* have, from *Don Juan*'s Canto II onwards, ceded their reign to images of spitting anti-heroes, leaky abdomens, ubiquitous diureses and – to put it in Popean terms which Byron must have been familiar with – 'smart[ing] and agoniz[ing] at every pore'.[153]

Juan's barrel-like porousness corresponds to the ship's leakiness. With the rudder torn off and the masts broken, the Trinidada quickly becomes a ship of arrant fools whose 'leak increase[s]' (*DJ* II, 299), accelerating the sinking of the ship as it is finally sucked down by the whirling waves. Although Byron's shipwreck scene in *Don Juan* takes its cue from well-known literary representations of maritime disasters such as Shakespeare's *The Tempest* (1611) or Coleridge's *The Rime of the Ancient Mariner* (1798), his depiction of the ship's accident is new and even more radical than Théodore Géricault's flamboyantly scandalous canvas *Le Radeau de Méduse* (1819), since Byron takes pleasure in laying bare the oozing entrails of both vessels, that of the ship and the human body. Regency readers become witnesses not only of the process that transforms men into ravenous beasts, but also of intense moments of vivisection when bodies are opened, eviscerated, consumed and eventually declared as waste products, regaling, as in the case of the pastor Pedrillo, two sharks. With this macabre episode, Byron provocatively shifts the emphasis from the impervious Romantic hero to the beast, from the heroic Prometheus of the Geneva period to the 'Promethean vulture' (*DJ* II, 596) that hacks man to pieces and reduces the Calvinistic dualism of election and damnation into a modern and blasphemous division of mankind into cannibalistic vampires and fodder.

As if to take the provocation even further, Byron sets out from the audacious assumption that the anti-Genesis narrative of man's regression into cannibals originates in porousness and that the human condition is shaped by an orifice which Horace, in his Satires, had openly identified as the 'teterrima belli/causa'.[154] Relying on his readers to know that Horace was outspoken and explicitly referred to Helena's vagina ('cunnus') as the cause of the atrocious Trojan War,[155] Byron uses his Horatian lines on the Russian Empress Catherine to digress on the female

---

[153] Pope, *An Essay on Man*, 198. *Poetical Works*, 246.
[154] Byron's *Don Juan* (*DJ* IX, 433) refers to Horace's *Satire* I.3.107f.: 'Nam fuit ante Helenam cunnus teterrima belli / causa'. See also Swift's *Tale of a Tub*, where the Princesse de Condé's genitals ('[cunnus]') are at the root of Henry IV of France's belligerent aspirations. *Tale of a Tub and Other Works*, 79.
[155] Cf. also Mole who refers to Byron's penchant for involving his readers in solving riddles (and thus making them accomplices in the narrator's dirty imagination). *Byron's Romantic Celebrity*, 146.

genitals as the gravitational centre of all human existence – the place where we come from and where we return to. While, in a Lacanian interpretation of this passage, Daniela Garofalo argues that Catherine is a 'hybrid thing', and that, in her nondescriptness and emptiness, she represents 'a gaping hole through which millions exit and enter',[156] readings like this tend to disregard the fact that Byron's focus in *Don Juan* lies not so much on vacancy as on the unutterable and dangerous ooziness of the female body.

Thus, what must have disquieted readers is not only the paradox that the vagina is the 'gate of life and death' (*DJ* IX, 434), the stage of 'our exit and our entrance' (*DJ* IX, 435), but most of all it is the irksome image of the souls being dipped in its 'perennial fountain' (*DJ* IX, 437) which must have elicited the disapproval of the Romantic writers who believed in Platonism or other forms of supernatural descent. Although the idea of the female genitals as fountains proves Byron's affiliation with Shakespeare and other early modern poets, Byron boldly amplifies Shakespeare's and the Cavaliers' erotic flippancies when he imagines women's vaginas not so much as holes, chasms or decorative water features (as, next to Garofalo, Mole also claims),[157] but as quasi-baptisterial basins where souls are initiated and 'dipt' (*DJ* IX, 436) into the porousness and juiciness of life. Deploying this extremely risqué imagery, Byron anticipates Gustave Courbet's scandalous painting *L'origine du monde* (1866, later privately owned by Lacan!) by approximately four decades (Figure 5); but while Courbet displays the genital openness of his truncated model as the origin of all human life, as the focal point of birth and procreativity, Byron is more interested in stressing the ambivalence of porous bodies, their blasphemous alpha and omega quality.

Thus, the vagina (familiarly apostrophized as 'thou nondescript!') is, on the one hand, the liminal place where life and death meet; on the other, it is an oxymoronic phenomenon, 'the sea of life's dry land' (*DJ* IX, 448), denoting life-preserving irrigation and gargantuan flooding at the same time. What these lines imply is far from all hallucinations about haunting female porosity up to then, since Byron imagines life as a precarious journey through and around women's genital orifices.[158] Challenging the sentimental concept of women's porous bodies at the mercy of phallocentric and transgressive rakes, Byron adroitly shifts the gender roles in this 'comedy of sexual role reversal'[159] and depicts men's parts

---

[156] Garofalo, *Women, Love, and Commodity Culture*, 89 and 90.
[157] Mole, *Byron's Romantic Celebrity*, 91.
[158] For Byron's tongue-in-cheek premise that man is biologically inferior to woman, see Franklin, 'Byron's *Don Juan* and the Woman Question', 624.
[159] Ibid., 627.

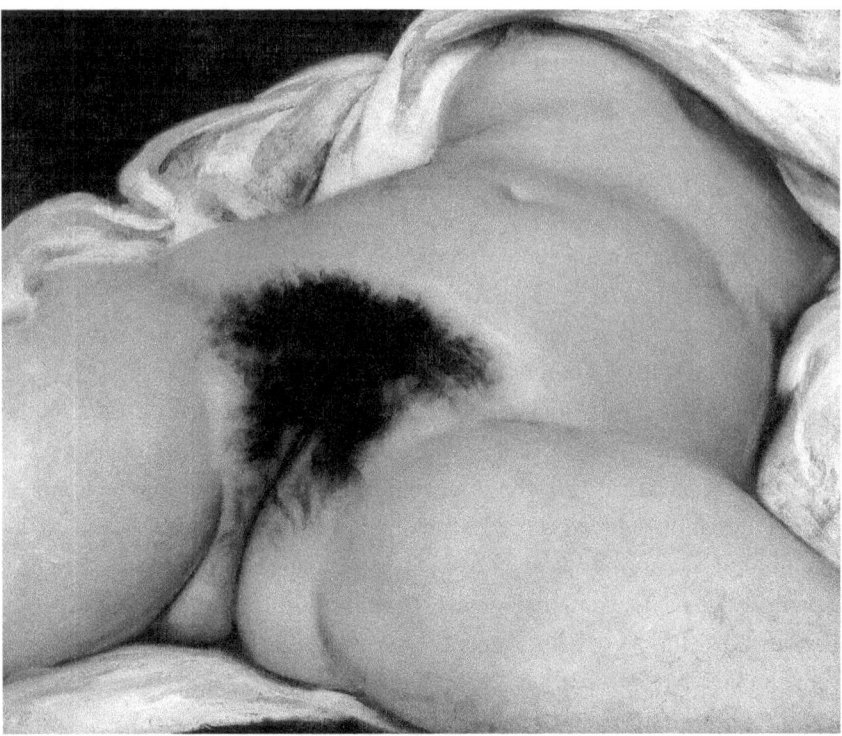

Figure 5 Gustave Courbet, *L'origine du monde* (The Origin of the World) (1866), Paris, Musée d'Orsay. Courtesy Fine Art Images/ARTOTHEK.

as those of Lilliputians in a grim 'gynocrasy' (*DJ* XII, 66), constantly in danger of being inundated and sucked in by 'succulent' (*DJ* IX, 491) giant women and their colossal genital vortices.[160] This idea is underscored by an image that, at first glance, looks like the harmless evocation of a Romantic sunset, but that, according to his habit of sexualizing stock-in-trade motifs of Romantic poetry, Byron turns into an allegory of a cosmic battle of the sexes culminating in man's post-coital nullification:

> [W]e can our native sun assuage
> In the next ocean, which may flow just then
> To make a twilight in, just as Sol's heat is
> Quenched in the lap of the salt sea or Thetis. (*DJ* IX, 549–52)

---

[160] In his conversations with Lady Blessington, Byron had voiced his disgust at 'coarse, fat ladies, à la Rubens', an indication that his genealogy of the gigantic women goes back to the Baroque. See Lansdown, 'A Marginal Interest? Byron and the Fine Arts', 279.

The most liminal of Romantic moments, twilight, is not only unduly mythologized, it is also etiologically explained as the result of a macrocosmic act of porous copulation. As in Keats's poem 'To Autumn', Byron's sun is also strongly sexualized and specifically related to each man's volatile level of testosterone ('our native sun'). Yet, in striking contrast to Keats's 'maturing sun', which, at least temporarily, was extremely penetrative and full of virility, the sexual heat of Byron's Sol seems to be scarcely resilient and is easily extinguished by the 'salt sea', by the Brobdingnagian and salty vagina ('lap') of the sea nymph Thetis.

While the imagery of the ocean in *Childe Harold* seems to be still untouched by this blunt genitalization of the aquatic, it is, before the backdrop of the verses in Canto IX, tempting and mandatory to reread the shipwreck scene in Canto II also as a nightmarish and distorted vision of man's encounter with the thalassian porousness of the female sex. In the context of this reading, the madmen's suicidal drinking of salt water suddenly takes on a new and submerged misogynist layer of meaning: in Shakespeare's *Venus and Adonis* advertised as a refreshing and 'pleasurable' stimulation for oral-genital activity,[161] genital oozings have now turned into a nightmarish flood of poison, into a liquid wrecking both body and mind. What is later, in the England Cantos, trivialized as the diminutive and cultivated '*petits puits d'amour*' (*DJ* XV, 538) in a catalogue of eroticized dishes is, in the shipwreck scene, shown as the ravenous and sucking abyss of the female genitalia, which, not least on account of the French homophonic pun of *la mer – la mère*, is more often than not compared to a wide gendered ocean.

This reading of the ocean is supported by another aquatic reference, where, at the beginning of Canto VI, Byron takes a quotation from Shakespeare's *Julius Caesar* ('There is a tide in the affairs of men / Which taken at the flood leads on to fortune')[162] and reworks it into a misogynist pun: 'There is a tide in the affairs of women / "Which taken at the flood leads" – God knows where', playing here on the double meaning of 'tide' as time and flood and reverting to the early modern (but also early nineteenth-century) connotation of 'affairs' as female genitals.[163] Translated into Regency parlance and the rakes' inner-circle badinage, the line thus reads: 'There is a flood in the genitals of women / Which taken at high water leaves man in dire need of navigation.' The conspicuous 'under-valorisation' of love in *Don Juan* which Andrew Elfenbein comments upon[164] perfectly dovetails

---

[161] Fisher, 'Cunnilingus in *Venus and Adonis*', 345.
[162] *JC* 4.3.216–17. The 'full sea' (4.3.220) that Brutus refers to fits Byron's misogynist imagery.
[163] Cf. Williams' entry on 'affairs', *Glossary of Shakespeare's Sexual Language*, 26. This codified meaning of 'affair' as female genitals seems to have been well known to the letter-writer Keats. Gittings, *John Keats*, 651.
[164] Elfenbein, 'Byron: Gender and Sexuality', 71.

into the anti-teleological structure of the poem in which the genital tides of women (and 'women' persistently rhyming with 'seamen'/semen) are one of the striking leitmotifs epitomizing man's absurd circle of life: man is launched into life through the porousness of the monstrous female body (with Catherine's 'great *whole*' [*DJ* IX, 459, my italics] becoming increasingly menacing), is perilously navigated by its unpredictable tides and eventually sucked into it again, there to have his vigour and the spark of his life '[q]uenched' for ever.

In his magisterial study *Perverse Romanticism*, which is deeply influenced by Laqueur's one-sex model, Richard C. Sha posits the intriguing hypothesis that Byron uses the Shakespearean terminology of 'affairs' and 'tide' to refer to sexual hybridity, to the fluidity of the boundaries between the penis and the vagina.[165] Since Byron evinces a certain fondness for dallying with and challenging traditional ideas of 'anatomical localization',[166] this reading of the passage is tempting, but it takes too little account of Byron's edgy misogynist satire that pervades the entire poem. Juan's conspicuous femininity, the epicenism of the poem which, at one point, threatens to transform Juan into a Juanna (a process of emasculation which he can only stop by asserting his phallic identity and stinging Dudù in her sleep) could also be understood to the effect that the gravitational forces dragging men back to the women's genital abyss are constantly at work and hampering the boy's initiation into manhood.

Passages and cantos like these substituting Byronic effeminacy for heroism, and female genital flooding for Niobean stoic dryness bear testimony to the fact that Byron's *Don Juan* was not only an erratic block of smutty poetry, but also, as Sha proves, a specimen of iconoclastic epic puberty that fitted neither into Romanticism nor into the dawning age of Victorian hero worship. Carlyle's persistent attempt to dissuade the Victorians from reading Byron and to foreground Goethe can be ascribed to the fact that Byron's poetry was not only too blasphemous and nihilistic, but also too concerned with liminality, genital porousness and man's unacknowledged lack of self-containment. The image of the epic hero as a nondescript individual adrift on the oceans of fluids produced by leaking female genitals was even too scandalous in the context of frivolous Regency society, which dramatists such as T. W. Moncrieff revealingly saw in dangerous proximity to Charles II's porous and effeminate court.[167] The image of Catherine as a dizzying maelstrom, with her head as a whirlwind and her voracious body as 'a whirlpool full of depth and danger' (*DJ* IX, 507), conjures

---

[165] Sha, *Perverse Romanticism*, 252.
[166] Ibid.
[167] See Cochran, 'The Mainstream Juans and Byron's Juan', 174–78.

up Rochesterian visions of female bodies that are no longer victimized by penetrative looks, but threaten to engulf dwarfed and feminized men in their corporeal floods.

In Byron's *Don Juan*, the porousness of the female sentimental body has assumed the quality of a deluge washing away Romantic concepts of femininity and inflating Swift's Brobdingnagians into monstrosities which reverberate not only in Swinburne's larger-than-life ladies of painful porosity, but also in Alfred Jarry's Mère Ubu or Joyce's towering Bella Cohen.[168] That these women are revenants from (pre-) Byronic times come to challenge the numerous persistently dry and self-contained angels in their ascetic houses makes the Victorian age highly controversial and tension-laden.

---

[168] For the genealogy of the monstrously gigantic female body, see also Menninghaus, *Disgust*, especially the chapter 'The "Hypergigantic" Sex of the "Colossal Woman,"' 75–78.

3

Far from the madding Romantic crowd: The anti-porous turn in the Victorian age

From body to stone: The myth of Pygmalion reloaded in Victorian fiction

The sister as Pygmalion: *Goblin Market*

Byron's large-scale epic *olla podrida* with its numerous indigestible images of porous women, cannibalistic men and bestialized bodies was quickly anathematized by the Victorians and duly replaced by a more mature Victorian Don Juan.[1] Having turned their backs not only on cynical Byronism, but also on the profligacies of the Regency court with its newly crowned king, George IV, as the prime example of decadent and obese porosity, the Victorians readily reverted to Jane Austen's legacy and subscribed to what Terry Eagleton termed as her 'culture of reticence'.[2] Surrounded as she was by all sorts of weeping men of feeling and consumptive, drug-addicted and eminently porous poets, by an impressive range of perforated, evaporating and leaking females, Austen saw herself in the vanguard of a new movement that wanted to close the female body, ridiculed all relapses into Niobean porosity and charted new 'maps of health'.[3]

Yet, even if with 'one stroke of that vaginal, virginal, pen', Austen ejects sexuality from her novels, as Susan Morgan argues, putting 'the guiding catalyst of a penis' hopelessly out of reach,[4] the austerity of Austen's novels, despite fostering the 'safe, beloved auntie myth',[5] more often than not resonates with a suppressed porosity, with a tension that in rare irrational moments seeks relief in ambivalent tears. Preceding the Victorian age by more than a generation,

---

[1] In Charles Daly's 1852 illustrated edition of *Don Juan*, Don Juan has sideburns and a moustache. See Mole, *What the Victorians Made of Romanticism*, 55–58.
[2] Eagleton, *The English Novel*, 111.
[3] See Wiltshire, *Jane Austen and the Body*, 23.
[4] Morgan, *Sisters in Time*, 39.
[5] Looser, *The Making of Jane Austen*, 5.

Austen's novels, thus, laid the foundation for a pattern which was to structure later Victorian culture in its entirety: the latent, but highly fraught conflict between women's porousness and men's heroic attempts at self-containedness, the unbridgeable gap that was thought to exist between the women's lingering Romantic affinity with water and the Victorian men's penchant for stone, ice and the sculptural. With the Victorians' normative body being 'middle-class, male, closed, and active'[6] gaining more ascendancy, writers and artists (of both sexes) express their special interest in the myth of Pygmalion (as best shown in Jean-Louis Gerôme's 1890 painting; Figure 6), albeit in a reversed form: in their

Figure 6 Jean-Louis Gerôme, *Pygmalion et Galatée* (Pygmalion and Galatea) (1890), Metropolitan Museum of Art, New York. Courtesy ARTOTHEK.

[6] Gilbert, *Victorian Skin*, 110.

self-understanding as the sculptors and shapers of the malleable female sex, Victorian Pygmalions seem to be less attracted by the moment when women are released from their petrification than by the process in which they achieve the retransformation of their porous Galateas into senseless (and innocuous) blocks of stone.

It is this rabid fear of the female body's porosity, of the body's exuding and absorbing fluids, that also informs Christina Rossetti's narrative poem *Goblin Market* (1862), a long ballad-like allegory that essentially revolves around the question of how to seal the orifices of a young woman who is on the point of becoming too porous and too much of a threat to Victorian moral hygiene. The protagonists are, as in Austen's *Sense and Sensibility* (1811), two diametrically opposed sisters: Laura, much more akin to rebellious Marianne than to the numerous angelic women in the wake of Petrarch's Madonna Laura, and Lizzie, the true descendant of Elinor, the guardian of Victorian duty, in vigilant control of what Sedgwick tropes as the 'sphincter' of her will.[7] It is the latter who takes over the (pseudo-) Pygmalion responsibility of readjusting her sibling in line with Victorian gender conventions.

Accordingly, both respond differently to the dizzying list of enticingly exotic 'gourmet fruits'[8] that the goblin men, little animalized imps in the tradition of Autolycus in *The Winter's Tale*,[9] seem to have imported from Keats's poem 'The Eve of St Agnes' (1819). The 'heap of candied apple, quince, plum, and gourd', the 'lucent syrups, tinct with cinnamon; / Manna and dates',[10] all the 'delicates' which Porphyro uses to lure his beloved Madeline away from her hostile home is enriched in Rossetti's poem by the choicest specimens of Victorian globalization. Yet, while Porphyro's arrangement of fruit is the oneiric prelude of an erotic union ('Into her dream he melted [...] / Solution sweet')[11] that releases the lovers from captivity, in *Goblin Market*, the display and consumption of fruit are tantamount to addiction and bondage. The moment Laura buys a mouthful of fruit in exchange for a 'precious golden lock' of hers (*GM*, 125), she notices not only that she is compelled to go on sucking more and more fruits, but also that

---

[7] Sedgwick, 'Jane Austen and the Masturbating Girl', 818–37.
[8] Carpenter emphasizes the fact that the fruits are 'fruits of the empire' and a clear indication of the extent to which 'capitalistic exploitation of the poor' is linked with the commodification of the female body. 'The Consumable Female Body', 427.
[9] For the intertextuality between the imps and Autolycus, see the latter's enticing that Rossetti translates into an erotic context: 'Come buy of me, come, come buy, come buy, / Buy, lads, or else your lasses cry. Come buy!' *WT* 4.4.230–31.
[10] 'The Eve of St Agnes', 264–65/267–68. *Complete Poems*, 320.
[11] Ibid., 320 and 322.

the absorption of and overindulgence in so much juice have made herself watery and leaky as well: 'I ate and ate my fill, / Yet my mouth waters still' (*GM*, 165–66).

This allegorical imagery has provoked many critical readings, all of which are vexingly speculative, with two major camps of criticism emerging: one camp tends to read the poem in terms of the dichotomy of women's fallenness and purity, the other camp asserts that both sisters are on a par and equally '"redeemed" by [the] confrontation with the goblins'.[12] More convincing, however, seems to be another reading of the poem that is intriguingly suggested by Anna Krugovoy Silver. Reading the poem in the context of Rossetti's sympathy with religious fasting, she underscores the fact that women's refusal to eat 'fits snugly alongside secular cultural ideologies about the repression of sexual desire'.[13] Positing the 'inherent rottenness of the flesh'[14] and conflating sexual desire with the idea of the deadly sin of gluttony, Rossetti uses the tantalizing list of seductive food as a code in the margins of which she warns her female readers about the self-destructive dangers of sloppy, hedonistic and non-reproductive (auto-)sexuality.

The nexus between Laura's consumption of the goblin men's fruit and the lack of control of her body is clearly underlined by the ambiguous reference to the fact that, in her listlessness, Laura no longer cares about 'her pitcher dripping all the way' (*GM*, 264). Although Christina Rossetti was – unlike her brother Dante Gabriel – the epitome of Victorian austerity and 'a devout Anglo-Catholic spinster'[15] all her life, as a poet on the critical fringes of the Pre-Raphaelite movement, she must have been conversant with the codified language of sexuality and the iconography of the broken or dripping pitcher. As a symbol of the loss of virginity and the female body's inception of sexual porosity, the broken pitcher has always had unequivocal connotations. It is Rossetti's achievement that, in her poem, she translates this eighteenth-century imagery of erotic gallantry into her strait-laced Victorian times and that, from her gloomy perspective, a Victorian girl's experience of juicy sexuality is turned into an obsessive *psychopathia sexualis*, into a pathological condition which leaves her open to recurrent attacks of madness:

> Then [she] sat up in a passionate yearning,
> And gnashed her teeth for baulked desire, and wept
> As if her heart would break. (*GM*, 267–69)

---

[12] See Carpenter, 'The Consumable Female Body', 425.
[13] Silver, *Victorian Literature and the Anorexic Body*, 137.
[14] Ibid., 145.
[15] Carpenter, 'The Consumable Female Body', 418.

Niobean grief has now become a syndrome of severe pre-Freudian hysteria. At this moment of crisis, when Laura seems to be 'knocking at Death's door' (*GM*, 322), Lizzie makes up her mind to save Laura by revisiting the goblin men and effecting a cure in which she undergoes a nightmarish process of similar temptations. In sharp contrast to her sister, who willingly yielded and opened herself to the luscious fruit that the imps proffered, Lizzie personifies the ideal of the closed and petrified female body of the Victorian age, which invites comparison not only to an unwavering 'lily in a flood' (*GM*, 410), but also to 'a rock of blue-veined stone' (*GM*, 411), uncompromisingly impervious to the raging surge around it. When she is finally likened to a 'royal virgin town / […] / Close beleagured by a fleet' (*GM*, 419/21), her predicament seems to be modelled on that of Lucrece in Shakespeare's *Rape of Lucrece* who is imagined as a stony bastion, with breasts like 'turrets',[16] all of which, however, prove ineffectual in the face of Tarquin's transgressively phallic battering ram. Beset by a horde of devilish and satyr-like men who violently (albeit less belligerently) try to break open her body, Lizzie is much more successful than Lucrece in exercising her volitional sphincter and in keeping her body inviolate and shut. Despite the fact that she is maltreated by these nightmarish representatives of crude sensuality, she never swerves from her plan to frustrate the imps and to preserve her bodily intactness:

> Lizzie uttered not a word;
> Would not open lip from lip
> Lest they should cram a mouthful in:
> But laughed in heart to feel the drip
> Of juice that syruped all her face,
> And lodged in dimples of her chin,
> And streaked her neck which quaked like curd. (*GM*, 431–37)

Although Simon Humphries stresses Rossetti's thorough knowledge of Bunyan's *Pilgrim's Progress* and tries to highlight the Eucharistic language of the poem, the overwhelming extent to which this poem is resonant with hidden sexual meaning cannot be ignored in passages like the one quoted above. Lizzie, anything but a 'queen of curds and cream' like Shakespeare's Perdita,[17] manages to keep her mouth impervious to the sticky juices which, in this context, clearly transcend the meaning of fruity syrup and denote viscous seminal fluids.

---

[16] *Luc*, 441. *Shakespeare's Poems*, 437.
[17] *WT* 4.4.161.

Refusing to 'open lip from lip' to prevent the goblin men from 'cram[ming] a mouthful in' (*GM*, 431–32), Lizzie is shown shielding her body, her upper and lower labia, from being raped, from an act of sexual violence which leaves not only stains and telling traces in her dimples, but also caked 'curd'-like fluids on her neck. Interpreted by Humphries as references to 'the two kinds of Communion, bread and wine',[18] the '[g]oblin pulp and goblin dew' (471) hardly fit into Eucharistic patterns, but must rather be understood as the ambivalent ingredients of a cocktail of spermatic juices, which, no sooner are they sucked from Lizzie's face than they turn into bitter-tasting wormwood.

This is the critical moment when the Victorian policing of (female) bodies turns fantasies of sexual openness and fluidity into bitterness and into what Carpenter even calls a 'masochistic orgy'.[19] The fact that it is wormwood, a plant that, as legend has it, 'sprang up in the track of the serpent as it writhed along the ground when driven out of Paradise'[20] (and at that time was also commonly used to wean infants from being breastfed) is revealing. Like the ominous person from Porlock in Coleridge's auto-sexual reverie in 'Kubla Khan', Lizzie brings about and accelerates a process of sexual weaning which at first looks like a deflection of Laura's heterosexual desire into same-sex and incestuous love: 'Hug me, kiss me, suck my juices / Squeezed from goblin fruits for you' (*GM*, 468–69). But the subsequent lines make it amply clear that Lizzie's erotic intervention is part of a censorious act, the prelude to an ordeal with which the grim Pygmalions of Victorian society refashioned and reclaimed adolescent girls who were on the point of succumbing to the desire to open their bodies and to listen to the luring voices of their riotous minds.[21]

Having taken its readers through a cathartic process, the poem eventually ends on a reassuring note of conformity to Victorian values and to family bonds. What is unsettling, however, is that it is also a bitter plea against the sexualization of the female body, its vexing permeability and alleged tendency to absorb juices that are likely to turn into 'poison in the blood' (*GM*, 556). Without being able to learn more about the poison, which can only be neutralized by a 'fiery antidote' (*GM*, 560), the reader is invited to read the juices in terms of stigmatizing (male or female) bodily fluids which Victorian women, in their role of angels in the house, were supposed to be closed to, to deny categorically and to

---

[18] Humphries, 'Notes', *Poems and Prose*, 439.
[19] Carpenter, 'The Consumable Female Body', 429.
[20] See the entry 'wormwood' in *Brewer's Dictionary of Phrase and Fable*, 1282.
[21] Marantz Cohen interprets the goblin men as 'internal forces' prompting anorexia. 'A Paradigm for Nineteenth-Century Anorexia Nervosa', 7.

treat as a *res tacenda*. The Victorians' panic-stricken reaction to girls' (and boys') sexual awakenings, and in particular to masturbation as a form of self-inflicted porousness, is certainly at the core of this symbol-laden poem. In his cultural history of masturbation, Thomas Laqueur fails to consider Rossetti's poem, when he expands on the Victorians' abhorrence of solitary and uncontrollable desires, to which numerous pamphlets since Samuel Auguste Tissot's 1760 French treatise *L' onanisme* had given the pathological tag of 'nymphomania'.[22] In both medical and moral theological discourses, masturbation came to be seen as a severe act of self-pollution which was supposed to disintegrate boys' brains and to make girls dangerously aware of their scandalous openness, of their aquatic nature which proved to be disconcertingly elusive of firm Pygmalion moulds.

Pygmalion and the genre of the *Bildungsroman*: *Jane Eyre* and *David Copperfield*

Read in the context of Rossetti's poem of sexual panic, Victorian literature – both its poetry and its comparatively new genre of the *Bildungsroman* – 'privileges themes of self-enclosure'[23] and is, thus, alarmingly replete with girls (and boys) who are trained to conceal their porousness and to regard their bodies as a waxy and fluid substance that desperately needs moulding, hardening and (re-)shaping. In this respect, two almost contemporaneous protagonists prior to Laura and Lizzie deserve special attention: Charlotte Brontë's Jane Eyre and Charles Dickens's David Copperfield. Self-educated and solaced by eighteenth-century novels such as *Pamela*, *Roderick Random* or *The Expedition of Humphry Clinker*, Jane and David are, from the very beginning of their stories, equally exposed to intimidating personifications of Victorian solidity: to Mr Brocklehurst's marble immobility (engraved in his face like 'a carved mask, placed above the shaft by way of capital', *JE*, 40), and to Mr Murdstone's eponymous conflation of death and stoniness, respectively.

The men's stony inhumanity is, in both novels, abetted by the unnatural petrification and hardness of women who, as spinsters or embittered widows, seem to fulfil the position of the collaborators and androgynous henchmen of their male superiors. While Miss Murdstone's hard steel purse – kept 'in a very jail of a bag which hung upon her arm by a heavy chain' (*DC*, 58) – also reveals that she is a character in the sad likeness of Marley in 'The Christmas

---

[22] Laqueur, *Solitary Sex*, 262.
[23] Gilbert, *Victorian Skin*, 178.

Carol', enchained by her belief in commercialism and victimized by sexual self-negation,[24] Mrs Reed, endowed with an 'eye of ice' (*JE*, 45) in *Jane Eyre*, is far more active, detrimental and transgressive in her basilisk-like personality. While, on the one hand, her icy gaze is intent on suppressing Jane's Romantic rebelliousness, it is, on the other, meant to freeze all emotional and sexual secretions in her ward's intractable body. The conspicuous opaqueness of Mrs Reed's skin, emphasized as a sign of her impervious robustness, irreconcilably clashes with Jane's adolescent porosity, her (verbal) proximity to water, which the Victorians were overeager not only to freeze, but also to confine to claustrophobic interiors: attics, cellars or other relentless red-rooms of correction.[25]

Given the aquatic nature of the young female bodies on the threshold of their sexual awakening, it is hardly coincidental that images of frost and congealed water are so prominent in Victorian depictions of adolescence and school life. In Lowood, pitchers and jugs are not so much broken (as in Rossetti's poem) as vessels whose contents are frozen. Assuming that Charlotte Brontë was also familiar with the iconography of pitchers, the reader is well advised to interpret the omission of the 'ceremony of washing', the icy wind 'whistling through the crevices' in the dormitory and the useless pitchers (*JE*, 63) as parts of a ruthless pedagogical strategy to seal the girls' bodies, their orifices and to nip their sexual awakening in the bud. Despite the absence of pitchers and the relative scarcity of references to ice in Salem House in Dickens's *David Copperfield*, even the boys are not exempt from both the 'hoar frost' (*DC*, 133) of the foggy morning and from anti-corporeal fundamentalism in the classroom. The graphic descriptions of the stiff, numbed hands in both novels are sympathetically juxtaposed not only with the 'burning tears' (*DC*, 134) shed by David and by Helen Burns (whose very name seems to oppose the ice of Victorian pedagogy with the ardour of religion), but also with the fallacious thaw of a spring, which instead of causing the regeneration of the children's bodies brings about the paralysing news of the death of David's mother and opens the girls' bodies to 'the effluvia of mortality' in *Jane Eyre* (*JE*, 90).

Closely modelled on Bunyan's *Pilgrim's Progress*, as most of the Victorian *Bildungsromane* are, the Lowood episode in *Jane Eyre* can be read as the progress of a young, plain girl from a regimen of ice and stone to the spurious liberation

---

[24] Especially the purse that 'shut[s] up like a bite' (*DC*, 58f.) seems to have the quality of a sterile, but canine *vagina dentata*.
[25] The fact that one of the teachers in Lowood is called Miss Temple, evocative of the forbidding sterility of ecclesiastical buildings, certainly fits into this context. See also, Gilbert and Gubar's classic study, *Madwoman in the Attic*, 341 and 345.

of her body in a vernal and mammal *locus amoenus* ('a pleasant site [...] bosomed in hill and wood' *JE*, 89), which, however, abruptly turns into a *locus horribilis* of contagion and death. Images such as 'the cradle of fog' breeding pestilence deliberately lead readers astray and open semantic fields where the idea of maternity (and its multifarious associations of lactating porousness) is conflated with miasmatic seepage. While the school episode eventually ends on a note of anarchy and openness – '[c]lasses were broken up, rules relaxed' (*JE*, 89) – Jane is still far from achieving a relaxation of her body's rigidity. Arriving at the next stage of her pilgrimage, at Thornfield Hall, she is again subjected to frozenness and admitted to a house whose 'chill and vault-like air' (*JE*, 113) seems to recapture the ecclesiastical atmosphere of many Victorian houses. The fact that Jane and Mr Rochester meet on a sheet of ice for the very first time (*JE*, 129) is thus more than consistent and emblematic of the iciness on which communication between the sexes was expected to be based in the nineteenth century. At first intimidated by Rochester's Byronic attitude and by his piercing eyes that are expressive of wrath, Jane is scarcely aware of the fact that it is Rochester's arrival that brings a certain ambiguous porousness into the sombre and quiescent house: 'a rill from the outer world was flowing through it; it had a master' (*JE*, 135). It does not take long for Jane to see that the positive meaning of her figurative language is soon translated into sober reality, that the house's new porousness is not only of a convivial kind (of which Jane in her 'hunger artistry' never partakes),[26] but also carries all sorts of implications of danger and bodily dissolution.

With Rochester's pseudo-Gothic arrival, a new porousness affects both sexes at Thornfield Hall which, irrespective of rules of decorum, makes Jane transgressively rush into Rochester's room and extinguish the flames of his burning bed. This nocturnal incident is not only another example of a Victorian woman in the conventional role of a guardian angel, but also an active and unconsciously indecorous attempt to melt the inter-sexual ice which Rochester seems to have expanded on when explaining to Jane a painting of a 'pinnacle of an iceberg piercing a polar winter sky' (*JE*, 143). The burning bed, the flames and the increasing hotness of the Rochester household[27] are thrown into sharp relief with Lowood's iciness and stony rigidity. Yet, since any indications of a period of emotional and sexual thaw have to be duly anathematized in accordance with what Robert W. Richgels identifies as a 'culture of control',[28] Jane's act of

---

[26] See here Renk, 'Jane Eyre as Hunger Artist', 7.
[27] See here Maynard, *Charlotte Brontë and Sexuality*, 93.
[28] Richgels, 'Masculinity and Tears in 19th-Century Thinking', 140.

inundating Rochester's bed (with her own water-jug!) is predictably translated into the Rossettian language of religious purification. That the imagery of fire and water exceeded the pale of religious discourse and was also expressive of an 'alarming revolution' going on was clear not only to prolific Mrs. Oliphant, but also to Gilbert and Gubar:[29] by 'delug[ing] the bed and its occupant [...], baptiz[ing] the couch afresh', she manages not only to rescue her master, but also to reacquaint him with an element that had been exclusively seen in terms of elusive and porous femininity. After his first prostration before Jane on the slippery road, Rochester now finds himself sprawled amid the fragments of a pitcher, 'fulminating strange anathemas' at the vexing fact that he is lying 'in a pool of water' (JE, 169). Apart from the typological meaning which the close juxtaposition of words bracketing the Old and the New Testament ('deluge' and 'baptise') conveys, this passage is also conceived of as a revolutionary rite of passage which melts the iceblocks keeping the Victorian genders in a deadlock position and reveals the redemptive qualities of the female fountains and their hitherto denounced leaking jugs.

Having transgressively brought about a thaw in her icy relationship with Rochester, Jane progressively yields to the aquatic nature of her quasi-Romantic life which, as the text seems to suggest, is perilously devoid of Victorian mechanisms of restraint. Seeing herself tossed about 'on a buoyant but unquiet sea' (JE, 172) she is – judged by Victorian standards – not only in a condition of indecent libertinism, but also too dangerously close to Byron's reckless idea of life as a 'nautical existence'. Even in traditionally female places, such as the secluded orchard, Jane is exposed to troubling insecurity and to various erotic temptations that beset her unbounded and unchaperoned life. Luscious fruit and 'dewy orchard trees' (JE, 243) are more evocative of the realm of the sexualized goblin men in Rossetti's later poem than of ideals of corporeal closure. That Thornfield Hall is a place that vibrates with thorny passion and leaves Jane adrift and porous on a sea of sexual anarchy is almost imperceptibly revealed by small symbolic details and signs that later on make up a semiotics of erotic turmoil and gender confusion.

Set on 'Midsummer-eve' (JE, 278), the orchard episode is charged with a transitory atmosphere of erotic solemnity (with roses 'yielding their evening sacrifice of incense', JE, 279) in which the abundance of blossoms and fruit, however, jars with subtle intertextual hints at grief, wounds and painful porousness. Repeated references to the nightingale, 'warbling in a wood half

---

[29] Gilbert and Gubar, *Mad Woman in the Attic*, 337f.

a mile off' (*JE*, 279), are meant to remind the attentive reader of the myth of Philomela, who in Ovid's *Metamorphoses* is a victim not only of rape and mutilation, but also of porousness and bloodshed. Mr Rochester's libertinism and bigamous marriage proposal are about to abruptly turn the spell of Midsummer-night levity and dalliance into a nightmare of victimization in which Jane, like the 'great moth' (*JE*, 279), circles around him waiting to have her wings seared and to be implicitly aligned with an impressive range of sexual victims such as Philomela, Danaë ('with the golden shower falling daily around me'; *JE*, 301), Daphne ('the laurel-walk'; *JE*, 285) and Ophelia. In accordance with Shakespeare's suicidal anti-heroine, Jane is left not only drenched and 'shaking the water out of [her] loosened hair' (*JE*, 287), but also, in the aftermath of the disrupted wedding, in a state of self-abandonment, in an imaginary 'dried-up bed of a great river' (*JE*, 331) waiting for the torrential floods to engulf her.

Despite the fact that this passage is closely related to the biblical book of Psalms, and here in particular to Ps 69, 1–2, where the speaker sinks 'in deep mire'[30] and struggles against the diluvian flood of his penitential tears, Jane's image of seeing herself drowning in the crashing floods is only tangential to the Bible and owes much more to Byron's idea of the *conditio humana* as a shipwreck adroitly conflated with Ophelia's death as a mermaid. In light of the fact that Steven Connor goes so far as to see 'a general defensive closing of the pores' since the end of the medieval period (a time frame that is too inclusive),[31] Sedgwick's unusual image of the volitional sphincter again proves to be useful, especially when one considers the slackness of Jane's muscles, the relaxation and effortlessness with which she passively waits for the floods (of tears and desperation) to engulf her: 'I heard a flood loosened in remote mountains, and felt the torrent come: to rise I had no will, to flee I had no strength. I lay faint; longing to be dead' (*JE*, 331).

Having gone through the first watery phase of her pilgrimage and been left in the Havisham situation of being a deserted bride, Jane is then subjected to the quasi-Pygmalion process of having her unruly and porous Ophelian body moulded and hardened. That this task is undertaken by characters that are the extreme (or extremist even) opposite of the Byronic and rakish Rochester, the religious fundamentalist St John Rivers and his sisterly paragons of (pagan and Christian) chastity, Diana and Mary, is part of the (temporary) ordeal. Finding the hard patterns of the German language in Schiller's pre-Romantic play *Die*

---

[30] Ps 69, 2. *The Bible*, OT, 676.
[31] Connor, *The Book of Skin*, 22.

Räuber (The Robbers)[32] now pitted against the mellifluous cadences of French in Rochester's amoral household, divested of her dripping clothes and put into 'a warm, dry bed' (*JE*, 378), Jane is put through the first stage of being weaned from her watery self-abandonment and Ophelian inclinations. Her first encounters with St John Rivers, whose name is a glaringly ironic misnomer for this modern St John the Baptist[33] and neurotic campaigner against everything aquatic and feminine, leave Jane in no doubt that she is expected to adapt to a new, sternly Victorian concept of life which, as the cluttering /c/-alliterations later suggest, defines men in terms of 'cold cumbrous column[s]' (*JE*, 438) and women as malleable soft creatures, in dire need of shaping. As if to belie the aquatic allusions of his name, he meets all the requirements of Victorian petrification, best shown in his face that resembles an ancient piece of sculpture:

> [I]t was like a Greek face, very pure in outline; quite a straight, classic nose; quite an Athenian mouth and chin. (*JE*, 386)

Not unlike the cold philosopher Apollonius in Keats's poem 'Lamia', whose steadfast gaze pierces and annihilates his victim, St John uses his fascinating, 'blue [and] pictorial-looking' eyes (*JE*, 386) not only to proselyte and influence Jane, but eventually to recast her life into that of a missionary's wife. To what extent mercurial, once passionate and Romantically free-flowing Jane is fashioned and reconverted into a lifeless block and object is made clear by various expressions, all of which stress the various phases and intensity of the 'freezing spell' (*JE*, 443) that St John is ruthlessly casting over her. That the 'marble kisses, or ice kisses' (*JE*, 444) which he imprints onto her face are also part of an experiment ('his was an experiment kiss'; *JE*, 444) reveals that there is more to his art of persuasion and that, as a hubristic pseudoscientist, he belongs in the category of the numerous nineteenth-century vivisectors who try to manipulate and tamper with the sinews, tubes and orifices of man and animals. Obsessed with the idea that he, in the mode of a statuesque sculptor, can transform a lively human being into an icy or marble effigy (with an 'iron shroud' around her, *JE*, 449), St John neatly fits into the impressive array of mid- to late nineteenth-century (would-be) creators – Wilde's Lord Henry, Wells's Doctor Moreau and Shaw's Professor Higgins – who, by reusing the early impetus given by Mary Shelley's *Frankenstein*, fashion women, men and animals into dolls, sculptures, paintings

---

[32] 'Crabbed but glorious Deutsch' (*JE*, 374) provides the apt sound pattern for the Rivers' (anti-)Pygmalion project, which is, however, so glaringly out of tune with Schiller's fiercely revolutionary impact of the play.

[33] Gilbert and Gubar, *Mad Woman in the Attic*, 365.

and avatars, always driven by the egotistic need to turn the 'other's' disturbing fluidity into decorative and lifeless art.[34]

While Jane is rescued from the clutches of this paralysing preacher and manipulator by means of telepathy and an inexplicable deus-ex-machina recourse to Romantic supernaturalism, other protagonists, petrified and coerced into Victorian patterns by similar fundamentalists and mock-Pygmalions, are left to fend for themselves and called upon to find new and subversive ways to allow for the porosity of their bodies. This culture of pitiless astringency and petrification put enormous pressure on the young generation, a fact which is evidenced not only by John Stuart Mill's complete breakdown, but also by imploring voices such as that of Matthew Arnold pleading for the cultural ban on weeping (and porousness) to be lifted in his gloomy poem 'Stanzas from the Grande Chartreuse' – 'Sons of the world, oh, allow our tears'[35] – or Alfred Lord Tennyson uttering the hope that the Byronic 'deep vase of chilling tears' might break[36] and release a wave of unwept tears. One of these 'deep vase[s]' of repressed emotion is the young David Copperfield who not only finds comfort in eighteenth-century picaresque characters such as Smollett's Roderick Random, but also guidelines on how to refrain from crying in desperate situations. Sorely beset with institutions and harbingers of correction which seem to specialize in painfully sealing and petrifying children's bodies, David manages to take some pressure off his inner reservoir of tears when he subversively finds opportunities where, without being spied upon, he lets himself 'occasionally [be] seized with a stormy sob' (*DC*, 74). Equipped as he is with a truly sentimental heritage, David's educational process is mainly concerned with negotiating Romantic space in the Victorian city of the dead (an image that Christina Rossetti aptly used),[37] and finding a poise between Victorian rigour and belated relapses into excessive and monstrous sentimentalism.

The novel being thus (like *Jane Eyre* and *Goblin Market*) constructed on dichotomies, David finds himself flung between the Murdstones' impenetrable and metallic imperviousness and what can be seen as a spooky relic of Gothic porosity, the liminal figure of Uriah Heep. Compared to a bat, a vulture and a baboon, Uriah Heep, the 'red-headed animal' (*DC*, 389), not only irritatingly wavers between humanity and animality, he is also characterized by a degree of

---

[34] Lennartz, 'Figurative Literalism', 521–33.
[35] Arnold, 'Stanzas from the Grande Chartreuse', 162. *Selected Poetry*, 125.
[36] *In Memoriam A.H.H.* (1850), 4, 11. *The Major Works*, 206. The image of the 'deep vase' of chilling and unwept tears clearly attests to Tennyson's reading of Byron.
[37] See 'The Dead City' and its 'stony guest[s]', 263. *Poems and Prose*, 3–11.

unmanly porousness that provokes David's (and the reader's) revulsion. When David finds him reading a book, he is fully convinced of the fact that Uriah's fingers leave 'clammy tracks along the page (or so I believed) like a snail' (*DC*, 243). Having cast some doubt on the image of Uriah as a slimy snail (and thus dealt with the reader's longing for realism), David nevertheless insists on the veracity of his observation – '[i]t was no fancy of mine about his hands' (*DC*, 244) – that Uriah's palms are excessively sweaty and that he is often seen pressing his palms against each other and 'wiping them, in a stealthy way, on his pocket-handkerchief' (*DC*, 244).

It is the stealthiness with which he wipes his hands that makes the reader acutely aware of the perversity of Uriah Heep's porosity.[38] More often than not related to a slimy fish (*DC*, 246), Uriah seems to be a belated and gender-crossing descendant and mutation of the Romantic sirens and mermaids, but also an ominously incontinent relative of slime- and oil-secreting characters such as Mr Chadband or Krook in *Bleak House*. At first unaccountably attracted by Uriah Heep as his monstrous doppelgänger and immediately alerted to his bestial orifices such as his nostrils, which 'had a singular and most uncomfortable way of expanding and contracting themselves' (*DC*, 243), David is painfully made to see that Uriah Heep's porosity is of a dangerous and kinky nature and that his cavernous bodily openings pose a threat that must be neutralized and exorcized out of his life. In what can be seen as one of the climactic episodes of the story, as a Gothic Walpurgis Night, David takes Uriah Heep into his lodgings and even goes so far as to offer him his bed. In moments of hallucination and delirium, which make him perceive Uriah Heep in distorted and gigantic dimensions ('He seemed to swell and grow before my eyes', *DC*, 389), David is repeatedly haunted by the idea of stabbing his guest with the red-hot poker, of penetrating him and 'running him through with it'. What at first glance looks like a violent fantasy of 'a homosexual rape',[39] as a severe physical reaction to Heep's treacherous way of seeping into him, turns out to be one of David's strategies to keep his mental health and to make his inflated and oozing opponent burst like a balloon. With Uriah Heep becoming too oppressive and his presence turning into an unbearably puffed-up Fuselian nightmare, the narrator finally chooses the most incisive, but also hygienic instrument which he has at hand and which characters in the wake

---

[38] David's revulsion at Uriah's sweaty hand is nowadays even related to David's exteriorization of his homosexual and masturbatory desires. Cf. Rees, *The Romance of Innocent Sexuality*, 245.

[39] Cohen, 'Interiors', 17. For the wider context and aspects of queer Dickens, see Furneaux, *Queer Dickens*, 10.

of the sentimental novel, Lizzie, Laura or Jane Eyre, were so glaringly lacking: the exorcizing, deflating and trenchant power of humour and caricature.

Seeing the impish and goblin-like Uriah Heep spread-eagled on the floor, 'gurglings taking place in his throat' (*DC*, 391), David fixes his attention on his guest's most prominent porous feature: the open mouth, which he, with an auto-diegetic narrator's retrospective flourish of cathartic humour, compares to an open 'post-office' (*DC*, 391) and thus, on account of the inappropriate simile, makes it innocuous and ridiculous. Neutralizing Uriah Heep's Gothic and grotesque porosity (with the open mouth and the cavernous nostrils as vaguely Bakhtinian reminders of the carnivalesque) by a sudden relapse into eighteenth-century caricature, David learns to free and distance himself from the Gothic onsets of porous liminality. To read the hilariously improper image of the oscular post office in terms of one of the many keyholes in the novel, as a perilously 'pervious membrane between himself [= Heep] and Copperfield', as William Cohen does,[40] is, however, a problematic way of disregarding Dickens's cleansing humour.

Left with a clean slate of his life, disentangled from all Romantic (Dora) and Gothic (Heep) affiliations that might have hampered his development as a budding Victorian writer, David is eventually lost in dejection, suffering from a 'wound' which his 'undisciplined heart' (*DC*, 819) is unable to heal. Although comparatively late in the plot, Dickens also resorts to the motif of crisis and collapse to convey the idea of the strain that constant disciplining of the heart and the exercising of the volitional sphincter put on the Victorians. Seeing the pattern and grid of his life reduced to 'a ruined blank and waste, lying wide around me, unbroken, to the dark horizon' (*DC*, 819), David decides to go abroad, briefly impersonating Byron's Childe Harold when he, in his dissatisfaction, '[roams] from place to place, carrying my burden with me everywhere' (*DC*, 820). What David's melancholy pilgrimage through Italy and Switzerland, his Victorian version of the Romantics' Grand Tour, teaches him in spite of its absurd purposelessness is the bitter lesson that his Victorian policing of his wife's porous Romantic body, that his victory over goblin ooziness, does not eventually lead to lasting satisfaction.

In his seminal biography of Dickens, Michael Slater finds it 'noteworthy' that after Wordsworth's death in April 1850 Dickens bought a copy of *The Prelude*.[41] And since, according to John Worthen, Wordsworth's poetry has the function

---

[40] Cohen, 'Interiors', 17.
[41] Slater, *Charles Dickens*, 316.

of being 'pontific',⁴² we can see here *The Prelude* bridging the wide gap that presumably existed between the Romantic and the Victorian age. In a passage that, on a more modest scale, rewrites Book VI of Wordsworth's *Prelude*, David not only imbibes the sublime beauty of the Swiss Alpine scenery, he is now, due to his grief, also able to benefit from and to understand the language of its nature. In a valley which epitomizes the Romantic cult of sublimity, he sees 'forests of dark fir, cleaving the wintry snow-drift, wedge-like, and stemming the avalanche' (*DC*, 821), an interesting objective correlative of his emotional situation, since it illustrates the critical moment before the precarious balance between retention and yielding tilts in the latter's favour. It is here that the wedges and bars recede and that Tennyson's 'deep vase' of collected tears breaks. That it is in a Romantic setting outside Britain that David, like Arnold's speaker at the French Grande Chartreuse, releases his emotional avalanche is no coincidence and clear criticism of the Victorians' stern politics of body surveillance:

> All at once, in this serenity, great Nature spoke to me; and soothed me to lay down my weary head upon the grass, and weep as I had not wept yet, since Dora died! (*DC*, 821)

It is a sentimental valve that Dickens (both here and elsewhere) uses to deflate Victorian concepts of rigid and stony masculinity. Yet, by mitigating the awe-inspiring effects of Romanticism and intermingling the sublime elements of the 'craggy steeps, grey rock, bright ice' (*DC*, 821) with pastoral components, 'shepherd voices' (*DC*, 821), Dickens seems eager to tone down the emphatic Romantic voice of the story and to reconcile it with Victorian, albeit kitschy, demands. It is consistent with Dickens's efforts at pegging down the high-strung Romantic key that, at the very moment when David succumbs to his torrential flood of tears, he is reclaimed from his Romantic vagaries by being reminded of a parcel of Agnes's letters (which, as a lucky charm, was in his hands all the time). It is intriguing to notice that, with Agnes's epistolary appearance, the language veers from the diction of Romantic self-centredness and melancholy to the Victorian discourse of physiological and mental salubriousness. 'Strength', 'purpose' and 'robust exercise' (*DC*, 823) are now the very catchwords of David's new existence after his porous Romantic spell abroad. Renouncing his chequered past, David puts his confidence solely in Agnes, the *agnus Dei* that 'point[s] to that sky above me, where, in the mystery to come, I might yet love her with a love unknown on earth' (*DC*, 849), and thus finally reenters the Victorian realm

---

⁴² Worthen, *Wordsworth: A Critical Biography*, 450. For Wordsworth's 'pervasive presence' with the Victorians, see also Kaplan, *Sacred Tears*, 41.

of bodiless love, where marriage is a nondescript 'mystery', devoid of sensuality, bodily fluids and goblin-like temptation.

While, by the end of *David Copperfield* and *Jane Eyre*, both protagonists are shepherded into the safe haven of marriage (with David particularly enjoying its 'rock'-like quality, *DC*, 869), there are several marriages, families and couples in Victorian works where the rockiness, the stony imperviousness, is precisely the problem that oppresses and destroys them.[43] While the Dombeys in Dickens's *Dombey and Son* (1848) are about to undergo a metamorphosis into stony blocks, there is a variety of icy matrimonial automata or effigies such as the Dedlocks in *Bleak House* (1853), those 'magnificent refrigerator[s]' (*BH*, 623) or George Meredith's stony couple in *Modern Love* (1862) that turn marriage into icy non-communication and themselves into a grim petrified parody of Pygmalion and Galatea.

Marital mausoleums, sepulchral beds and tragic masks in damp times

The Gorgon in the Victorian marriage bed

In his book on *The Social Life of Fluids*, Jules Law seems to undertake the paradoxical task of proving that the Victorian age is – despite its various images of dryness, petrification and iciness – threatened and destabilized by an overabundance of fluids, juices and oozings. Without taking into consideration the fact that the Victorian age became a byword for stoniness and retention, he even goes so far as to maintain that '[f]luids are the principal symbolic and material vehicles of sociality in Dickens's novels' and that novels such as *Dombey and Son* (1848) are 'virtually under siege by forces of dampness'.[44] A close look at Dickens's novels seems to prove Law right and shows that, next to images of stoniness and iciness, there is an all-pervading humidity and wateriness that, by insidiously seeping into all conceivable nooks, provide striking evidence for Law's argument. What these images of seepage, however, emphatically show and what eludes Law's criticism is that the Victorians' obsession with a wide range of fluids is indissolubly linked with their obsessive concern with creating counter-worlds of stony longevity, of withdrawing into impervious, dry and dehydrated recesses

---

[43] Cf. Hager, *Dickens and the Rise of Divorce*, 131ff. In this context, Armstrong aptly uses the term 'claustrophobic households'. 'When Gender Meets Sexuality', 177.
[44] Law, *The Social Life of Fluids*, 30 and 32.

of jealously guarded privacy. It is in these rooms, sanctuaries of domesticity and marital mausoleums that the Victorians felt safe (albeit unhappy) and protected from fluids, fogs and miasma that seemed to penetrate into all chinks, crevices and pores.

The perilous porousness of Victorian life is symbolized by public buildings that are paradigmatically shown in a state of incredible permeability: in the introductory chapter to *Bleak House* (1853), the court of Chancery is so densely filled with fog (and the nebulousness of ignorance) that everybody's perception and health are severely impaired. This public porosity is then transferred onto the private houses which are threatened by seepage, dampness and mould exempting nobody, not even the most notable of families, the Dedlocks, whose manor house is alarmingly surrounded and permeated by wetness. The air is dangerously 'moist', and, as a good example of Dickens's blurring the lines between humans and objects, the small church in the park proves to be not only 'mouldy', but also at its most porous when, as a sign of its worm-eaten ricketiness, the pulpit 'breaks out into a cold sweat' (*BH*, 56). With objects becoming grotesquely human in their sweatiness and porosity, human beings are conversely metamorphosed into parasitical vegetative or crustacean forms, either into 'extraordinary specimens of human fungus' (*BH*, 426) that, in their nightmarish deformity, grow and sprout out of the slum's porous stones, or into oysters which thrive on the dampness, but use all their muscles to keep their shell-like bodies tightly shut. Lady Dedlock's special inclination for the sartorial and the icy, her habit of falling 'not into the melting, but rather into the freezing mood' (*BH*, 57), neatly fits into this reiterative Victorian pattern: the more the Victorians saw their life threatened by ecological, social or even sexual seepage and ooziness (aptly symbolized by Rossetti's goblin men or Dickensian monsters such as Fagin in *Oliver Twist* or Uriah Heep), the more they felt constrained to transform their domestic spheres into sealed tombs, to turn their bodies into stony, frozen or oysterous artefacts concealed behind rigid masks.[45]

In their panic-stricken efforts to keep their asphyxiatingly sepulchral homes as dry and anti-porous as possible, they hired wet nurses to buy their freedom from breastfeeding, from an offensive ooziness which Victorian women detested and saw as an embarrassing flaw in the image of the immaculate angel in the house. That in their attempt to keep their domestic spheres sanitized and vacuum-sealed, well-to-do Victorian women were prepared to have their revulsion at lactation

---

[45] For the use of masks in Dickens's novels, see Hollington, 'Dickens and the Commedia dell'arte', 46–52.

dearly compensated for by what class-conscious critics saw as the infiltration of the upper classes' offspring by the vulgar, adulterated and 'transindividual' fluid of working-class milk[46] is certainly a good example of an irony in an otherwise so irony-free age. The rumours that were spread about the wet nurses (denigratingly labelled as 'common fountain[s]' in contrast to Victorian women as dried or frozen fountains)[47] were echoed in *Bleak House* by (muffled) cries that bewailed not only the loss of the old 'landmarks of the cohesion by which things are held together' (*BH*, 628), but also the perfunctoriness in the policing of the Victorians' individual bodies.

Lady Dedlock's tragedy is that of the failure of the marital tomb, of bodily fluids being able to transgress social boundaries and to engender a bastard (Esther Summerson, one of the focalizers of the story) between socially incompatible classes: between that of Captain Hawdon, the drug-addicted suicide victim 'Nemo', and Sir Leicester's wife. Although Dickens's narrators are not unsympathetic towards Lady Dedlock's misery and her claustrophobic life in the Lincolnshire mausoleum, they do not fail to insist on the desperate efforts that Victorians were forced to take to keep the membranes of their bodies impervious both to the infiltrations of public fluids (sewerage, pollution) and to the sentimental cross-class contaminations caused by illicit sex. For the Victorians, it did not suffice to make their households waterproof (or to be more precise: tear- and milkproof), even the potential nucleus of porousness in the house, the marriage bed, had to be converted into a cold sculptural environment, aseptically devoid of passion and lust, hygienically drained of all bodily fluids and frantically scrubbed. Thorough readings of Victorian novels and poems, however, make it amply clear that it is the novelists' or the poets' subversive task to reveal the flaws in these monumental constructions, to show that the (fallacious) control of the porous body was obtained at the exorbitant cost of self-entombment and death in life.

From this perspective, it is intriguing to reread George Meredith's 1862 collection of poems, *Modern Love*, where, as a Victorian (and autobiographical) riposte to Donne's conceit of the ecstatic lovers as 'sepulchral statues',[48] Meredith creates the image of a married couple as stony unecstatic effigies supine on their marriage sepulchre: 'Like sculptured effigies they might be seen / Upon their

---

[46] Ibid., 5. For the idea of 'cross-class contamination', see also Klimaszewski, 'Examining the Wet Nurse', 328.
[47] *Dombey and Son*, 89. For the image of the frozen, tearless fountain, see Rossetti, 'A Better Resurrection', 13: 'My life is like a frozen thing'.
[48] Donne, 'The Extasie', 18. *Poetical Works*, 46.

marriage-tomb, the sword between.'[49] Given the fact that marriage beds of the past and present were imagined as being focal points of sexual activity and, by definition, as reservoirs of sexual fantasy and fluidity, 'seas / where we would dive for pearls',[50] it is one of the striking features of the Victorian age that marriage beds were easily transformed into vaults or at least into places of austere self-containment. As so often in this survey of porosity, the counter-narrative of anti-porous frustration is supplied by the Romantics: Blake coins the term 'marriage-hearse' in his 1794 poem 'London' and, in *Epipsychidion* (1821), Percy Bysshe Shelley allegorizes his sexual dissatisfaction into the image of a 'chaste cold bed' that leaves him 'nor alive nor dead'.[51] Following in the Romantic key, Meredith (and other Victorians more or less sotto voce) defines the marriage bed as a zone of sterility and petrifying non-activity. With a rigorous ban on all bodily liquids, even tears seem to be ruthlessly checked in the Victorian beds, so that, in the face of separation and jealousy, even the lowest sobs are stifled and 'strangled mute, like little gaping snakes, / Dreadfully venomous' to the speaker.[52]

It is before this cultural backdrop that texts ranging from Mr Dombey's second stony marriage to Angel Clare's somnambulant interment of his new wife Tess into an ancient sepulchre in Hardy's *Tess of the d'Urbervilles* (1891) must be read. As the epitome of emotional frostiness, who, on the occasion of his son's christening, sheds such an influence of coldness on the people present that the party seems to be 'gradually resolving itself into a congealed and gelid state' (*DS*, 66), the widower Paul Dombey senior is shown clumsily falling in love. The chosen woman is Edith Granger, an unprecedented woman in Dickens's universe, who, in her unwonted self-reliance, defies the image of the woman as an angelic nonentity and clearly paves the way for the advent of the various new and impervious women in the wake of Ibsen's Nora. Contrasting grotesquely with her mother, a decrepit old woman in a wheelchair, who coquettishly imitates and is ludicrously fawned upon as a modern Cleopatra (who is, every night, deconstructed by her maid in an outrageously Swiftian manner), Edith is not only uncommonly on a par with her future petrified husband; she is also the closest that Dickens ever got to portraying a Byronic heroine.[53]

---

[49] *Modern Love* I, 14–15. *Selected Poems*, 30.
[50] That is the way Duffy imagines Shakespeare's second-best bed in her dramatic monologue 'Anne Hathaway', 2f. *Collected Poems*, 256.
[51] *Songs of Experience* VIII, 'London', 16. *Complete Poems*, 214 and *Epipsychidion*, 299–300. *Poetical Works*, 418. For Shelley's strategy of refining porous corporeality into 'deliberate artistry', see Callaghan, *Shelley's Living Artistry*, 214.
[52] *Modern Love* I, 5–6.
[53] See Lennartz, 'Dickens as a Modern Romantic', 105–25.

Switching off her emotional, Niobean side Edith surpasses characters such as Jane Eyre or Lady Dedlock and gets to a stage of stoniness and frostiness that was thought to be exclusively reserved for men. Assuming the role of a Victorian Gorgon she reacts devastatingly to her icy wedding and honeymoon and turns everything into stone. In this respect, Edith is strikingly unlike Meredith's Madam, who, as the hostess of a dinner, keeps up pretences under '[w]arm-lighted looks, Love's ephemerioe' and manages to conceal the deceptive 'Love's corpse-light'.[54] The Gorgon Edith, by contrast, makes no effort to play the social hypocrite and communicates her erotic frigidity via the dinner table and its food, both of which metonymically reflect what is (not) happening in the sensual realms of her funereal marriage-bed. The extent to which the 'installation dinner' (*DS*, 530) becomes the perversion of what used to be the tradition of juicy agape and symbolizes the disharmony and rigor mortis of the cold bodies of the newlyweds is revealed by the fact that nobody takes notice of the array of delicacies on the sideboard and sweeps past them as if they were 'heaped-up dirt' (*DS*, 530). The absence of a detailed description of the food with its indisputably erotic overtones which it had in Byron's 'England' Cantos in *Don Juan* or in Rossetti's *Goblin Market* is expressive and conveys a meaningful impression of the mausoleum-like atmosphere of the Dombey household. While Mr Dombey does not object to this ambience of anti-corporeality – 'being a good deal in the statue way himself' (*DS*, 530) – he even seems to be pleased that his wife is motionless and preserves a cold hauteur that ostensibly matches his Victorian concept of stony and sterile matrimony.

While the Dombeys' first matrimonial repast seems to be the inauguration of a ritual that passes without 'any warmth or hilarity' (*DS*, 530), Edith prefers to sit there 'like a statue, at the feast' (*DS*, 530) – a simple fact whose ominous reverberations neither her husband nor most of Dickens's readers seem to be aware of. Referring to the 'marble statue of Don Guzman' in *Don Giovanni* as early as in his 1842 *American Notes*,[55] Dickens, probably remembering burlesque adaptations of the opera such as Thomas Dibdin's *Don Giovanni, or the Spectre on Horseback* (first staged in 1817), was more than familiar with the motif of the stony guest at the banquet. What seems to be an ironic twist of the Don Juan theme is that Dickens has a woman retaliate against an elderly Victorian gentleman, who, to cap it all, is utterly devoid of donjuanesque ambitions.[56] Not realizing to what extent his wife conflates the Gorgon with the stony Commendatore in her

---

[54] *Modern Love* XVII, 12 and 16.
[55] *American Notes*, 99.
[56] See also, Lennartz, 'Dickens as a Modern Romantic', 114f.

vindictive personality, Mr Dombey is oblivious to the fact that his downward spiral into the hell of a mismatch (and attendant bankruptcy) has just started. In her 'unfeminine recalcitrance'[57] and resemblance to 'a marble image' (*DS*, 535), Edith is not only the contrastive foil to the vegetative and leaking Florence, she is also the cool, Byronic scourge of the Victorian patresfamilias who, in compliance with Evangelical expectations, used to freeze their wives and lovers into marble icons. That the barren iconicity of her body is the result of painstaking effort and still remote from the immaculate facade of the later dandies is, however, underlined by the hint that, at critical moments, she has to work hard to repress her tears and to show her 'composed face' for what it really is: a construction, like her mother's borrowed identity from a Shakespearean heroine, 'a handsome mask' (*DS*, 536).

The mad and porous woman in the tomb

The ubiquity of masks in Victorian fiction is still a neglected field of Victorian studies. In the context of the Victorian household as a mausoleum and the marriage bed as a tomb, it is also important to see the many references to masks in terms of a rekindled interest in death masks. The death mask, in its double function of sealing and immortalizing a dry and juiceless face, is the epitome of anti-porousness and petrification. With the rigorous emphasis that Victorians placed on sculptural dignity and self-monumentalization, the (death) masks in Victorian literature are instruments to freeze facial expressions and to block all channels of detested porousness: tears, perspiration, mucus and saliva. What the proto-Ensorian evocation of masks in works by writers as different as Dickens, Hardy or Wilde, however, shows is that the loss or the reckless removing of the masks is always dangerous and almost tantamount to self-annihilation. Thus, on the analogy of Tennyson's Lady of Shalott, who by destroying the cocoon of her woven tapestry also eliminates her own shadowy existence, there are a considerable number of women who, by rebelling against their disembodiment and their premature entombment in the Victorian house, dare to tear off their masks and consequently face the threat of their social (and existential) nullification.

It is owing to Edith's uniqueness in Dickens's work that her end is (or has the potential of being) different from that of the Lady of Shalott and the various broken-backed or coffined women listed in Dijkstra's seminal study *Idols of*

---

[57] Surridge, *Bleak Houses*, 71.

Perversity.⁵⁸ Sitting in a profusion of jewels and finery, 'feathers, jewels, laces, silks and satins' (*DS*, 596), which are all meant to endorse her transformation into an inanimate piece of decoration, Edith is about to break the fetters that enchain her to the tomb-like Dombey house: 'The very diamonds – a marriage gift – that rose and fell impatiently upon her bosom, seemed to pant to break the chain that clasped them round her neck, and roll down on the floor where she might tread upon them' (*DS*, 596). Her panting bosom becomes the icon of her feminine rebellion and of her imminent resurrection as a proud, vital, but also eminently Nemesian woman. In an unparalleled episode of female resistance in Victorian fiction, she repays her husband's attempts to artificialize her into a nonentity, harangues him and then treats him like an 'odious object', a squashed insect, 'forgotten among the ignominious and dead vermin of the ground' (*DS*, 602). Almost a generation prior to August Strindberg's harrowing plays of gender warfare,⁵⁹ Dickens shows matrimony as a ruthless battle for positions raging behind the mausolean walls of Victorian houses. Insisting on unstinted obedience and surrender in the old Victorian style, Mr Dombey eventually meets with a Jovian flash of lightning which seems to radiate from his wife's 'haughty brow' (*DS*, 601) and which lays bare what is behind Dombey's pompous self-fashioning, behind the stony and frosty composition of his death-mask: Victorian man's ossified regulations, stale verbosity and the inveterate dislike of anything juicy and vegetative (such as Dombey's daughter Florence).

The beginning of chapter 47 neatly encapsulates the deadlock situation of their barren marriage when, 'in their flinty opposition, [they] struck out fire [...] burned up everything within their mutual reach, and made their marriage way a road of ashes' (*DS*, 683). The 'road of ashes' underlines Edith's affiliation with Byron's Niobe covered in dust; and the concessions that Dickens makes to an audience 'spoiled by floods of kitschy melodramatic works'⁶⁰ when he has Edith's eyes temporarily suffused with tears cannot deceive the reader into believing that Edith might revoke her shrew-like position and melt in repentance. When Dickens leaves her self-immured in a dark grave-like room (*DS*, 919) and thus like a blot on the text's unachieved closure,⁶¹ he seems to be doing what Charlotte Brontë's Mr Rochester was simultaneously doing to the mad Creole in the attic, Bertha Mason: entombing the species of the rebellious 'new' women who had grown tired of their angel-like masks and, by emphatically rejecting their roles

---

⁵⁸ Dijkstra, *Idols of Perversity*, 50–63 and 97–109.
⁵⁹ For Dickens's influence on Strindberg, see Lindblad, 'Dickens in Sweden', 430–45.
⁶⁰ Lennartz, 'Dickens as Modernist Romantic', 121.
⁶¹ Surridge, *Bleak Houses*, 65.

as the self-sacrificing oozy Ophelia, revealed shocking evidence of masculine stoniness or vampiric ferocity.

Reading Dickens's and Brontë's novels through the lens of anti-porous femininity might also shed new light on Angel Clare's unconscious act of entombing his wife Tess in Hardy's later novel. Having moulded her into the pagan goddesses that neatly fit into the mise en scène of his pastoral world – 'He called her Artemis, Demeter, and other fanciful names half teasingly' (*T*, 130) – Angel is shattered when, on their wedding night, he watches her divesting herself of the mythological trappings and masks and, in the wake of her confession, assuming the real shape of a fallen and sexually porous woman. Although the narrator mentions Tess's mask-like countenance which, even at crucial moments, keeps her from emotional outbursts, she is guilty of a sexual leakiness which never tallies with Angel's high-flown concepts of feminine deification. No longer able to reconcile the former misconstrued Tess – '[a]nother woman in your shape' (*T*, 229) – with what he sees as her fallen and tainted doppelgänger, Angel sets about turning her into an insipid object and burying her in the remains of a sarcophagus in a ruined abbey church. The fact that he undertakes the entombment of his wife in the liminal state of somnambulism is tragically revealing: unable to get rid of the 'vein of metal in [the] soft loam' of his constitution (*T*, 241), even in his sleep, Angel refuses to accept Tess in her outrageously sexual (and moral) porousness. Murmuring words of endearment, which before, in moments of rational lucidity, failed to pass his lips, Angel is urged by the hard, metallic substratum of his Victorian personality to turn the honeymoon into an eerily Gothic event[62] and to seal up Tess's scandalously open and seeping body in the stony confines of a tomb, an 'empty stone coffin of an abbot, without a lid' (*T*, 249).

That the sarcophagus lacks a proper lid and thus a proper device to keep Tess's body successfully repressed is only an ironic twist to the multifarious disconcerting stories of Victorian men's abortive attempts to keep the female bodies subjected to the fundamentalist regimes of their sepulchral homes. Only six years after the publication of Hardy's controversial novel, women more effectively rebelled against their entombment and emerged from their marital sarcophaguses in the gruesome shape of eroticized vampires in Bram Stoker's *Dracula* (1897), whereas other inveterate Victorians enlisted the help of Mrs Grundy and brought the proverbial 'stiff upper lip' to perfection, turning the permissive Yellow Nineties into the heyday of stoicism and self-monitoring dandyism.

---

[62] Cf. Michie, *Victorian Honeymoons*, 184.

The advent of the stony stoic

A stoic in distress: *Tess of the d'Urbervilles*

Immured in crinolines, in 'ballooning garments' and cages of steel,[63] Victorian women's porousness was deemed manageable as long as they were able to regulate their emotional and physical pressure in cathartic bouts of weeping and swooning. Any comparable forms of pressure equalization were rigorously denied to men. While some women ventured to throw off their corsets and crinolines and recklessly ran the risk of being labelled as liminal, 'negotiating a thin line between comfort and mannishness',[64] men rejecting the constraints of male dress and pleading for male porosity were immediately relegated to the margins of patriarchal society, there to live in a state of freakish seclusion,[65] in a similar state of ostracism to Frankenstein's monster that without inhibition gives vent to its tears.[66]

Among the most despotic controllers of the people's volitional sphincters was the fictitious, invisible, but alarmingly omnipresent Mrs Grundy. Originally taken from Thomas Morton's forgotten Romantic play *Speed the Plough* (1798) and elevated to the position of a dictatorial 'Victorian deity',[67] Mrs Grundy (in a fateful alliance with bluff John Bull) came to incorporate the Victorians' obsessive fear of sensuality and, by the end of the century, assumed the haunting figure of a Big Sister that was always watching the people and admonishing them to keep their genital porousness in check. How strict Mrs Grundy's regime was can be gauged by the fact that, in Dickens's novels, men desperately seek refuges to indulge in a few furtive tears. As if acting upon Mark Antony's advice in Shakespeare's *Julius Caesar*, 'get thee apart and weep',[68] Mr Dombey, Mr Jarndyce, but also harsh Mr Scrooge, give free rein to their bouts of porosity in the closet (the latter even in the double seclusion of his curtained four-poster bed), because in public life they all felt obliged to obey Mrs Grundy's imperatives and, like Lady Dedlock, meekly

---

[63] Munich, *Queen Victoria's Secrets*, 64.
[64] Ibid., 62
[65] For this species of 'new men', the way they were ridiculed and marginalized, see MacDonald, *The New Man, Masculinity and Marriage*, 2.
[66] See the monster's narrative, chapter XI: 'feeling pain invade me on all sides, I sat down and wept'. *Frankenstein*, 103.
[67] Houghton, *The Victorian Frame of Mind*, 397.
[68] JC 3.1.282–85. For the Victorians' reading of Shakespeare see Poole, *Shakespeare and the Victorians*, 116–53.

go through 'that destructive school which shuts up the natural feelings of the heart, like flies in amber' (*BH*, 812).[69]

Inspired by or improving on Byron's image of a dry and decaying Niobe devoid of tears and bodily fluids, Victorian novelists, in particular towards the end of the nineteenth century, rediscovered the figure of the stoic of both genders who, in the face of destruction or bodily infiltration, not only suppressed their tears, but also decided to endure all torments without any sign of Niobean grief or pain. With Byron's recalcitrant rebels (Prometheus, Manfred, Haidée and the bride of Abydos, in the guise of 'a younger Niobe'[70]), but also Shakespeare's stoics as their matrixes, it is novelists of Thomas Hardy's generation in particular who go further than Dickens and show characters bereft of any retreat and fully exposed to circumstances that Hardy allusively calls 'the ache of modernism' (*T*, 124), but which should more aptly be labelled as Mrs Grundy's grim retaliation.

Introduced into the story as 'a mere vessel of emotion' (*T*, 15), which, in a moment of coarsely anti-Romantic Darwinism, is forcefully opened and then later turned into a 'marble term' (*T*, 78) of disgrace, right from the start, Tess, the eponymous heroine of *Tess of the d'Urbervilles* (1891), is shown as being endowed with a body that tragically lacks the necessary safeguards to keep it stoically self-contained; prone to an almost narcoleptic tendency to fall asleep at crucial moments, she is doomed to fail to protect her fragile (and anachronistically noble) body from the corrosive and tainting juices of Alec d'Urberville's transgressive vulgarity. In a world that is progressively dominated by ruthless careerists and by Machiavellian egotism that Dickens still saw limited to shark-like Mr Carker and his ilk, Tess's fate is inevitable. No longer sufficiently armed against the liquids of the vulgar, the uncouth and the Darwinistically fittest, her enfeebled aristocratic body is, according to Hardy's concepts of degeneration,[71] made dangerously porous, receptive and impregnable. Due to a string of accidents (triggered by her father's consumption of alcohol), Tess is drenched with the blood of her impaled horse Prince ('splashed from face to skirt with the crimson drops', *T*, 33) in a highly symbolic scene of fatalistic baptism: as in a negative process of bloody initiation (conflating the 'horror of menstrual trauma' and fatalistic stigmatization),[72] Tess's virginal body is now for the first time subjected to corrosion, which eventually culminates in Alec's

---

[69] In this context, Stedman writes about the 'pronounced tendency to "fix" the feelings by defining and classifying them'. *Stemming the Torrent*, 27f.
[70] *The Bride of Abydos*, 496. *CPW*, 3, 139.
[71] For Hardy's reading of Herbert Spencer, see Millgate, *Thomas Hardy*, 229.
[72] Mulvey-Roberts, 'Menstrual Misogyny and Taboo', 155.

treacherous attempt to penetrate the delicate 'vessel' with his sleeping potion and subsequently with his defiling semen.

Tess's first encounter with Alec on the precincts of the parvenu's garden is emblematic: 'the touches of barbarism' (*T*, 40) about Alec's face show that, in Hardy's universe, ancient fatalism has now assumed the shape of modern Darwinism, leaving Tess at a disadvantage before Mrs Grundy's gender-biased tribunal. Inducing her to open her mouth in a 'symbolic rape through food',[73] he has her submissively eat the juicy strawberries which he, now in the guise of a dandified goblin man, offers and compels her to eat. In his annotations to the Penguin edition of the text, Tim Dolin highlights the striking similarities between this passage and Rossetti's *Goblin Market* and shows Tess in the role of Laura.[74] Yet, while the pollution of Laura's body is self-inflicted, the result of her sexual curiosity, and rocky Lizzie comes to her sister's rescue with the aid of her insuperable Victorian discipline, Tess, as the daughter of stupefied and alcohol-soaked parents, is fatalistically (and genetically) deprived of all harnesses and mechanisms to keep her fragile body shut. In this context, Lyn Pykett draws our attention to the seductiveness of Tess's open mouth,[75] to the red and enticing orifice of her body which not only spellbinds the male narrator, but also invites Alec to cram his sexualized fruit into it. Only after suffering the infusion of his goblin liquids into her body does Tess manage to flee his satyr-like dominance (albeit pregnant with a sickly, death-bound child). The next time they fatally meet, the tables are ostensibly turned when, in a moment of relinquishing her role of stoic Niobean suffering, she makes his body porous and elicits blood from him. Yet, with poetic justice unevenly poised over her life, it is his juices again, this time his blood in the shape of 'a gigantic ace of hearts' (*T*, 382), that stigmatize her and bring a premature end to her life, which had always been seen in terms of a fatalistically thwarted game of cards (the treacle running down the Queen of Spade's body influencing and maligning the cards of her short life).

Hoping to (re-)translate her raped and porous body into an impervious marble state, Tess is blinded to the fact that fate antagonistically flings her into places that, by being full of juices and seminal fluids, undermine her stoic self-fashionings. The alleged *locus amoenus* of Talbothays with Mr Crick's dairy farm is such an alarmingly porous place, which, in its profusion of milk, stands in ironic contrast to Tess's wish for marble self-containment and to her new role

---

[73] Michie, *The Flesh Made Word*, 23.
[74] Dolin, 'Annotations' to *Tess of the d'Urbervilles*, 410. In this context, Dolin also refers to Claridge's essay 'Tess: A Less than Pure Woman', 324–38.
[75] Pykett, 'Ruinous Bodies', 159.

as a dry and bereft Niobean mother. The irreconcilable clash between nature's porosity and the pressure exercised by Victorian Grundyists to keep women's bodies rigorously sealed, the chasm between the cornucopian plenty of the idyllic valleys and the stoic's mask of renunciation – these are the conflicts in which Tess finds herself checkmated. It is thus bitterly ironic that the first impression that Tess in her post-maternal pursuit of bodily rehabilitation gets of the farm is the bucolic array of cows – 'prime milchers' (*T*, 106) – displaying '[t]heir large-veined udders', their 'teats sticking out like the legs of a gipsy's crock' and milk oozing forth and falling in heavy drops to the ground (*T*, 106). The contrast between Tess's barrenness and this milky land of Cockaigne could not be starker, and, by falling asleep to the sound of 'the measured dripping of the whey' from the cheeses (*T*, 113), Tess lets herself be lulled again and is imperceptibly drawn into the absorbing rhythms of fertility and fermentation.

As if impregnated by nature and Angel Clare's overtures, Tess is, over the next few days, less and less able to sustain her mask of marble stoicism and aloofness. Although casting herself in the role of a damsel in distress and mustering all her strength to negate her body's wishes ('I should refuse him, as I should refuse any man', *T*, 146), her sudden and sole fit of weeping ('her tears running down', *T*, 146) proves that her argument is invalidated in the face of transgressive and all-impregnating nature. Like the other dairymaids, who are at the mercy of their bodily desires, Tess is about to be hopelessly absorbed by the 'oozing fatness and warm ferments of the Var Vale', by 'the rush of juices' (*T*, 149) that inevitably galvanizes and fertilizes all female vessels in an almost Keatsian manner. Swayed by 'cruel Nature's law' (*T*, 147), Tess eventually succumbs to Angel's entreaties, to what Elisabeth Bronfen calls his male 'allegorising gaze'.[76] This translation of her body into 'a trope', into a disembodied sign,[77] is, however, incompatible with the verbal porousness that ensues on the occasion of her (physically anti-porous) wedding night and which goes back to what Michel Foucault diagnoses as the Christian compulsion to confess, to become 'a confessing animal'.[78] In stark contrast to Pamela's eighteenth-century epistolary porousness and efficient way of channelling her bodily juices into (at times masturbatory) flows of ink, Tess's terse confessions (written and oral) are not only devoid of erotic overtones, but also dismally abortive and eventually conducive to the loss of her temporary and undreamt-of sexualized paradise.

---

[76] Bronfen, *Over Her Dead Body*, 240.
[77] Ibid.
[78] Foucault, *The History of Sexuality*, 1:59.

Suddenly thrown back into harsh and prohibitive Victorian reality, Tess is ready to face the ostracism that, from the perspective of the double-tongued Evangelical guardians of sexual morals, was inevitably in store for fallen, deserted and genitally porous women. Socially dead and deposited by her husband into an empty sepulchre during an episode of somnambulism, Tess is – according to Andrew Hewitt[79] – exposed to a relentless process of 'mineralisation' and granted the purgatorial existence of a revenant, when, in the fifth part of the novel, she is transported to the hellish *locus terribilis* characterized by hardness, stoniness and frost: Flintcomb-Ash. What at first might look appropriate for her wish for an unmolested, asexual existence ironically reveals itself as its grim opposite, the stony fields composed of 'loose white flints in bulbous, cusped, and *phallic* shapes' (*T*, 285, my italics) functioning as sarcastic reminders of her own fatal porousness. As is evident, Tess is unable to escape sexualized nature which, however, in blatant contrast to the impregnating ooziness of Talbothays, is now solidified, barren, but not less incisive. Anonymized as nondescript flies, the girls crawl over the surface of the stony fields and feel their bodies viciously attacked and penetrated by horizontal rain in the form of phallic 'glass splinters' (*T*, 286) and by a moisture that does not so much have a seminal as a freezing quality which 'made their bones ache [and] penetrated to their skeletons' (*T*, 288). The inverted and cynical eroticism of Flintcomb-Ash's nature even includes the wind, which, unlike the fertile zephyrous breezes in Romantic poetry, smells of 'icebergs, arctic seas, whales and white bears' and 'lick[s]' the land in a deceptively sensual, but also congealing manner.

The silence following the murder of Alec which is interrupted by the regular beat of the blood drops – 'Drip, drip, drip' (*T*, 382) – makes it acoustically evident that Hardy's novel ends neither on T. S. Eliot's visions of regenerative rain in *The Waste Land* nor on the sounds of redemptive or cathartic Niobean tears. That Tess is eventually found not in a muddy river (like Eustacia Vye in *The Return of the Native*), but arrested on the stony slabs of Stonehenge fits the novel's semiotics of stoicism which – contrary to Hewitt's idea of petrification as a disease[80] – clearly separates her from the multifarious Ophelian suicides in late Victorian fiction and art. Without shedding tears and being absorbed by water, letting out no more than 'a suppressed sob' (*T*, 394), Tess regains her Hamletian stoicism ('I am ready', *T*, 396), advises Angel to do what in *Hamlet* was condemned as incest: to marry her sister, and then sacrifices her body to the

---

[79] Hewitt, 'Galatea in the Hintocks', 99.
[80] Ibid., 90.

anonymous power of justice, as it is reified by the buttress-like octagonal tower of the Shakespearean theatre of grim justice: the prison.

Chased by the dandyish rake and grim metaphysical justice, Tess, porous against her will, has a chequered genealogy: Hamlet (like her wavering and stabbing someone in a frenzied moment), Byron's dry and bereft Niobe, but also Persephone, raped and abducted by a Hades-like libertine,[81] now a Mr B in a new Darwinian garb. The fact that Hardy insisted on seeing porous and guilty Tess as a 'pure woman' (as he indicates in the subtitle) set the followers of vindictive Mrs Grundy on edge and turned the novel into a succès de scandale in the wake of Flaubert's *Madame Bovary* (1857).

The failure of stoicism and dry Niobean convulsions: *Jude the Obscure*

The inadequacy of the mask of stoicism in the face of transgressive nature and relentless fate is also the experience of Jude in Hardy's last and most controversial novel *Jude the Obscure* (1895). While Elaine Showalter's characterization of the last part of the nineteenth century as 'decades of sexual anarchy'[82] still implies chaotic arbitrariness, it is more appropriate to consider the end of the Victorian age in terms of rampant sexual Darwinism, in which the weaker sex is redefined as that which is subjugated by the sexually fittest, by the most ruthless rapist (who, in Hardy's last novel, is, to the patriarchy's unutterable dismay, no longer stereotypically male). Attempting to fortify himself against nature's relentlessness and its porous logic with books and vast amounts of knowledge, Jude, a delusional Romantic misfit, a rural Peter Pan,[83] united by a 'magic thread of fellow-feeling' to birds and other animals (*JO*, 15) is suddenly interfered with in his puerile dreams of academic fame by Arabella Donn, a liminal figure and goblin woman, who not only embodies the carnal principle of life, but also stands for the oozing and primordial processes of crude nature.

Despite the critics' rabid tirades of disgust at the novel's 'hoggishness,'[84] it is consistent with Arabella's role in the novel that, from her first transgressive

---

[81] Radford, 'The Making of a Goddess', 202–32.
[82] Showalter, *Sexual Anarchy*, 3.
[83] By creating a character who does not want to grow up ('If he could only prevent himself growing up! He did not want to be a man', *JO*, 18), Hardy precedes J.M. Barrie's *Peter Pan* (1904) by almost a decade.
[84] *World* (13 November 1895), 15, quoted in Millgate, *Hardy*, 341. For further references to Hardy's reception and to the novel's alleged proximity to Émile Zola's scandalous novel *La Terre*, see also Millgate, *Hardy*, 340–45.

appearance, she is associated with water, blood and with the dirty entrails of pigs. Conflating the mythological figures of the Parcae (being in the company of two other young women) with Circe, the sorceress transforming Odysseus's companions into grovelling swine, Arabella not only entrances Jude with her 'magnetism' (*JO*, 41), but also fulfils her nature-ordained job of dragging the would-be stoic into the paradoxical depths of procreative matter (hatching eggs in her bosom) and into the realms of oozing death (killing pigs and bleeding them). The autodidactic scholar Jude is so repulsed by the 'dismal, sordid, ugly spectacle' of blood (*JO*, 65) that he is hardly aware of the fact that this 'baptism of blood' – 'steaming liquid […] splashed over the snow' (*JO*, 65) – is not only akin to that which Tess went through with her horse,[85] but also about to wash away his plan of a Cartesian existence, devoid of bodily needs, feminine liquids and shaming porousness.

What makes Arabella so exceptional and inviting to Victorian criticism is that she epitomizes the reintroduction of the long-banned grotesque female body into literary history. Challenging the concept of the anti-corporeal Victorian angel in the house, Arabella is remarkable for her sensual and protuberant body, which owes more to the body of Jonson's Ursula, the pig woman in *Bartholomew Fair*, than to those wasp-waisted and flat-chested bodies commonly associated with nondescript Victorian heroines.[86] Highlighting the fact that Arabella's bosom is exceptionally voluminous ('capacious' and 'inflated') and that she is deeply immersed in blood and pigs' innards, Hardy reverts to long-forgotten Rabelaisian categories, but not without making the concession to his late Victorian audience that he never shows her in moments of 'vulgar' porousness. Subjecting others to baptismal immersions in blood or other fluids, she is one of Hardy's typical catalyst figures who instigates others' porousness without being porous, sweaty or bloody herself. In contrast to Tess's (decorously concealed) lactating breasts, Arabella's 'capacious bosom' seems to be strikingly barren and almost as fake ('inflated') as are her dimples and her long tail of false hair which, to Jude's dismay, she displays in conjunction with her confession that her pregnancy was a mistake. That Arabella unwittingly accompanies this shattering revelation with a (slightly altered) quotation from Lady Macbeth – 'What's done can't be undone' (*JO*, 61)[87] – can, in this context, be read as an ominous hint that

---

[85] Casagrande even goes as far as to say that 'Sue is a female Angel, Jude a male Tess, Arabella a female Alec', 'Hardy's Creative Process and the Case of *Tess* and *Jude*', 31.
[86] The 'aristocracy of wasp waists' came under even more pressure in the Victorian age. Cf. Samuel Smiles, *Physical Education* (1838), quoted in Langland, *Nobody's Angels*, 37f.
[87] The correct quotation reads 'What's done, is done', *Mac* 3.2.13, confirming Lady Macbeth's fatalistic determination before the banquet scene.

she, like childless Lady Macbeth, sees herself as an emissary of sterile fate and that she has, unbeknownst to him, initiated Jude's embarkation on his inevitably and irreversibly downward spiral into crude and porous materialism.

Jude's sojourn in Christmister, where he enters the profession of a stonemason (!), is a good contrast which enables him to regain his stoic distance from the crude ooziness of nature. The narrator, however, leaves the reader in no doubt that the city, which Jude had idealized and endowed with a halo since his boyhood, is in reality nothing more than a proliferation of dead stones, an assortment of 'ancient mediæval pile[s]' (*JO*, 79), which have been drained of their vitality and assumed the character of a ruinous necropolis with 'doorways of enriched and florid middle-age design, their extinct air being accentuated by the rottenness of the stones' (*JO*, 79). It is ironic, but also revealing that, in this atmosphere of dryness and claustrophobic stoniness, Jude meets Sue Bridehead, a young virginal woman with nebulous neopagan aspirations, who not only emphatically maintains that the 'most passionately erotic poets have been the most self-contained in their daily lives', but also proudly flaunts her disinclination to have sex and display her naked body ('cold-natured, – sexless', *JO*, 149).[88] Fitting into Hardy's dualistic or even antagonistic pattern of Arnoldian Hebraism versus crude materialism, Sue, with her 'small, tight, apple-like curves of her bodice' (*JO*, 187), is the direct Hebraist (and feigned Hellenist) opposite of Arabella and her – at first glance – pagan, Rubens-like and mellow body.

To what extent Arabella's sensually prominent body proves to be an alluring, but ashen Sodom's apple that haunts Jude's life becomes evident when she temporarily returns from Australia, as careless about her bigamous life as Defoe's Moll Flanders was in the eighteenth century. As if she intends to be more than instrumental in Jude's transformation into 'a tragic Don Quixote' (*JO*, 205), she gives him to understand that she will send over to him a boy who, despite the fact that he was born in Australia, is purported to be Jude's son (and diminutive doppelgänger). The reader is never given any clear evidence of the boy's parentage and is rather inclined to see the boy as a fatal intruder coming to wreak havoc on Jude's and Sue's pseudo-married life. His ominous nickname, Little Father Time, his tragic face ('like the tragic mask of Melpomene', *JO*, 280) and the reference to the atrocities of the house of Atreus (*JO*, 283) are all meant to prepare the reader for the ultimate catastrophe of the plot: Little Father Time's suicide and the murder of his siblings within walking distance of a college fittingly called 'Sarcophagus College'.

---

[88] For Sue's submerged sexuality, see Wood, *Passion and Pathology*, 208.

What is, in this context, most intriguing is how Hardy tries to reconcile his ideas of stoicism with the episode which seems to be most closely predicated on the story of Niobe's loss of her children. Sue's tragic flaw is, however, not overreaching pride, but a contagious despondency which she confronts her stepson with, insinuating, in a fit of misdirected Malthusianism, that children are an economic burden in the world and only the result of a blind 'law of nature' (*JO*, 333). Fate's (in conjunction with Mrs Grundy's) response is immediate and pitiless in Hardy's novels: boiling eggs (as a possible rejoinder to Arabella's hatching them in her bosom), Jude is startled by Sue's shriek and relentlessly faced with the destruction of his offspring. What in comparison to Niobe's grief is now illuminating is that the shattering sight of 'the triplet of little corpses' (*JO*, 336) elicits strangely subdued reactions, stressing the fact that the Victorian stoic's grief is distressingly fluidless, non-cathartic and reminiscent of Tennyson's image of the vase of repressed tears. Completely unhinged and paralysed by 'the grotesque and hideous horror of the scene' (*JO*, 335), neither Jude nor Sue is able to weep and is rather struck by what Hardy inappropriately circumscribes as 'grotesque', as the logical outcome of Jude's fatal fascination for Arabella's grotesque body. As with Tess, the stoic's mask is stiflingly tight, allowing for no relief apart from 'convulsive agony' (*JO*, 336) and 'spasmodic breathing' (*JO*, 337). Faced with a new generation of Schopenhauerian children, most of them (notably, boys), as the doctor laconically says, infected with 'the coming universal wish not to live' (*JO*, 337), Sue and Jude, the 'masochistic dyad',[89] are left writhing under 'uncontrollable fit[s] of grief' (*JO*, 337), as involuntary actors in a 'tragedy' (*JO*, 336) of Attic dimensions.

The grim fatalism vaguely derived from Aeschylus's *Agamemnon* eventually revolves around an irresponsible mother who by refraining from succumbing to 'pleasant untruths' (*JO*, 338) sacrifices the budding next generation to the harsh truth in the same manner as the adults did Iphigenie in the Greek drama, or adolescent Hedwig in Henrik Ibsen's grim problem play *Vilanden* (The Wild Duck, 1884).[90] Unable to find relief in tears, Sue's pent-up emotional pressure discharges itself in a miscarriage and in the auto-destructive wish to release the accumulated grief (and guilt) not so much by weeping as by masochistically opening and injuring her body with pins: 'I should like to prick myself all over with pins and bleed out the badness that's in me!' (*JO*, 345). This recourse that she wishes to have to the non-stoic act of lacerating one's body and eliciting its blood

---

[89] Jarvis, *Exquisite Masochism*, 111.
[90] Hardy was 'enthusiastically aware of Ibsen's arrival on the English stage'. Millgate, *Hardy*, 307.

is seen by Hardy in the context of a rigorous Catholicization of the Church of England which Sue willingly subscribes to by exposing herself to the narcotizing fumes of incense in St Silas's church and to the ideology of 'self-abnegation' and the mortification of the sexually porous flesh. Sue's seeking solace in the church ultimately culminates in her prostration and utter disembodiment underneath a gigantic crucifix. While porous maternity and utter sexlessness had always competed within her, the miscarriage, the ejection of everything that is sappy and lively from her body, ushers in a process of total anti-corporeality, at the end of which stands the (symbolic) disappearance of her body in what appears to be 'a heap of black clothes'. Reduced to the sound of her mere voice, Sue ends up as a 'sobbing' nonentity that is scarcely discernible under her clothes: 'It was his Sue's form, prostrate on the paving' (*JO*, 349).

Sue's desire for bleeding and self-laceration belongs to the realms of both fanaticism and the 'easy mechanics of ritual',[91] with blood becoming more and more a precious fluid that needs to be not only economized, but also shielded from insidious attacks by monsters, intruders or parasites rallying to contaminate and drain the Victorians' physical or political bodies. Punished, drained and eventually disembodied by Mrs Grundy's ruthless avengers, Sue is brought back from her Hellenist extravagances and reintegrated into the flock of anaemic and sexless women bemoaning the death of their children in a subdued Niobean fashion. The fact that Mrs Grundy's power was on the wane, however, becomes visible when Arabella escapes her clutches and, while Jude is in his death throes (randomly quoting from the book of Job), is shown on the prowl for her next victim. When she resorts to a 'love-philter' (*JO*, 401) to make the quack doctor Vilbert pliant to her overtures, she proves to be in the same, new category as Alec in *Tess*: the category of parasites, vampiric creatures that attach themselves to the bodies of weakened and vulnerable misfits, only to leave them porous, contaminated and doomed to death. These parasites and blood-suckers not only show themselves as being immune to the tradition of stoicism and its milestones from Seneca to Epictetus so diligently imbibed by Jude; they are also unassailable by Grundyism, since their legislator is blind and self-sufficient nature, aptly hypostasized by Hardy in the passive hostility of Egdon Heath.

With Arabella triumphant at the end of the novel, Hardy's Darwinistic vampire and blood-soaked Circe ushers in a new phase of late and decadent Victorianism whose harnesses and carapaces no longer prove unimpregnable to parasites, viruses and other (sexual) corrosives. In this respect, Hardy paves

---

[91] Wood, *Passion and Pathology*, 210.

the way for Bram Stoker's turn-of-the-century novel *Dracula* (1897) and its new and unprecedented quality of porosity: not so much directed at the individual porousness of a fallen woman or a rustic Quixote, Stoker's novel alarmingly shows the extent to which the entire Victorian body politic is suddenly threatened by an indefinite, almost pandemic trans-civilizational 'other' that is about to undermine the tottering ideal of the Victorians' self-idolization as a chosen, robust and pithy people. Finding their narrative of the vigorous nation jeopardized and corroded by a vampiric and exotic predator, the Victorian Establishment in the novel feels called upon to embark on its last crusade for the inviolability of the private and public body, aware of the grim fact that this battle had an apocalyptic flavour and called for something more belligerent and heroic than was commonly (mis-)understood as Kingsley's muscular Christianity.

Vampiric agents of porosity

While, since early Victorian times, the threat of porous alterity had been neatly confined to certain (Gothic) situations, abnormal figures or grotesque specimens of the unruly female sex, Stoker's *Dracula* is alarmingly different insofar as it shows the 'other' no longer tidily encapsulated in scapegoat-like brutes (such as Bertha Mason, Uriah Heep or Arabella Donn), but spreading maliciously through Victorian circles like a highly contagious virus. Although the novel can be read along different lines, as a symbolic treatment of the nineteenth-century scourge of consumption and phthisical wasting,[92] or, as the various references to Dracula's aquiline nose suggest, in terms of Victorian anti-Semitic and racist prejudices that frequently flared up in the 1890s,[93] its major deconstructivist potential, however, lies in its depictions of porous, kinky, 'unacceptable sex',[94] and in the extent to which it revolutionizes and wipes away the entrenched ideas of the caged Victorian female body. Close to various pop-cultural texts of Victorian pornography that were traded under counters or exchanged in smutty *chambres séparées*, *Dracula* is not only drippingly sensuous, but also cunningly subversive, since it daringly sexualizes the hitherto priggish Victorian novel (with its annoying omissions and dashes), aggressively tackles the concept of the asexual and demure Victorian woman and openly metonymizes blood as a

---

[92] See Byrne, *Tuberculosis and the Victorian Literary Imagination*, 126.
[93] Cf. Halberstam, *Skin Shows*, 86.
[94] Tracy, 'Loving You All Ways: Vamps, Vampires, Necrophites', 41.

sexual fluid freely plied between an exotic goblin monster and the haloed British angels in the house.[95]

Although ideologically disparate, the Victorian angelic wife, the female stoic and the New Woman in the wake of Ibsen's Nora and Hedda Gabler have at least one thing in common: they are conspicuously reticent about sexuality and seem to go to great lengths to keep their bodies closed and to channel their genital porosity into various domestic or political activities. When Hardy's Sue Bridehead buys two statuettes, one of Venus and one of Apollo, in order to rebel against the codes of Victorian morality, she does so not only furtively in the awareness of committing a breach of sexual taboo, but also under the obligation to give her trespasses an intellectual touch with quotations from Swinburne's 'Hymn to Proserpine'. Lucy Westenra in Stoker's novel is, by contrast, free from intellectual aspirations and rather indulges in an inappropriate degree of frivolity, which even culminates in utopian ideas of sexual openness and promiscuity. In what she characterizes as 'a very sloppy letter in more ways than one', she even poses the provocative and scandalous question: 'Why can't they let a girl marry three men, or as many as want her, and save all this trouble?' (D, 58).

Lucy's 'sloppy' letters are preceded by Jonathan Harker's diary entries which are meant to underline the separation of the men's public sphere from that of the domestic sphere snugly inhabited by the Victorian women. As an estate agent, Jonathan has started his descent into the heart of the monstrous 'other'[96] and, as the scene with the three female vampires (analogous to Lucy's indecorous longing for three men) shows, into the 'infinitely liquid world'[97] of his subconscious desires. Hidden and held captive in Dracula's Gothicized castle, reduced to the state of being a panicky male Pamela writing cassiber, Jonathan undergoes the rapid destabilization of his Victorian masculinity.[98] On the critical point of letting go, Jonathan even succumbs to the sexual dominance of the three animalized and porous women and, in a moment of effeminate abandon and state of arousal, waits for their rapists' bite: 'I could feel [...] the hard dents of two sharp teeth, just touching and pausing there. I closed my eyes in a languorous ecstasy and waited – waited with beating heart' (D, 39).

---

[95] For the seminal connotations of blood, see also Stevenson, 'A Vampire in the Mirror', 144.
[96] For this context, see Aydemir who reads Dracula as Harker's 'barbaric or savage other'. 'Blood Brothers', 162.
[97] See Sage's convincing essay 'Dracula and the Codes of Victorian Pornography', 69.
[98] Spear, 'Gender and Sexual Dis-Ease in Dracula', 187.

Hoping to keep the Transylvanian record of his emasculation (and onanism?[99]) locked in his diary, Jonathan is not aware of the velocity with which the vampire's germ of sexual destabilization was spilling over into Europe and corrupting the very texture of Victorian society. As a friend and addressee of Lucy's sloppy letters, Jonathan's wife Mina is painfully aware of the fact that, as a quasi-chaperon, she is unable to contain Lucy's sloppiness which consists of risky somnambulist flights from the confines of Grundyism, to stray to the cemetery to fornicate with the vampire. Starting her diary entry for 11 August with an account of their sojourn at an old-fashioned inn, Mina tries to comment facetiously on what Carol Senf terms 'Stoker's binaristic vision of femininity',[100] on the difference between Lucy, herself and the New Women, the latter being for her an epithet for grim fanaticism. With the equivocal line, 'I believe we should have shocked the New Woman with our appetites' (*D*, 85), she not only conflates eating with sexual lust, but also insinuates that, in contrast to the anti-hedonistic New Woman, she and Lucy now belong to the new category of the lascivious and sexually voracious sinners in the house. Even though critics such as Elizabeth Miller voice their misgivings about 'the slippery slope of reductive textual nitpicking' which a close reading of the sexual innuendoes of the text might lead to,[101] there is no doubt that Stoker continues the long tradition of employing a codified sexual language in order to show the porous decomposition of the twilight of the Victorian age: the 'long, heavy gasps' (*D*, 87) which Lucy emits, the secrecy surrounding her 'sleep-walking adventure' (*D*, 88) and the wounds in the shape of two 'pin-pricks' on her throat oozing blood create a ramified semantics of sexuality and show Lucy's defloration not so much as a painful sacrifice, but as an orgasmic adventure and a trespass on the territory of taboo.

As one of the last nineteenth-century epistolary novels in English, *Dracula* is generically related to and a radicalized version of Richardson's *Pamela*. While Pamela channels her Niobean tears into 'sloppy' and pathetic cassibers ostensibly to ensure her sexual containment (and inadvertently attracting Mr B with her inky and lachrymal juices), Lucy and Mina are not only provocatively open and frivolous in their letters and diaries, but also subversive in the way they seem to retranslate Rossetti's story about the goblin men into a shocking narrative of unrestrained, animalized sex. Fetishized by all letter writers,[102] in the

---

[99] Sellers argues that Jonathan Harker's yielding to emasculation is also aggravated by a strong proclivity for auto-sexual satisfaction: 'he [= Jonathan] is a plausible onanist'. 'Dracula's Band of the Hand', 150.
[100] Senf, '*Dracula* and Women', 117.
[101] Miller, 'Coitus Interruptus: Sex, Bram Stoker and *Dracula*' (accessed 11 November 2018).
[102] Halberstam, *Skin Shows*, 91.

guise of a great bat, or some indefinite ornithological creature, 'something that looked like a good-sized bird' (*D*, 90), Dracula provides the eerie Hitchcock-like background to Mina's text and induces the reader to guess the degree to which the Transylvanian 'other' has already (at that time still unbeknownst to the patriarchal Establishment) seeped into the British body politic. With Lucy's wounds (readable as displaced genital orifices) being 'open, and if anything, larger, than before' (*D*, 91), the contaminating substances of the parasitical 'other' are slowly corrupting, opening and draining the female body, the former icon of decorum, obedience and chastity. In one of Mina's diary entries, Lucy eventually verbalizes this experience of perforation in imagery that is as remote from Pamela's vigilant rationality as from evocations of Gothic horror and rather invests Ophelia's mermaid-like death with an ecstatic and orgasmic quality:

> I have a vague memory of something long and dark with red eyes […]; and then something very sweet and very bitter around me at once; and then I seemed sinking into deep green water, and there was a singing in my ears, as I have heard there is to drowning men; and then everything seemed passing away from me. (*D*, 93)

As if being sucked into water, Lucy depicts her sexual union with the vampire as a moment of bodily dissolution, as a near-death by drowning, from which Mina's interference agonizingly brings her back. Lucy's mermaid-like and porous body with its 'little white dots with red centres' (*D*, 91) attracts Dracula in a variety of metamorphoses which, to a certain extent, link him with and give a demonic twist to Jove in Ovid's *Metamorphoses*. When Stoker has Dracula seduce Lucy in the multifarious shapes of a bird, bat or a wolf, he seems to count on his readers' knowledge of the various narratives of woman-beast intercourse in Antiquity. When Lucy is finally penetrated by a red-eyed mist, the narrator even uses conventions of erotic Renaissance art and, via Correggio's Ovidian painting *Io e Giove* (1532–33), underscores the Jovian power of Dracula's kinky sexuality.

Lucy's sexual (and culturally relevant) encounters with bestial Dracula leave her drained, haggard and 'chalkily pale' (*D*, 113), in a debilitated condition that late Victorian writers tended to associate with the consumptive results of the self-inflicted porousness of masturbation, the 'evil doppelgänger of Enlightenment'.[103] Lucy's sexualized porousness is so alarming that it eventually calls for a significant masculine counterpoise, for iron heroism, best embodied by the Dutchman, Professor Van Helsing, a metaphysician, philosopher and

---

[103] Cf. Laqueur, *Solitary Sex*, 274. For the connection between masturbation and consumption as 'transmissible disorders', see Mason, *The Secret Vice*, 52.

scientist who scandalously induces men such as Quincey Morris, Dr Seward and Lucy's fiancé Arthur to refill her body with their own blood. In a barely codified symbolism, he acts as a pimp and invites men to have a form of blood-transmitted (and necrophiliac) sexual intercourse with a 'wan-looking' (D, 120), corpse-like young woman. At this point, Lucy's earlier flippant remark about desiring to marry three men has been ironically translated into the reality of a dark, quasi-pornographic *ménage à quatre*, a bohemian arrangement which overtaxed the Victorians' patience by suggesting unconventional sex as a restorative.

While playing on the negative and risqué connotations which blood transfusions had had since the late seventeenth century (when blood was lethally transfused from a sheep to a divinity student),[104] correspondents such as Dr Seward are acutely aware of the fact that there was more to a blood donation than medical discourses expressed – 'No man knows till he experiences it, what it is to feel his own life-blood drawn away into the veins of the woman he loves' (D, 120) – and that the promiscuous mixture of three men's blood in Lucy's weak body also had grossly promiscuous and even homoerotic overtones. Subjecting the young men (and himself) to a scientific form of vampirism, Van Helsing is not reluctant to use Lucy's body as a passive and leaking vessel to be repeatedly filled by male fluids; and since the blood passing through Lucy's body is finally consumed by Dracula, Van Helsing tacitly approves of the fact that, via Lucy, the men are also turned into weakened (and porous) vessels, catering to the libertinistic and bisexual desires of the vampire. In the end, there is even a competition among the young men and 'bloody' lovers as to the quantity of blood that is taken and instilled into Lucy (and into the vampire).

As a Gothicized rewriting of the sentimental novel, *Dracula* confronts its readership with a breathtakingly modern reinterpretation of the porous man of feeling: the man vying with others to exhaust himself not so much in streams of tears and ink as in transfusions of (seminal) blood. All efforts to refill Lucy's voracious body with different men's blood, however, prove to be futile; replenishing a porous or Niobean body turns out to be a Sisyphean task which drains the Victorian man and eventually leaves him in a state of weakness, quasi-castration and vulnerability that so blatantly clashes with the display of the age's new technological accomplishments (medical progress, telegrams, phonographs). The modern world of science and engineering seems to be checkmated in the face of primitivism, savagery and monstrous otherness.

[104] See Porter, *The Greatest Benefit to Mankind*, 234.

Lucy's death is inevitable, a punishment for her transgressive sexuality and openness. Yet, the Victorians' expectation of seeing Lucy quickly converted into a beautiful corpse, into an innocuous and sculptural artefact of Poe's conception, at first remains unfulfilled, as Van Helsing's scream of horror (typically in German, "'Mein Gott!'" *D*, 149) at her metamorphosis underlines. The strange beauty of her Juliet-like corpse is marred by her canine teeth which seem to have grown longer and more fang-like; it is through the acquisition of these phallic attributes that she undergoes an unsettling process of fantastic transgendering. After the transformation of her body into that of a male predator (beyond the scale of Hardy's Arabella), Lucy assumes a degree of liminality that was commonly associated with the freakish and masculine New Women, the unsexed feminists, suffragettes and 'amazon[s] of the clitoris'.[105] While children mistake her for the 'bloofer lady' (*D*, 166), thus conjuring up inter-textual reminiscences of the 'boofer lady' in Dickens's 1865 novel *Our Mutual Friend*, Lucy, as a vampire, multiplies the threat posed by the New Women when, in a perversion of her role as a potential mother, she turns into a predatory paedophile, luring away children and, instead of nursing or breastfeeding them, inflicts sexualized wounds on them.

That the exorcism of the vampire is, as a *contrappasso*, itself a highly sexualized (and porous) act becomes patently obvious when Van Helsing and the others turn into creepy grave desecrators and, like the monk Ambrosio a century before them, pay a nocturnal visit to the churchyard and thus transfer the *Liebestod* motif of *Romeo and Juliet* into the last nineteenth-century Gothic novel. Not only by the fact that the men climb over the churchyard wall is the reader made aware of a necrophiliac eroticism that links Shakespeare's play to the novel, but also by the fact that they enter the Westenra tomb (albeit not with a crowbar, but with a key) is evidence of the sexual transgressiveness that also characterized the young Montague.

The sexual symbolism of the graveyard scene becomes unmistakable when Van Helsing's candle produces not so much wax as 'sperm'[106] that drops 'in white patches' (*D*, 183) onto the coffin and underscores the crude sexualization of this scene. And while during daytime the dead Lucy is a harnessed female corpse, a decorative and blessed damozel inviting hagiographic worship – 'more radiantly

---

[105] See Leatherdale, *Dracula. The Novel & the Legend*, 143 and Craft, 'Gender and Inversion in Bram Stoker's *Dracula*', 104.

[106] In his annotations, Luckhurst refers to the *spermaceti*, to the fat that sperm whales (known at least since Melville's *Moby Dick*) produce which was used in the manufacture of candles, 383. Stoker seems to be fully aware of the ambiguities of the term and dallies with the phallic connotations of candles.

beautiful than ever' (*D*, 186) – at night, her angelic beauty is transformed into a ghastliness which mirrors the indomitable sexual revolt which men believed to be seething beneath New Women's rigid serenity and which they felt called upon to destroy. Coming across her when she has a child in her vampiric clutches, the three men are suddenly faced with the outcome of Lucy's frivolousness, with her nightly metamorphosis from a beautiful, corpselike nonentity into a snarling and voluptuous Krafft-Ebingian vamp, who tries to entice her male (and puerile) victims into the realms of an unknown *psychopathia sexualis*, which markers such as 'the coils of Medusa's snakes' (*D*, 197) or the 'passion masks of the Greeks and Japanese' (*D*, 198) only give a vague and exotic idea of. Turned into a fiendish femme fatale, solely driven by carnal lust and almost on a par with other female sexual rebels of that time, Wedekind's Lulu, Zola's Nana or Wilde's Salomé, Lucy trespasses on a masculine domain when she addresses her fiancé as 'my husband' and, Salomé-like, invites and inveigles him to have sex with her – 'My arms are hungry for you. Come, and we can rest together. Come, my husband, come!' (*D*, 197).

While it takes a small golden crucifix to stave off this particular threat of perverse female sexuality, it requires a true Victorian hero (with the resonant name of the Arthurian legend) to fight against the proliferating hosts of the undead, to combat feminine disorder and to fully reconvert the vamp(ire) into an impervious angelic creature. In an act of unsurpassed brutality, Victorian man is urged to undergo the painful ordeal of restoring sexual order, putting an end to all blurry and liminal conditions, closing the female body (the 'Thing') and of subjecting it to a drastic form of violence that reasserts the man's phallic dominion over the overreaching female sex. Before this backdrop, it is an undeniable fact that, as Craft highlights, 'the failure of the hypodermic needle necessitates the stake':[107]

> The Thing in the coffin writhed; and a hideous, blood-curdling screech came from the opened red lips. The body shook and quivered and twisted in wild contortions; the sharp white teeth champed together till the lips were cut and the mouth was smeared with a crimson foam. But Arthur never faltered. He looked like a figure of Thor as his untrembling arm rose and fell, driving deeper and deeper the mercy-bearing stake, whilst the blood from the pierced heart welled and spurted up around it. His face was set, and high duty seemed to shine through it. (*D*, 201)

---

[107] Craft, 'Gender and Inversion in Bram Stoker's *Dracula*', 106.

In Rossetti's poem it is Lizzie, the sister, who takes on the duty of the painful exorcism and weans Laura from the addiction to the goblin men's dripping fruits of sexual knowledge. This sisterly bonding is now irreconcilable with the persistent phallocentrism of Stoker's novel, which, after so many instances of female sloppiness and a rampant 'feminization of writing' in late nineteenth-century writing, now resurfaces with vehemence.[108] As if cuckolded by the different blood streams that had mingled in Lucy's porous and promiscuous body, it is now Arthur's 'high duty' to assert his phallic power in an act which Leatherdale reads as 'a thinly disguised account of passionate intercourse',[109] witnessed and acclaimed by his friends and blood brothers around him. While Dijkstra claims that it takes 'a little show of monogamous masculine force' to (re-)fashion 'the polyandrous virago' into the paragon of Victorian virtue,[110] the 'little show', the peak of sexual sadism in the book and in Victorian fiction,[111] turns out to be so toilsome and devastatingly orgasmic that Lucy's 'screech' is answered by Arthur's post-coital exhaustion, by the '[g]reat drops of sweat' (*D*, 201) that become visible on his forehead and his gasp-like breath. The act of driving the phallic stake into Lucy's heart ('her symbolic maidenhead')[112] and draining her of promiscuous fluids is also part of a punitive ritual that is unprecedented in the Victorian novel. As a precaution against Lucy's resuscitation as an uncontrollable porous revenant, her (maiden-)head is severed from the body (in a metonymic form of cliterodectomy),[113] her facial (and vaginal) mouth filled with garlic and the leaden coffin soldered up in a way that reminds readers of Roderick Usher's futile attempts to inter and suppress his mad doppelgänger in a metallic coffin.

With the key of the tomb in his custody and thus reinstituted into his phallic rights over Lucy, Arthur is, however, only temporarily strengthened. From his superhuman performance as a Thor-like sexual avenger, he suddenly collapses into a state of unrestrained porousness which, from Mina's perspective, takes him through various retrogressive stages to infancy. In contrast to Lucy who challenged his masculinity with her sexual openness and her sympathies for the devilish vampire, Mina triggers his dissolution in a different way and leaves him

---

[108] Felski, *The Gender of Modernity*, 91–114.
[109] Leatherdale, *Dracula: Novel & Legend*, 152. It is certainly ironic that their only incident of sexual intercourse 'is not a private affair'.
[110] Dijkstra, *Idols of Perversity*, 346.
[111] Leatherdale, *Dracula: Novel & Legend*, 152. Mulvey-Roberts intriguingly interprets the staking scene as an allegory for medical surgery which Victorians inflicted on hysterical women, 'chronic masturbators' and other unruly female patients. *Dangerous Bodies*, 94–98. The staking as a 'performance of a Gothic version of caesarean section' is, however, far-fetched. Kibbie, *Transfusion*, 211.
[112] Leatherdale, *Dracula: Novel & Legend*, 345.
[113] See also Senf, '*Dracula* and Women', 119.

in a similar situation of impotence to that in which she subjects her husband Jonathan to total prostration. Prompting him to find 'a vent' for his agony, Arthur grows 'quite hysterical' (*D*, 214) and eventually slips into the role of 'a wearied child' (*D*, 214) sobbing on Mina's shoulder. When Mina invokes 'the mother-spirit' and compares the weeping Arthur to the 'baby that some day may be on my bosom' (*D*, 214), she proves to be as menacing to Victorian ideas of masculinity as Lucy was. Both women call men's solidified position as a hero and paterfamilias into question, with Lucy trying to lure Arthur into the trap of vampiric, perverse and diseased sex and Mina smothering Arthur's manhood between her maternal breasts.

Mina's role in the novel is highly ambivalent: according to the Lizzie-Laura dualism, she is Lucy's Grundyist guardian, but unable to protect her from the sexual attacks that Count Dracula levels against her. What is more, Mina herself loses control of her orifices and yields to the vampire's phallic assaults. This shift in her personality is understandably not recorded in her diary, but registered by the authoritative Dr Seward who gives his correspondent a shocking insight into the Harkers' bedroom. The scenario that he reveals is not only radically different from the gloomily funereal one in Meredith's *Modern Love*; it tallies more with what adepts expected to find in the pornographic library of the otherwise stalwart Victorian Henry Spencer Ashbee:[114] as if composed as an erotic still, the scene shows Jonathan lying inert on the bed, this time not at the mercy of three female vampires, but 'breathing heavily as though in a stupor' (*D*, 262), while his wife, '[k]neeling on the near edge of the bed', seems to be engaged in what critics have come to see as an 'upward displacement of a forced fellatio' with Count Dracula[115] – 'his right hand gripped her by the back of the neck, forcing her face down on his bosom' (*D*, 262). The ambivalent connotation of the word 'bosom' is revealing: while Mina's bosom was instrumental in dismantling Arthur's masculinity and in reducing him to the position of an ersatz baby, Dracula's bleeding bosom conjures up different ideas of maternity,[116] the imagery of Christ as a pelican nourishing man, which is, however, blasphemously inverted into an icon of domineering male lust and abusiveness.[117] Compelled to watch his wife's sexual activities, finding himself only passively involved in a threesome constellation which exceeds the Victorians' idea of reproductive sexuality,

---

[114] See Marcus, *The Other Victorians*, 60–63.
[115] Spear, 'Gender and Sexual Dis-ease', 184.
[116] Craft also sees here an intermingling of male and female bodily fluids; and the fellation is here blended with 'a lurid nursing'. Craft, 'Gender and Inversion in Bram Stoker's *Dracula*', 110.
[117] Dracula as 'an analog of Christ' is a challenging hypothesis. See O'Malley, *Catholicism, Sexual Deviance*, 158–59.

Jonathan is the hypnotized witness to the way women are proselytized for a new form of sexual hedonism which put an irrevocable end to Patmore's outdated legend of the angel in the house.

While it was easy to consign the Transylvanian female vampires to the category of monstrous and witch-like aberrations of the British paragon of virtue, Mina, the conventional Victorian wife, turns out to be disquietingly Janus-faced when she deceives her husband in his presence, and sexually pledges her troth to Dracula and his growing harem of carnally aggressive women. Although the narrator tries to downplay the sexual tenor of this bedroom scene – 'The attitude of the two had a terrible resemblance to a child forcing a kitten's nose into a saucer of milk to compel it to drink it' (*D*, 262) – it is eventually the image of the kitten (as the symbol of the female genitals) lapping up the milk which highlights and reinforces the oral-genital implication of the scenario. This is also supported by the fact that, when Mina recapitulates her nocturnal apostasy from Victorian mores, she is so traumatized and guilt-ridden that she is unable to give proper expression to what had spurted out of Dracula's pelican wound. Considering the fact that she mentions the word 'blood' before, one must assume that the substance and quality of what she was forced to 'swallow' was so different and genital-related that, woken up from her sexual revels, she is inarticulate and augments the repository of nineteenth-century evasive dashes in literature: 'When the blood began to spurt out, he took my hands in one of his, holding them tight, and with the other seized my neck and pressed my mouth to the wound, so that I must either suffocate or swallow some of the – ' (*D*, 268).

Far from being just 'a virtuous footstool to do man's bidding in the world of scientific accomplishment and intellectual evolution',[118] Mina turns into a dangerous rebel against Victorian concepts of self-containment and, in the privacy of the bedroom, she reveals what is beneath the facade of a meek and loving wife. The horror of this scene thus lies in the sobering insight that even staunch Victorians are not immune to the lure of atavism and that Dracula's sanguine ejaculation is one of the last quasi-sacrilegious acts that demolished the myth of the Victorian age as an era of discipline and disembodied virtue. Embodying the oxymoronic conflict between whore and angel, Mina eventually contributes to the further emasculation of her male companions, when, by the end of her plea for the vampire, she moves them to tears and turns them into men of feeling, scandalously indulging in their tears publicly: 'We men were all in tears now. There was no resisting them, and we wept *openly*' (*D*, 287; my italics).

---

[118] Dijkstra, *Idols of Perversity*, 346.

As if to rescue the novel from an all-pervasive sloppiness and porosity Stoker ultimately reverts to concepts or 'anchor[s]' (*D*, 288) that are coarsely archaic and starkly incompatible with the dawn of modernity. In the face of women wallowing in the 'Vampire's baptism of blood' (*D*, 299) and becoming embroiled in a strange confusion of satanic religion and kinky sexuality, the Victorian men in the novel hope to retrieve their (and society's) solidification in the fundamentalist idea of pronouncing themselves as 'ministers of God's own wish' and 'old knights of the Cross' (*D*, 297). The moment when Van Helsing, Quincey, Arthur and Jonathan kneel down to take an oath and pledge to exorcize the erotic poison in Mina's veins themselves, the reader is instantly reminded of the scene in *Hamlet*, in which Claudius's antagonists swear to have the murder of Hamlet's father redressed. In this respect, the array of weapons (garlic, crucifix and stake) that the Victorians were able to muster for their Armageddon battle ('butcher work', *D*, 344) was disquietingly archaic and likely to provoke facetiousness and parody. That this 'sloppy' work was only effective with vampires, but evidently of no consequence with another figure of the late Victorian age, the dandy, becomes clear when the dandies of the Yellow Nineties are reconsidered in the context of porous bodies and shown deceptively wavering between rigorous self-containment and a vampiric relish for their victims' porous bodies.

The importance of being self-contained: Victorian dandies

While French writers such as Baudelaire saw Britain as the native land of dandies, naming Richard Brinsley Sheridan, Beau Brummell and even Byron as prototypes,[119] the Victorians saw dandies as another foreign influence, as a new species of insidious cultural Trojan horses sent from France to weaken and undermine their stronghold of Grundyism. Thus, the Victorians, steeled by Carlyle's hero worship, refused to see dandyism in terms of heroism[120] and, in their novels, preferred to foreground a vicious pattern according to which the Victorian dandies paraded their immaculate aestheticist bodies before the spectacular backdrop of their victims' mortifying porosity.

Frantically eager to keep their bodies impervious, to denigrate sex as the lyricism of the masses and never to lose control of their invisibilized orifices, the dandies exercised their volitional sphincters more rigorously than the

---

[119] Baudelaire, 'Le peintre de la vie moderne' IX 'Le Dandy'. *Œuvres complètes*, 2:712.
[120] Ibid., 2:711.

staunchest Victorian stoics. But while the latter subjected themselves to this regime of anti-porosity finally to comply with Grundyist principles, the dandies propagated their idea of aestheticist surveillance, of living and sleeping in front of a mirror,[121] for the sake of an artistic solipsism which not only transfers porosity to others, but even thrives on the unheeded openness of their victims' bodies. Alec d'Urberville, at one point explicitly identified as a dandy (*T*, 327), owes his existence as one of the obscenely rich and bored parvenus not only to his money, but also to his cultural and physical vampirism, to the fact that he sticks to Tess's aristocratic and porous body like the suffocating 'Druidical mistletoe' which gradually smothers and saps the nobility of the 'aged oaks' (*T*, 38).[122]

In 1891, in the same year as Hardy's *Tess of the d'Urbervilles* was published, Oscar Wilde confronted his Victorian readership with another, this time urban and sophisticated, but no less dangerous and vampiric dandy, when, in the novel *The Picture of Dorian Gray*, he has Lord Henry Wotton tempt Dorian Gray into discarding his role as a young and innocent male muse and change him into an *homme fatal*. In a true Mephistophelean manner, Lord Henry seems to scan his victim's body and to search its surface for flaws into which he can pour his malicious juices, fluids that ambiguously oscillate between intellectual and physical infiltrations.[123] The first encounter between Dorian and Lord Henry, thus, happens in a walled-in garden (analogous to the 'enclosure' in *T*, 58), as a modern re-enactment of the biblical scene of Eve's temptation in a new and shocking same-sex situation. In contrast to the traditional *horti conclusi* in the wake of the book Genesis, Wilde's dandyish garden is characterized not only by its conspicuous lack of women, but also by its supreme artificiality that creates the illusion that all (feminized) orifices and natural outlets are duly varnished, painted and closed. In accordance with Wilde's anti-Romantic and anti-feminine image of nature, the foliage in the garden, like the dandy's body, is devoid of pores and holes, polished, sealed and with the fresh leaves replaced by 'the green lacquer leaves of ivy' (*PDG*, 10). The profuse lacquered ivy that grows in the dandy's garden is more than a first revelatory hint that the aestheticist garden is built on two principles: on the idea of *l'art pour l'art* and on that of a vampirism that leaves other plants stunted, overgrown and nullified. As if to match the

---

[121] Baudelaire, 'Journaux intimes' III. *Œuvres complètes*, 1:678.
[122] 'Le peintre de la vie moderne' IX 'Le Dandy', 2:710. See also Gagnier, 'Productive, Reproductive and Consuming Bodies', 43–57.
[123] For the Faust theme in Wilde's novel, see also Pinyaeva, 'Faustian Motifs and Transformations of Modern Myths', 60–63.

artificiality of the dandy's garden, the narrator stresses Dorian's sculptural qualities, his 'finely-chiselled nostrils' (*PDG*, 17) and later his 'chiselled lips' (*PDG*, 72), showing that the dandy is part of a male-dominated tableau vivant, free of pores or porous indentations and with a physiognomy that is lifeless and displays a mask-like immobility.

While in the context of dandyism women were considered to be the epitome of natural drives and porosity, thus the alarming opposite of the dandy, 'espèce d'idole, stupide peut-être, mais éblouissante, enchanteresse',[124] English texts apparently diverge from the well-trodden paths of French dandyism, when readers learn that Lord Henry is married to a Wagner enthusiast, a nonentity with a 'nervous staccato laugh' (*PDG*, 37). Allocating his wife the same position as a superfluous curio in a cabinet, Lord Henry takes more interest in a new masculine hedonism, in being the satanic corrupter and vampiric opener of Dorian's virginal mind (and body). To make this young and innocent lad receptive to his demonic insinuations, Lord Henry not only focuses on his ears, but is also keen on infiltrating his victim's body with a seductively fruity drink ('something iced to drink, something with strawberries in it'; *PDG*, 16), whose strawberries overwrite Eve's biblical apple and remind the reader of Alec stuffing Tess's mouth with strawberries as an oscular overture to what follows genitally later.

The moment Dorian has imbibed Lord Henry's theories and iced potion, something that looks like a dandy's dream suddenly comes true: art and life coalesce to such an extent that they swap positions, turning Dorian into a work of art. With the portrait changing into the reflection of his dissipated life, leaving the canvas a porous mass of decomposing and dripping particles, the dream has, however, at Lord Henry's instigation, turned into a Gothic nightmare. Fallaciously believing in the idea that the devil's pact leaves him unimpaired and impervious to the pernicious influences of old age and to the porousness of the human condition, Dorian never notices that Lord Henry has subtly subjected him to an experiment that cunningly combines vampirism with the Pygmalion project. Highlighting the image of a 'furry bee' that preys upon the flowers and blossoms and is then shown creeping and penetrating deep into (the sexualized) 'stained trumpet of a Tyrian convolvulus' (*PDG*, 19), the narrator goes on to describe Lord Henry's approach towards piercing and creeping into Dorian's body and mind in the guise of a modern scientist. As an adherent of the pseudoscientific method of vivisection, Lord Henry is eager to apply this kind

---

[124] Ibid., X 'La femme'. *Œuvres complètes*, 2:713.

of anatomy to Dorian and, in what is a strange combination of psychology and homoerotic desire, to probe his virginal body. The innocent image of the flower and the furry bee thus supplies the reader with a natural dumb show of what is happening on a different level: Dorian's (mental and bodily) defloration, the penetration of his porous body, with the name of the flower vaguely conjuring up associations of the female vulva.

While Dracula involves his victims in provocatively sexual spectacles and undergoes fantastic metamorphoses to be able to tap their bodies and to feed on their juices, Lord Henry seems to penetrate Dorian's body verbally, but, like Iago in Shakespeare's *Othello*, he clearly draws on the knowledge that ears used to be seen as receptive and almost vaginal organs. Having engendered a dandyish sort of 'monstrous birth'[125] through Dorian's ear, Lord Henry prefers to watch him and to see the effects of his verbal rape. In glaring contrast to the atavistic Dracula, Lord Henry as the epitome of the supracultural vampire, takes care that, according to his idea of life as a stylish pageant, Dorian's wounds are never – like those of Lucy and Mina – frayed or ugly, but always aestheticized as 'red roses' (*PDG*, 47). With gender roles still allocated traditionally in the battle of the sexes in Stoker's novel, *The Picture of Dorian Gray* depicts an exclusive men's world, in which the dirty work of blood transfusions, impaling and beheading female bodies is unthinkable (and unnecessary), since women have, once and for all, been neatly classified as the 'decorative sex', as sumptuous accoutrements in the salons, eviscerated, shallow, puppet-like and 'psittacine'.[126] In this context, it is small wonder that the only Niobean and porous figure, Sibyl Vane, the typical Gretchen figure and impersonator of Shakespearean heroines at a little seedy East-End theatre, is deprecated as being 'absurdly melodramatic' (*PDG*, 72) when she sheds tears after Dorian's cruel desertion. While her porousness and fragility would have attracted traditional vampires of all sorts, in a novel about dandyish vivisection and homosocial vampirism she is not only completely useless, but also a drooling nuisance: 'Her tears and sobs annoyed him' (*PDG*, 72).

In a cosmos deprived of women and where vampiric dandies seem to thrive on the poisonous theories that they treacherously instil into the minds of young, androgynous men, Niobe has become not so much dry, ventriloquial and superfluous as superseded by more self-referential and homoerotically exploitable mythological foils. Hence, the dandyish Pygmalion no longer produces and falls in love with his Galatea, but now gives birth to a doppelgänger

---

[125] *Oth* 1.3.403.
[126] Davies focuses on Sibyl Vane in the context of Wilde's parrot imagery and his 'investment in this ventriloquial continuum'. *Gender and Ventriloquism*, 101.

of himself, to modern Narcissus who, becoming so amorous of himself (or his progenitor), starts or 'feign[s] to kiss, those painted lips that now smiled so cruelly at him' (*PDG*, 86–87).[127] As the 'most magical of mirrors' (*PDG*, 87), the portrait constantly entices Dorian to lose his poise and to be Narcissus-like absorbed into the depths of the painting. When the painting gradually becomes a cruel reflection of his hideous moral and bodily disintegration, Dorian loses his dandyish and narcissistic 'self-enclosure'[128] and opens himself up to another penetration by his satanic mentor. Faced with his portrait as a hideous clone of himself, as a loathsome heap of geriatric horrors in which the rosy wounds seem to have changed into foul, oozing 'leprosies of sin' (*PDG*, 129), Dorian accepts another dose of poison that the devilish dandy Lord Henry injects into his blood. While Dracula's assaults are of the utmost physicality, drinking, contaminating and emitting blood in moments of orgasmic communion, Lord Henry's venomous insemination becomes more and more subtle, rational and perfidious, especially when for the conception of his ideas in Dorian's mind he, in the second part of the novel, no longer relies on the impact of his voice on the young man's ear, but now rather on the corruption that the infectious matter of printed letters causes in Dorian's eyes. The mysterious yellow book, ostensibly Joris-Karl Huysmans's breviary of *À rebours* (Against the Grain) (1884), into which Dorian instantaneously immerses himself,[129] has an immediate narcotic and hypnotizing effect, and instead of liquids, it is now the text's 'heavy odour of incense' (*PDG*, 103) and the monotonous rhythm of the sentences which penetrate his body and thrust him further into the hell of Lord Henry's Frankensteinian laboratory.

It is more than an ironic barb to the entire story that, by its end, Lord Henry, the vivisector and penetrator of Dorian's sculptural body, imagines his victim as 'the young Apollo' and himself as Marsyas listening to him in raptures. Relying on his interlocutor to know that Marsyas was flayed and deprived of his protective skin for challenging Apollo to a musical competition, Lord Henry perfidiously seems to suggest that it is he who has to bear the brunt of the vivisection, whereas Dorian has been empowered by him to translate his life into art: 'You have set yourself to music. Your days are your sonnets' (*PDG*, 178). Thus, it is an overwhelming shock for Dorian when he, the alleged conflation of Apollo and Narcissus, recognizes that the magical mirror of the portrait reveals

---

[127] '*Dorian Gray* is a study in narcissism', see Bruhm, 'Taking One to Know One: Oscar Wilde and Narcissism', 170–88.
[128] Ibid., 177.
[129] For the influence of Huysman's *À rebours* and Gautier's *Mademoiselle de Maupin*, see Raby, 'Poisoned by a Book', 159–67.

what he is beneath the lacquered surface: a hideous, monstrous Marsyas, with his skin perforated, torn apart and oozing with blood: 'There was blood on the painted feet, as though the thing had dripped' (*PDG*, 182).

It is not too far-fetched to argue that Wilde's novel ends on a similar note to Stoker's: next to the restoration of order, there is the violent death of the monster and the emphatic closure of the body, the difference being that it is not so much the women's as the dandy's porous body in the painting that is eventually closed and re-varnished. While Wilde is thus ready to (partially) meet Victorian expectations of poetic justice at the end of his controversial novel (notwithstanding that he lets the satanic tempter escape and Narcissus's female echo be muted in suicide), the intimate genre of his poetry more often than not arrives at different conclusions, thereby underscoring the fact that the Yellow Nineties were particularly responsive to the general feeling of disintegration and to the haunting image of bodies in the disquieting process of melting, dissolving and corroding in water. It is in this more intimate framework of the poetic genre that Victorians such as Wilde dare to eschew their dandyish statuesqueness and are ready to succumb both to the fascination of the disintegrating aquatic element and to the subversion of female tears. What the inveterate Victorians surreptitiously did in the privacy of their Growleries, Wilde was ready to do in the private rooms of his poems, as, for instance, in 'The Grave of Keats'.[130]

Written around 1880, two years prior to his lecture tour of America as a figurehead of British aestheticism, when Wilde was on the point of adopting the mask of the impervious dandy, he freely expresses his admiration for Keats and sees in the Romantic poet a precursor of (homoerotic) porousness which the Victorians' ideal of corporeal iciness and taxidermist manipulation of the skin sternly prohibited. For Wilde, Keats is in a long line of artistic, moral (and even sexual) martyrs starting with Saint Sebastian who is supposed to prefigure Keats not only in his beauty and in the fate of an untimely death ('Fair as Sebastian, and as early slain'),[131] but also in the bodily leakiness that was brought about by his enemies' venomous arrows. Weeping nature – 'gentle violets weeping with the dew' (7) – irrigates ever-blossoming chains of flowers around his bones, while, in the privacy of the sonnet, the speaker forgets his dandyish mask and contributes his tears to the freshness of Keats's memory: 'And tears like mine

---

[130] Najaran also refers to reading Keats in terms of sexual embarrassment and something which was preferably done in the privacy of the closet. *Victorian Keats*, 18–25.
[131] 'The Grave of Keats', 5. *Complete Poetry*, 23. For more details on this 'male homoerotic vision of Keats's and another of Wilde's revered Romantic martyrs, Thomas Chatterton, see Bristow and Mitchell, *Oscar Wilde's Chatterton*, 137–40.

shall keep thy memory green,/As Isabella did her Basil-tree' (13–14). The very last line not only introduces a ghastly Gothic element into the elegiac poem, it also shows that Wilde was enthusiastic about Keats's most gory and porous poem and that Isabella's kissing Lorenzo's severed head became an inspiration for the climactic scene in his later one-act play *Salomé* (1892).

The idea of the martyr is incompatible with that of the dandy and aestheticist: while the dandy insists on the immaculateness of his body and aspires to the state of a work of art, the martyr is keen on exhibiting the gashes and openness of his maltreated body. Having come across Guido Reni's *San Sebastian* in the Palazzo Rosso in Genoa in 1877 (Figure 7), Wilde was enthusiastic

Figure 7 Guido Reni, *San Sebastian* (Saint Sebastian) (1615), Genoa, Palazzo Rosso. Courtesy Niday Picture Library/Alamy Stock Foto.

about the painting,[132] since it seems to reconcile the ever-jarring Arnoldian dichotomy between Hebraism and Hellenism. Christian medievalism is, for Wilde, synonymous with blood, lacerations of the body and sadomasochistic porousness – 'its love of self-torture, its wild passion for wounding itself, its gashing with knives, and its whipping with rods'[133] – whereas Reni's painting combines the Hellenist beauty of the body with the Hebraist notion of martyrdom and aestheticizes the martyr's wounds as marks of distinction and nobility, without the Grünewaldian ostentation of seepage and porous dissolution. The Arnoldian division which Reni and other Renaissance artists bridged also seems to determine Wilde's life and shows him torn apart and unsuccessfully in pursuit of a reconcilement of two extreme positions. While in the public role of the dandy and 'theoretikos' Wilde casts himself as a Hellenist, dissociated from the world 'in dreams of Art/And loftiest culture',[134] in the privacy of his poetry, Wilde does not refrain from revealing himself as a Hebraist who, in subversive defiance of the Victorians' concept of masculinity, exhibits his dripping wounds and is not ashamed to show his Niobean tear-stained face.

Although Wilde had resorted to Christian imagery before and written about the terrifying feeling of 'drowning in a stormier sea/Than Simon on thy lake of Galilee',[135] it is Wilde's very last poem, *The Ballad of Reading Gaol* (1898), published after his traumatic two years in prison, which pinpoints Wilde's radical shift both from Hellenism to Hebraism and from the public exposure of the Victorian stage to the seclusion of the ballads in the wake of François Villon and other poètes maudits. In the Dantean circle of outcasts and prisoners, the speaker has discarded both his Hellenism and vampiric dandyism and no longer sees any occasion to suppress his porousness; quite the contrary, by defining life as the imitation of Christ's Passion, he shows himself familiar with 'the bloody sweats'[136] with which he eventually hopes to corrode the stony facades of the Victorian Establishment. In the vague context of Psalm 51, Wilde, the renegade dandy, has his persona plead for the rehabilitation of tears, blood and bodily fluids, because they alone, so the Hebraist's argument, have the power to erase the mark of Cain:

---

[132] Ellmann, *Oscar Wilde*, 68.
[133] *The Soul of Man*, 34.
[134] 'Theoretikos', 12–13. *Complete Poetry*, 29.
[135] 'E Tenebris', 2–3. *Complete Poetry*, 26.
[136] *The Ballad of Reading Gaol*, 393. *Complete Poetry*, 152–72.

> For only blood can wipe out blood,
> And only tears can heal:
> And the crimson stain that was of Cain
> Became Christ's snow-white seal. (633–36)

The healing and restorative power of tears and blood stands in marked contrast to the sanitary measures which the authorities (as sham advocates of Hebraism) had taken to blot out the moral or physical stains which the executed criminal might leave behind. As if afraid of the balladic array of revenants or spectres that by bleeding 'great gouts of blood' (431) might persecute them as portents of their guilt, the prison warders scatter quicklime which is supposed to eat 'flesh and bone away' (463–64). In *The Picture of Dorian Gray*, it was the dandy himself who blackmailed the chemist Alan Campbell into atomizing Basil Hallward's body and to erase all vestiges of bodily fluidity; in the poem, the voice of the dandy has been silenced, and the position of anti-corporeal sterility seems to have been occupied by the typified representatives of the Establishment, by the Chaplain, the Sheriff, the spokesmen of order, Grundyism and censorship. As in *Tess of the d'Urbervilles*, the prison becomes less a site of justice than of exorcism, a place where, in the name of cold and fundamentalist Hebraism, moral and bodily porosity is stopped, where blood, tears and all fluids are combatted and turned into '[t]he shard, the pebble, and the flint' (489). After his manifesto of a new Hedonism and a return to the Hellenic ideal in the novel, Wilde's last poem can best be understood as a plea for a new Hebraism which, however, denounces bigotry and hypocrisy and which retains a few traces of sensual Hellenism (as Reni had so wonderfully accomplished in his seventeenth-century paintings of Saint Sebastian).

4

(Re-)Liquefaction at the dawn of the twentieth century

Rebirth of carnivalism in James Joyce's *Ulysses*

Modernist language as a laxative

Although the nineteenth century is framed by two examples of subversive textual porosity, Lord Byron's stew-like *Don Juan* and Stoker's 'sloppy' *Dracula*, the Victorians are notorious for their figures of self-containment and for the rigid formal moulds into which they were accustomed to casting their ideas and sentiments. In this respect, Dante Gabriel Rossetti's definition of the formally strict sonnet as a moment's monument, as a verbal sculpture carved 'in ivory or in ebony'[1] chimes in with Victorian ideas of monumentalization and longevity, even though Rossetti's poem does not tally with the Victorians' understanding of literature as edification and Grundyist instruction. Given the Victorians' obsession with form, structure and solidification in their biographies, but also in art and fashion, the emergence of the dandy in the nineteenth century is logical (albeit seen with great misgivings), and as such (after Wordsworth's stony poetics) one of the last Deucalion stones in the looming blurriness and liquefaction of Impressionism and related movements. While Walter Pater succinctly describes the dawn of a new epistemology as a disquieting process of melting and dissolving – 'all melts under our feet'[2] – and indefatigably seeks to congeal this Heraclitean flux into gem-like moments of supreme artificiality, he nevertheless seems to adumbrate a new period in which leakiness becomes a temporary benchmark of avant-gardist innovation.

In this context, James Joyce's epitome of the porous novel *Ulysses* (1922) not only emphatically marks the end of Victorian dandyism and its concepts

---

[1] Introductory Sonnet to *The House of Life*, 6. *Selected Poems and Translations*, 23.
[2] Pater, 'Conclusion' in *The Renaissance: Studies in Art and Poetry*, 152.

of unperturbed stoicism, it also dispenses with the idea of literature as commemorative architecture and surprisingly ushers into the modernist novel what Celan later called a 'porous structure' ('Porenbau'). But while Celan's poetic 'Porenbau' is a paradoxical combination of porosity and crystalline fragments, Joyce's novel reintroduces into the art of novel writing a multilayered porosity that comprises the syntactic sloppiness of Molly Bloom's masturbatory stream of consciousness (with eight sentences sprawling impressionistically over thirty pages) in the same way as it promotes the carnivalesque with all its forgotten features of abdominal pleasure and reopened sluices of bodily fluids.

Modernists such as Joyce and D.H. Lawrence not only turned into the angry young men of their lost generation, holding (as Lawrence did in his fierce poem 'The Deadly Victorians') the Victorians accountable for their unremitting petrification of oozy bodies, they are also credited with relocating the focus of man's porousness from (metonymic) eyes to the real genital regions. Whenever the Victorians thematized the odium of genital porosity, they invariably did so in vaguely allegorical terms, shamefacedly referring to dripping pitchers, sloppy letters, prick-hole wounds or the like. In this respect, the Victorians had been in the bad habit of doing what René Magritte's provocative painting *Le Viol* (1945, Figure 8) suggests and provides a good *post-festum* interpretative key for: starting from the erroneous assumption that a woman's face and body are exchangeable or that her facial features have a close correspondence to the female trunk and its genitals, Magritte's painting invites readers to reconsider rape scenes (*viol*) from *Pamela* to *Tess* and *Dracula* and induces them to read the extreme disproportion between the torrents of female tears and the taciturnity about sexual matters in a different light. While Magritte's painting sheds an intriguingly retrospective light on displaced, repressed and misdirected porosity from the Victorian age to Surrealism, it is to the merit of Lawrence's and Joyce's texts that they cease to rely on metonymies and that they teasingly reacquaint their readers with the time-honoured, but long-neglected congruence between sexual things (*res*) and their crude names (*verba*). Lady Chatterley's shocking, but frank question 'What is cunt?' (*LCL*, 178)[3] inaugurates a new age, where women are no longer 'fetishistic oddit[ies],'[4] but (re-)acquainted with the abdominal regions of their bodies (a terra incognita for most Victorian women raised as asexual angels in the house). They are also made to learn that the old tacit assumption that there is a hushed correspondence between their mouths and genitals is a myth of bygone times.

---

[3] See also Lawrence's plea for the liberation of stigmatized language in 'Pornography and Obscenity'. *Selected Literary Criticism*, 32–51.
[4] Garrington, *Haptic Modernism*, 52.

Figure 8 René Magritte, *Le Viol* (The Rape) (1934), Menil Collection, Houston. Courtesy Peter Willi/ARTOTHEK.

In *Ulysses* (1922), this new linguistic straightforwardness is, to a certain degree, personified by Molly Bloom, the wife and companion of the Jewish flâneur Leopold. Right from the outset, Molly refuses to comply with circumlocutions and euphemisms in the same way as she rejects the Niobean role model of the preceding Victorian age, the role of the mute mourner spending her fluids in a profusion of tears. In accordance with the mythological slant of the novel, the picture over her bed, *The Bath of the Nymph*, clearly suggests that Molly's function is no longer that of an ever-mourning mother (even though the loss of the Blooms' son Rudy is a constantly traumatizing Niobean subtext of the novel), but rather that of a lascivious nymph or a sleeping Venus in the manner of Titian.[5] Neither Niobe nor any other goddess, Molly is an autonomous woman who not

---

[5] Ibid., 84.

only relegates her husband to the role of a servant, an unwitting Leporello in her promiscuous Don Giovanni universe (a fact which is incompatible with her traditional role of Zerlina), but, in her obscene volubility, she also makes it clear that her marriage is no longer based on phallic aggression (as in Arthur's and Lucy Westenra's perverse wedding rite in the graveyard), but on the mutual understanding that each partner has the freedom to indulge in their (linguistic and corporeal) porosity and to enjoy their release from Mrs Grundy's tight shackles.

As if intending to challenge the preceding literary models from Homer to Shakespeare and Tennyson, Joyce shows the protagonist of his epic 'encyclopaedia'[6] as a porous Jew in anti-Semitic Dublin, whose relationship with the world is, right from the outset, defined not only along abdominal lines, but also in terms of an unparalleled desire for ooziness and (as yet) shockingly distasteful fluids. Accordingly, when Leopold Bloom, the modern Ulysses, embarks on his circuitous one-day journey of Dublin (leaving his alleged Penelope behind in bed), the zest and almost voluptuousness that he shows for interior and subcutaneous things, for organs and their secretions, constitute his (and Joyce's) large-scale programmatic renunciation of what the Victorians had championed and stood for. Instead of facades, sartorial negations of the body and self-effacing masks, Bloom, as a hero of porosity and campaigner for carnivalism, is ready not only to tackle the body in its stark nudity, but also to go beneath the skin, to probe its pores and to celebrate what Garrington calls 'a litany of epidermic adventures'.[7]

At the beginning of part II, Bloom is introduced as a hearty eater ('Mr Leopold Bloom ate with relish', *U*, 53), who, unlike the late Victorian dandies and anorexic aestheticists, does not despise food and rather evinces an unbridled appetite for 'the inner organs of beasts and fowls'. The list of food that follows might have not only a vertiginous, but also a sickening effect on the (post-modern, belligerently vegan) reader – 'thick giblet soup, nutty gizzards, a stuffed roast heart, liver slices fried with crustcrumbs, fried hencods' roes' (*U*, 53) – but it is also meant to convey Bloom's coarse and animal-like tastes which, with a carnivalesque flourish, are pitted against the ideas of dandyish artificiality, but also against the homosocial visions that poets such as Rupert Brooke had of athletic warriors leaping in early Riefenstahl manner into pools of heroic cleanness.[8] It is thus hardly surprising that among the inner organs that he prefers most, he has a special penchant for

---

[6] Letter from Joyce to Carlo Linati, 21 September 1920. Gilbert, *Letters of James Joyce*, 146.
[7] Garrington, *Haptic Modernism*, 108.
[8] Brooke, '1914 I Peace'. *Poetical Works*, 19.

(grilled) mutton kidneys, just on the grounds that they epitomize abdominal porosity and give to 'his palate a fine tang of faintly scented urine' (*U*, 53). That the mythic Daughters of Erin later even invoke Bloom's kidney as a patron saint – 'Kidney of Bloom, pray for us' (*U*, 470) – is thus consistent, albeit reductionist and highly absurd. The enormous extent to which (genital) porosity is a leitmotif in Bloom's perambulations through Dublin, but also at home, in the Penelope cosmos, is repeatedly illustrated by various vignette-like episodes; what used to be the clean, above-waist hemisphere in preceding ages, chiefly in the Victorian *Bildungsroman*, has now been replaced by throbbing bodies (private and politic) that incessantly ooze, drip and exude fluids which, since Rabelaisian forays into the body in early modern times, had been considered opprobrious.

That in this highly porous and carnivalesque context the text veers off to deal extensively with a cat at first looks like an inconsistency, but then perfectly fits into the Blooms' genital universe. Although Joyce distances himself from the Victorians' codification of language and seems freely to express what contemporaries called his sexual and 'cloacal obsession',[9] he seizes every opportunity, and if necessary, even hackneyed imagery, to underline the fact that the Blooms' household gravitates towards genitals and their exudations: the '"Milk for the pussens"' and the cat's tongue on which he meditates – 'all porous holes' (*U*, 54) – certainly remind the attentive, intertextuality-alert readers of the genitalized kitten in *Dracula*, but also of the small progress that Joyce is making in his liberation of literature from the clutter of Victorian iconography.

While the cat holds sway over the kitchen and Molly's invisible zone of influence, Bloom is drawn from the outside, allured by 'the lukewarm breath of cooked spicy pig's blood' (*U*, 57) at the butcher's. Almost mesmerized by the sight of the last kidney on the meat counter, he finds his attraction heightened by the fact that the kidney, displayed as it is in Dlugacz's shop, seems to be both an agent and an object of extreme porousness, dramatically 'ooz[ing] bloodgouts on the willowpatterned dish' (*U*, 57). The purchase of the last kidney, that 'moist tender gland' (*U*, 58), not only triggers incoherent thoughts in Bloom about female bodies which he stereotypically prefers to see in terms of moist and oozy meat; it also clashes with a poster for a Zionist colony in Palestine which Bloom sees advertised in the shop. Preoccupied with his abdominal universe of kidneys and milk-splashed vaginal cats in microscopic Ireland, Bloom imagines the Orient as being an apocalyptic wasteland, as a world of extinction, '[a] dead sea in a dead land, grey and old' (*U*, 59). Resorting to the traditional idea of female

---

[9] For Wells's diagnosis of 'cloacal obsession', see also Anspaugh, 'Powers of Ordure', 81.

bodies as topographies, Bloom cannot help visualizing the Old Testament world around 'Sodom, Gommorah [sic], Edom' (*U*, 59) as being an old and withered woman's body, with the former fountainhead of mankind now being reduced to the shrivelled genitals of a 'bent hag': 'the grey sunken cunt of the world' (*U*, 59). Absorbed by the image of the revolting dryness of old women's genitals and suddenly affected by premonitions of petrifying old age ('age crusting him with a salt cloak', *U*, 59), Bloom suddenly leaps from his negative thoughts about Lot's wife into the present ('Well, I am here now'), with its odd assortment of brick houses and his wife's, Molly's, life-affirming 'ample bedwarmed flesh. Yes, yes' (*U*, 59).

Leaving images of the decrepit, blocked and withered (Biblical and Victorian) past behind, Bloom re-immerses himself into the positive porous cosmos of kidneys, sausages and milk-lapping pussens, to which his wife so essentially belongs: introduced into the story as a amorphous 'bulk' of porous and milk-yielding flesh ('bubs', *U*, 61), Molly clearly stands for a new type of woman who counters the Victorian women's dryness (and their phobia of lactation) with the luxuriance of a juicily buxom body that, under her nightdress, takes the indistinct form of 'a shegoat's udder' (*U*, 61). Far from being squeezed into Grundyist carapaces of corsets and crinolines, Molly seems to pique the male imagination, which cannot help representing her as a pile of warm and sensuous flesh that not only mingles her fragrance with that of the tea, but that is also as open and bulky as the bulgy pot from which she so generously pours her tea. Reverting to the well-known literary situation of a man in a woman's boudoir and vaguely counting on his readers to remember the horror that Swift's explorer of Celia's bedroom felt, Joyce has Bloom freely rummage through Molly's 'soiled drawers' (*U*, 61) and ransack her garters, only to find that the book she has been reading has slipped off the bed and 'sprawls against the bulge of the orangekeyed chamberpot' (*U*, 61).

Here the first small narrative unit comes full circle: Bloom's peregrination from the horror of the dry sunken 'cunt' of the leaflet leads to the urine-scented kidney (still sizzling in the pan) and from there to Molly's chamber pot as one of the gravitational Grail-like centres of the story. The reference to the chamber pot is, however, not only an indication of Bloom's 'fetishistic concern with feces, menstrual blood, urine, and bodily secretions',[10] it is also a devastating comment on the intellectual aspirations of modernist women who – in the symbolism of flutes – are later provocatively equated with the instrument's holes ('Three

---

[10] Henke, 'Joyce's New Womanly Man', 46.

holes, all women', *U*, 273). As the twentieth-century reincarnation of the female leaky vessel, Molly is shown treating books as the leaky receptacles of words, essentially on a par with chamber pots; both collect the spillage that man exudes through physical or intellectual orifices. The additional fact that Molly unashamedly selects her books by the phallic associations that the author's name conjures up – 'Get another of Paul de Kock's. Nice name he has' (*U*, 62) – further supports the argument that Molly has left the irksome stage of questions behind and at least six years prior to Lady Chatterley sees the world through the lens of genital porousness.[11]

What looks like a misogynist jibe against women trying to reconcile the intellectual sphere with the carnival of their bodies also seems to be applicable to Bloom, who is a misfit in more than one sense: as a Jew, a cuckold and a porous man, he is the epitome of the effeminate anti-hero, so outrageously contrasted with the petrified men of Victorian descent. When, after the consumption of the kidney, he feels 'a gentle loosening of his bowels' (*U*, 65), the reader escorts him to the toilet where Bloom is less interested in appreciating the words of an old number of *Titbits* than, in a gesture of the outsider's ignorance of mainstream culture, in unceremoniously wiping his bottom with the acclaimed literary prize story, *Matcham's Masterstroke*. While Bloom, the abdominal man, is clearly shown lacking aesthetic discrimination and seems to be more impressed by the author's remuneration of 'three pounds thirteen and six' (*U*, 67), Joyce uses the concluding paragraphs of the 'Calypso'-chapter as an unparalleled attack on the literary consumer culture of the Establishment. Conflating the acts of defecating and reading so ingeniously, Joyce, via Bloom, leaves his reader in the proverbial dark of the jakes, wondering what kind of porosity is meant, that of the protagonist's own digestion or that of the nondescript prize-winning writer, both of which are, from a longitudinal perspective, nothing more than carnivalesque waste:

> [...] he allowed his bowels to ease themselves quietly as he read, reading still patiently that slight constipation of yesterday quite gone. Hope *it*'s not too big bring on the piles again. No, just right. So. Ah! Costive one tabloid of cascara sagrada. Life might be so. *It* did not move or touch him but *it* was something quick and neat. Print anything now. Silly season. He read on, seated calm above his own rising smell. (*U*, 66; my italics)

---

[11] That Bloom is also familiar with Paul de Kock's novels, especially his 1878 novel with the telling title *La femme aux trois corsets* (translated by Joyce into English as *The Girl with Three Stays*), is clear from his masochistic fantasies in the 'Circe' episode (*U*, 441) and sheds an interesting light on his double-edged view of literary mass production and literary incontinence. See also Pease, *Modernism, Mass Culture*, 114.

Refusing to clarify what the pronoun 'it' refers to, confusing the word 'tabloid' (a newspaper) with tablet (here a pill as a mild laxative), and giving defecation and reading a vexing simultaneity,[12] Bloom seems to insinuate that words, even in the sophisticated sense of *litterae*, have something excremental about them which one cannot help discharging. While a whole phalanx of Modernist authors saw the preceding age of Victorian culture as a period of blockage, stagnation and intellectual constipation, they all seem to emphasize that, with that 'constipation of yesterday' being gone, all restrictions and restraints have vanished and an all-pervasive and cathartic porosity has set in, radically revising key concepts of language, literature and the arts. Given the fact that Victorians only reverted to porosity in the narrow context of ecological and pathological disorders (thus conflating public fluids with laxatives, emetics and blood-letting) and that, beside anorexic non-consumption, codified images of constipation and obstruction were paramount features in nineteenth-century culture, Modernists around Joyce were ready to use literature and art as a cultural Dadaist purgative and – as Marcel Duchamp did with his pioneering urinal bowl turned upside down, *Fountain* (1917) – by restarting the disused bodily fountains, to resuscitate the concept of the laxative carnivalesque after its deep post-Jonsonian slumber.

The descent into the porosity of death

If we follow Bakhtin and simplifyingly define the carnivalesque as the discovery of and the gargantuan joy at the ready display of all sorts of bodily fluids and excrements in literature,[13] Joyce certainly qualifies as an eminently post-Rabelaisian writer (a consideration of his literary works should suffice here and not necessitate a nosey glimpse into his private correspondence with his wife Nora).[14] As a narrative meant to effect a cleansing of Victorian obstruction, Joyce's *Ulysses* refocuses its readers' attention on the abdominal parts of the body, with all its fluids and oozings, but, what is more, it approaches the hallowed Victorian topics of maternity, marriage and death (the 'hatches, matches and despatches' as they used to be advertised in Victorian newspapers) from a radically corporeal perspective. In this quasi-epic cycle, death is no longer the ultimate end of the heroic story, but it is rather interspersed into the juicy

---

[12] See also Cheng, 'James Joyce and the Literature of Excrement', quoted in Brienza, 'Krapping Out', 123.
[13] Bakhtin, *Rabelais and His World*, 317.
[14] Anspaugh's consideration of Joyce's 1909 love letters in order to triumphantly state that 'we *know* that Joyce was a coprophile' is too reminiscent of gossipy Positivist readings. Anspaugh, 'Powers of Ordure', 80 (italics in the original).

chapters of everyday life, and – this must have proved to be most irksome for the last supporters of the Victorian mores – it succeeds defecation and Bloom's self-centred reflections about (and presumably masturbatory rubbings of) his flaccid penis in the tepid water of a public bath: 'the limp father of thousands, a languid floating flower' (*U*, 83).

While death is, for the Victorians, the ultimate triumph of petrification, the consummation of the intractable body's closure (staged in lavish, monumental *pompes funèbres* and commemorated in bombastic tomb architecture), Bloom's descent into the shadowy world of death is wedged between life-affirming and carnivalesque processes of eating, defecating, masturbating and giving birth. This is, on the one hand, underscored by the fact that Bloom's reminiscences about Molly singing Rossini's *Stabat Mater* (an oblique hint at Mary's and Molly's Niobean tears about their dead sons) are suddenly diverted into reveries about his genitals in the bath, and, on the other, that the bathtub as the 'womb of warmth' (*U*, 83), where his navel as the 'bud of flesh' eventually blossoms into the flower of his penis, is as conducive to procreativity as the many porous graves in the 'Hades' cemetery.

From the contemplation of Bloom's virility, the reader is thus catapulted into Paddy Dignam's funeral cortege, with Martin Cunningham's aggressively stiff Victorian top hat contrasting oddly with Bloom's detumescent penis in the previous chapter. The detumescence of his penis is also linked with the sad fact that, almost as a stigma of his Jewish 'otherness', Bloom is painfully reminded of his life-framing losses: the suicidal loss of his father and the premature loss of his infant son: 'Dwarf's body, weak as putty, in a whitelined deal box' (*U*, 92). Navel, penis, womb and tomb seem to be oddly connected in Bloom's carnivalesque life, which, not only on account of his vegetative name, is so at variance with the petrified dignity of his male company.

From the politically incorrect (and at one point even openly anti-Semitic) carriage banter, the novel moves straight into the darkish, repellent and abject viscera of human existence. On their way to the cemetery, Martin Cunningham recalls an accident, in which a hearse is said to have capsized, upset the coffin and flung the corpse onto the street. Bloom readily takes up the idea and visualizes Dignam's corpse not so much as complying with Victorian ideas of the *ars moriendi*, but rather as a shocking sight, gruesome in its obscene openness: 'Looks horrid open. [...] Much better to close up all the orifices. Yes, also. With wax. The *sphincter loose*. Seal up all' (*U*, 95, my italics). In radical contradistinction to Sedgwick's image of the closed volitional sphincter in nineteenth-century literature, sphincters of the body (and mind) tend to become so 'loose' in early twentieth-century arts that even a spokesman of porosity such as Bloom vociferously calls for wax and other means to seal up the gaping orifices. While Bloom here recoils from this post-mortem nightmare of sphincterless porosity, in the following paragraphs, and here in provocative contrast to the mummification of Victorian bodies and their porousness congealed into the smoothness of marble effigies, Joyce lets Bloom reinvent the cemetery as a heterotopian place par excellence[15] where the living are fascinated by the juiciness of death, and where the dead are no longer disembodied sculptures, but porous organisms that live on and undergo grotesque metamorphoses. The Simnel cakes that a vendor sells at the gates turn out to be the *entrée-billets* to a modernized Hades, where not only Cerberus has been radically commercialized and propitiated by cheap '[d]og-biscuits' (*U*, 97), but death has also been divested of its dark fin-de-siècle atmosphere and turned into the mass processing of cartloads of porous bodies: 'Must be twenty or thirty funerals every day. […] Funerals all over the world everywhere every minute. Shovelling them under by the cartload doublequick. Thousands every hour' (*U*, 97).

This radical carnivalization of Hades as a place of sphincterless porosity implicates a translation of the Homeric underworld into a nightmarishly absurd scenery that seems to be more indebted to paintings by Bosch and Breughel than to any ancient text. Thus, the first object of Bloom's carnivalization of Hades is the priest: straddling the boundaries between man and animal, but also precariously open to and impregnable by the unwholesome miasmatic atmosphere of the cemetery, the priest, in Bloom's vivid imagination, takes on various shapes, ranging from a toad and a puffed up 'sheep in clover' to an inflated 'poisoned pup' (*U*, 100). Convinced of the fact that it is the infectious air of the place that, via the pores, penetrates into the priest's body, Bloom cannot help thinking that modernist Hades is an intestinal place, a receptacle full of flatulence, gases and stenches. While the toilet episode focuses on post-constipational relief, on yielding and discharging, in the cemetery, Bloom is temporarily stuck in a place where gases do not evaporate, but infiltrate into the people, and where the living and the dead continue to interact via vapours and bodily fluids. Thus, it is no surprise that Bloom is immediately reminded of Molly's flatulence, of the fact that 'Molly gets swelled after cabbage' (*U*, 100). Like the cabbage that so indecorously works on Molly's anti-Victorian bowels, the dead exude toxic gases that bloat the priest and turn him into a liminal and flatulent being: 'Must be an infernal lot of bad gas round the place' (*U*, 100).

[15] Foucault, 'Of Other Spaces', 22–27.

Bloom's kinky imagination, however, does not stop here: in the labyrinthine intestines of the cemetery, the dead are also responsive to the sexual atmosphere that other inhabitants of and visitors to the Hades, such as the undertaker, seem to radiate. Mixing up Shakespeare's idea of a humanized and highly sexualized death in the last act of *Romeo and Juliet* with Robert Browning's poem 'Love among the Ruins' (1855), Bloom turns the Modernist cemetery not only into a large and coiled intestine, but also into a site of disturbingly erotic desires: 'Love among the tombstones. Romeo. Spice of pleasure' (*U*, 104). It is this 'spice of pleasure' that seems to keep the dead tantalizingly awake and in a state of constant titillation. That the graveyard triggers erotic feelings in Bloom – 'Whores in Turkish graveyards. Learn anything if taken young' (*U*, 104) – is not just evidence of his perversity, it is rather another good example of his circular view of porous and juicy existence, where '[b]oth ends meet' (*U*, 104). Only in this context is it logical that it is here that Bloom thinks about exhibitionistic sex with Molly, about the conception of his son Rudy ('Molly wanting to do it at the window', *U*, 104), in whose brief existence life and death also tragically meet.

While in this paragraph the dead are visualized as Tantalus figures, thrilled by the sexual activities of the living in the same manner as the starving are teased by the smell of inaccessible grilled beefsteaks, in the subsequent section, Bloom argues that porosity does not end with death, but continues, so that he imagines the corpses being subjected to a process of inexorable and porous metamorphosis. Contributing to the fertility of the soil of the cemetery, 'quite fat with corpse manure' (*U*, 104), the dead bodies, in Bloom's overactive imagination, not only turn green and pink, they also change into a condition of softness that he, for want of more precise terminology, depicts as 'a kind of a tallowy kind of a cheesy' (*U*, 104). While Victorian literature tended to depict corpses as rigid and sculptural objects (as things 'straight as an arrow'),[16] Joyce, via Bloom, describes death as an explosively carnivalesque process, in which corpses are involved in constant oozy transformations.

These post-mortem metamorphoses, which even out-Ovid Ovid, strikingly clash with Bloom's previous ideas of the cemetery as a scrapyard, where stray organs, dissociated from their bodies, 'lungs, hearts, livers' are scattered and wait for their ultimate destruction: 'Old rusty pumps' (*U*, 102). Bloom's short-lived and inconsistent forays into the eighteenth-century lore of the *homme machine* are immediately followed by the Baudelairean obsession with the oozy vitality of

---

[16] *Jude the Obscure*, 407. For the Victorian age as a corpse in rigor mortis, see also Hardy, 'The Darkling Thrush', 9–10. *Complete Poems*, 150.

putrefaction. While Baudelaire frames the revolting description of a putrefying dog's sweating carcass into a pornographic monstrosity,[17] and addresses it as a memento mori poem to a young lady who one day will predictably resemble the fly-blown, porous abomination, 'cette ordure',[18] Joyce's porous (human) corpses do not have this expostulatory effect, but are rather meant to be a drastic illustration of the abjectness of everlasting material life. Accordingly, Bloom's meditations on death do not stop at the glaring discoloration of the body, but, irrespective of the European tradition of the vanitas motif, take the reader through the various stages of the body's mutations, from its 'cheesyness' to that in which the body starts a further level of porosity, when 'treacle [is] oozing out' of it (*U*, 104). The last stage of Bloom's inverted eschatology is, however, reached, when the phase of porosity is left behind and the body has been reduced to a cadaverous lump, squeezed dry with deathmoths rising from its empty husk. In a novel whose raison d'être is the parodic reversal of traditions, this image is evocative of the ancient allegory of man's teleological purpose: having undergone the transformatory process from the earth-bound caterpillar to the death-like stasis in a cocoon, man was believed to ultimately reach the soul-like stage of a butterfly (Psyche) soaring to eternity. In his aversion to ideas of linearity, Bloom persistently resorts to images of circularity and, by the end of his ruminations on life's crude biologism, comes up with the shocking idea of an organic automatism in which cells incessantly change and, in a vague allusion to Ulysses's image of the monstrously lupine and self-devouring body politic in Shakespeare's *Troilus and Cressida*,[19] propel a relentless process of life-sustaining auto-cannibalism: 'Live for ever practically. Nothing to feed on feed on themselves' (*U*, 104).

The funereal descent into hell, the Hamletian graveyard scene ends with an 'obese grey rat' (*U*, 110) safely disappearing under the plinth of a tomb. While 'rats' hiding behind arras curtains in *Hamlet* ran a high risk of being killed, rats in Joyce's graveyard seem to partake of the luscious carnivalism and to cultivate their obesity. With his imagination running riot, Bloom visualizes the rats drilling holes into the porous coffins, gnawing the bones of the corpses and thus not only nullifying any hope of corporeal resurrection, but reducing human existence to the deplorable state of '[s]altwhite crumbling mush of corpse: smell, taste like raw white turnips' (*U*, 110). With this image of pulpy and amorphous porosity on his mind, Bloom re-emerges from the cemetery, feels his commitment to life strengthened and exults in his conviction that there is '[p]lenty to see

---

[17] Cf. 'Une charogne', 5–6, *Les fleurs du mal. Œuvres complètes*, 1:31–32.
[18] Ibid., 1:37.
[19] *TC* 1.3.121–24.

and hear and feel yet' (*U*, 110). Drawing a clear demarcation line between the realm of the dead 'in their maggoty beds' and the '[w]arm beds' of his sexual vitality, Bloom has taken a shuddering glimpse at death as an un-Victorian, carnivalesque and porous spectacle. Teeming with vermin ('swirling' with maggots, *U*, 105), dripping with fluids and filled with gases, Joyce's Modernist graveyard is an intricately woven intestinal construction in which Sedgwick's volitional sphincter has become utterly loose and ineffectual. In the role of a new and Rabelaisian *psychagogos*, Bloom leads readers into the porous cavities of the thanatotic underworld and exposes them to the unsettling fact that the human condition's porousness transcends death and breeds new life.

In a little blasphemous quatrain, Ezra Pound wrote the line 'Sweet Christ from hell spew up some Rabelais, / To belch […]' which appropriately captures the liberating and anarchic effect that Rabelais was to have on post-Victorian Modernist culture and which Pound saw re-embodied in Joyce's *Ulysses*.[20] While, in the late nineteenth century, English translations of Rabelais's *Gargantua et Pantagruel* (1532–35) were, as Gowan Dawson writes, attracting 'the vigilant attentions of the Society for the Suppression of Vice',[21] a rapid Rabelaisation of culture seems to gain ground after Queen Victoria's death, encouraging writers such as Joyce to trespass upon hitherto forbidden ground and to explore realms that had unnoticeably been inhabited by other Rabelaisian experimenters and iconoclasts, the most notorious among whom had been the practitioner of pataphysics, the Breton Alfred Jarry.

'After us the savage god', or the explosion of the new porous women

Witnessing the first night of Alfred Jarry's *Ubu Roi* at the Paris Théâtre de l'Œuvre in 1896, William Butler Yeats could not help exclaiming 'After us the Savage God'[22] to express his bewilderment at and confusion about characters who not only dragged the tragedy of *Macbeth* to the level of a raucous Punch and Judy show, but also reinvested drama with a hitherto forgotten quantity of scatophilia, porousness and obscenity. Jarry, who was a pioneer of the carnivalesque on the stage, not only introduced the excrementally porous (with the toilet brush and the slightly distorted word 'merdre' as its emblems) into

---

[20] Pound, *Culture*, 2:13, 'Monumental', 96. See also Perelman, *The Trouble with Genius*, 94.
[21] Dawson, *Darwin, Literature and Victorian Respectability*, 202.
[22] Yeats, *Autobiographies*, 348.

dramatic literature, he also brushed away the numerous overly intellectual and disembodied Ibsenite New Women and supplanted them by the monstrous and coprophilic caricature of Mère Ubu, a proto-Dadaist transformation of sinister Lady Macbeth into unsexed grotesqueness. Jarry's inroad into the Rabelaisian carnivalesque (with its unprecedented instances of porous violence in the shape of the Machine à Décerveler)[23] even overtaxed the French audience's patience and, after two tumultuous performances, the play was taken off the bill. While Jarry's influence on British literature ostensibly remains negligible and in the case of Joyce has only been acknowledged with reference to *Finnegans Wake* (1939),[24] it is not groundless to claim that Joyce's (and, to a lesser degree, even Lawrence's) work has an impact on early twentieth-century literature that was either fuelled by or was in the spirit of what later came to be recognized, if not appreciated, as the Ubuesque.

Faced with a multitude of Noras, Hedda Gablers and Mrs Erlynnes rebelling against the objectification of the decorative female sex, the Modernists were not the first to perceive women as being sexless and dispassionate, as rigorously in control of their genital orifices as their angelic sisters in the Victorian houses had been. Some of the New Women (ranging from Dickens's Mrs Jellyby in *Bleak House* to Hardy's Sue Bridehead) even eclipsed their Victorian demure predecessors in their fanatical negation of the body. When, in the last act of his travesty, Jarry has his remake of Lady Macbeth maimed on stage, her buttocks ripped apart, her bladder opened and, in an act of raging infantile sadism, her entire body eventually torn into fragments,[25] he seems to be proposing not only a bizarre strategy of how to deal with the clichéd images of these bossy unsexed women, but also an anarchic way of confronting his audience with the forgotten fleshy and porous materiality of the (female) body.

While Jarry, in an almost infantile fury, smashes the concept of the New Woman to pieces, Joyce and Lawrence are more subtle, but scarcely less radical. As Suzette Henke argues, Bloom personifies the new concept of the womanly man and in chapters such as the 'Circe'-episode there is not only a 'plurality of signs confirming Bloom's androgynous aspect',[26] but also a clear indication that Bloom is ruthlessly subjected to a fate that, on the Parisian stage, Mère Ubu had been forced to endure. This concern about man's

---

[23] See Fisher, *The Pataphysician's Library*, 97.
[24] Corcoran, 'Drawing our Attention to Jarry, Duchamp and Joyce', 659–71. Jarry is, in this context, considered 'an enormous unacknowledged source' whose plays, novels and biography feed into Joyce's late œuvre.
[25] *Ubu Roi* 5.1. *Œuvres Complètes* 1:394–95.
[26] Henke, 'Joyce's New Womanly Man', 50.

increasing androgyny (so easily and grotesquely solved by Jarry) is also shared by D.H. Lawrence. As an ardent reader of Hardy's novels, Lawrence saw the Jude-Arabella relationship as negatively ground-breaking and as a prototype of a dualism that exchanged bygone Arnoldian dichotomies for a crude gender antagonism where women were deprecated as being 'cock-sure' and men as womanish, anxious and 'hen-sure'.[27]

This swapping of gender roles, which, for Joyce, is part of a carnivalesque Walpurgis Night and for Jarry the trigger of farcical fantasies of dismemberment, is, for Lawrence, at the core of 'the tragedy of the modern woman' who '[f]rightened of her own henny self, [...] rushes to mad lengths about votes, or welfare, or sports, or business', and tries to be 'marvellous, out-manning the man'.[28] Refusing to be fertile and to hatch eggs (as Arabella, the Circean woman, so deceptively did), the new 'cock-sure' women have now proceeded to hatch votes, ink-bottles or other 'absolutely unhatchable object[s]' and sealed up their reproductive and oozy orifices in favour of male cognitive faculties. The 'vast human farmyard', which Lawrence considers society to be, seems to have become a monstrosity with men withdrawing into their 'hen-like tremulousness' and women transforming themselves into monstrous androgynous nonentities, devoid of the juiciness and fecundity that Joyce and Lawrence so decisively associated with the female sex. Flung into a 'farmyard' in which an inverted pecking order has created a wasteland of barrenness and sexual insecurity, men are shown as either being cuckolded (Bloom), crippled (Sir Clifford Chatterley) or reduced to old, doddering and marginalized figures who, like Tiresias in Eliot's *The Waste Land*, have reached the ultimate stage of emasculation and, as hen-like 'old m[e]n with wrinkled dugs', are condemned to live in a dubious state of liminality.[29]

What, from different perspectives, Lawrence and Joyce undertake to do is not so much a remoulding (or even maiming) of the 'cock-sure' woman as adopting a critical approach to the onerous heritage of the Victorian age and hence to rethink gender roles in breathtakingly new ways that more often than not verge on Rabelaisian and Ubuesque radicalism. This concept of dealing with and, in the case of Joyce, playfully partaking of the prevalent gender confusion aims not only to resuscitate ideas of primeval womanhood, but also to question obsolete notions about manly petrification and self-containment. The novels

[27] Lawrence, 'Cock-sure Women and Hen-sure Men'. *Late Essays and Articles*, 125.
[28] Ibid., 127.
[29] Eliot, *The Waste Land* III 'The Fire Sermon', 228. *Collected Poems*, 72. See also Apollinaire's Ubuesque play *Les mamelles de Tirésias* (1918).

that originated in the turmoil of European Dadaism and Surrealism, *Ulysses* (1922) and *Lady Chatterley's Lover* (1928), make it disquietingly clear that the unveiling and unmasking of the New Women also resulted in the shattering of men's encrusted roles and in forcing them to take cognisance of the fact that female bodies (like that of Mère Ubu) were bewildering conglomerations of porous parts that openly defied men's rigorous control. Freed of the Grundyist harnesses of skirts, crinoline and Victorian misconceptions of femininity, women now demanded not only intellectual rooms of their own, but also opportunities to have their bodies demystified and their hitherto shameful openness acknowledged. While Jarry reverted to the genre of knock-about farce to reintroduce Rabelaisian female porosity onto the stage, Joyce and Lawrence embarked on different discourses and, instead of menacingly wielding toilet brushes, they devised episodes and revitalized languages of genital and anal porousness which would have been inconceivable without Jarry's iconoclastic Ubuism and his vital reinterpretations of Rabelais's grotesque novels.

Having escaped two fatal attractions, death's smutty seepage in the Hades scene and the advertised 'grey sunken cunt' of the Jewish-Oriental world, Bloom redirects his attention to the fruitful and procreative openness of his Irish world. Chiming in with the post-Victorian clamorous calls for youth and a new Bergsonian *élan vital*, Joyce (via Bloom) and Lawrence (via Oliver Mellors) seem to posit that the decade around the memorable Bloomsday of 1904 marks the end of late Victorian mourning, death and decadence and, in accordance with what later came to be called Jugendstil (art nouveau), focuses on birth, labour and juicy reproduction. Although there is a tacit assumption that Victorian *Bildungsromane* start ab ovo, with the birth of their protagonists, they are strikingly devoid of episodes in which heroes are actually born. After the scene of Tristram Shandy's bungled conception in Laurence Sterne's eighteenth-century experimental novel (the first novel literally and vexingly starting *ante ovum*), Victorian protagonists are enveloped in the 'blank of [their] infancy', a phrase that the autodiegetic narrator of *David Copperfield* noticeably uses twice.[30] Despite the veneration of maternity in the Victorian age, an opaque cloak of silence and discretion seems to be thrown over all things that are even remotely linked to pregnancy, labour and confinement.[31] Accounting for the first months after childbirth as an unduly victimization of the mother 'caused

---

[30] *David Copperfield*, 24 and 25.
[31] See Hanson, *A Cultural History of Pregnancy* which makes it unmistakably clear that textual or 'visual representations of pregnancy are rare in this period', 79.

by her baby vampire'.³² Victorian women were clearly obsessed and angst-ridden with a vampirism that defined sex, pregnancy, birth and lactation in terms of an intolerable consumption and draining of the female body, which they consequently expected to bypass discreetly in the novels they usually read for entertainment. Lawrence's and Joyce's novels are, thus, bracketed by the Victorians' Gothic horror of birth and Samuel Beckett's later iconic equation of birth with death, especially when, in *Waiting for Godot* (1952), Vladimir, trapped in absurd circularity, envisions the porous act of birth performed 'astride of a grave'.³³

The depiction of a woman giving birth had, thus, always been taboo, a forbidden insight into creatural leakage. In this respect, Lawrence leaves Constance Chatterley in an advanced state of pregnancy, whereas the birth scene in *Ulysses* seems to be shockingly foregrounded, with Mina Purefoy not only in labour, 'on the stools, poor body, two days past her term' (*U*, 379), but also in the moment of impending porosity, on the point of pushing a huge, obstructing block out of her body. The use of the word 'stools' indicates that Bloom is not reluctant to establish a connection between defecation (cucking stool) and the utensils in the delivery room. While not only the Victorians, but also post-war writers such as Beckett prefer to focus on the thematic cluster of obstruction, constipation and blockage, Joyce pinpoints the hidden links between faeces, birth and creative fluidity.³⁴ But while Joyce writes smoothly about defecation and anal matters and, in line with the scatophilic tradition since Jarry's Rabelaisian play, has Bloom delightfully linger on the cusp between self-restraint and yielding, it is odd that he seems to have some reservations about being too explicit in his description of what is euphemistically called the 'happy *accouchement*' (*U*, 399). Not only by reverting to French terminology, but also by having his various speakers in the maternity ward adopt the style of a classical obstetrics manual (which contains 'all the cases of human nativity which Aristotle has classified in his masterpiece with chromolithographic illustrations', *U*, 391) does the narration create a certain misogynist distance to the explosive porousness which Mina Purefoy is about to undergo.

---

[32] *Mrs. Beeton's Book of Household Management* (1868), quoted in Flanders, *Victorian House*, 22. In this context, see also Esther in Moore's novel: 'suckling her child seemed to draw all strength from her'. *Esther Waters*, 138.

[33] *Waiting for Godot* 2.58. What makes the image even more uncannily Gothic is that the obstetrician and the grave-digger are identical: 'Down in the hole, lingeringly, the grave-digger puts on the forceps' (58).

[34] See for this context, Brienza, 'Krapping Out', 117.

The simple fact that Mina's waters break and that, in glaring contrast to all self-contained women of the Victorian age, she is at her most porous and Ubuesque is surprisingly expressed in the dry and detached scientific idiom that Joyce puts into the mouths of a group of inebriated medical students: 'the premature relentment of the amniotic fluid' (*U*, 391). In the cacophony of voices, which Bloom reluctantly listens to while waiting in the ante-chamber, the long catalogue of obstetric problems which might accompany pregnant women's porosity leaves the impression that the porous (and cathartic) affair of giving birth – and in particular in the case of the 'distressing manner of delivery called by the Brandenburghers [sic] *Sturzgeburt*' (*U*, 391) – is an aberration and instance of disgust. Despite the fact that the noisy visitors and brawling students are preoccupied with and, in their smutty conversations, constantly revolve around the phenomenon of birth, they prefer to flaunt a repugnance of feminine porousness which Bloom, however, refuses to share and which strikes him as glaringly contrary to the carnivalesque joy of bodily liquidity that he has been feeling in various respects since the matinal eating of the grilled kidney. Earlier interspersed references to the Christian dogma of the Immaculate Conception, the Virgin's 'pregnancy without joy' and her 'belly without bigness' (*U*, 374) make it sufficiently clear that Christianity's scepticism of the body casts a long shadow on Catholic Irish life and for a while even interferes with Bloom's thoughts about the porosity of birth, which, in the peculiarly riotous *mundus inversus* of Bloomsday, follows the carnivalism of death.

Notwithstanding the semantic inhibitions that are attendant upon Mina Purefoy's confinement, the actual birth scene has, as Patrick O'Donnell stresses, an unusually unleashing and untrammelling effect,[35] and in this respect comes close to Mère Ubu's fragmentization and the cathartic bursting of her bladder. In the same way as defecating sets free creative impulses (and invites analogy-hunting critics such as Brienza to find 'litter in literature [and] potty in poetry'),[36] there is undeniably a strong link between the eruptive porosity of birth and the 'babel or "hubbub" of language'[37] which is even enhanced in the passages that follow 'the prescribed ceremony of the afterbirth' (*U*, 390). Here, as in the subsequent chapter, Bloom's monologue is drowned in an unleashed chaos of conflicting voices, idioms and styles. Like a bubble (or Mina's amniotic sac) that has actually burst and released a diluvian quantity of fluids, all (Victorian-related) restraints seem to have been lifted from the speakers' thoughts, words

---

[35] O'Donnell, *Echo Chambers*, 76.
[36] Brienza, 'Krapping Out', 125.
[37] O'Donnell, *Echo Chambers*, 76.

and fantasies, especially as the novel approaches midnight, the chaotic Walpurgis Night of the 'Circe' episode, where hallucinations, dreams and metamorphoses succeed each other rapidly and merge into a tumult of sexual anarchy.

As if to compensate for the restrictions that Joyce had imposed upon himself by limiting the delivery to offstage and to the sparse 'news of placentation' (*U*, 402), he has the riotous company at the National Maternity Hospital (among them Stephen Dedalus) frequently use comparisons and analogies from nature and thus deflect the reader's attention from their covertly salacious fantasies about the porousness of birth onto natural phenomena. The air into which they rush on their way to Burke's pub 'is impregnated with raindew moisture' (*U*, 402), but even before, the tense atmosphere in the antechamber is likened to the liminal and ominously quiet moments, when a storm is approaching and the pregnant clouds are about to burst, meaning sotto voce Mina Purefoy's womb:

> But as before the lightning the serried stormclouds, heavy with preponderant excess of moisture, in swollen masses turgidly distended, compass earth and sky in one vast slumber, impending above parched fields and drowsy oxen and blighted growth of shrub and verdure till in an instant a flash rives their centres and with reverberation of the thunder the cloudburst pours its torrent, so and not otherwise was the transformation, violent and instantaneous, upon the utterance of the Word. (*U*, 401)

The 'preponderant excess of moisture', the 'swollen masses' of clouds, as they seem to be hanging oppressively over the dry fields, and the 'torrent' of water neatly capture the situation in the delivery room, where Mina, shielded from the inquisitive eyes of both the readers and the boisterous 'wastrels' (*U*, 373), eventually discharges her uterine and genital fluids. The reference to 'the Word', which, in accordance with Dedalus's foray into theology, gives the passage an overt allusion to the (porous) birth of Christ and takes up the reference to the nativity scene with the shepherds and angels around the crib in Bethlehem, underlines the epiphanic impact of the birth process, but also the artist's labour (in a twofold sense) that, after months of gestation, explodes into a cascade of words. As early as in *A Portrait of the Artist as a Young Man* (1914–15), Stephen had become aware of 'a soft liquid joy', a kind of nocturnal emission that fertilized the 'virgin womb of his imagination'[38] (the result being a villanelle). One novel later, Joyce's motley crew of vociferous drinkers around Stephen, 'winefizzling ginfizzling booseguzzling existences' (*U*, 406), not only poke fun at Mina Purefoy's husband and his anti-Malthusian procreativity, they also, in an

---

[38] *A Portrait of the Artist as a Young Man*, 190 and 182. Cf. also Weir, 'A Womb of His Own', 218.

academic idiom of learned euphemism, continue to conflate religion, sexuality and artistic creativity in a daringly offensive manner. The clouds' preponderant fullness and their watery gravidness (to a certain degree, reminiscent of Keats's imagery of swollen and pregnant fruit) are recaptured in the image of Mina's udder-like and full-to-bursting breasts:

> It displodes for thee in abundance. Drink, man, an udderful! Mother's milk, Purefoy, the milk of human kin, milk too of those burgeoning stars overhead, rutilant in thin rainvapour, punch milk, such as those rioters will quaff in their guzzlingden, milk of madness, the honeymilk of Canaan's land. (*U*, 403)

Linking Mina's full breasts to animal udders superficially suggests a comparison to Molly's voluminous, but now milkless and self-sufficient breasts; but the speaker of this passage, ostensibly the inebriated Dedalus, still encumbered with his Victorian heritage, goes even further when he puts the everyday act of lactation, the 'displod[ing]' of both the female body and its full breasts, into the mock-heroic tradition of literary, mythological and biblical satire. Being unable to find proper words for Mina's porous delivery and lactating breasts, Dedalus conceals the tightness of his own Victorian volitional sphincter behind a badinage of erudite witticisms. Accordingly, Mina is not only metamorphosed into the parodic incarnation of jealous Hera, who by pulling her nipple out of Hercules's mouth inadvertently gave birth to the Milky Way ('those burgeoning stars overhead'), but she is, in Dedalus's temporarily disorderly mind, also the modern successor to the full-breasted Roman caritas nourishing her elderly, Dickensian 'Doady' ('fifty odd', *U*, 379). As such, she becomes the embodiment of 'the honeymilk of Canaan's land' and poses a juicy and porous Irish contrast not only to her husband, but also to the turn-of-the-century Palestinian country which Bloom had earlier visualized as the desiccated and withered 'sunken cunt of the world'.

The attendant theme of emasculation which runs through the entire novel finds its first peak when Theodore Purefoy is not only envisaged as an elderly man drinking an udderful of mother's milk and claiming kin with the breastfed men in the Cavalier poetry of Richard Lovelace; it is also referred to in the intertextual allusion to 'the milk of human kin', which conjures up Lady Macbeth's (and hence Mère Ubu's) denigration of her husband, who with his excessively uxorious 'milk of human kindness' failed to live up to her adopted masculinity, or, in Lawrence's terms, 'cock-sureness'. While looking for a new language for gynaecological processes beyond what Jarry suggested in his infantile vision of Mère Ubu's dismemberment and feeling stuck in a gibberish-like mixture of French and German, Joyce seems to be preparing his readers for the climactic fact that the Modernist idea of porous birth entails not only the thundering explosion of the female body, the appreciation of its oozing fecundity, but also the painful (re-)birth of a species that had already, in the context of the Baroque feminization of Christ, created heated controversies: the porous, 'pregnant' and penetrated man, shockingly deprived of all mind-forged manacles and Grundyist sphincters.

Porousness unleashed: Unsexing Bloom

While Lawrence saw his main task in the restoration of man's cock-sureness, in the (re-)birth of a phallus-proud man,[39] Joyce did not flinch from using his Modernist rewriting of Homer's *Odyssey* as a deconstruction of long-established ideals of masculinity. Leaving Theodore Purefoy, the 'old patriarch' (*U*, 403), in the abject position of a suckling infant (at least in the facetious minds of the brawlers), imbibing his wife's milk that is 'hot and sweet and fattening', Joyce sends his protagonists to the 'Bawdyhouse' (*U*, 406), a place of ordeal and deconstruction, where, instead of asserting their phallic power, they are made to undergo a thorough and painful redefinition of their gender roles. Joyce's letter of 13 March 1920 to Frank Budgen must certainly be taken with a pinch of salt, when Joyce defines Bloom's role in the 'Oxen in the Sun'-chapter in terms of a 'spermatozoon', the hospital as a womb, the nurses as the ovum and Stephen ultimately as the 'embryo'.[40] Yet what the radical reduction of Bloom to the status of a sperm cell or that of Stephen as an embryo implies is that both their sexes and their gender roles are, at that stage of the novel, in a blurry state of non-definition and that the complaint about the loss of heroes in the wake of Byron's *Don Juan* is now given a further dimension by the hero in *statu nascendi*, by his search for his porous sexual identity.

If the 'Oxen in the Sun'-chapter deals with the heroes' conception, with their re-conceptualization ab ovo, the subsequent 'Circe'-chapter launches them, after their painful gestation and the surrealist or Bosch-like moment of their birth, into an absurd and Ubuesque world. Burrowing their way through Joyce's library, critics have been eager to identify the origins of the hallucinatory mode in this episode and have convincingly shown that Joyce took inspiration from a

---

[39] See here and also later Ruderman's chapter 'Lawrence's Sexual Fallacies' in *D.H. Lawrence and the Devouring Mother*, 75ff.
[40] Gilbert, *Letters of James Joyce*, 139.

variety of multilingual works that deal with the fluidity and almost psychedelic transformations of the human character: Joyce was, thus, familiar with Goethe's *Faust* II (1832), Flaubert's *La tentation de Saint Antoine* (The Temptation of St Anthony, 1874), Hauptmann's *Hanneles Himmelfahrt* (Hannele's Ascension, 1893) and Strindberg's *Spöksonaten* (The Ghost Sonata, 1908). In the context of the radical paradigm shift from the traditional image of virile man to that of the porously feminine man of the early twentieth century, the 'Circe'-chapter is also heavily dependent on two books which, as early as in the second half of the nineteenth century, challenged the Victorian heritage of the petrified and phallocratic man, while relegating the idea of the emasculated and porous man to the realm of sexual kinkiness: Leopold von Sacher-Masoch's *Venus im Pelz* (Venus in Furs, 1870) and Krafft-Ebing's *Psychopathia Sexualis*, the compendium of subversive, non-reproductive forms of sexuality that had eluded Mrs Grundy's regime of surveillance.

That Joyce writes this episode in the dramatic mode of a (screen)play, with a surrealist proliferation of the dramatis personae including animated things and plants such as The Yews, The Pianola or The Gasjet, anticipates Antonin Artaud's pioneering Théâtre de la Cruauté, but is also reminiscent of the absurd cast in *Ubu Roi* which, next to the ominous Machine à Décerveler, lists a Bear, a Horse and a Coach among its characters. The episode also reveals that what is about to happen in and around the brothel is of a highly theatrical nature, a nightmarish spectacle or avant-gardist film noir in which Bloom is brutally unsexed and Dedalus eventually reborn as Bloom's son, the Homeric Ulysses's Telemachus. That the mélange of controversial books that contribute to what Henke (inappropriately) calls a 'Levitical holocaust'[41] is also augmented by Otto Weininger's writings, by a treatise so rabidly infused with anti-Semitism and misogyny, makes the entire chapter highly explosive.[42] In the widely read (and acclaimed) book *Geschlecht und Charakter* (Sex and Character, 1903), Weininger had written extensively on the lack of sexual differentiation in embryos and harangued on the new womanly man, whom he, himself of Jewish descent, interpreted as a detrimental effect of Jewishness, of the fact that Jews were 'more saturated with femininity' than Aryans.[43] It is in this extraordinary diatribe (running through twenty-six editions by 1925!) that Joyce is also familiarized with the prejudice that Jews are 'always more absorbed by sexual matters'

---

[41] Henke, 'Joyce's New Womanly Man', 50.
[42] See Ellmann, who maintains that Joyce's 'pet theory' that Jews were by nature womanly men was 'borrowed' from Weininger's *Sex and Character*. *James Joyce*, 463.
[43] Weininger, *Sex and Character*, 306.

than other ethnic groups,[44] a fact which might explain the choice of his Jewish protagonist with Masoch's first name as a city-roaming sex maniac. Although readers are informed that what they are witnessing is a 'midsummer madness', a 'ghastly joke' (*U*, 465), or a temporary carnival of Freudian dimensions which explores the hidden recesses of the human mind, the metamorphoses that the protagonists, and most of all the allegedly effeminized Jew, undergo are bewildering and shocking, all the more so, since the dream-like sequence of images never shows the demarcation line between reality and phantasmagoria.

As a prelude to the oncoming orgy of ooziness, the sparse stage directions mention a navvy who, as a quasi-dramatic one-man chorus, comments on the porousness of Bloom's odyssey into the darkest regions of his body by ejecting 'from the farther nostril a long liquid jet of snot' (*U*, 412); but the 'midsummer' surrealism is further underlined by the brothel's location and its proximity to the river, to an area that seems to be perforated by 'drains, clefts, cesspools, middens' (*U*, 412). It is these cavities that produce miasmatic fumes and, at least since the emergence of crudely misogynist poetry in early modern times, had served as the matrixes for the toxic swampiness of absorbing female genitals.

It is in this steamy and strangely porous atmosphere that, quite in the manner of the apparitions from the witches' cauldron in *Macbeth*, Bloom sees and interacts with a weird succession of people and objects, among them not only his wife Molly, Mrs Breen, the butcher Dlugacz and the dead Paddy Dignam, but also a hobgoblin, the cake of soap that he bought before the funeral, bells and a hollybush. In this preliminary dizzying and cruel whirl of images and metamorphoses, Bloom himself even becomes a cauldron when he is made to bear 'eight male yellow and white children' (*U*, 466). The more the readers are faced with this kaleidoscope of absurdities (which Martin Esslin labelled as one of the outstanding early examples of the Theatre of the Absurd),[45] the more they are at a loss to decide whether Bella Cohen, the 'massive whoremistress' (*U*, 494), is real or just another facet of Bloom's overwrought imagination. Clothed in a 'threequarter ivory gown', sweatingly porous ('I'm all of a mucksweat', *U*, 495) and flaunting a moustache, Bella Cohen is unnervingly liminal, a conglomeration of diverse roles in which Shakespeare's bearded Weird Sisters, mythological Circe and Wanda, the red-haired sadistic Venus in Sacher-Masoch's novel, are astonishingly conflated. In order to intensify her intimidating sexual monstrosity, certain parts and accessories of Bella's – the fan, her 'plump buskined hoof' (*U*,

---

[44] Ibid., 311.
[45] Esslin, *The Theatre of the Absurd*, 354.

497) – turn into agents and address Bloom in a coarsely colloquial idiom: 'If you bungle, Handy Andy, I'll kick your football for you' (*U*, 497). What is even more uncanny in this nocturnal Grand Guignol is that Bella's sex is liable to change and that she is suddenly transformed into the satyr-like Bello, who, as an 'imperious semitic circus master'[46] and with a petrifyingly 'hard basilisk stare' (*U*, 497), brings about Bloom's metamorphosis into the epitome of abjection, into the hybrid mixture of a grunting truffle pig and a female slave desperately waiting for her/its sexual subjugation: 'I promise never to disobey' (*U*, 498).

While brothel scenes in the wake of Cleland's *Fanny Hill* tend to stage men in the role of phallocentric aggressors, Joyce (almost in anticipation of Jean Genêt's 1956 play *The Balcony*) sets about the pioneering task of showing the bawdy house as a place of gender deconstruction, role playing, carnivalesque anarchy and the painful penetration of the hitherto sacrosanct male body. In the course of the sexual chaos in Bella/Bello Cohen's brothel, Bloom is degraded, insulted, revealed as a coprophile ('Dungdevourer!' *U*, 498), infantilized as a pet ('ducky dear', *U*, 499), and ultimately exposed to the threat of becoming victimized in a luscious cannibalistic bacchanal ('slaughtered and skewered', *U*, 499). But this trajectory of degradation is not complete until Bloom is finally turned into a 'cockhorse', transformed into and dressed up as a Victorian whore:

> BELLO (points to his whores): As they are now, so will you be, wigged, singed, perfumesprayed, ricepowdered, with smoothshaven armpits. […]. You will be laced with cruel force into vicelike corsets of soft dove coutille, with whalebone busk, to the diamond trimmed pelvis, the absolute outside edge, while your figure, plumper than when at large, will be restrained in nettight frocks, pretty two ounce petticoats and fringes and things stamped, of course, with my houseflag. (*U*, 502)

Although associated with prostitutes here, the oxymoronic 'vicelike corsets of soft dove coutille' and the relentless 'whalebone busk' stand for a relapse into Victorian discipline and Grundyist rigour, which also proved to be stimulants for adherents of sadomasochistic sex. It is ironically in this disguise of Victorian self-containedness that Bloom, now turned into a Modernist drag queen, tries to get rid of the last remnants of the Victorian trauma of the volitional sphincter. As if taking the cue of his Circean taskmaster who (as a farcical parody of Tilla Durieux's famous impersonation of Circe as a femme fatale)[47] had, in the middle

---

[46] Henke, 'Joyce's New Womanly Man', 50.
[47] Durieux played Circe in 1912 and inspired the German painter Franz von Stuck to paint her in this role as a seductress.

of the cockhorse ride, 'uncorke[d] himself' and farted loudly (*U*, 501), Bloom confesses to wetting himself and to soiling the lingerie which he had, since the days as an actor of a female role in a High School play, enjoyed wearing. Bloom is immediately reprimanded for this 'insubordination' (*U*, 503) and, in what seems to be a modern Freudian revival of the medieval morality play, finds not so much the Seven Deadly Sins as his own Sins of the Past rising against him and denouncing his kinkiness and perversity.

This mechanism of confession and punishment seems to be, as Joseph A. Boone argues, echoed by Joyce's obstinate wish to exercise his textual authority over the 'proclamations of polymorphous fluidity'.[48] The long and accurate stage directions which are narrative intrusions into the text are felt by Boone to be expressions of 'extreme authorial exhibitionism' and amount to what he calls 'acts of masturbatory display.'[49] Before the text culminates in Joyce's 'own textual-narratological orgasm',[50] Bloom (clearly still in Victorian female garb) is subjected to a severe ritual of perforation and porousness which ambivalently oscillates between lust and torment. While Bloom is at first prevailed upon to wash the whores' underclothes, to become absorbed in their menstrual secretions and to clean their latrines with his 'dress pinned up and a dishclout tied to [his] tail' (*U*, 504), he is, in Bella's/Bello's subsequent speech, further debased and transformed into an abject leaky vessel, forced to imbibe the prostitutes' and the Seven Sins' urine: 'Ay, rinse the seven [pisspots] of them well, mind, or lap it up like champagne. Drink me piping hot' (*U*, 505). While this speech ends on an overtly pornographic note and shows Bloom being ultimately brutally penetrated, 'elbowdeep', in what is his most feminine attribute, 'Bloom's vulva' (*U*, 505), it also shows emphatically that, in Bloom's and Stephen Dedalus's 'quest on toward their common Grail',[51] Bloom has finally attained his transmutation into a female bowl, into a vaginal receptacle which recaptures the various cup-like or grail-like objects in the novel that at least since Eliot's sexualized mythology in *The Waste Land* had been waiting to be filled and reunified with their phallic lances.[52] This act of transformation and transsexualization was not only unprecedented in literary history, it was also an assault on other Modernists (among them Joyce's brother Stanislaus who defined the 'Circe'-chapter as 'the last inspection of the stinkpots'[53])

---

[48] Boone, 'Representing Interiority', 75.
[49] Ibid.
[50] Ibid., 76.
[51] Froula, *Modernism's Body*, 136.
[52] For Eliot's indebtedness to Weston's *From Ritual to Romance*, see *Collected Poems*, 80.
[53] Letter from Stanislaus Joyce to James Joyce, 26 February 1922. Ellmann, *Letters of James Joyce*, 3:58.

who saw their priority not so much in the unleashing of men's porosity as in the restoration of the male sex's lost phallic confidence. In this context, Stephen's ventriloquizing of the female character Gerty also emphasizes the scandalous porous femaleness is the ultimate goal that Joyce's one-day *Bildungsroman* (with its progress from the spermatzoon to the newly born baby) aspires to.

A crescendo of chaotic voices, figures and apparitions finally explodes into a Black Mass which is clearly indebted to one of the most indecent books that made up the stock of Joyce's early library of about 1900, Joris-Karl Huysmans's occultist novel *Là-bas* (Down There, 1891).[54] But in contrast to Huysmans who stages the satanic desecration of the Host in his novel just for the sake of sacrilege, Joyce uses the Black Mass as another formative, or even maieutic stage that helps Bloom 'to body forth the repressed woman within himself'.[55] While men in the wake of Laertes did everything to exorcize the porous woman out of their bodies, Bloom – '*weep[ing] tearlessly*' (*U*, 509) – runs the whole gamut of emasculation in Nighttown finally to emerge as the infantile and beastly Jewish mother/whore Ruby Cohen.[56] The reappearance of Mina Purefoy on the altar stone of the Black Mass, still in the bubble-like state of pre-confinement, 'naked, fettered, a chalice resting on her swollen belly' (*U*, 556), not only reiterates the vaginal symbolism of cups and bowls, it is also the dark foreshadowing of Bloom's absurd confinement of a son, a surreal conflation of Rudy and Stephen, with Stephen lying in a strikingly embryonic position ('*doubling himself together*', *U*, 564) on the pavement, still overpowered by the lascivious witches' sabbath and its blasphemously palindromic replacement of God with the sacrilegious idea of a porous and urinating dog. It is dogs in their canine porosity and preoccupation with urine that seem to run through the novel as a leitmotif: watching two copulating dogs inspired Molly and Bloom to have sex and to engender their son Rudy; and while 'dog-biscuits' were the obolus to the nether world of the cemetery, the entire novel seems to gravitate towards Molly's oracular monologue, delivered in the role of the 'dearest Doggerina' (*U*, 706). While Michael H. Begnal refers to and summarizes the massive problems that critics have had with Hester Stanhope's epistolary salutation to Molly,[57]

---

[54] Ellmann, *James Joyce*, 75. Joyce became increasingly impatient with Huysmans' formlessness and his tendency to turn his books into something 'more obviously comedian'.
[55] Froula, *Modernism's Body*, 145.
[56] See here, Harrison, 'Bloodsucking Bloom', 789.
[57] Begnal, 'Molly Bloom and Lady Hester Stanhope', 71.

there is no denying that Molly and her straying husband stand for the ooziness of a doggish and bestial life.[58]

The extent to which father and son, Bloom and Stephen as his Telemachus, converge in the post-'Circe' chapters and recognize each other in Joyce's redefinition of an *anagnorisis* is open to debate. While Froula argues that, by sharing a cocoa refined by the 'viscous cream' ordinarily reserved for Molly's breakfast, they relish Molly's 'maternal cream' in a parody of the Eucharist and thus 'incorporate Molly as fetishized female body',[59] father and son are conspicuously apart in their attitude towards the most female of elements, water. In accordance with his fascination for all sorts of fluids, Bloom feels attracted by water and is a 'waterlover' (*U*, 624), which, as Don Gifford suggests, might also be an indication of the fact that he is an Aquarius.[60] Written in the sober style of a scientific questionnaire, the 'Ithaca'-text even becomes exuberant and overflowing when it characterizes Bloom's admiration for water and porosity. Thus, Bloom is not only enraptured by the various manifestations of water – 'torrents, eddies, freshets, spates, groundswells, watersheds, waterpartings, geysers, cataracts, whirlpools, maelstroms, inundations, deluges, cloudbursts' (*U*, 625) – he is also impressed by 'its persevering penetrativeness' (*U*, 625) and by the irrefutable fact that, in its ubiquity, it constitutes '90% of the human body' (*U*, 625) – a fact that neither impressed the Romantics nor affected the Victorians in their concept of the (male) body as a stony and solidified object.

Designated as a 'hydrophobe' (*U*, 625), Stephen still retains a retentive Victorian substratum in his character that makes him hate 'partial contact by immersion or total by submersion in cold water' (*U*, 625). Stephen's aversion to all sorts of 'aqueous substances', to 'aquacities of thought and language' (*U*, 626), is an impediment not only to his quest for new parental adoption (in particular, since both Leopold and Molly Bloom epitomize modernism's 'aquacities of thought and language' in their unbridled streams of consciousness), but also to his attitude towards his own physiological porousness. While Brienza interprets the moments antecedent to the vision of a drowned man's body by the end of the 'Proteus'-chapter, the tidal pools gathering off Sandymount – in 'long lassoes from the Cock lake the water flowed full [...]' (*U*, 49) – as an 'act of micturating', as Stephen's poetic reinvention of his penis as 'a lake holding water',[61] the passage

---

[58] Boone calling Molly's stream of consciousness 'a self-contained monologue' is here misleading. 'Staging Sexuality', 192.
[59] Froula, *Modernism's Body*, 160–61.
[60] Gifford, *Ulysses Annotated*, 569.
[61] Brienza, 'Krapping Out', 120 and 121.

can also be read as an onomatopoeic and almost Dadaist evocation of the sucking and nullifying effects of the life-erasing water, 'a fourworded wavespeech: seesoo, hrss, rsseeiss ooos' (*U*, 49). Reservations about Brienza's (otherwise compelling) reading of the text are also justified on account of the disgust that both the water and the corpse arouse in Stephen. Faced with the '[b]ag of corpsegas sopping in foul brine', with the fish that flit through 'the slits of [the dead man's] buttoned trouserfly' (*U*, 49), Stephen gives a lyrical, but also emphatic expression to his detestation of the watery element and dismisses his own abject existence as nothing more than an abhorrent rehash of dead, porous and excretory matter.

In the light of Stephen's view of life as a 'urinous offal' and his dislike of 'aquacities' of all sorts (opining that aquacity is incompatible with 'the erratic originality of genius', *U*, 626), the act of Bloom's and Stephen's joint urination in the 'Ithaca'-chapter resonates with ambivalence.[62] Both urinate in darkness, 'in penumbra', standing close to each other, but shielding their penises from each other's sight with their hands. While there is no gainsaying that, for Joyce, 'micturition' is associated with poetic creativity, the language is as remote from carnivalesque hilarity as it can possibly be and rather echoes the shameful uneasiness which post-Victorians, the 'gelded third and fourth generation',[63] must have acutely felt at such moments of intense male bonding. Placing this episode as a coda to the glaring theatre of cruelty and sexual anarchy in Bella's Circean arena, Joyce not only parodies the sentimental tradition of joint Niobean weeping, of forging erotic chains of tears, but also pinpoints the striking incompatibility of the two protagonists. Thus, it is consistent that the 'trajectories of their, first sequent, then simultaneous, urinations' (*U*, 655) are divergent and that Bloom and Stephen have irreconcilably different attitudes towards their organs of porosity (both of which turn out to be alarmingly dysfunctional): while Bloom had already contemplated his penis in terms of a blossoming (and feminized) flower (punning on 'flow-er'),[64] by the end of his tiresome odyssey through Dublin, after the emasculating and excruciating 'Circe'-ordeal, he cannot help facing his genital limitations, the persistent 'problems of irritability, tumescence, rigidity [...]' (*U*, 655), which, as a disappointing finale, culminate in the abortive fact of an 'approximate erection' at the sight of sleeping Molly's 'plump mellow yellow smellow melons of her rump' (*U*, 686).

Stephen, by contrast, is unable to see his penis detached from religious controversies and is immediately induced to raise seventeenth-century questions

---

[62] See also, Lavers, 'Poetry and Urination in *Ulysses*', 297–306.
[63] Lawrence, 'The Deadly Victorians', 7. *Complete Poems*, 521.
[64] Brienza, 'Krapping Out', 121.

on Christ's circumcision and the problem of the 'divine prepuce' (*U*, 656). The chain of scholastic issues that the act of shamefaced urination triggers in Stephen's mind proves that both generations and both creeds are still, to a certain degree, encumbered with the leaden Victorian heritage of anti-corporeality. If one additionally takes into account that, in Joyce's novel, uninhibited carnivalesque porousness is restricted to secluded and heterotopian places such as the toilet, the public bath, the cemetery or Bella Cohen's Nighttown brothel, one cannot help feeling that the long censorious shadow of the Victorians is still present. While at the end of a similarly riotous night and wild tour d'horizon of his repressed monstrous desires, the Oxford student in Wilde's poem 'The Sphinx' still seizes the chance to cling to his time-worn crucifix and its 'pallid burden' of Christ's weeping body,[65] Joyce ends Bloom's narrative on a note of religious loss, sexual impotence and miscarriage: Stephen, the son conceived and born under tormenting pain in Bella's torture chamber, leaves the story as the 'centrifugal departer' and Bloom, the 'centripetal remainer' (*U*, 656), now himself in the role of an infant, nestles up to Molly's sensual bulk of female body, guiltily conscious of his deficiencies as a husband, owing to 'a period of 10 years, 5 months and 18 days [...] without ejaculation of semen within the natural female organ' (*U*, 687). With Molly having the last – albeit mentally porous and chaotic – say in the novel, Joyce underlines the cogency of his argument that the old world of the Victorian paterfamilias has been successfully eclipsed by pervasive gynomorphic structures, laws and a visible semiotics of female porousness.

Re-enter Mrs Grundy: Lawrence's rekindled puritanism

Misogynist wrath

Subscribing to the same project of demolishing the outdated Victorian concepts of the body and of releasing its dormant carnivalesque potential, Joyce and Lawrence struggled with the same encumbrances under the weight of Mrs Grundy's heritage. Although supporters of the same cause, both writers were astonishingly reticent about each other's literary achievements. While Joyce hardly deigns to take notice of Lawrence, just condensing his disapproval of the latter's work into one abrasive French sentence 'Cet homme écrit vraiment

---

[65] Wilde, 'The Sphinx', 173. *Complete Poetry*, 151.

très mal',⁶⁶ Lawrence is repelled by the crude materialism and sexual perversion of various chapters in *Ulysses*. To express his displeasure at Joyce's catch-all novel, Lawrence even reverts to the term of 'a stupid *olla podrida*' and thus interestingly links the kaleidoscopic range of Joyce's text, the 'stewed-up fragments of quotation in the sauce of a would-be-dirty mind,'⁶⁷ with Byron's *Don Juan*, where the image of the literary stew originated and the leitmotif of bodily porosity came to be reflected in the porous and corrosive structure of the meandering poem.

Apart from its numerous vulgar ingredients and 'sloppy English',⁶⁸ Lawrence must have been exasperated by Joyce's delight in transexualizing his protagonists and about his joy in giving an exuberant depiction of Bloom's (real or imagined) initiation into the porousness of a female body. The discovery (and brutal penetration) of Bloom's vulva in the surreal Walpurgis Night of Bella Cohen's brothel is as incompatible with Lawrence's plea for man's restoration to cocksureness as the derisive image of Theodore Purefoy being suckled at his wife's oozing breasts in the 'Oxen in the Sun'-chapter. While in his famous essay 'Pornography and Obscenity' Lawrence vociferously argues for the end of censorship of allegedly obscene and pornographic words and objects to the continuation of the Victorians' rigorous policy of castrating and cleansing their body politic, he betrays a striking squeamishness when pornography becomes self-sufficient or – as in Bloom's case – runs counter to traditional ideas of gender. Still trying to evade the long shadow of Grundyism and feeling paralysed by the 'excruciating torment of hopelessness, helplessness, listnessness',⁶⁹ Lawrence finds himself involved in the exhausting dilemma which, on the one hand, induces him to free the English language of the Victorian clutter of euphemism, but, on the other, to denounce pornography as a disease of the body politic, as a 'hidden sore or inflammation'.⁷⁰ If one considers the additional fact that Lawrence's wife, Frieda von Richthofen, paradoxically calls the succès de scandale *Lady Chatterley's Lover* (1928) 'the last word in Puritanism',⁷¹ there is some justification in assuming that in Lawrence's work sexual provocation is peculiarly linked to a new, revivified Grundyism and that, beneath the sparse

---

⁶⁶ Ellmann, *James Joyce*, 615.
⁶⁷ Letter to Earl Brewster, [15 August 1928]. *Letters*, 6:507.
⁶⁸ Quoted in Bowen, '*Lady Chatterley's Lover* and *Ulysses*', 11.
⁶⁹ 'The Deadly Victorians', 4.
⁷⁰ 'Pornography and Obscenity'. *Late Essays and Articles*, 40.
⁷¹ Quoted in Williams, *Sex in the Head*, 105. Ladenson even refers to Lawrence's 'idiosyncratically reactionary bent' that, in the words of Anthony Burgess, would have made him shudder at the fact that 'he had become a prophet of the so-called sexual revolution'. *Dirt for Art's Sake*, 132.

language of genital frankness, there are hidden and calcified layers of self-banned eroticism. While, in this context, Anthony Burgess flippantly dubs Lawrence a prim *noli me tangerine*,[72] Linda Ruth Williams goes so far as to assert that *Lady Chatterley's Lover*, Lawrence's most notorious and emphatic plea for female porosity, is 'a gateway text',[73] key to the author's repressed homosexuality and, as such, an interesting testimonial to the way a discourse of (partially) overt sexuality can paradoxically be allied to a sudden resurfacing of astringent puritanism.

While Joyce is Rabelaisian in his almost infantile delight in flinging abdominal matter at the Victorians and in provocatively offering to supplant their Evangelical dryness with a zesty and juicy Byronic *olla podrida*, Lawrence more often than not assumes the role of a preacher[74] and of a therapist, so radically out of tune with the nonchalant attitude of Joyce, the Parisian man of letters and enfant terrible. Highly prolific in various genres and disciplines (and as the painter of a urinating man at his most Joycean),[75] Lawrence instrumentalizes his texts as vehicles of a protracted *j'accuse*, of a harangue that allows the speaker to give vent to his pent-up fury; the lines of his poems are thus unrhymed linguistic bullets shot against the smooth and anti-porous facades of the post-Victorians, meant to jostle them out of their complacency. Although himself a regular contributor to Edward Marsh's collections of Georgian Poetry, poems such as 'Medlars and Sorb-Apples' (1923) hardly fit into the Georgians' neo-Romantic concept. The poem shows its speaker temporarily wallowing in the '[d]elicious rottenness' of the fruit, in the '[a]utumnal excrementa'[76] of their pulp. But while Joyce wields his Ubuesque toilet brush with the relish of an obstreperous child, Lawrence can scarcely conceal a jarring tone of misogynist disgust, in particular when the reader becomes aware of the oblique intertextual reference to *Romeo and Juliet*, where Mercutio expands on the morbid lusciousness of the medlar and its resemblance to the foul female genitals, or to what Renaissance girls apparently used to call an 'open-arse'.[77]

Following Williams's intriguing assumption that Lawrence is a 'closet queen', hiding his same-sex desires either behind images of women as fragile, flowery

---

[72] Burgess, *Flame into Being*, 63.
[73] Williams, *Sex in the Head*, 107.
[74] Mehl and Jansohn, 'The Reception of D.H. Lawrence in German-Speaking Countries 1922–1945', 50.
[75] Cf. *Dandelions*, or *Le pisseur* (as its original title), see also Ellis, *D.H. Lawrence: Dying Game*, 409–10.
[76] 'Medlars and Sorb-Apples', 2 and 17. *Complete Poems*, 220. See also the poem on the female 'Figs' that are eaten in the 'vulgar way', by 'put[ting] your mouth to the crack', 7–8. *Complete Poems*, 93.
[77] *RJ* 2.1.38.

Baudelairean *charognes* or a quasi-heterosexual veneration for women's puerile posteriors, for 'button-arsed lasses',[78] one is scarcely surprised to see that sexes and genders in Lawrence's works hardly tally. Fuelled by a good quantity of Strindbergian truisms, most of his novels aim to show that the sexes are locked in battles which are fiercely waged between representatives of porous sensuality and those of puritan self-containedness. This dualism cutting across sexes, genders and classes is a late consequence of the Arnoldian polarity between Hebraism and Hellenism, and as such, part of the complex Victorian heritage that Lawrence was struggling with. This strife, this dichotomy and oxymoronic feeling are best illustrated by novels from the beginning and the end of Lawrence's short period of productivity: *Sons and Lovers* (1913), an early spin-off of Zola's grim Naturalism and *Lady Chatterley's Lover* (1928), his last and most scandalous novel which in its final version is the result of a conspicuously long process of rewritings and various stages of self-censorship.

Translating the spirit of Zola's dark novel *Germinal* (1885) into England, *Sons and Lovers* is set in a mining village in Nottinghamshire where Lawrence was born and grew up. Right from its beginning, it conjures up the dismal atmosphere of modern industrialized hell: workers live in 'Hell Row' (*SL*, 5), they suffer from the claustrophobic feeling of being 'buried alive' (*SL*, 10), when, in drunken torpor, they trudge along paths that are troped as 'trough[s] of darkness' (*SL*, 10). While hell in the shape of the infernal Dublin cemetery seems to be a place of morbid and necrophilic sensuality in Joyce's 'Hades'-episode, with death as a carnivalesque and porous interlude in the everlasting cycle of human porosity, Lawrence's hell is of an Evangelical austerity, inhabited by people who not only emulate the Apostle Paul and, like him, flaunt an ignorance of all 'sensuous pleasure', but most of all concur in being inveterate 'puritan[s]' (*SL*, 15). Raised in this atmosphere, Gertrude, Paul Morel's mother, is the epitome of sternness, 'contemptuous of dancing' (*SL*, 15) and suspicious of everything that might catch her off guard and in a state of uncontrollable porousness. Thus, it is consistent that, in this world of pits, mines and a puritan work ethic, both her body and soul have 'crystallized out hard as rock' (*SL*, 18) and assumed a degree of petrification and edgy hardness which Lawrence's narratives dwell so much on. The birth of her son Paul is only hinted at – 'he came on quickly' (*SL*, 19) – and, in accordance with Victorian standards, dealt with as an incident which has to be duly concealed from the reader's prurient eyes. The contrast to Mina Purefoy's confinement in *Ulysses* could not be greater, although even Joyce seems to have

---

[78] Williams, *Sex in the Head*, 108.

had second thoughts about it and shielded the porosity of birth behind a screen of erudite and (pseudo-) scientific language.

In Lawrence's 'pandemonium' (*SL*, 43) where temporary obstetric openness is immediately eclipsed by persistent hardness and hatred, porousness is only mentioned as a consequence of transgression and violence. When Gertrude's husband Walter, inarticulate with rage, flings a drawer at his wife and inflicts a gaping wound on her, the facade of her strict self-composure is momentarily broken and her left brow is shown 'bleeding rather profusely' (*SL*, 48). What this Strindbergian view of matrimonial hell seems to convey is that the tyranny of the Victorian volitional sphincter can only be slackened by irrational violence. The intricate image of Gertrude in her Niobean stoniness, 'cold and impassive as stone, with her mouth shut tight' (*SL*, 49) and so different from her namesake Gertrude's Niobean tearfulness in *Hamlet*, dripping blood on the head of her newborn is full of symbolism and clearly insinuates that there is more than just a blood relationship between mother and child. The drops of blood not only fall from the wound into the child's downy hair; they are almost soaked into the baby's scalp, making it visibly clear that the mother's painful bloody ooziness penetrates into the child's absorbent skin and strengthens a bond that conflates Niobean grief with Oedipal desire. In this respect, the tragic loss of her eldest son, William, does not elicit Niobean tears, but triggers the wish to take possession of her younger son, to merge with his body and to drain his life sap almost like a parasite or maternal vampire: 'The two knitted together in perfect intimacy. Mrs Morel's life now rooted itself in Paul' (*SL*, 162).

Before the backdrop of this exclusive mother-son relationship, the advent of Miriam is seen in terms of an intrusion, of a threat that is about to disrupt Paul's and his mother's symbiotic existence. Given the fact that post-Victorian depictions of women tend to be hyperbolic and extremist, and that Joyce prefers to portray women in *Ulysses* as being disconcertingly porous, libidinous and dangerously on a par with milk-producing cattle, Lawrence is haunted by the extreme opposite, by two types of women who, in their perverse cocksureness, are either despotic, fanatical, unimpregnable ('flat-chested, crop-headed, chemicalised women, of indeterminate sex'), or belong to the category of harpies, endowed with maiming vaginal teeth or beaks.[79] Miriam, in Lawrence's floral imagery, one of the post-Victorian 'chill Lent lilies',[80] is a

---

[79] Cowan cites Ursula Brangwen in *Women in Love* and Bertha Coutts, Mellors's former wife in *Lady Chatterley's Lover*, as typically Lawrentian women with beak-like *vaginae dentatae*. *D.H. Lawrence: Self and Sexuality*, 86–87.

[80] 'Craving for Spring', 14. *Complete Poems*, 214–17.

complex character: deeply imbued with a Wordsworthian stony Romanticism and with a penchant for Scott's novels, on the one hand, she is, on the other, one of the religious fanatics who 'treasure religion inside them' (*SL*, 165) and who see themselves as self-contained vessels or sealed treasure troves which no one is entitled to open. The additional fact that Miriam enjoys reading *Macbeth* intriguingly accounts for Miriam's hatred of her femininity, for her eager desire to be 'unsexed' and for her fierce wish 'that she were a man' (*SL*, 178). Despite her fantasies of a transsexualized body, Miriam paradoxically hates the male sex and, to Paul's dissatisfaction, tries hard to scorn him. Locked in this dead-end situation of a stark hatred of men and unlimited self-loathing, living in a world in which literature and religion fuel the disapproval of the genital openness of her body, Miriam tragically (and more than Sue Bridehead before her) incorporates the lingering dualism of the Victorian age: with her body squeezed into a high-collared blouse 'with a tiny ruff', she manages to destroy the impression that she has developed into a 'full-breasted and luxuriously formed' (*SL*, 247) young woman.

With Hebraism and Hellenism so unevenly balanced in her body, it is barely surprising that her face has assumed the paradoxical appearance of a 'soft rich mask' (*SL*, 247): the unusual softness of the mask seems to insinuate that Miriam is stuck in a double-bind condition, where pliancy and rigidity, fertile porousness (breasts) and anti-sexuality (collar/ruff), or femininity and masculinity are still painfully in abeyance. The entire novel resonates with the antithetical mixture of Miriam's character and, in glaring contrast to Joyce's women, shows the unflinching grip that Mrs Grundy still had on Lawrence and his characters. Accordingly, we find Miriam walking 'in her proud humility' (*SL*, 171) and learn that her body lacks the flexibility and 'looseness' (*SL*, 178) which Joyce's animalized Molly has as a prerequisite for her unbridled physiological and linguistic porousness. Instead, '[e]verything was gripped stiff with intensity' and Miriam's effort 'overcharged, closed in on itself' (*SL*, 178). It is these few words which neatly encapsulate Lawrence's difficulties in coming to terms with corporeality, porousness and femininity, revealing Miriam as a true descendant of Lady Dedlock's, like her lifelessly stuck in the amber of convention and hopelessly out of touch with modernist *provocateuses* such as Clara Dawes in the novel or Nancy Cunard and Edith Sitwell in reality.

It is a sign of the oppressiveness of post-Victorian puritanism that, when Paul terminates his relationship with Miriam (meanwhile having had his body transformed into 'one weapon, firm and hard against her', *SL*, 249), there is no sense of freedom that he can enjoy. Feeling likewise caged, crippled and stiflingly sealed up by his own virginity, he continues to suffer from the ideological beliefs that the Victorians had cherished and transmitted to him in the shape of the angelic woman, Miriam (the Hebraist version of Mary), the immaculate woman who 'had no body, only a voice and a dim face' (*SL*, 321) and who eventually self-effacingly awaits sex as an 'immolation' (*SL*, 328). Finding no sustenance in a subversively Hellenist spell with the married Clara (who programmatically wears no stays) and falling back on the old Oedipal ties which connect him to his mother, he suddenly learns that the smooth and impenetrable facade of his mother's body has become severely disfigured by 'a bit of a tumour' (*SL*, 417).

The cancerous 'lump' perverts and thwarts all expectations of catharsis, since it not only stands for blockage, but also malignantly erodes the Victorian body from within and, not unlike consumption in the nineteenth and early twentieth centuries, makes it mortally porous and crumbling. Katherine Byrne stresses the fact that, in nineteenth-century literature, there is a strong tendency to feminize diseases and thus, to Lawrence's later dismay, to link consumption to women's main causes of leakiness, menstruation and breastfeeding.[81] Although such an overtly feminized view of cancer did not exist, there was, however, no doubt that cancerous tumours were conducive to the body's porousness and instrumental in insidiously undermining the ideal of Victorian self-containedness. With reference to Emily Gosse's story of suffering from breast cancer, Judith Flanders quotes a longish passage in which not only the eruptive power of the 'malignant lump in the breast' is described, but its leakiness is also more than graphically rendered: 'exuding the stench of foul fluid that oozed constantly from its ever-widening circumference'.[82]

In Lawrence's novel, the grim hope that it is ultimately the disease's power that might shatter the mythical facade of Victorian femininity is sorely disappointed when Gertrude reacts to the disease with an unparalleled rigidity that ironically links her with her most inveterate adversary, Miriam: 'that hard, utterly lonely and stubborn clenching of her mouth, which persisted for weeks' (*SL*, 435). The end of Lawrence's dark Oedipal novel strikingly reverses the Niobean situation: in the manner of stern Zolaesque Naturalism, Paul and his sister Annie feed the dying mother with a cocktail of hot milk and an overdose of morphine pills; but while death finally restores Gertrude's facade of youth and maiden

---

[81] Byrne, *Tuberculosis*, 31.
[82] Flanders, *Victorian House*, 311. The (female) leakiness of diseases is also foregrounded in Zola's novel *Nana* where the men's world of progressive belligerence is contrasted with Nana's fin-de-siècle body disintegrating into an amorphous mass of suppurating pustules. In a letter to Catherine Carswell, 23 November 1916, Lawrence expressly orders Zola's *Nana* to be sent to him.

immaculateness, it is her offspring that, with uncontrollable fits of weeping, by 'tear-drops falling on the pavement' (*SL*, 435) deconstruct the masks and edifices of the Victorian age which, with the First World War and chaos looming large,[83] was finally limping to its end.

Paul's mercilessly unsentimental education (with the name Morel bringing back memories of Flaubert's Frédéric Moreau) ends on an ambivalent note in which bleak pessimism blends with stubborn confidence: crushed and annihilated by two female emissaries from the Victorian age, eclipsed by Miriam's 'anguished sweetness of self-sacrifice' (*SL*, 471), Paul's existence dwindles to the insignificant presence of a 'tiny upright speck of flesh', a tiny 'spark' (*SL*, 473) that is on the point of being extinguished by walls of excruciating silence. This image not only captures the smothering, emasculating atmosphere which the Victorians bequeathed to the twentieth century; it also nullifies the hope that the Modernists are able to shake off the ballast of Victorian taboos. Whimpering 'mother! [...] mother!' (*SL*, 473), Paul eventually decides to turn his back on the claustrophobic darkness of his town, on the misogynist hell of his milieu and to bend his steps in the direction of what is idealized as 'the city's gold phosphorescence' (*SL*, 474). But since Paul's fists are shut and 'his mouth set fast' (*SL*, 474), one cannot forget the impression that Paul's Modernist pilgrim's progress towards his 'glowing town' of liberation, towards the acceptance of a free, porous and disemburdened sexuality might turn out to be an adventurous journey, with many traps and perilous sloughs of despair lurking ahead.

Therapeutic porosity in *Lady Chatterley's Lover*

It is highly speculative whether the Heavenly Jerusalem of Paul's pilgrimage is finally reached at the end of *Lady Chatterley's Lover*, but the (blasphemous) reference to the 'pentecost flame' which Constance and Oliver Mellors 'fucked [...] into being' (*LCL*, 301) seems to suggest that the dense cloud of Victorian puritanism had been dispelled, making the nineteenth-century strategies of policing, covering and 'gelding' the bodies less forceful and despotic. Set in the same northern region as *Sons and Lovers*, but with Wragby jealously guarded from the Morels' mining village, the novel is chronologically situated in the years after the First World War, a period identified by Lawrence's narrator as a 'tragic age' (*LCL*, 5) and conspicuously remote from what came to be known as the

---

[83] In this respect, Theweleit intriguingly connects the horrors of the front with the slackening of the sphincter. *Male Fantasies*, 396–97.

frivolous roaring twenties with their 'silly generation'.[84] As in his early novels, but now even more emphatically, Lawrence structures his text using a pattern of contrasts and dichotomies: Married to Sir Clifford, Constance is permitted to enjoy a one-month honeymoon period (about which Lawrence is tellingly silent), before her husband returns from the battlefields in Flanders, 'with the lower half of his body, from the hips down, paralysed for ever' (*LCL*, 5). Paralysis, which Joyce diagnoses as the disease of his Irish compatriots in the *Dubliners* (1914), is here synonymous with the stagnation and strait-lacedness that the descendants of the Victorian age were afflicted with. Not only (like Paul) a 'spiritual cripple' (*SL*, 318), but also a bodily, psychological and sexual fragment, Sir Clifford is one of the chipped pillars of post-war society, the failed 'soldier-male dam',[85] who stands in marked contrast to his twenty-year-old wife, a completely new kind of New Woman. No longer anaemic, aloof and endowed with a diffuse intellectualism (as the 'old' new women of Sue Bridehead's or Miriam's calibre were supposed to be), Constance not only has a 'ruddy' complexion, but also a 'sturdy body' in which a lot of 'unused energy' (*LCL*, 6) seems to lie dormant.

While the traditional antagonism between the sexes was beguilingly captured by Virginia Woolf in the image used in the novel *To the Lighthouse* (1927) of Mrs. Ramsay as a sponge 'sopped full of human emotions' and her husband as a creature related to things that are hard, metallic and lacerating – 'the beak of brass, the acid scimitar of the male'[86] – Lawrence's novel is propelled by the wish to show that these gender dichotomies have become obsolete or that they are in dire need of reconsideration. The aristocratic manor house Wragby – 'a warren of a place without much distinction' (*LCL*, 13) – is still the objective correlative of the leaden stagnation and stifling claustrophobia that the twentieth century inherited from the Victorians. '[T]he stench of this sulphureous combustion of the earth's excrement' (*LCL*, 13), which so annoyingly fills the house, strengthens Constance's impression of living in an infernal outpost. Apart from the furnaces nearby emitting soot 'like black manna from the skies of doom' (*LCL*, 13), the hell of Wragby is particularly marked by its Victorian lack of physicality, by the absence of porosity and the pervading feeling of existing 'in the void' (*LCL*, 18). While the hellish mining town in *Sons and Lovers* was an impasse without the possibility of a refuge, there is, in *Lady Chatterley*'s dualistic world, a wood, a

---

[84] Wilson, *After the Victorian Age*, 230–41. As an example of the levity of the 1920s, Wilson refers to Noël Coward's *This Year of Grace* (1928) and its 'migraine of a song': 'Dance, dance, dance, little lady' (230).
[85] Theweleit, *Male Fantasies*, 266.
[86] *To the Lighthouse*, 45 and 53.

'sanctuary' (*LCL*, 20), where Constance is able to cope with the restlessness and pressure that affects her not only psychologically, but most of all physiologically 'in her womb' (*LCL*, 20).

The wood as a heterotopian place of anarchy and freedom is a symbol that has a long tradition and is best deployed by Shakespeare in *As You Like It*. In the forest of Arden, people not only assume different roles and identities, they are also ready to sympathize with creatures that are evidently not ashamed to give vent to their inner pressures and become the exemplars of a cathartic and healthy porousness. The 'poor sequestered stag' in Act II is a good case in point: its sartorial attributes such as 'his leathern coat' or its 'velvet' skin make it clear that the wounded deer stands for the courtier who has temporarily escaped from the court's public sphere. Meant as a parabola, the interpolated story signifies that it is only in the sheltered wood that the creature can feel free to give expression to its groans and that, being relieved of the pressure whose 'discharge did stretch his leathern coat/Almost to bursting', he is finally able to yield to some 'big round tears' without shame.[87] Read in the context of the Shakespearean antecedent, the wood in Lawrence's novel turns into a limited carnivalesque space, into a small counter-world where Constance can escape from the dry, aseptic and 'mechanical cleanliness' (*LCL*, 17) of her husband's world. The alluring otherness of the wood is not only stressed by the fact that its vegetation is sexually overcharged, it is also personified by the figure of a gamekeeper who progressively takes over the role of a preacher and instructor sent to initiate Constance (and her readership) into the mysteries of sexuality and to familiarize her with the cathartic porosity of her (hitherto meaninglessly drooping) body.

The sexual liquidity of her body which Constance is about to explore differs greatly from the detrimental psycho-pathological porousness that subcutaneously festers in her social environment. This inward and hidden porosity, as Lawrence aptly points out by repetition, is the result of a gaping wound that, due to the atrocities of the war, defies probing: 'The bruise was deep, deep, deep – the bruise of the false and inhuman war' (*LCL*, 50). What is even more perilous though than the severe and deep psycho-pathological contusion of the Wragby society's body is that its arteries are obstructed by a 'vast black clot of bruised blood' which it either takes generations to dissolve or leads to unexpected death by a kind of psychological embolism. Lawrence differs from Joyce and Woolf not only by pointing to a hidden rupture in the body politic,

---

[87] *AYL* 2.2.33–38.

to a dangerous reservoir of blood, but also by specifying the disease as a life-endangering blood clot, as a cultural thrombus or a festering tumour (spreading from Gertrude's breast)[88] which only a special type of man can heal and dissolve into a wholesome fluidity. While the cancerous lump in the early novel proves to be a lasting and terminal blight on the Morel family, in his final novel, Lawrence strives to overcome the determinism of Naturalism and, as shocking therapy, offers the porosity of a mutual orgasm.[89]

The idea of Mellors as a therapist and healer of a moribund society still has hints of Lawrence's temporary sympathy with the concept of the (Fascist) leader in his heavily criticized 'leadership novels'.[90] Although the uncouthness of Mellors's behaviour and his addiction to four-letter words are scarcely compatible with ideas of 'eroticized fascism' and 'fascist mesmerism',[91] there are, next to the 'element of bullying' in Mellors,[92] identifiable traces of a leader who is ready to attack the ossified culture which Constance and the sterile enclosure of Wragby stand for. In comparison to the effete representatives of an exhausted age, Clifford and Michaelis (the latter being Constance's first and frustrating adulterous affair), Mellors stands for physical prowess, for superhuman and ithyphallic power which fit more with Tommaso Marinetti's unleashed Futurist eulogies of aggression, with 'the furious coitus of war',[93] than with the whimperings of a decadent and paralysed culture. While Clifford is a torso of the post-Victorian age, a human being reduced to disjointed 'bits' (*LCL*, 5), Michaelis is a relic of the artificialized fin de siècle, an example of an effete sexuality that seems to have 'loosened itself from its moorings in the natural body' and had been appropriated by degenerate male aesthetes.[94] Disillusioned and impatiently waiting for Brooke's swimmers in the pool of cleanness, Constance is made to see that the masculine relics of the Victorian age are characterized by physiological dryness and a striking deficiency in erotic creativity and performance.

While dandies of Wilde's type favour yellow gloves and pink carnations, the would-be dandy Michaelis appears in Wragby Hall 'in a pale-coloured suit and white suède gloves, with mauve orchids for Connie' (*LCL*, 51). Michaelis's present of orchids has an ironic significance, because the etymological root of

---

[88] 'Pornography and Obscenity', 243.
[89] See, Cowan, *Lawrence: Self and Sexuality*, 93.
[90] For the broader context, see Frost, *Sex Drives: Fantasies of Fascism*, 38ff.
[91] Ibid., 6.
[92] Sagar, quoted in Ruderman, *Lawrence and the Devouring Mother*, 164.
[93] See the pamphlet *Uccidiamo il Chiaro di Luna!* (1909), translated as *Let's Murder the Moonshine!* Quoted in Frost, *Sex Drives: Fantasies of Fascism*, 4.
[94] Felski, *Gender of Modernity*, 94–95.

the word 'orchid' comes from the Greek *órkhis* (= testicles) and suggests a sexual performance which clashes with his bodily diminution and immaturity, with 'his small-boy's frail nakedness' (*LCL*, 53). Accordingly, sex with a feminized or puerile dandy proves to be disappointing and, instead of having a healing effect on Constance, Michaelis's poor performance (topped by coarse, ungentlemanly accusations) aggravates her frustration and leads her to lose faith in modern men's practice of mechanized copulation. With the 'empty treadmill' (*LCL*, 55) of her barren, desexualized life going on, the 'black clot' of congealed blood is stuck more firmly than ever in her and modern society's body; for a generation that considers sex either a sterile cogwheel mechanism or in terms of an extravagantly mixed and superfluous 'cocktail' (*LCL*, 64) porousness and Joycean carnivalesque sexuality is a messy disease that civilization has succeeded in marginalizing.

The lowest point in Constance's Victorian hell of dry, sterile anti-porousness is reached when some visitors to Wragby link civilization with the process of mankind forgetting their bodies; one of the New Women utterly out of touch with Mina Purefoy's life of continuous pregnancies even loudly clamours for the 'breeding-bottle' as a triumph of science over detested bodily porousness: 'Only hurry up with the breeding-bottle, and let us poor women off' (*LCL*, 75). Although one of the guests takes the *à rebours*-position of calling for both the 'resurrection of the body' and for the veneration of the phallus as the last conceivable bridge over the 'bottomless pit' of chaos (*LCL*, 75), the novel suddenly embarks on a discourse that was shared by a phalanx of Modernist phallocratic writers such as Weininger and his followers who preferred to understand the phallus less as a symbol of seminal porosity than as an icon under which all those rallied who deplored a lack of assertive maleness, Fascist control and cocksure hardness.

In this context, Lawrence's obsession with phallic hardness and strength must be seen in a different light which is even intensified by the fact that he places severe strictures on male masturbation. The phallus seems only to be acceptable as long as it is like the hard fasces (the bundle of rods from which the word Fascism is derived), inflexible and symbolic of patriarchal supremacy. While later Fascists and Nazis tend to be more lenient about masturbation,[95] Lawrence's moralistic harangue on the dangers of auto-eroticism in his essay on 'Pornography and Obscenity' is uncompromisingly rigoristic, especially when, in the essay, he sees adolescent masturbators trapped in what he calls a vicious

---

[95] Herzog, *Sex after Fascism*, 116.

'narcissus-masturbation circle',[96] and, adopting the voice of 'an omniscient Old Testament God'[97] and legislator, he exhorts young men to try to contain themselves. This cult of self-contained manliness in conjunction with the deprecation of masturbation as the 'most dangerous sexual vice that a society can be afflicted with'[98] (leaving young men as empty 'shells') betrays Lawrence's congeniality with other strict disparagers of masturbation such as Lord Baden-Powell, the founder of the Boy Scout Movement,[99] or James Harvey Kellogg, the co-inventor of Kellogg's Cornflakes; and it shows that his campaign for liberated sexuality is, despite its (at that time) utopian ideas of a mutual orgasm, strangely allied with a new puritanism and a passionate crusade for the sanitization of the (male) body.

Decrying masturbation as an evil and its practitioners as perverts,[100] Lawrence's texts not only unwittingly foster blood clots, but even help to magnify a phenomenon whose dangerous pathological potential is conveyed by the image that one of the visitors to Wragby brings up: the 'cerebral stone' (*LCL*, 75).[101] What at first looks like the modern version of the medieval fool's stone, 'the cerebral stone' threatening to clog up passages in post-Victorian minds is a different metaphor for Sedgwick's volitional sphincter and an appropriate image for the life-endangering re-petrification that was imperceptibly happening in the minds of the Modernists who, after getting rid of the oppressive paperweight of Queen Victoria,[102] prided themselves on being open to all sorts of ideas, philosophies and religions. One of these belated Victorians is Sir Clifford who resists the unblocking of his pores and refuses to drive out all pathological stones, clots and coagulations of Grundyism and, as a consequence, increasingly metamorphoses into a Kafkaesque 'creature with a hard, efficient shell', into one of the 'invertebrates of the crustacean order, with shells of steel' (*LCL*, 110). In contrast to Kafka's isolated beetle, supine, stigmatized and detested as it is by its family, Sir Clifford can rely on the fact that, in his metamorphosis, he is not a monad, but partakes of a well-established majority of crustacean creatures that

---

[96] 'Pornography and Obscenity', 47.
[97] On Lawrence, Freud and masturbation, see Cowan, *Lawrence: Self and Sexuality*, 99.
[98] 'Pornography and Obscenity', 245.
[99] On Baden-Powell's repressiveness on tears and fluids, see also Wilson, *The Victorians*, 597–601.
[100] Joyce is supposed to have been 'an avid and unrepentant onanist'. See Gillis, 'James Joyce and the Masturbating Boy', 612.
[101] For Lawrence as 'one of the most ardent pathologizers of modernity', see Schaffner, *Modernism and Perversion*, 182.
[102] For H.G. Wells's characterization of Queen Victoria's impact on culture, see MacKenzie, *The Time Traveller*, 101.

abhor any tendency towards porosity and (as in the case of the masturbating Bloom) vegetative softness.

While the cultural space of Wragby Hall is, thus, one of obstruction, calcification and pathology, nature is the diametric opposite, a counter-world of porosity where Constance can almost feel 'the huge heave of the sap in the massive trees' (*LCL*, 121), where, in sharp contrast to crippled or boyish impotence, everything seems to flaunt an unflagging tumescence and where the 'tide' of orgasmic juices permeates everything. It is in this natural context that she meets the gamekeeper as a purveyor of a new phallic reality, that her inward stones and clots start to dissolve and that she experiences an orgasm which is not aided by mental exertions (as it was with Michaelis), but whose overpowering and dissolving climax Lawrence appropriately depicts in a 'sexualized syntax',[103] in an accumulation of present participles taken from the contrastive semantic fields of water and fire:

> [T]here awoke in her new strange thrills rippling inside her, rippling, rippling, like a flapping overlapping of soft flames, soft as feathers, running to points of brilliance, exquisite, exquisite, and melting her all molten inside. (*LCL*, 133)

Orgasms in literature had always been problematic and writers had been at a loss either to catch the liminal experience that saw men stuck between emasculating expenditure and aggressiveness or to encapsulate into words something like a female orgasm that was considered to be non-existent or part of a semiotics of silence, at best rendered by a mute dash or a few insignificant dots. Like Stoker before him, who scandalously verbalized the female, vampire-induced climax as a way of drowning, Lawrence comes up against the limits of his language when he tries to convey the flowing and porous feeling of the female orgasm in a repetitive, lyrical and assonantal diction (which, however, never exonerated him from the accusation of being a phallocentric writer).[104] In the last story of the *Dubliners*, 'The Dead', Joyce tries to catch the process of dying in an equally flowing and progressive language, verbally conjuring up the swooning effect of a *Liebestod*. Joyce's early interest in death by snow as an illogical way out of stagnation and paralysis is, in Lawrence's novel, duly translated into a semantics of orgasmic flowing which no longer neatly differentiates between the elements of water and fire. While at one point Constance's womb is compared to a 'sea-anemone under the tides' (*LCL*, 133), the flames also make the reader associate

---

[103] Schaffner, *Modernism and Perversion*, 193.
[104] Lawrence and (to a certain degree) Stoker, two pioneers in the representation of female orgasms, are not mentioned in Muchembled's cultural history of the orgasm: *Orgasm and the West*.

her uterus with a furnace, where the obstructive clots and stones are eventually turned into hot liquids. This reading is supported by passages where she feels a new self coming alive in her, 'burning molten and soft and sensitive in her womb and bowels' (*LCL*, 135).

While, in the wood episodes, Constance's blockages are liquefied and the paralysis of her reproductive system yields to a new energetic flow – '[i]n her womb and bowels she was flowing and alive now' (*LCL*, 135) – Lawrence leaves his readers in no doubt that Lady Chatterley's porousness is still restricted to her interiority and that the moltenness of her limbs and uterine organs is still susceptible to onsets of rational encrustation and sudden relapses into aristocratic atrophy. Oscillating between Wragby Hall and Mellors's lodge, Constance is like a pawn hotly contested by two opponents in an erotic chess game; and as long as she still evinces a feeling of revulsion at bodily fluids and even takes a critical stance towards the porousness of the male orgasm, Constance is still more tightly in the grip of Clifford's sterile and puritan anti-corporeality than she might have thought possible.

Her ironic Maupassantian distance is, however, only a brief downward slope in the zigzagging curve of her sexual awakening. Before long her facade of aristocratic haughtiness is shattered in a kind of dialectical process which brings about her social death and her rebirth as a new character. This is revealed in a passage that shows that sexuality is not so much a Baudelairean surgical intervention[105] (that bypasses the clots and stones) as a death-inflicting, annihilating (and fluid-producing) piercing of the female body by the sword-like penis: 'It might come with the thrust of a sword in her softly-opened body, and that would be death' (*LCL*, 173). Given the fact that the hygienic site of Baudelaire's sex scenario (with the 'chemicalised women') has now been exchanged for a battlefield, the penetration of her body by the thrusts of the male sword-like penis (a stock-in-trade image of sexuality from Shakespeare to Cleland) has a new irenic quality ('a strange slow thrust of peace', *LCL*, 174), but, what is more, it releases a sea of juices and waves of genital liquids in which Constance drowns and loses her former self, only then to emerge as a new Aphrodite-like woman:

> And it seemed she was like the sea, nothing but dark waves rising and heaving, heaving with a great swell, so that slowly her whole darkness was in motion, and she was ocean rolling its dark, dumb mass. [...] She was gone, she was not, and she was born: a woman. (*LCL*, 174)

---

[105] See Baudelaire's definition of love as a torture and a surgical operation, 'Fusées' III. *Œuvres complètes*, 1:651.

While Byron imagines thalassian women as insatiable graves, absorbing and smothering their male sexual partners, Lawrence reverts to the imagery of the ocean, on the one hand, to illustrate the regenerative power of unleashed sexuality, and, on the other, to illustrate a paradigm shift from ever-mourning and petrified Niobe to the ooziness of a modern Venus Genetrix. At the end of a long array of personifications of porosity, temporarily culminating in Bella Cohen's destructive Ubuesque power, Lawrence's Lady Chatterley stands for a new regenerative porosity, which, in her later ritualized bacchantic dance in the pouring rain, she celebrates. While Molly's bulkiness almost dwarfs Bloom and leaves him clinging to her rump like an undersexed child, Constance, despite her negligible spell of irony, is shown by Lawrence as always being in deferential awe of the gamekeeper's penis, whose short intervals of flaccidity are impressively succeeded by the 'momentous, surging rise of the phallos' (*LCL*, 175). In contrast to Joyce who hails the advent of the porous and female man (with weird mythical connotations of Jewish menstruation),[106] Lawrence reinstates the phallic, cocksure man in what is left of the human farmyard.

Yet, while Lawrence's earlier texts had provoked harsh criticism and morphed their author into feminism's bête noire, the alternation between tumescence and detumescence of Mellors's penis underlines that, in the last phase of his work, Lawrence's veneration for the Priapic phallus was undergoing a change, with the penis occasionally being attributed the feminine qualities of tenderness, moistness and softness. When Constance is ready to see Mellors's penis in vegetative terms and to refer to it as 'the primeval root of all full beauty' (*LCL*, 175), the gamekeeper's masculinity temporarily approximates the androgynous and floral view that Bloom had of his penis.[107] Although Lawrence refrains from following Joyce in staging the penis as a fountain, a blossoming spout or 'flower', in Mellors's natural habitat, resuscitated Mrs Grundy's iron grip of puritanism seems to be slowly slackening and paving the way for a less biased view of (male) porousness.

Linguistic Pentecost or a new word-prudery?

With the post-Victorian 'gelding' being restored to his lost phallic power in *Lady Chatterley's Lover*, the gamekeeper (as Lawrence's mouthpiece) sets about

---

[106] For the wider context of the Jewish blood libel and stories of Jews' menstruation, see Briggs, 'Why Leopold Bloom Menstruates', 41–61.
[107] For the new notion of masculinity embodied by Mellors and Bloom, see Ingersoll, 'Constructing the "New Man"', 49.

the project of retrieving a linguistic code that, as a signifier of porousness and stark bodiliness, had been relegated to the banned sphere of gross vulgarity and countercultural communication. While Joyce uses vulgar four-letter words, and in particular the long-repressed 'c'-word, in the subtext of the Blooms' interior monologues and situates these gross indecencies at the blurry intersection between reality and imagination or, as in the case of Molly's chaotic flow of stream of consciousness, between waking, masturbating and sleeping, Lawrence has the gamekeeper not only resort to a broad and rustic dialect; he also has him address Constance in a crude pornographic idiom, with the aim of destroying her last Victorian moorings and of confronting her with a language that openly defies all forms of stratification: "'Tha'rt good cunt, though, aren't ter? Best bit o' cunt left on earth'" (*LCL*, 177). The fossilized 'word-prudery', so Lawrence's argument in his essay on 'Pornography and Obscenity',[108] is a phenomenon of the past that, like other hasty and restrictive dealings with sex, has to be abolished. The old habit of replacing four-letter words with ominous dashes (as even Byron did in the intertextual reference to Horace's odes) or with far-fetched circumlocutions is symptomatic of the clots and cerebral stones which the majority of people in their 'mob-habit' cherish.[109] Lawrence's liberation of the clotted language, of the tumours of repressive culture, is, thus, part of a long therapeutic process, which is diametrically opposed to the Victorians' pornographic subculture of postcards, jokes and dirty limericks. In this context, Lawrence feels called upon to extend his diagnosis from the singular diseased bodies (such as that of Paul's mother or that of Sir Clifford) to the entire body politic with its cancerous tumours of linguistic taboos which, as he sermonizes, only a 'natural fresh openness about sex' can remedy.[110]

As Margot Norris argues in her comparison between *Ulysses* and *Lady Chatterley's Lover*, both novels translated the nineteenth-century adultery novel into modernity and released Molly and Constance from the suicidal punishment that had been in store for Emma Bovary or Tolstoy's Anna Karenina.[111] While Norris subjects both novels to an ecocritical reading, she appears to overlook the divergent tones of the two novels and to comment on the radically different linguistic codes of the two protagonists Bloom and Mellors. While Bloom is a self-centred soliloquist on the streets of Dublin, Mellors relies on an interlocutor who helps him to eradicate the superfluous offshoots of the moribund aristocracy

---

[108] 'Pornography and Obscenity', 239.
[109] Ibid.
[110] Ibid., 40.
[111] Norris, 'Love, Bodies, and Nature', 29.

as represented by the impotent Clifford. In light of the fact that industrial man's body has been sucked dry by 'motor-cars and cinemas and aeroplanes' (*LCL*, 217) and that a new species of mechanized and unimpregnable human beings – 'with indiarubber tubing for guts and tin legs and tin faces' (*LCL*, 217) – is about to be generated, Mellors combines the rediscovery of Constance's hidden bodily orifices with a new assault on the Chatterleys' language. That this rediscovery coincides with a heavy shower of rain which, in her stark nakedness, Constance accepts as a kind of baptism is made instantaneously clear when she rushes into the rain and has her naked, unimpeded body washed by the rejuvenating rain. This baptism or rite of passage is indissolubly linked with the acquisition of a new layer of language, a pornographic jargon that goes beyond her pudendum and is devoted to the exploration of 'the two secret openings to her body' (*LCL*, 223), the last, hitherto forbidden and, in Mrs Grundy's reign, non-existent regions of the female body's topography. In the scatological delight that Mellors feels he is briefly on a par with Bloom, but while, in his abdominal joy, Bloom is only anarchic and riotously Ubuesque, Mellors's admiration for Constance's anus is fuelled by rage, by the revenge that he seems to have sworn to take on the Victorians' ideology of repressing, destroying and concealing the human body in wiry, class-dictated cages.

While Joyce, not least due to his Weiningerian view of women,[112] restricts his representations of Molly's body to some debasingly animal functions and rather concentrates his subversively anal liberties on the effeminized and coprophilic Bloom, Lawrence is eager to rewrite literary and cultural history when he, quite in the manner of seventeenth-century writers of scatophilic erotica,[113] emphasizes that Constance's body is not exempt from producing waste and that her genital and anal openness is the source of exceedingly erotic attraction: '"An' if tha shits an' if tha pisses, I'm glad. I don't want a woman as couldna shit nor piss"' (*LCL*, 223). Seen before the backdrop of literary history, Mellors stands in a long line of notable predecessors: ready to use a new idiom to highlight the fact that Constance's body is remote from angelic immaculateness, Mellors aims to give a belated response to and an overdue correction of Strephon's horrible insight in Swift's poem 'The Lady's Bedroom' in which the lover is shocked to find that his paramour Celia is subject to the human condition and 'shits'.[114] While Swift's

---

[112] See also, Pöder, 'Molly *Is* Sexuality', 227–35.
[113] See Toulalan, *Imagining Sex*, 230–31.
[114] Lawrence explicitly refers to this significant eighteenth-century pretext in 'A Propos of "Lady Chatterley's Lover"' published in 1929 as an introduction to the Paris edition of the novel and added to the Penguin edition of *Lady Chatterley's Lover*, 305–35.

references to excrements are still deeply rooted in rationalist concepts of bodily disgust, or in the Cartesian 'mind's terror of the body',[115] Lawrence uses Mellors as a spokesman for what Robert Muchembled aptly expresses in the phrase of 'anal rejoicing'.[116] Mellors's enthusiasm for Constance's excremental orifices – "'Here tha shits an' here tha pisses: an' I lay my hand on 'em both, an' I like thee for it'" (*LCL*, 223) – echoes that of a pioneer who has burrowed his way through layers of heavy cloth, steel and fishbone (and encrusted language)[117] and finally unveiled the deepest mysteries of the genital terra incognita. And even if the image of Constance's 'ivory-gleaming legs' (*LCL*, 223) seems to be a relapse into diehard aestheticist ideas of women's sculptural decorativeness, it is the naturalness and openness of Constance's body that, after her bodily and linguistic rebirth, are repeatedly referred to.

Katie Gramich argues that Constance, reborn and endowed with a new language, follows the trajectory from the austerity of the civilized Apollonian body to the excess of the Dionysian body, in the end revelling in the latter's 'primeval fecundity'.[118] This Nietzschean dichotomy informs Lawrence's novel via Thomas Mann's 1912 novella *Der Tod in Venedig* (Death in Venice), which, as Gramich convincingly puts it, Lawrence passionately objected to because Mann, in the guise of the Neo-Classicist writer Gustav von Aschenbach clearly favoured the Apollonian idea of the body and, in the interpolated dream about the elevation of the 'obscene symbol' of the phallus, saw a nightmarish orgy of utter degeneration.[119] As if to give his misgivings about Mann's work additional weight, Lawrence shows the Apollonian world of Clifford's aristocracy less in terms of classical serenity than as a grotesque assembly of 'professorial corpses' (*LCL*, 234) and gabbling automata. While, by the end of the novel, Constance is reborn as a natural human being and, as a token of her porousness, is made pregnant by Mellors, Clifford, the Apollonian, rapidly regresses into the state of a child whose crippled body is sponged down by Mrs Bolton, the nurse and late descendant of Mrs Grundy. As Gerald Doherty writes, 'the "backward" telos'

---

[115] Ibid., 309.
[116] My translation of the French term 'jubilations anales' in Muchembled, *L'invention de l'homme moderne*, 55. Mellors's anal enthusiasm is, however, contradicted by Lawrence's differentiation between sex as a 'creative flow' and the 'excrementory flow' as its opposite: 'dissolution, de-creation'. 'Pornography and Obscenity', 39.
[117] A fashionable Victorian woman was supposed to be 'carrying thirty-seven pounds of clothing'. See, Flanders, *Victorian House*, 268.
[118] Gramich, 'Stripping Off the "Civilized Body"', 153.
[119] Ibid., 155.

of the Clifford-Bolton affair 'provides the perfect counterfoil for the dynamic "forward" telos' of the Constance-Mellors relationship.[120]

Before Mellors appears on the scene, the strange *ménage à trois* between Clifford, Mrs Ivy Bolton and Constance is intriguingly compared to a horticultural monstrosity, to 'a bulb stuck parasitic' (*LCL*, 83) on the sappy tree of life, whereas Constance's later pregnancy is dithyrambically celebrated as a new sign of healthiness. Constance's pregnancy and healthy porousness thus contrast so flamboyantly with the various symptoms of sordid and barren decadence, as they are represented or indicated by the 'ivy'-like, mammal intimacy between Clifford and his nurse, by the oft-quoted Swinburne in the image of the infertile 'Niobean womb' in 'Ave Atque Vale'[121] and by Mann's Venice in general, which, as a farewell to the fin de siècle, she visits with her sister Hilda. Here, she is repelled by the 'conglomerate mass of nearly nude flesh on the Lido' (*LCL*, 259), and by the donjuanesque and deceptive verbosity, so glibly recited by the Italian gondolier Giovanni, 'pining to prostitute himself, dribbling like a dog, wanting to give himself to a woman' (*LCL*, 260).

It is here that the Modernist concept of porousness finally comes full circle: while Molly Bloom is trying to come to terms with a few Italian lines from Mozart's opera *Don Giovanni* and herself embodies the sensual libertinism of the gigantic and all-engulfing women in Byron's *Don Juan*, Constance is not only sick of 'the easily-overflowing' Giovanni, she also comes to detest all ideas of a repetitive, self-referential and doggish sexuality.[122] Inspired by her mentor Mellors, she eventually endorses a kind of mystical fertility, which, even in its enforced chastity (defined as 'the pause and peace of our fucking', *LCL*, 301), is to be preferred to the cloying and aporetic voluptuousness of Don Juanism:

> What a misery to be like Don Juan, and impotent ever to fuck oneself into peace, and the little flame alight, impotent and unable to be chaste in the cool between-whiles, as by a river. (*LCL*, 301)

Although Joyce's *Ulysses* ends on repeated affirmations of life and its porousness (programmatically shown by the word 'Yes' that brackets Molly's final monologue), references to sexual dysfunctionality abound, and right to the end, Molly and feminized Leopold remain a couple haunted by memories of

---

[120] Doherty, 'The Chatterley/Bolton Affair', 378.
[121] Swinburne, 'Ave Atque Vale', 192. *Selected Poems*, 160–65. In her moments of deep frustration in Clifford's Wragby, Constance is an eager reader of Swinburne's poems, see *LCL*, 85.
[122] For Molly/Penelope 'exercis[ing] a sexuality, a sensate eroticism, that often proves sufficient unto itself', see Boone, 'Staging Sexuality', 211. The omnipresent dog in *Ulysses* is here clearly given a negative connotation of fawning, dribbling and anti-human ooziness.

irreparable Niobean loss. *Lady Chatterley*, by contrast, concludes on a note of epistolary sentimentalism, with Mellors adopting the role of an early Romantic letter writer who, in his anti-donjuanism, translates Donne's cold concetto of the pair of compasses in 'The Extasie' into the Pentecostal 'forked flame between me and you' (*LCL*, 301) and thus suggests a rethinking of Niobe as a porous, pregnant and happy woman, as a conflation of Venus and the Madonna gravida.

While both novels of the turbulent 1920s focus on periods of short-lived carnivalesque riot, there is no denying that these novels are also deeply imbued with intimations of failure and finality. While the spokesman of unleashed porousness in *Ulysses* is an outsider, a Jewish flâneur on the fringes of straitlaced Irish society, Stephen, the poet's alter ego, is a hydrophobic intellectual and, not unlike Sir Clifford, only partially and shamefully aware of his body's porous nether regions. While Joyce takes delight in the Ubuesque maxim of épater les bourgeois, Lawrence's novels are inspired by a disproportionate and insistent didacticism, or, in Zack Bowen's words, *Ulysses* 'plays a Sancho Panza to Lawrence's Quixote',[123] inviting critics to put special emphasis on Lawrence's latent, 'beastly' bourgeoiserie,[124] on his chagrined puritanism that was modelled on readings of Savonarola[125] and clashed so blatantly with Joyce's anarchic boisterousness. Like Lawrence's ferocious in-yer-face poems, Mellors's sentences, and in particular his final letter, have a naggingly sermonizing quality that is more Victorian than an indication of Bloom's iconoclastic Dadaism or Ubuism. The fact that Mellors complains about the bodily limpness of the industrial people and implicitly contrasts them with Constance's and his own anthroposophic nudity (indulged in their eurythmic dances in the rain) makes it clear that Lawrence's dramatization of the naked body is more programmatic of and indebted to Brooke's athlete-warrior, or to the pre-Fascist German fascination for sanitized physicality in the wake of Turnvater Jahn, Rudolf Steiner or Hugo Höppner, aka Meister Fidus.

Epitomizing the interludal mood of the roaring 1920s, Lawrence's and Joyce's novels tie in with the Bloomsbury frivolity that had been in evidence since Lytton Strachey's transgressive bantering about 'semen',[126] but also precede (and, to a considerable degree, even sow the seeds of) a counter-discourse that, in the 1930s, 40s and 50s, not only reinstalls the image of the sealed and captivated body, but also reformulates the concept of the Niobean body along the lines of

---

[123] Bowen, '*Lady Chatterley's Lover* and *Ulysses*', 27.
[124] Cf. the poem 'How Beastly the Bourgeois Is'. *Complete Poems*, 348.
[125] Burgess, *Flame into Being*, 104.
[126] For the anecdote of Lytton Strachey's confronting Virginia Woolf with the word 'semen' see, Adams, 'Victorian Sexualities', 125.

incessant, irremediable absurdity. With the defiant and shocking avant-gardes of the Futurists, the Dadaists and the Surrealists proving to be iridescent, but extremely short-lived flashes in the cultural pan, the carnival of porosity on the singular Bloomsday of 1904 and the sylvan spell of oozing sexuality in Sherwood Forest were soon to be forgotten, put on the Grundyists' index and decried as smutty outpourings of diseased and expatriated minds.

5

Niobean reverberations in post-war literature

The fact that this survey of the porous bodies ends on a positive note of pregnancy and an expected birth seems to be a happy reversal of its point of departure, Macduff's horrifying news about the death of his family, which suddenly confronted a soldierly man with the unprecedented situation of finding himself forced into the role of a male Niobe. Between Lady Chatterley's provocative pregnancy and Macduff's shattering bereavement there is an interval of more than three centuries, in which attitudes towards porosity – in its entire diversity from tears to blood, sweat and seminal fluids – ran the whole gamut from suspicion and disgust to certain spells of delight, delectation and joy. What proved to be constant though was the association of uncontrollable porousness with women, whereas men were mostly forced to hide their porous bodies behind masks of stern authority, and even in brief periods which upturned traditional gender associations of porosity such as the decades of Metaphysical poetry or the Age of Sentimentality men were always at risk of being ridiculed, denigrated and seen as infected by foreign perversion.

As a mythological figure who was said to reconcile both sides, female porousness and the male imperative for petrification, Niobe became an unseen presence in many discourses of the body, sometimes appearing in the limelight of shame (as in *Hamlet*), sometimes taking on the guise of a tear-bereft stoic (as in Byron's visualization of Rome) and sometimes becoming an artistic expression of heartfelt grief (as in Isidora Duncan's Niobe performances after the accidental deaths of her children in 1913).[1] The oxymoronic idea of a stone that sheds copious tears inspired some writers and artists to become new Pygmalions and to turn their shockingly porous women back into dry lifeless blocks of marble, and even if some poets were blissfully unaware of Niobe and her fate, their poetry was nevertheless primarily concerned with attempts to transfer the unsettling ooziness of (female) nature into firm stanzaic structures whose

[1] Preston, *Modernism's Mythic Pose*, 182–83.

mausolean character often resembled the mummification of clothes with which the Victorians tended to conceal the porous nether regions of female bodies.

For the Victorians in particular, Niobe evinced an alarming ambivalence: on the one hand, she dovetailed perfectly into the cult of grief that Queen Victoria paraded after Prince Albert's death as 'an exemplar of chronic grief'[2] (with Frederick Tennyson idolizing Victoria in his heavy-handed 1891 poem 'Niobe' as 'a living fount of tears', on the verge of the fourth decade of excessive mourning).[3] On the other hand, she produced an uncontrollable torrent of tears that Victorian men were unable to cope with and that Mrs Grundy was called upon to stop or to relegate into the category of hysteria. Casting Niobe into Victorian bric-à-brac, into a decorative statue, 'veiled in hair to her slender hips, gazing at the pool she had wept',[4] was thus a way not only of Christianizing her (conflating her with Mary Magdalene in her penitential veil of hair), but also of freezing her fluids which Victorians and Edwardians felt so ill at ease with. When Joyce and Lawrence resuscitated and galvanized these frozen Victorian bodies and even supplanted the idea of the Niobean woman in favour of a life-throbbing Venus, Circe and even a promiscuous Penelope, the volitional sphincter seemed to be loosened and a new carnivalism (with all its Ubuesque revelries) was about to make the 1920s even more roaring than the visual arts suggest. That the 1920s were, however, a transitional age was not only a fact that was corroborated in the sphere of politics and economy, it also manifested itself in the representation of the (female) body which was quickly subjected to a new puritan scepticism and soon recast as a fanatically sanitized and deodorized object.

The Kulturkampf that had been raging between supporters of porosity and their staunch opponents for ages and that seemed to have ended with the defeat of Mrs Grundy suddenly flares up again, leaving the post-Joycean and post-Lawrentian reader with an even stricter harness of Grundyist rules. In this respect, Michel Foucault can hardly be accused of exaggerating when he captions his history of twentieth-century sexuality as 'We Other Victorians' (but definitely not in Steven Marcus's sense) and thus characterizes the years after the Second World War as decades of 'medical prudence', of a yearning for 'precautions in order to contain everything, with no fear of "overflow"'.[5] This new culture of reticence is ubiquitous, especially in the Theatre of the Absurd where dysfunctional, maimed, puppet-like torsos are not only confined to dustbins and

---

[2] Jalland, *Death in the Victorian Family*, 321
[3] Frederick Tennyson, *Daphne and Other Poems*, 362.
[4] Galsworthy, *The Forsyte Saga*, 529
[5] Foucault, *History of Sexuality*, 1:5.

reduced to immobility, but are also shown as practising 'dry sex in a dry land'.[6] Although Beckett's Pozzo reverts to a rare moment of Niobean lyricism when he says that 'the tears of the world are a constant quantity',[7] the characters who are porous enough to weep them have long since shrivelled into oblivion. What in Victorian times used to be a dichotomy between Hebraism and Hellenism has now become a monochromatic consensus where glaring colours are avoided and fragmentary bodies gradually come to be seen in the light of dehumanized and sterile automata.

In this context, it is intriguing to note that John Fowles's novel *The French Lieutenant's Woman* (1969) shows the alarming extent to which the year 1969, despite the onset of porosity in pop culture (Woodstock), is a revival, if not a continuation of the year 1869, in which the novel is set. Adroitly combining cultural studies and fiction, Fowles insinuates that the threshold situation, 'the beginning of a revolt against crinoline and the large bonnet' (*FLW*, 5) not only turned out to be short-lived, eventually culminating in Lady Chatterley dancing naked in the pouring, baptismal rain; it also inaugurated a fierce backlash and a relapse into new forms of astringency, as is shown in Fowles's novel in the character Ernestina (a Wildean allusion to the Victorians' proverbial earnestness) who, when tempted to dance a few frivolous steps in front of a mirror, is immediately reminded of another myth of grief: Laocoon and his sons in their excruciating death throes.

That Ernestina's fiancé Charles is an amateur palaeontologist perfectly fits into the binary structure of Victorians genders. His pseudoscientific concentration on fossils, stones and petrified relics of the past matches the atmosphere of sexual frustration which hangs over their relationship and which allows them no premarital sexual interaction other than a few chaste kisses, 'with lips as chastely asexual as children's' (*FLW*, 83). When the deviant, darkish and water-obsessed Sarah Woodruff intrudes upon this mausolean relationship like a catalyst figure, Victorian conventions start to crumble, only to open up new vistas in which Constance Chatterley and Molly Bloom become utopian figurations of unleashed porosity. Since Fowles looks on the twentieth century as 'our own deodorized century' (*FLW*, 443), he tries to blend the nineteenth and twentieth centuries and implicitly posits that the Victorians' 'schizophrenic outlook on society' (*FLW*, 255) has been bequeathed to his own generation, making it shudder bashfully

---

[6] Brienza, 'Krapping Out', 130.
[7] Beckett, *Waiting for Godot*, 1.22

at 'excretory functions' (*FLW*, 269) while simultaneously boosting a blossoming pornographic industry.

In 1969, similar mechanisms of compensation seem to be working as they did in the 1860s or even in Shakespeare's *Macbeth*: like Macduff, or the later Victorians, the young people of the 1960s saw parts of their generation disputing it like men in Vietnam and pouring their vases of pent-up bodily fluids into violence and aggression. Criticizing the Victorians' strategy of 'pour[ing] their libido into […] other fields', Fowles even goes so far as to formulate the bold, but plausible hypothesis that the Victorians' (and twentieth-century man's) fetishization of competitive progress is causally linked with the frenzied act of negating the Niobean body, with damming up genital fluids and obstructing the natural flow of juices: 'We need some progress, so let us dam and divert this one great canal [of bodily juices] and see what happens' (*FLW*, 269). The diversion of the libido into technical progress is, according to Fowles's narrator, the main reason for the Victorians' lack of a dialectical mind. While the Romantics depended on contradictions and some of them derived enormous power from urging (feminized) porousness into (masculine) patterns of stony rigidity, the Victorians, so Fowles, flatly refused to 'think naturally in opposites, of positives and negatives as aspects of the same whole' (*FLW*, 250). Considering the fact that the irreconcilable Arnoldian dichotomy between Hebraism and Hellenism or Lord Tennyson's two contrastive voices underlie numerous Victorian works, Fowles takes too myopic a view of the Victorian age. Yet, what is indisputable is the fact that the Victorians partook of (and passed on) a long tradition of suppressing and sublimating bodily juices which inevitably led to pathological records of women and womanish dandies refusing to eat, to sweat and to urinate, thus, seeking relief by means of technical devices such as catheters (*FLW*, 235).

The more we are ready to see the post-Victorian decades as reproductions of the nineteenth century in which the tyranny of the Cartesian mind seems to be paramount, the more we are able to understand that Lawrence's and Joyce's experimental novels are exotic rarities in an ongoing discourse that targets the abolition of the human condition with all its atavistic porosity and ultimately defines artificial intelligence as the final triumph of mind over oozing matter. When Fowles focuses on the Victorians' 'claustrophilia', on their inveterate habit of interring themselves in the double seclusion of their 'mummifying clothes' and in the darkness of 'narrow-windowed and -corridored architecture' (*FLW*, 177), we tend to see the twentieth century differing here, not only in the provocative models in miniskirts in 1969 (unthinkable for the Victorians, even though their rigorous strictures on naked ankles are now seen as anecdotal 'old chestnut[s]'[8]), but also in the staging of stark nakedness in fashion, film and photography. What is, however, paradoxical is the fact that the ostentatious display of naked skin in post-1969 decades does not result in more porousness: as if vying with the magazines for the glossiness in which nakedness is paraded, naked bodies have become tableaux vivants, lacking exudations, remote from carnivalesque riot and receptive only to the designs of tattoo artists. In this respect, nudity becomes synonymous with a new aestheticism in which art, performance and a new paradigm of body scepticism coalesce and in which any indication of porousness is rigorously concealed or even photoshopped.

With Niobe being briefly eclipsed by Venus and Circe in the early twentieth century, it is intriguing to notice that myths revolving around (erotic or transgressive) interaction are inevitably supplanted by mythological frames that stress solipsism and self-veneration. Muchembled's survey of the orgasm (and, to a certain degree, of the body's porosity) ends on the challenging assumption that Narcissus has become the mythological figurehead of our troubled and self-centred age: 'Narcissism [...] is everywhere the rule.'[9] As already shown by Wilde and his idea of the portrait as the gravitational centre of narcissist egotism (reducing women to bodiless voices), the narcissist's love for his reflection propagates the fallacy of erotic autonomy. It is this ideal of self-isolation that Lawrence criticized as a vicious circle, pillorying men who indulge in masturbatory fantasies instead of celebrating sexuality as a mutual 'give and take'.[10] Seen before this backdrop, Lady Chatterley's bacchanal in the rain is meant to be a eulogy of interactive porous sex, and, as such, differs significantly from Joyce's Walpurgis Night revels in the brothel (although Bloom is here confined of his new son, Stephen), from the masturbatory vagaries which dandies are aroused to when touching the fetishistic artefacts around them, or from what countless women seem to experience when looking at their naked images in the various mirrors of nineteenth-century art.[11] While the narcissism of the postmodern era has undergone a disquieting process of democratization and led to an uncontrollable 'selfie' mania, the self-indulgent look in the mirror, either by the dandy or by languishing fin-de-siècle women, was a privilege of the supra-cultural narcissist, making sure that no pore eluded the vigilance of their self-amatory look.

---

[8] Sweet, *Inventing the Victorians*, xii.
[9] Muchembled, *Orgasm and the West*, 246.
[10] 'Pornography and Obscenity', 245.
[11] See Dijkstra, *Idols of Perversity*, 129–46.

With the loss of dandyism and supra-cultural elitism in the wake of two atrocious world wars and the emergence of twentieth-century mass production, narcissism seems to have infiltrated all strata of society. TV productions, talk shows and the proliferation of social media daily give unsettling insights into an apotheosis of the self which US psychoanalysts such as Heinz Kohut started to explore as early as in the 1970s. While, in his pathology of narcissism, Kohut highlights four main features, such as 'perverse fantasies', 'an inability to form and maintain significant social relationships', 'lack of humour' and an inclination for profound hypochondria,[12] there is one symptom conspicuously missing in his list: the lack and repression of tears and other bodily fluids. This is not only due to a widespread emotional dehydration (which also accounts for a lack of empathy for other people's concerns), but most of all due to a pandemic loathing of the human condition whose fluids, pores and cavities twentieth- and twenty-first-century narcissists frantically try to deodorize, to ignore or to freeze into body-hostile works of art.

With Narcissus as the dominant cultural paradigm of our time, it is not only the porous body that is effaced in the idealized mirror projection of the beholder, it is also most dramatically the female body with its apertures that is marginalized and nullified. The trajectory of the porous female body from the early modern fountains to the effigies in Victorian marriage beds, from the milk-producing cattle in Cavalier poetry to Lady Chatterley's pregnant body is a zigzagging arch that, from a male perspective, inevitably leads to the nonentity of an Echo (as evidenced with little variation in the novels and plays by John Braine, Kingsley Amis, Harold Pinter and many others). If in male narcissist fantasies women dwindle to nothing or only inadvertently echo male discourses, the question arises as to what happened to the goblin men, the numerous perforators and rapists that so glibly catered to the stereotypical ideas of masculinity and in their mad pursuit of women attested to a non-narcissistic dependence on the female other. The fact that vampires such as Count Dracula had no mirror reflection is a clear hint that narcissism outside the sphere of the Frenchified dandies played no significant role in late nineteenth-century literature: more Jovian than narcissistic, the vampire was the last transgressor of Victorian sexual politics and a ruthless perforator of female bodies in the vein of Don Juan. If Kohut's diagnosis of prevalent narcissism is right, the fact that there has been a rekindled interest in vampires, bloodsuckers and goblin suitors of innocent women since the 1950s seems to be a contradiction. Films

---

[12] Kohut, *The Analysis of the Self*, paraphrased by Muchembled, *Orgasm and the West*, 251–52.

starring Christopher Lee as the perennial Count Dracula or parodies such as Roman Polanski's *The Fearless Vampire Killers* (1967) prove that vampires are an indispensable element in twentieth- and twenty-first-century pop culture and that narcissism seems to coexist with forms of predatory Jovian lust (in both cases relegating women to mute victims). With Stephenie Meyer's highly controversial saga of 'vegetarian' and sexually temperate vampires *Twilight Saga* (2005–08), we eventually (re-) enter the territory of bodily conservatism where vampiric transgression is mitigated and translated into glossy schoolgirl magazines leaving the (chiefly female) readers thrilled by the new aestheticism of scintillating and photoshopped vampires. More than a century after the end of what Joss Marsh characterized as 'the golden age of euphemism',[13] Dracula, the ruthless parasite and thriver on bisexual porosity, has been turned into a monogamous young man, palatable to an audience unaccustomed and averse to the carnivalism of flowing bodily juices.

What is, however, intriguing to see in post-war literature and culture is the striking imbalance between bodily closure and the increasing amorphism and openness of the media authors resort to. While writers in the wake of Shakespeare tried to contain onsets of corporeal porousness in tightly knit structures, such as the well-wrought play, the rigorous form of the sonnet or the monumentalized stanza of the epitaph, the novel dissolving into a multitude of sloppy, tear-drenched letters or fuzzy chapters increasingly became the genre that was best suited to reflect the intensifying porosity of its characters. Novels by Dickens, Hardy and Wilde are thus concerned with representing the conflict between porousness and containment in a narrative structure that in its looseness left so many loopholes and apertures that readers waiting for the next instalment were faced with a problem that Shakespeare's theatregoers were blissfully ignorant of: that of literature's porousness. Byron captured this dilemma best when he squeezed the meandering and digressive story of his modern Don Juan into the prescriptive grid of the ottava rima and at the same time announced that the poem might be inflated into more than fifty irregular cantos. Gottfried Benn's thought-provoking idea of the 'form-fordernde Gewalt des Nichts' (the form-demanding power of nothingness)[14] is challenged here *avant la lettre*, because the attempted rigorism of the form (and its forced rhymes) tellingly reveals the porousness of the poem and clashes with the outrageous depictions of transgressively porous bodies.

---

[13] Marsh, *Word Crimes*, 215.
[14] Benn, *Gesammelte Werke*, 8:1913.

Byron's chatty, never-ending poem satirizes (and imitates) the gossipy ooziness of the nineteenth-century gazettes, reversing the effort that some of the Romantics took to give lasting shape and contours to their lives that they often felt were only writ in water. With the forms and media becoming more and more porous over the nineteenth century (culminating in the sloppiness of Stoker's epistolary novel), there is, however, a contrasting tendency for the bodies to become more rigorously closed, sculptural and strikingly reticent about fluids and bodily functions. With the exception of the carnivalesque spell in Joyce's and (to a lesser extent) in Lawrence's novels, bodies are shown aspiring to a new ideal of petrification in genres that are vexingly open, fragmentary, porous and liquefied. Plunging his readers into hell, 'the ooze full of morsels,/ lost contours, erosions', Ezra Pound, in one of his *Cantos* (1917–71), shows his hell guide admonishing his entourage to '[c]lose the pores of your feet' and to pray to Medusa who, according to the narrator's manipulation of the mythological story, petrifies the soil by the shield.[15] Pound's *Cantos* are the acme of poetic porousness or osmosis opening the poem to a Babelian plurality of languages, Asian semiotics and a palimpsest of texts, but the wish to keep the body intact from all assaults of cultural dissolution is a pervading feature of this poetic monstrosity. The fact that, despite his obsessive interest in mythological conflations, Pound does not allude to Niobe, the epitome of porous grief, is not coincidental, since she would have undermined the Modernists' paradox of striving for hard, imagist imperviousness in disintegrating and dissolving forms.

In the course of 300 years of bodily and textual porosity, Niobe proved to be a reliable guide through cultural periods and a precise indicator of the extent to which liquidity and petrification attracted or even repulsed each other. While some periods cherished paradoxes and tended to bring together the Niobean dichotomy in the shape of weeping and sentimental men, other periods widened the contrast so drastically that women and men became almost two different species bereft of the comfortingly connecting part in Donne's image of the compasses in 'The Extasie'. Even when conflated with or parodied by other myths such as Pygmalion's Galatea or Pandora, or even re-embodied by Mary Magdalene, Niobe and her oxymoronic grief were underlying concepts which helped to ascertain to what degree Mrs Grundy and her emissaries were successful in clamping down on rivulets of tears or their metonymic fluids.

After being relegated to a museal piece of art in Galsworthy's *Forsyte Saga* and, subsequently, eclipsed by more fertile and life-generating myths such as

---

[15] Pound, *The Cantos*, XIV–XV, 62 and 66.

Lawrence's rain-born Venus or Joyce's Molly as a Diana Multimammia, Niobe seems to have been retrieved from post-war oblivion in two pop-cultural media, in the open-ended graphic novel (programmatically titled) *NIOBE: She Is Life* (2015) and in Guido Argentini's silver photo series. In the comic strip, Amandla Stenberg and Sebastian A. Jones, now provide Niobe Ayutami with a surname and, thus, with a full female identity. As the heroine of a narrative of black female heroism, she is no longer descended from Greek misogynist mythology, but as an orphaned elf and a human warrior, she is a hybrid figure on a quest for self-discovery and female empowerment. When interviewed by Aysha Khan, Stenberg states that she 'was drawn to give voice to Niobe and co-write her story',[16] she puts exclusive emphasis on Niobe's strength and astonishingly omits Niobe's proverbial grief, impotence and porosity from the story. Armed with a knife or a lance (which is no longer one of straw as in Shakespeare's *Taming of the Shrew*), towering triumphantly over her adversary, Niobe suddenly assumes the position of a female St Michael, combatting and subjugating (male, bald-headed) evil, her shock of snaky dreadlocks underlining Niobe's new resemblance to vindictive Medusa. Childless, self-contained and fully in control of her casually dressed body, the twenty-first-century re-impersonation of Niobe is that of a 'badass girl',[17] of a Nemesis who resists all male, gender-biased ascriptions of female porosity.

Resorting to a well-established myth, Stenberg's and Jones's graphic novel engages with a parodic iconoclasm that redefines feminism in terms of exhibiting young black women as being independent, transgressive and devoid of stigmatizing female porosity. The Italian photographer Guido Argentini, by contrast, reverts to the figure of Niobe to re-emphasize the photoshopped immaculateness of the mythological figure's body: in his silver-coated Cellini-like female nudes of his 2003 silver series, he has his models re-enact the mythological scene of Aedon and Niobe. Two highly artificialized silver nudes show the interwovenness of their mythological fates: with her body propped up and her legs spread-eagled, Niobe lets her genitals be covered by the head of Aedon, her sister-in-law, who is reported to have envied her fertility and, by coincidence, to have killed her own child, Itylos. The mythological imbroglio of jealousy, treachery and erroneous murder is only vaguely hinted at, but what in this context is of prime significance is that neither Niobe's nor Aedon's aesthetic and athletic bodies show any trace of porousness.

[16] Khan in The Tempest interview with Stenberg in https://thetempest.co/2015/10/31/entertainment/niobe-bringing-badass-girls-comics/ (accessed 1 June 2019).
[17] Ibid.

With her body immersed in and her pores sealed by liquid silver, Niobe seems to have found one of her twenty-first-century representations: devoid of all signs of porosity, vaguely reminiscent of the dehydrated Niobes in the wake of Byron's *Childe Harold's Pilgrimage* and on a new aestheticist level remote from Stenberg's feminist avenger, Argentini's Niobe (in conjunction with the envious Aedon) epitomizes our longing for a cool, deodorized and almost metallic body that is perfectly shaped, flawless and without the cavities and protuberances of a throbbing and oozing body. In this respect, the Swiftian rationalists' disgust at oozy bodies and their preference for smoothly polished silver statues has found a spectacular update, making it patently obvious that the narrative of porous bodies is never a linear, but always an erratic one in which apparently irregular and short phases of carnivalesque exuberance alternate with longish spells of reticence, revulsion and bodily dissatisfaction. What a new carnivalism and a revisiting of the porous Niobean body will look like in the future remains a matter of speculation, but it highlights the fact that books on porosity also clearly belong to the genre of porous textual corpora.

Bibliography

Primary texts

Arnold, M. (1994), *Selected Poetry*, ed. K. Silver, Manchester: Carcanet Press.
Barnes, J. (2012), *Flaubert's Parrot*, London: Vintage.
Barthes, R. (1972), *Critical Essays*, trans. R. Howard, Evanston: Northwestern University Press.
Barthes, R. (2010), *A Lover's Discourse: Fragments*, trans. R. Howard, New York: Hill and Wang.
Baudelaire, C. (1976), *Œuvres complètes*, 2 vols, ed. C. Pichois, Paris: Gallimard.
Beckett, S. ([1952] 1980), *Waiting for Godot*, New York: Grove Press.
Benn, G. (1960–68), *Gesammelte Werke*, ed. D. Wellershoff, Wiesbaden: Limes.
The Bible. The Authorised King James Version with Apocrypha (1998), ed. R. Carroll and S. Prickett, Oxford: Oxford University Press.
Blake, W. (1989), *The Complete Poems*, ed. W. H. Stevenson, London: New York, Longman.
Braddon, M. E. ([1862] 1998), *Lady Audley's Secret*, ed. D. Skilton, Oxford: Oxford University Press.
Bright, T. (1586), *Treatise on Melancholy*, London: Thomas Vautrollier.
Brontë, C. ([1847] 2003), *Jane Eyre*, ed. M. Mason, London: Penguin.
Brooke, R. (1970), *The Poetical Works*, ed. G. Keynes, London: Faber and Faber.
Burton, R. ([1620] 1994), *The Anatomy of Melancholy*, ed. T. C. Faulkner, N. K. Kiessling and R. L. Blair, Oxford: Clarendon Press.
Byron, L. [G. Gordon] (1977), *Byron's Letters and Journals*, 13 vols, ed. L. A. Marchand, London: John Murray.
Byron, L. [G. Gordon] (1980–93), *The Complete Poetical Works*, 7 vols, ed. J. J. McGann, Oxford: Clarendon Press.
Byron, L. [G. Gordon] (1977), *Byron's Letters and Journals*, 13 vols, ed. L. A. Marchand, London: John Murray.
Carew, T. (1949), *The Poems of Thomas Carew*, ed. R. Dunlap, Oxford: Clarendon Press.
Castiglione, B. ([1560] 1974), *The Book of the Courtier*, trans. Sir T. Hoby, London: Dent.
Celan, P. (1971), *Speech-Grille and Selected Poems*, trans. J. Neugroschel, New York: E. P. Dutton and Co.
Chapman, G. (1970), *The Plays of George Chapman. The Comedies: A Critical Edition*, ed. A. Holaday and M. Kiernan, Chicago: University of Illinois Press.
Chapman, G. (1982), *The Revenger's Tragedy. Three Jacobean Tragedies*, ed. G. Salgado, Harmondsworth: Penguin.

Cleland, J. ([1748] 1986), *Memoirs of a Woman of Pleasure*, ed. P. Sabor, Oxford: Oxford University Press.
Coleridge, S. T. (1956), *Collected Letters of Samuel Taylor Coleridge*, ed. E. L. Griggs, 6 vols, Oxford: Clarendon Press.
Coleridge, S. T. (1957), *The Notebooks of Samuel Taylor Coleridge*, ed. K. Coburn, vol. 1 (1794–1804), New York: Pantheon Books.
Coleridge, S. T. (1990), *The Notebooks of Samuel Taylor Coleridge*, ed. K. Coburn and M. Christensen, vol. 4 (1819–26), London: Routledge.
Coleridge, S. T. (1997), *The Complete Poems*, ed. W. Keach, London: Penguin.
Crashaw, R. (1957), *The Poems, English, Latin and Greek of Richard Crashaw*, ed. L. C. Martin, Oxford: Clarendon Press.
Crooke, H. (1616), *Microcosmographia: A Description of the Body of Man*, London: W. Jaggard.
Dickens, C. ([1853] 1988), *Bleak House*, ed. N. Page, London: Penguin.
Dickens, C. ([1842] 2000), *American Notes*, ed. P. Ingham, London: Penguin.
Dickens, C. ([1838] 2003), *Oliver Twist*, ed. P. Horne, London: Penguin.
Dickens, C. ([1850] 2004), *David Copperfield*, ed. J. Tambling, London: Penguin.
Dickens, C. ([1848] 2008), *Dombey and Son*, ed. A. Horsman, Oxford: Oxford University Press.
Donne, J. (1979), *Poetical Works*, ed. H. J. C. Grierson, Oxford: Oxford University Press.
Dowson, E. (1962), *The Poems of Ernest Dowson*, ed. M. Longaker, Philadelphia: University of Pennsylvania Press.
Duffy, C. A. (2015), *Collected Poems*, London: Picador.
Eliot, T. S. (1963), *Collected Poems*, London: Faber and Faber.
Foucault, M. (1978), *The History of Sexuality*, vol. 1, *The Will to Knowledge*, trans. R. Hurley, London: Penguin.
Foucault, M. (1986), 'Of Other Spaces', trans. J. Miskowiec, *Diacritics* 16:22–27.
Fowles, J. (2004), *The French Lieutenant's Woman*, London: Vintage Books.
Galsworthy, J. (2008), *The Forsyte Saga*, ed. G. Harvey, Oxford: Oxford University Press.
Hardy, T. (1976), *The Complete Poems*, ed. J. Gibson, London: Macmillan.
Hardy, T. (1980), *The Collected Letters of Thomas Hardy*, ed. R. Little Purdy and M. Millgate, 7 vols, Oxford: Clarendon Press.
Hardy, T. ([1895] 1998), *Jude the Obscure*, ed. D. Taylor, London: Penguin.
Hardy, T. ([1891] 1998), *Tess of the d'Urbervilles*, ed. T. Dolin, London: Penguin.
Hazlitt, W. (1825), *The Spirit of the Age; or, Contemporary Portraits*, London: Henry Colburn.
Jarry, A. (1972), *Œuvres Complètes*, 2 vols, ed. M. Arrivé, Paris: Gallimard.
Jonson, B. (1932), *Ben Jonson*, ed. C. H. Herford and P. Simpson, Oxford: Clarendon Press.
Joyce, J. (1957), *Letters of James Joyce*, ed. S. Gilbert, London: Faber and Faber.
Joyce, J. (1966), *Letters of James Joyce*, ed. R. Ellmann, London: Faber and Faber.
Joyce, J. ([1922] 1998), *Ulysses*, ed. J. Johnson, Oxford: Oxford University Press.

Joyce, J. ([1915] 2000), *A Portrait of the Artist as a Young Man*, ed. J. Johnson, Oxford: Oxford University Press.
Keats, J. (1958), *The Letters of John Keats 1814-1821*, ed. H. E. Rollins, Cambridge MA: Harvard University Press.
Keats, J. (1972), *The Poems of John Keats*, ed. M. Allott, New York: W. W. Norton.
Keats, J. (1987), *The Complete Poems*, ed. J. Barnard, Harmondsworth: Penguin.
Lawrence, D. H. (1960), *Selected Literary Criticism*, ed. A. Beal, London: Heinemann.
Lawrence, D. H. (1991), *The Letters of D. H. Lawrence*, vol. 6, ed. J. T. Boulton and M. H. Boulton, Cambridge: Cambridge University Press.
Lawrence, D. H. ([1913] 1998), *Sons and Lovers*, ed. D. Trotter, Oxford: Oxford University Press.
Lawrence, D. H. (2002), *Complete Poems of D. H. Lawrence*, ed. D. Ellis, Ware: Wordsworth Editions Limited.
Lawrence, D. H. ([1928] 2006), *Lady Chatterley's Lover*, ed. M. Squires, London: Penguin.
Lawrence, D. H. (2006), *Late Essays and Articles*, ed. J. T. Boulton, Cambridge: Cambridge University Press.
Lewis, M. G. ([1796] 2008), *The Monk*, ed. H. Anderson, Oxford: Oxford University Press.
Lovelace, R. (1974), *Ben Jonson and the Cavalier Poets: Authoritative Texts and Criticism*, ed. H. Maclean, New York/London: W. W. Norton.
McEwan, I. (2016), *Nutshell*, London: Vintage.
Meredith, G. (1988), *Selected Poems*, ed. K. Hanley, Manchester: Carcanet.
Moore, G. ([1894] 1995), *Esther Waters*, ed. D. Skilton, Oxford: Oxford University Press.
Ovid (1916), *Metamorphoses*, Loeb Classical Library, vol. 1, trans. F. J. Miller, Cambridge MA: Harvard University Press.
Pater, W. ([1873] 1986), *The Renaissance: Studies in Art and Poetry*, ed. A. Phillips, Oxford: Oxford University Press.
Pepys, S. (1985), *The Shorter Pepys*, ed. R. Latham, London: Penguin.
Pope, A. (1966), *Poetical Works*, ed. H. Davies, Oxford: Oxford University Press.
Pound, E. (1938), *Culture*, Norfolk: New Directions.
Pound, E. (1986), *The Cantos*, London: Faber and Faber.
Radcliffe, A. ([1797] 2004), *The Italian, or the Confessional of the Black Penitents*, ed. R. Miles, London: Penguin.
Radcliffe, A. ([1794] 2008), *The Mysteries of Udolpho*, ed. B. Dobrée and T. Castle, Oxford: Oxford University Press.
Richardson, S. ([1740] 2001), *Pamela, or Virtue Rewarded*, ed. T. Keymer and A. Wakely, Oxford: Oxford University Press.
Rochester, Earl [J. Wilmot] (1994), *The Complete Works*, ed. F. H. Ellis, London: Penguin.
Rossetti, D. G. (1991), *Selected Poems and Translations*, ed. C. Wilmer, Manchester: Cacarnet.

Rossetti, C. (2008), *Poems and Prose*, ed. S. Humphries, Oxford: Oxford University Press.
Shakespeare, W. ([1604–05] 1997), *King Lear*, ed. R. A. Foakes, London: Thomas Nelson.
Shakespeare, W. ([1599] 2002), *Julius Caesar*, ed. D. Daniell, London: Thomson Learning.
Shakespeare, W. ([1594] 2004), *Titus Andronicus*, ed. J. Bate, London: Thomson Learning.
Shakespeare, W. ([1600] 2005), *King Henry 5*, ed. T. W. Craik, London: Thomson Learning.
Shakespeare, W. ([1606–07] 2006), *Antony and Cleopatra*, ed. J. Wilders, London: Thomson Learning.
Shakespeare, W. ([1600] 2006), *As You Like It*, ed. J. Dusinberre, London: Thomson Learning.
Shakespeare, W. ([1609] 2006), *Shakespeare's Sonnets*, ed. K. Duncan-Jones, London: Thomson Learning.
Shakespeare, W. ([1602] 2006), *Troilus and Cressida*, ed. D. Bevington, London: Thomson Learning.
Shakespeare, W. (2007), *Shakespeare's Poems*, ed. K. Duncan-Jones and H. R. Woudhuysen, London: Cengage Learning.
Shakespeare, W. ([1634] 2007), *The Two Noble Kinsmen*, ed. L. Potter, London: Thomson Learning.
Shakespeare, W. ([1597] 2009), *Richard 3*, ed. J. R. Siemon, London: Methuen.
Shakespeare, W. ([1596] 2010), *The Merchant of Venice*, ed. J. Drakakis, London: Methuen.
Shakespeare, W. ([1594] 2010), *The Taming of the Shrew*, ed. B. Hodgdon, London: Methuen.
Shakespeare, W. ([1595] 2012), *Romeo and Juliet*, ed. R. Weis, London: Methuen.
Shakespeare, W. ([1597] 2013), *Richard 2*, ed. C. R. Forker, London: Bloomsbury.
Shakespeare, W. ([1608] 2013), *Coriolanus*, ed. P. Holland, London: Bloomsbury.
Shakespeare, W. ([1606] 2015), *Macbeth*, ed. S. Clark and P. Mason, London: Bloomsbury.
Shakespeare, W. ([1604] 2016), *Othello*, ed. E. A. J. Honigmann, rev. A. Thompson, London: Bloomsbury.
Shakespeare, W. ([1601] 2019), *Hamlet*, ed. A. Thompson and N. Taylor, London: Bloomsbury.
Shakespeare, W. ([1609] 2017), *Cymbeline*, ed. V. Wayne, London: Bloomsbury.
Shakespeare, W. ([1611] 2017), *The Winter's Tale*, ed. J. Pitcher, London: Bloomsbury.
Shelley, M. ([1818] 1998), *Frankenstein, or the Modern Prometheus*, ed. M. K. Joseph, Oxford: Oxford University Press.
Shelley, P. B. (1986), *Poetical Works*, ed. T. Hutchinson, Oxford: Oxford University Press.
Stoker, B. ([1897] 2011), *Dracula*, ed. R. Luckhurst, Oxford: Oxford University Press.
Swift, J. ([1726] 2008), *Gulliver's Travels*, ed. C. Rawson, Oxford: Oxford University Press.
Swift, J. (1983), *The Complete Poems*, ed. P. Rogers, Harmondsworth: Penguin.

Swift, J. ([1704] 1986), *Tale of a Tub and Other Works*, ed. A. Ross and D. Woolley, Oxford: Oxford University Press.
Swinburne, A. C. (1982), *Selected Poems*, ed. L. M. Findlay, Manchester: Cacarnet.
Tennyson, A. L. (2009), *The Major Works*, ed. A. Roberts, Oxford: Oxford University Press.
Tennyson, F. (1891), *Daphne and Other Poems*, London: Macmillan and Co.
Topsell, E. ([1607] 1973), *The History of Four-Footed Beasts* (1607), Amsterdam: Da Capo Press.
Weininger, O. ([1903] 1975), *Sex and Character*, authorized translation from the sixth German edition, London: William Heinemann.
Wells, H. G. ([1909] 1993), *Ann Veronica*, ed. S. Hardy, London: J. M. Dent.
Wilde, O. (1990), *The Soul of Man and Prison Writings*, ed. I. Murray, Oxford: Oxford University Press.
Wilde, O. ([1891] 1998), *The Picture of Dorian Gray*, ed. I. Murray, Oxford: Oxford University Press.
Wilde, O. (1998), *Complete Poetry*, ed. I. Murray, Oxford: Oxford University Press.
Woolf, V. ([1928] 1993), *Orlando*, ed. B. Lyons and S. M. Gilbert, London: Penguin.
Woolf, V. ([1927] 2000), *To the Lighthouse*, ed. M. Drabble, Oxford: Oxford University Press.
Woolf, V. ([1925] 2000), *Mrs Dalloway*, ed. D. Bradshaw, Oxford: Oxford University Press.
Woolf, V. ([1919] 2009), *Night and Day*, ed. S. Raitt, Oxford: Oxford University Press.
Wordsworth, W. (1988), *Poetical Works*, ed. T. Hutchinson and E. de Sélincourt, Oxford: Oxford University Press.
Wordsworth, W. (2014), *Wordsworth's Poetry and Prose: Authoritative Texts/Criticism*, ed. N. Halmi, New York/London: W. W. Norton.
Yeats, W. B. (1955), *Autobiographies*, London: Macmillan.
Yeats, W. B. (1989), *Yeats's Poems*, ed. A. N. Jeffares, London: Macmillan.
Young, E. ([1742–45] 1989), *Night Thoughts*, ed. S. Cornford, Cambridge: Cambridge University Press.

Critical literature

Ackroyd, P. (2001), *London: The Biography*, London: Vintage.
Adams, J. E. (2008), 'Victorian Sexualities' in H. F. Tucker (ed.), *A Companion to Victorian Literature and Culture*, 125–38, Oxford: Blackwell.
Adams, R. M. (1962), 'Bad Taste in Metaphysical Poetry: Richard Crashaw and Dylan Thomas' in W. Keast (ed.), *Seventeenth-Century English Poetry: Modern Essays in Criticism*, London/New York: Oxford University Press.
Alexander, L. (2014), '"Hearts as Innocent as Hers": The Drowned Woman in Literature and Art' in L. Dickson and M. Romanets (eds.), *Beauty, Violence, Representation*, 67–85, New York/London: Routledge.

Anspaugh, K. (1994), 'Powers of Ordure: James Joyce and Excremental Vision(s)', *Mosaic* 27:73–100.

Armstrong, N. (2013), 'When Gender Meets Sexuality in the Victorian Novel' in D. David (ed.), *The Victorian Novel*, 170–92, Cambridge: Cambridge University Press.

Aydemir, M. (2011), 'Blood Brothers', *Thamyris/Intersecting* 22:161–82.

Bakhtin, M. (1968), *Rabelais and His World*, trans. H. Iswolsky, Cambridge MA/London: MIT Press.

Bale, A. (2019), 'Where Did Margery Kempe Cry?' in A. M. Scott and M. D. Barbezat (eds.), *Fluid Bodies and Bodily Fluids in Premodern Europe: Bodies, Blood, and Tears in Literature, Theology, and Art*, 15–30, Leeds: Arc Humanities Press.

Bate, J. (2009), *Soul of the Age: The Life, Mind, and World of William Shakespeare*, London: Penguin.

Bate, J. (2019), *How the Classics Made Shakespeare*, Princeton/Oxford: Princeton University Press.

Bate, J. (2020), *Radical Wordsworth: The Poet Who Changed the World*, London: William Collins.

Begnal, M. H. (1996), 'Molly Bloom and Lady Hester Stanhope' in R. B. Kershner (ed.), *Joyce and Popular Culture*, 64–73, Gainesville: University of Florida Press.

Benthien, C. (2002), *Skin: On the Cultural Border between Self and the World*, trans. T. Dunlap, New York: Columbia University Press.

Blackwell, M. (2003), '"It stood an object of terror and delight": Sublime Masculinity and the Aesthetics of Disproportion in John Cleland's *Memoirs of a Woman of Pleasure*', *Eighteenth-Century Novel* 3:39–63.

Blakemore, S. (1998), 'Matthew Lewis's Black Mass: Sexual, Religious Inversion in *The Monk*', *Studies in the Novel* 30:521–39.

Boone, J. A. (1992), 'Representing Interiority: Spaces of Sexuality in *Ulysses*' in R. M. B. Bosinelli, C. M. Vaglio and C. van Boheemen (eds.), *The Languages of Joyce* (Selected Papers from the 11th International James Joyce Symposium, Venice 1988), 69–84, Philadelphia/Amsterdam: John Benjamins Publishing Company.

Boone, J. A. (1993), 'Staging Sexuality: Repression, Representation, and "Interior" States in *Ulysses*' in S. S. Friedman (ed.), *Joyce: The Return of the Repressed*, 190–221, Ithaca/London: Cornell University Press.

Bourke, J. (2008), 'Sexual Violence, Marital Guidance, and Victorian Bodies: An Aesthesiology', *Victorian Studies* 50:419–36.

Bowen, Z. (2015), '*Lady Chatterley's Lover* and *Ulysses*' in M. J. Kochis and H. L. Lusty (eds.), *Modernists at Odds: Reconsidering Joyce and Lawrence*, 11–27, Gainesville: University of Florida Press.

Brayton, D. (2012), *Shakespeare's Ocean: An Ecocritical Exploration*, Charlottesville/London: University of Virginia Press.

Brewer, W. D. (2004), 'Transgendering in Matthew Lewis's *The Monk*', *Gothic Studies* 6:192–207.

Brewer's Dictionary of Phrase and Fable (1999), ed. A. Room, New York: Harper Resource.

Brienza, S. (1992), 'Krapping Out: Images of Flow and Elimination as Creation in Joyce and Beckett' in P. Carey and E. Jewinski (eds.), *Re: Joyce'n Beckett*, 117–46, New York: Fordham University Press.

Briggs, A. (2009), 'Why Leopold Bloom Menstruates' in M. Beija and A. Fogarty (eds.), *Bloomsday 100: Essays on Ulysses*, 41–61, Gainesville: University of Florida Press.

Bristow, J. and R. N. Mitchell (2015), *Oscar Wilde's Chatterton: Literary History, Romanticism and the Art of Forgery*, New Haven/London: Yale University Press.

Bronfen, E. (1992), *Over Her Dead Body: Death, Femininity and the Aesthetic*, Manchester: Manchester University Press.

Bruhm, S. (1995), 'Taking One to Know One: Oscar Wilde and Narcissism', *English Studies in Canada* 21:170–88.

Bruhn, S. (1994), *Gothic Bodies: The Politics of Pain in Romantic Fiction*, Philadelphia: University of Pennsylvania Press.

Burgess, A. (2019), *Flame into Being: The Life and Work of D. H. Lawrence*, Cambridge: Galileo.

Byatt, A. S. (1997), *Unruly Times. Wordsworth and Coleridge in Their Time*, London: Vintage.

Bynum, C. W. (1982), *Jesus as Mother: Studies in the Spirituality of the High Middle Ages*, Los Angeles: University of California Press.

Byrne, K. (2011), *Tuberculosis and the Victorian Literary Imagination*, Cambridge: Cambridge University Press.

Callaghan, M. (2017), *Shelley's Living Artistry: Letters, Poems, Plays*, Liverpool: Liverpool University Press.

Capp, B. (2014), '"Jesus Wept" but Did the Englishman? Masculinity and Emotion in Early Modern England', *Past and Present* 224:75–108.

Carpenter, M. W. (1991), '"Eat me, Drink me, Love me": The Consumable Female Body in Christina Rossetti's *Goblin Market*', *Victorian Poetry* 29:415–34.

Carter, P. (2007), 'Tears and the Man' in S. Knott and B. Taylor (eds.), *Women, Gender and Enlightenment*, 156–73, Basingstoke: Palgrave Macmillan.

Casagrande, P. C. (1994), '"Something More to be Said": Hardy's Creative Process and the Case of *Tess* and *Jude*' in C. P. C. Petit (ed.), *New Perspectives on Thomas Hardy*, 16–40, Basingstoke: Palgrave Macmillan.

Casaliggi, C. and P. Fermanis (2016), *Romanticism: A Literary and Cultural History*, London/New York: Routledge.

Cherniak, W. (1995), *Sexual Freedom in Restoration Literature*, Cambridge: Cambridge University Press.

Claridge, L. (1986), 'Tess: A Less than Pure Woman Ambivalently Presented', *Texas Studies in Literature and Language* 28:324–38.

Cochran, P. (2013), 'The Mainstream Juans and Byron's Juan' in P. Cochran (ed.), *Aspects of Byron's Don Juan*, 144–88, Newcastle: Cambridge Scholars.

Cohen, P. M. (1985), 'Christina Rossetti's "Goblin Market": A Paradigm for Nineteenth-Century Anorexia Nervosa', *University of Hartford Studies in Literature* 17:1–18.

Cohen, R. (1995), 'Tears (and Acting) in Shakespeare', *Journal of Dramatic Theory and Criticism* 10:21–30.

Cohen, W. A. (2005), 'Interiors: Sex and Body in Dickens', *Critical Survey* 17:5–19.

Connor, S. (2004), *The Book of Skin*, London: Reaktion Books.

Corcoran, M. G. (1995), 'Drawing Our Attention to Jarry, Duchamp and Joyce: The Manuscript/Art of William Anastasi', *James Joyce Quarterly* 32:659–71.

Covington, S. (2009), *Wounds, Flesh, and Metaphor in Seventeenth-Century England*, Basingstoke: Palgrave Macmillan.

Cowan, J. C. (2002), *D. H. Lawrence: Self and Sexuality*, Columbus: Ohio State University Press.

Craft, C. (1999), '"Kiss Me with Those Red Lips": Gender and Inversion in Bram Stoker's *Dracula*' in G. Byron (ed.), *New Casebooks: Dracula*, 93–118, London: Macmillan.

Csengei, I. (2012), *Sympathy, Sensibility and the Literature of Feeling in the Eighteenth Century*, Basingstoke: Palgrave Macmillan.

Dabhoiwala, F. (2012), *The Origins of Sex: A History of the First Sexual Revolution*, Oxford: Oxford University Press.

Danahay, M. A. (1994), 'Mirrors of Masculine Desire: Narcissus and Pygmalion in Victorian Representation', *Victorian Poetry* 32:35–53.

Davies, H. (2012), *Gender and Ventriloquism in Victorian and Neo-Victorian Fiction: Passionate Puppets*, Basingstoke: Palgrave Macmillan.

Dawson, G. (2010), *Darwin, Literature and Victorian Respectability*, Cambridge: Cambridge University Press.

DeLong, A. (2012), *Mesmerism, Medusa and the Muse: The Romantic Discourse of Spontaneous Creativity*, Lanham: Lexington.

Dijkstra, B. (1986), *Idols of Perversity: Fantasies of Feminine Evil in fin-de-siècle Culture*, Oxford: Oxford University Press.

Dixon, T. (2017), *Weeping Britannia: Portrait of a Nation in Tears*, Oxford: Oxford University Press.

Doherty, G. (1998), 'The Chatterley/Bolton Affair: The Freudian Path of Regression in *Lady Chatterley's Lover*', *Papers on Language and Literature (PLL)* 34:372–87.

Dolin, T. (1998), 'Notes' in T. Dolin (ed.), *Tess of the d'Urvervilles*, 399–461, London: Penguin.

Eagleton, T. (2005), *The English Novel: An Introduction*, Oxford: Blackwell Publishing.

El-Gabalawy, S. (1988), 'The Trend of Naturalism in Libertine Poetry of the Later English Renaissance', *Renaissance and Reformation* 24:35–44.

Elfenbein, A. (2004), 'Byron: Gender and Sexuality' in D. Bone (ed.), *The Cambridge Companion to Byron*, 56–73, Cambridge: Cambridge University Press.

Elias, N. (2000), *The Civilising Process: Sociogenetic and Psychogenetic Investigations*, trans. E. Jephcott, London/Oxford: Blackwell.

Elkins, J. (2001), *Pictures and Tears: A History of People Who Have Cried in Front of Paintings*, New York/London: Routledge.
Ellis, D. (2011), *D. H. Lawrence: Dying Game, 1922–1930*, Cambridge: Cambridge University Press.
Ellmann, R. ([1959] 1983), *James Joyce*, Oxford: Oxford University Press.
Ellmann, R. (1987), *Oscar Wilde*, London: Penguin.
Endo, P. (1999), 'Seeing Romantically in *Lamia*', *ELH* 66:111–28.
Esslin, M. (1983), *The Theatre of the Absurd*, Harmondsworth: Penguin.
Felski, R. (1995), *The Gender of Modernity*, Cambridge MA: Harvard University Press.
Fisher, B. (2000), *The Pataphysician's Library: An Exploration of Alfred Jarry's Livres Pairs*, Liverpool: Liverpool University Press.
Fisher, R. L. (2017), *The Topography of Tears*, New York: Bellevue Literary Press.
Fisher, W. (2018), '"Stray[ing] Lower Where the Pleasant Fountains Lie": Cunnilingus in *Venus and Adonis* and in English Culture, c. 1600–1700' in V. Traub (ed.), *Oxford Handbook of Shakespeare and Embodiment*, 333–46, Oxford: Oxford University Press.
Flanders, J. (2003), *The Victorian House*, London: Harper Perennial.
Folkenflik, R. (2009), 'Memoirs of a Woman of Pleasure and the Culture of Pornography', *The Eighteenth-Century Novel* 6/7:103–25.
Folkerth, W. (2002), *The Sound of Shakespeare*, London/New York: Routledge.
Franklin, C. (1990), '"Quiet cruising o'er the Ocean Woman": Byron's *Don Juan* and the Woman Question', *Studies in Romanticism* 29:603–31.
Frost, L. (2002), *Sex Drives: Fantasies of Fascism in Literary Modernism*, Ithaca/London: Cornell University Press.
Froula, C. (1996), *Modernism's Body: Sex, Culture, and Joyce*, New York: Columbia University Press.
Fulford, T. (2015), *Wordsworth's Poetry 1815–1845*, Philadelphia: University of Pennsylvania Press.
Furneaux, H. (2009), *Queer Dickens: Erotics, Families, Masculinities*, Oxford: Oxford University Press.
Gagnier, R. (2000), 'Productive, Reproductive and Consuming Bodies in Victorian Aesthetic Models' in A. Horner and A. Keane (eds.), *Body Matters: Feminism, Textuality, Corporeality*, 43–57, Manchester: Manchester University Press.
Garofalo, D. (2012), *Women, Love, and Commodity Culture in British Romanticism*, Farnham: Ashgate.
Garrington, A. (2013), *Haptic Modernism: Touch and the Tactile in Modernist Writing*, Edinburgh: Edinburgh University Press.
Gay, P. (2002), *Schnitzler's Century: The Making of Middle-Class Culture 1815–1914*, New York: W. W. Norton.
Gifford, D. (with R. J. Seidman) (1989), *Ulysses Annotated: Notes for James Joyce's Ulysses*, Los Angeles/Berkeley: University of California Press.
Gigante, D. (2005), *Taste: A Literary History*, Boston: Yale University Press.

Gilbert, P. K. (2019), *Victorian Skin: Surface, Self, History*, Ithaca/London: Cornell University Press.

Gilbert, S. M. and S. Gubar (1979), *The Madwoman in the Attic: The Woman Writer and the Nineteenth-Century Imagination*, New Haven/London: Yale University Press.

Gill, S. (1989), *William Wordsworth: A Life*, Oxford: Clarendon Press.

Gillis, C. (2013), 'James Joyce and the Masturbating Boy', *James Joyce Quarterly* 50:611–33.

Gittings, R. (1986), *John Keats*, Harmondsworth: Penguin.

Goldstein, D. B. (2020), 'Liquid *Macbeth*' in K. Curran (ed.), *Renaissance Personhood: Materiality, Taxonomy, Process*, 163–85, Edinburgh: Edinburgh University Press.

Gramich, K. (2001), 'Stripping Off the "Civilized Body": Lawrence's *nostalgie de la boue* in *Lady Chatterley's Lover*' in P. Poplawski (ed.), *Writing the Body in D. H. Lawrence: Essays on Language, Representation, and Sexuality*, 149–61, Westport CO/London: Greenwood Press.

Greenblatt, S. ([1980] 2005), *Renaissance Self-Fashioning: From More to Shakespeare*, London/Chicago: University of Chicago Press.

Greenblatt, S. (2005), *Will in the World: How Shakespeare Became Shakespeare*, New York/London: W. W. Norton.

Greenblatt, S. (2011), *The Swerve: How the World Became Modern*, New York/London: W. W. Norton.

Guthke, K. S. (1999), *The Gender of Death: A Cultural History in Art and Literature*, Cambridge: Cambridge University Press.

Gwilliam, T. (1991), 'Pamela and the Duplicitous Body of Femininity', *Representations* 34:104–33.

Hager, K. (2010), *Dickens and the Rise of Divorce: The Failed-Marriage Plot and the Novel Tradition*, Farnham: Ashgate.

Hagstrum, J. (1980), *The Sister Arts: The Tradition of Literary Pictorialism and Poetry from Dryden to Gray*, London/Chicago: University of Chicago Press.

Hagstrum, J. (1985), *The Romantic Body: Love and Sexuality in Keats, Wordsworth and Blake*, Knoxville: University of Tennessee Press.

Halberstam, J. (1995), *Skin Shows: Gothic Horror and the Technology of Monsters*, Durham NC/London: Duke University Press.

Haley, B. (2003), *Living Forms: Romantics and the Monumental Figure*, New York: State University of New York Press.

Hanson, C. (2004), *A Cultural History of Pregnancy: Pregnancy, Medicine, Culture 1750–2000*, Basingstoke: Palgrave Macmillan.

Haraway, D. J. (2008), *When Species Meet*, London/Minneapolis: University of Minnesota Press.

Harrison, L. B. (1999), 'Bloodsucking Bloom: Vampirism as a Representation of Jewishness in *Ulysses*', *James Joyce Quarterly* 36:781–97.

Henke, S. (1991), 'Joyce's New Womanly Man: Sexual Signatures of Androgynous Transformation' in J. E. Dunleavy, M. J. Friedman and M. P. Gillespie (eds.), *Joycean*

Occasions: Essays from the Milwaukee James Joyce Conference, 46–58, Newark: University of Delaware Press.

Henkel, A. and A. Schöne, eds. (1996), *Emblemata: Handbuch zur Sinnbildkunst des XVI. und XVII. Jahrhunderts*, Stuttgart/Weimar: Metzler.

Heringman, N. (1998), '"Stones so wondrous Cheap"', *Studies in Romanticism* 37:43–62.

Herzog, D. (2005), *Sex after Fascism: Memory and Morality in Twentieth-Century Germany*, Princeton/Oxford: Princeton University Press.

Hewitt, A. (2016), 'Galatea in the Hintocks: Living Statues and Petrified Humans in the Work of Thomas Hardy', *Thomas Hardy Journal* 32:83–103.

Hochmann, B. (2001), *Getting at the Author: Reimagining Books and Reality in the Age of American Realism*, Amherst/Boston: University of Massachusetts Press.

Höfele, A. (2006), '*Bestiarum Humanum*: Lear's Animal Kingdom' in C. Jansohn (ed.), *German Shakespeare Studies at the Turn of the Twenty-First Century*, 84–98, Newark: University of Delaware Press.

Hollander, A. (1993), *Seeing Through Clothes*, Los Angeles/Berkeley: University of California Press.

Hollington, M. (2014), 'Dickens and the Commedia dell'arte' in N. Lennartz and D. Koch (eds.), *Texts, Contexts and Intertextuality: Dickens as a Reader*, 46–52, Göttingen: Vandenhoeck & Ruprecht.

Holmes, R. (1989), *Coleridge: Early Visions*, London: HarperCollins.

Holmes, R. (1998), *Coleridge: Darker Reflections*, London: HarperCollins.

Hopps, G. (2009), '"Eden's Door": The Porous Worlds of *Don Juan* and *Childe Harold's Pilgrimage*', *Byron Journal* 37:109–20.

Houghton, W. E. ([1957] 1985), *The Victorian Frame of Mind, 1830–1870*, New Haven/London: Yale University Press.

Humphries, S. (2008), 'Notes' in S. Humphries (ed.), *Christina Rossetti: Poems and Prose*, Oxford: Oxford University Press.

Ingersoll, E. G. (2015), 'The "Odd Couple" Constructing the "New Man": Bloom and Mellors' in M. J. Kochis and H. L. Lusty (eds.), *Modernists at Odds: Reconsidering Joyce and Lawrence*, 39–60, Gainesville: University of Florida Press.

Jalland, P. (1996), *Death in the Victorian Family*, Oxford: Oxford University Press.

Jarvis, C. (2016), *Exquisite Masochism: Marriage, Sex, and the Novel Form*, Baltimore: Johns Hopkins University Press.

Johnson, J. W. (2004), *A Profane Wit: The Life of John Wilmot, Earl of Rochester*, Rochester: University of Rochester Press.

Kaplan, F. (1987), *Sacred Tears: Sentimentality in Victorian Literature*, Princeton: Princeton University Press.

Khan, A., Tempest interview with Amandla Stenberg. https://thetempest.co/2015/10/31/entertainment/niobe-bringing-badass-girls-comics/ (accessed 1 June 2019).

Kibbie, A. L. (2019), *Transfusion: Blood and Sympathy in Nineteenth-Century Literary Imagination*, Charlottesville/London: University of Virginia Press.

Klimaszewski, M. (2006), 'Examining the Wet Nurse: Breasts, Power, and Penetration in Victorian England', *Women's Studies* 35:323–46.

Kneale, D. J. (1999), *Romantic Aversions: Aftermaths of Classicism in Wordsworth and Coleridge*, Montreal/Kingston: McGill-Queen's University Press.

Koschorke, A. (2008), 'Physiological Self-Regulation: The Eighteenth-Century Modernization of the Body', *Modern Language Notes* 23:469–84.

Kristeva, J. (1982), *Powers of Horror: An Essay on Abjection*, trans. L. S. Roudiez, New York: Columbia University Press.

Kubek, E. (2003), 'The Man Machine: Horror and the Phallus in *Memoirs of a Woman of Pleasure*' in P. S. Fowler and A. Jackson (eds.), *Launching 'Fanny Hill': Essays on the Novel and Its Influences*, 173–97, New York: AMS Press.

Kuchar, G. (2006), 'Andrew Marvell's Anamorphic Tears', *Studies in Philology* 103:345–81.

Kuchar, G. (2008), *The Poetry of Religious Sorrow in Early Modern England*, Cambridge: Cambridge University Press.

Ladenson, E. (2007), *Dirt for Art's Sake: Books on Trial from Madame Bovary to Lolita*, Ithaca/London: Cornell University Press.

Lange, M. E. (1996), *Telling Tears in the English Renaissance*, Leiden/New York: Brill.

Langland, E. (1995), *Nobody's Angels: Middle-Class Women and Domestic Ideology in Victorian Culture*, Ithaca/London: Cornell University Press.

Langley, E. (2009), *Narcissism and Suicide in Shakespeare and His Contemporaries*, Oxford: Oxford University Press.

Lansdown, R. (2018), 'A Marginal Interest? Byron and the Fine Arts' in N. Lennartz (ed.), *Byron and Marginality*, 271–90, Edinburgh: Edinburgh University Press.

Laqueur, T. (1990), *Making Sex: Body and Gender from the Greeks to Freud*, Cambridge MA: Harvard University Press.

Laqueur, T. (2003), *Solitary Sex: A Cultural History of Masturbation*, New York: Zone Books.

Lavers, M. (2013), '"To No End Gathered": Poetry and Urination in Joyce's Ulysses', *Joyce Studies Annual* 1:297–306.

Law, J. (2010), *The Social Life of Fluids: Blood, Milk and Water in the Victorian Novel*, Ithaca/London: Cornell University Press.

Leatherdale, C. (1985), *Dracula: The Novel & the Legend*, Wellingborough: The Aquarian Press.

Lennartz, N. (2009), 'Icarian Romanticism: On the Motif of Soaring and Falling in British Romantic Poetry', *Romanticism* 15:213–24.

Lennartz, N. (2009), *'My unwasht Muse': (De-) Konstruktionen der Erotik in der englischen Literatur des 17. Jahrhunderts*, Tübingen: Niemeyer/de Gruyter.

Lennartz, N. (2011), 'Porous Bodies in Romantic British Literature' in T. Morosetti and N. Lennartz (eds.), *Questione Romantica*, 3:55–67, Naples: Liguori Editore.

Lennartz, N. (2012), 'Dickens as a Modern Romantic: The Case of Edith Dombey in *Dombey and Son*' in F. Orestano and N. Lennartz (eds.), *Dickens's Signs, Readers' Designs: New Bearings in Dickens Criticism*, 105–25, Rome: Aracne.

Lennartz, N. (2014), 'Figurative Literalism: The Image of the Creator in Nineteenth-Century British Literature' in S. Prickett (ed.), *The Edinburgh Companion to the Bible and the Arts*, 521–33, Edinburgh: Edinburgh University Press.

Lindblad, I. (2013), 'Dickens in Sweden' in M. Hollington (ed.), *The Reception of Charles Dickens in Europe*, vol. 2, 430–45, London: Bloomsbury.

Looser, D. (2017), *The Making of Jane Austen*, Baltimore: Johns Hopkins University Press.

Lutz, D. (2006), *The Dangerous Lover: Gothic Villains, Byronism, and the Nineteenth-Century Seduction Narrative*, Columbus: Ohio State University Press.

Lutz, T. (2001), *Crying: The Natural and Cultural History of Tears*, New York/London: W. W. Norton.

MacCarthy, F. (2003), *Byron: Life and Legend*, London: Faber & Faber.

MacDonald, T. (2016), *The New Man, Masculinity and Marriage in the Victorian Novel*, New York/London: Routledge.

MacKenzie, N. I. and J. MacKenzie (1973), *The Time Traveller: The Life of H. G. Wells*, London: Weidenfels and Nicholson.

Maltzahn, N. von (2015), 'Rochester and the Satiric Underground' in M. C. Augustine and S. N. Zwicker (eds.), *Lord Rochester and the Restoration World*, 99–120, Cambridge: Cambridge University Press.

Mann, A. (2018), *Reading Contagion: The Hazards of Reading in the Age of Print*, Charlottesville/London: University of Virginia Press.

Marchand, L. A. (1987), *Byron: A Portrait*, London/Sydney: The Cresset Library.

Marcus, S. ([1966] 1985), *The Other Victorians: A Study of Sexuality and Pornography in Mid-Nineteenth-Century England*, New York/London: W. W. Norton.

Marsh, J. (1998), *Word Crimes: Blasphemy, Culture and Literature in Nineteenth-Century England*, Chicago: University of Chicago Press.

Martz, L. L. (2002), 'The Action of Grief in Herbert's "The Church"' in M. Swiss and D. Kent (eds.), *Speaking Grief in English Literary Culture: Shakespeare to Milton*, 119–35, Pittsburgh: Duquesne University Press.

Marwood, K. (2014), 'Imaginary Dimensions: Women, Surrealism and the Gothic' in M. Purves (ed.), *Women and Gothic*, 39–62, Newcastle: Cambridge Scholars.

Mason, D. (2008), *The Secret Vice: Masturbation in Victorian Fiction and Medical Culture*, Manchester: Manchester University Press.

Maynard, J. (1984), *Charlotte Brontë and Sexuality*, Cambridge: Cambridge University Press.

McColl, R. D. (2015), *Stirring Age: Scott, Byron and the Historical Romance*, Newcastle: Cambridge Scholars.

McEvoy, E. 'Introduction' in H. Anderson (ed.), *The Monk*, vii–xxx, Oxford: Oxford University Press.

Mehl, D. and C. Jansohn (2007), 'The Reception of D. H. Lawrence in German-Speaking Countries 1922–1945' in D. Mehl and C. Jansohn (eds.), *The Reception of D. H. Lawrence in Europe*, 23–52, London: Continuum.

Mellor, A. K. (1993), *Romanticism and Gender*, New York/London: Routledge.
Mengay, D. H. (1992), 'The Sodomitical Muse: Fanny Hill and the Rhetoric of Crossdressing', *Journal of Homosexuality* 23:185–98.
Menninghaus, W. (2003), *Disgust: Theory and History of a Strong Sensation*, trans. H. Eiland and J. Golb, New York: SUNY Press.
Michie, H. (1987), *The Flesh Made Word: Female Figures and Women's Bodies*, Oxford: Oxford University Press.
Michie, H. (2006), *Victorian Honeymoons: Journeys to the Conjugal*, Cambridge: Cambridge University Press.
Miller, E. (2006), 'Coitus Interruptus: Sex, Bram Stoker and *Dracula*', *Romanticism on the Net* 44, https://www.researchgate.net/publication/272718243_Coitus_Interruptus_Sex_Bram_Stoker_and_Dracula (accessed 11 November 2018).
Miller, W. I. (1997), *The Anatomy of Disgust*, Cambridge MA: Harvard University Press.
Millgate, M. (2004), *Thomas Hardy: A Biography Revisited*, Oxford: Oxford University Press.
Mills, D. (2016), '"Rankly digested, doth those things out-spue": John Donne, Bodily Fluids and the Metaphysical Abject' in N. K. Eschenbaum and B. Correll (eds.), *Disgust in Early Modern English Literature*, 183–99, London/New York: Routledge.
Mole, T. (2007), *Byron's Romantic Celebrity*, Basingstoke: Palgrave Macmillan.
Mole, T. (2017), *What the Victorians Made of Romanticism: Material Artifacts, Cultural Practices, and Reception History*, Princeton: Princeton University Press.
Morgan, S. (1989), *Sisters in Time: Imagining Gender in Nineteenth-Century British Fiction*, Oxford: Oxford University Press.
Muchembled, R. (1988), *L'invention de l'homme modern: Sensibilités, mœurs et comportements collectifs sous l'Ancien Régime*, Paris: Arthème Fayard.
Muchembled, R. (2008), *Orgasm and the West: A History of Pleasure from the Sixteenth Century to the Present*, trans. J. Birrell, Cambridge: Polity Press.
Mudge, B. K. (2000), *The Whore's Story: Women, Pornography, and the British Novel, 1684–1830*, Oxford: Oxford University Press.
Mudge, B. K. (2006), 'How to Do the History of Pornography' in R. C. Sha (ed.), *Historicising Romantic Sexuality*. https://romanticcircles.org/praxis/sexuality/mudge/mudge.html.(accessed 14 April 2019).
Mulvey-Roberts, M. (2005), 'Menstrual Misogyny and Taboo: The Medusa, Vampire and the Female Stigmatic' in A. Shail and G. Howie (eds.), *Menstruation: A Cultural History*, 149–61, Basingstoke: Palgrave Macmillan.
Mulvey-Roberts, M. (2018), *Dangerous Bodies: Historicising the Gothic Corporeal*, Manchester: Manchester University Press.
Munich, A. (1989), *Andromeda's Chains: Gender and Interpretation in Victorian Literature and Art*, New York: Columbia University Press.
Munich, A. (1996), *Queen Victoria's Secrets*, New York: Columbia University Press.
Najarian, J. (2002), *Victorian Keats: Manliness, Sexuality and Desire*, Basingstoke: Palgrave Macmillan.

Narayan, G. S. (2010), *Real and Imagined Women in British Romanticism*, Frankfurt/Berlin: Peter Lang.

Neu, J. (1987), 'A Tear Is an Intellectual Thing', *Representations* 19:35–61.

Norris, M. (2015), 'Love, Bodies, and Nature in *Lady Chatterley's Lover* and *Ulysses*' in M. J. Kochis and H. L. Lusty (eds.), *Modernists at Odds: Reconsidering Joyce and Lawrence*, 28–38, Gainesville: University Press of Florida.

Nussbaum, F. (1984), *The Brink of All We Hate: English Satires on Women, 1660–1750*, Lexington: University of Kentucky Press.

O'Donnell, P. (1992), *Echo Chambers: Figuring Voices in Modern Narrative*, Iowa: University of Iowa Press.

O'Malley, P. R. (2006), *Catholicism, Sexual Deviance, and Victorian Gothic Culture*, Cambridge: Cambridge University Press.

Otis, L. (1999), *Membranes: Metaphors of Invasion in Nineteenth-Century Literature*, Baltimore: Johns Hopkins University Press.

Page, J. W. (2015), 'Wordsworth on Gender and Sexuality' in R. Gravil and D. Robinson (eds.), *The Oxford Handbook of William Wordsworth*, 647–61, Oxford: Oxford University Press.

Parrish, P. (2002), 'Moderate Sorrow and Immoderate Tears' in M. Swiss and D. Kent (eds.), *Speaking Grief in English Literary Culture: Shakespeare to Milton*, 217–41, Pittsburgh: Duquesne University Press.

Paster, G. K. (1987), 'Leaky Vessels: The Incontinent Women of City Comedy', *Renaissance Drama* 18:43–65.

Paster, G. K. (1993), *The Body Embarrassed: Drama and the Disciplines of Shame in Early Modern England*, Ithaca/New York: Cornell University Press.

Peakman, J. (2004), *Lascivious Bodies: A Sexual History of the Eighteenth Century*, London: Atlantic Books.

Pease, A. (2000), *Modernism, Mass Culture and the Aesthetics of Obscenity*, Cambridge: Cambridge University Press.

Perelman, B. (1994), *The Trouble with Genius: Reading Pound, Joyce, Stein, Zukofsky*, Berkeley/Los Angeles: University of California Press.

Peterson, K. L. (2001), 'Fluid Economies: Portraying Shakespeare's Hysterics', *Mosaic* 34:35–59.

Peyré, Y. (2000), 'Niobe and the Nemean Lion: Reading *Hamlet* in the Light of Ovid's *Metamorphoses*' in A. B. Taylor (ed.), *Shakespeare's Ovid: The Metamorphoses in the Plays and Poems*, 126–34, Cambridge: Cambridge University Press.

Pfister, M. (1992), '"Man's Distinctive Mark": Paradoxical Distinctions between Man and His Bestial Other in Early Modern Texts' in E. Lehmann and B. Lenz (eds.), *Telling Stories: Studies in Honour of Ulrich Broich on the Occasion of His 60th Birthday*, 17–33, Amsterdam: Grüner.

Pigman, G. W. (1985), *Grief and English Renaissance Elegy*, Cambridge: Cambridge University Press.

Pincombe, M. (2001), *Elizabethan Humanism: Literature and Learning in the Later Sixteenth Century*, London/New York: Routledge.

Pinyaeva, E. (2016), 'Faustian Motifs and Transformations of Modern Myths in the Fictions of Oscar Wilde and Vernon Lee' in I. Grubica and Z. Beran (eds.), *The Fantastic of the Fin de Siècle*, 55–72, Newcastle: Cambridge Scholars.

Pöder, E. (1995), 'Molly *Is* Sexuality: The Weiningerian Definition of Woman in Joyce's *Ulysses*' in N. Harrowitz and B. Hyams (eds.), *Jews and Gender: Responses to Otto Weininger*, 227–35, Philadelphia: Temple University Press.

Poole, A. (2004), *Shakespeare and the Victorians*, London: Bloomsbury.

Porter, R. (1999), *The Greatest Benefit to Mankind: A Medical History of Humanity*, London/New York: W. W. Norton.

Porter, R. (2002), *Blood and Guts: A Short History of Medicine*, London: Penguin.

Porter, R. (2003), *Flesh in the Age of Reason: How the Enlightenment Transformed the Way We See Our Bodies and Souls*, London: Penguin.

Praz, M. (1979), *The Romantic Agony*, trans. A. Davidson, Oxford: Oxford University Press.

Preston, C. J. (2011), *Modernism's Mythic Pose: Gender, Genre, Solo Performance*, Oxford: Oxford University Press.

Pykett, L. (1993), 'Ruinous Bodies: Women and Sexuality in Hardy's Late Fiction', *Critical Survey* 5:157–66.

Raby, P. (2013), 'Poisoned by a Book: The Lethal Aura of *The Picture of Dorian Gray*' in K. Powell and P. Raby (eds.), *Oscar Wilde in Context*, Cambridge: Cambridge University Press.

Radford, A. (2002–03), 'The Making of a Goddess: Hardy, Lawrence and Persephone', *Connotations* 12:202–32.

Rees, G. (2011), *The Romance of Innocent Sexuality*, Eugene OR: Cascade.

Renk, K. W. (2008), 'Jane Eyre as Hunger Artist', *Women's Writing* 15:1–12.

Richardson, A. (2004), 'Romanticism and the Body', *Literature Compass* 1:1–14.

Richgels, R. W. (1994), 'Masculinity and Tears in 19th-Century Thinking: A Comparison of Novels in France and Britain', *Studies in Humanities* 2:134–46.

Richter, S. (2006), *Missing the Breast: Gender, Fantasy and the Body in the German Enlightenment*, Seattle/London: University of Washington Press.

Roe, N. (2012), *John Keats: A New Life*, New Haven/London: Yale University Press.

Roseman, E. B. (2003), *Unauthorized Pleasures: Accounts of Victorian Erotic Experience*, Ithaca/London: Cornell University Press.

Ruderman, J. (1984), *D. H. Lawrence and the Devouring Mother: The Search for a Patriarchal Ideal of Leadership*, Durham NC: Duke University Press.

Rummel, A. (2008), *'Delusive Beauty': Femmes fatales in English Romanticism*, Göttingen: Bonn University Press.

Sabine, M. (2007), 'Crashaw and Abjection: Reading the Unthinkable in His Devotional Verse', *American Imago* 63:423–43.

Sachdev, R. (2009), 'Of Paps and Dugs: Nursing Breasts in Shakespeare's England', *English Language Notes* 47:49–57.
Sage, V. (2005), '*Dracula* and the Codes of Victorian Pornography' in G. Menegaldo and D. Sipière (eds.), *Dracula: l'œuvre de Bram Stoker et le film de Francis F. Coppola*, 55–69, Paris: Ellipses.
Sandy, M. (2013), *Romanticism, Memory and Mourning*, Farnham: Ashgate.
Schaffner, A. K. (2012), *Modernism and Perversion: Sexual Deviance in Sexology and Literature, 1850–1930*, Basingstoke: Palgrave Macmillan.
Schulkins, R. (2014), *Keats, Modesty and Masturbation*, Farnham: Ashgate.
Sedgwick, E. K. (1991), 'Jane Austen and the Masturbating Girl', *Critical Inquiry* 17:818–37.
Sellers, J. (2005), 'Dracula's Band of the Hand: Suppressed Male Onanism', *English Language Notes* 43:148–59.
Senf, C. (2018), '*Dracula* and Women' in R. Luckhurst (ed.), *The Cambridge Companion to Dracula*, 114–22, Cambridge: Cambridge University Press.
Sha, R. C. (2009), *Perverse Romanticism: Aesthetics and Sexuality in Britain, 1750–1832*, Baltimore: Johns Hopkins University Press.
Shildrick, M. (1997), *Leaky Bodies and Boundaries: Feminism, Postmodernism, and (Bio) Ethics*, New York/London: Routledge.
Showalter, E. (1985), 'Representing Ophelia: Women, Madness, and the Responsibilities of Feminist Criticism' in P. Parker and G. Hartman (eds.), *Shakespeare and the Question of Theory*, 77–94, London: Methuen.
Showalter, E. (1990), *Sexual Anarchy: Gender and Culture at the Fin de Siècle*, London: Viking.
Silver, A. K. (2002), *Victorian Literature and the Anorexic Body*, Cambridge: Cambridge University Press.
Slater, M. (2009), *Charles Dickens*, New Haven/London: Yale University Press.
Spear, J. L. (1993), 'Gender and Sexual Dis-Ease in *Dracula*' in L. Davis (ed.), *Virginal Sexuality and Textuality in Victorian Literature*, 179–92, New York: State University of New York Press.
Stallybrass, P. and A. White (1986), *The Politics and Poetics of Transgression*, London: Methuen.
Stanton, L. K. (2014), *Shakespeare's 'Whores': Erotics, Politics, and Poetics*, Basingstoke: Palgrave Macmillan.
Stapleton, M. L. (2000), 'Aphra Behn, Libertine', *Restoration: Studies in English Literary Culture, 1660-1700* 24:75–97.
Staub, S. C. (2007), '"My throbbing heart shall rock you day and night": Shakespeare's Venus, Elizabeth, and Early Modern Constructions of Motherhood' in S. C. Staub (ed.), *The Literary Mother: Essays on Representations of Maternity and Child Care*, 15–31, Jefferson NC/London: McFarland and Company.
Stedman, G. (2002), *Stemming the Torrent: Expression and Control in the Victorian Discourses on Emotions, 1830-1872*, Farnham: Ashgate.

Stevenson, J. A. (1988), 'A Vampire in the Mirror: The Sexuality of *Dracula*', *PLMA* 103:139–49.
Stone, L. (1990), *The Family, Sex and Marriage in England 1500–1800*, London: Penguin.
Strong, R. (1998), *The Renaissance Garden in England*, London: Thames & Hudson.
Stubbs, J. (2017), *Jonathan Swift, the Reluctant Rebel*, London: Penguin.
Surridge, L. (2005), *Bleak Houses: Marital Violence in Victorian Fiction*, Athens OH: Ohio University Press.
Sweeney, A. R. (2006), *Robert Southwell: Snow in Arcadia/Redrawing the English Landscape, 1586–95*, Manchester: Manchester University Press.
Sweet, M. (2001), *Inventing the Victorians*, London: Faber and Faber.
Targoff, R. (2014), *Posthumous Love: Eros and Afterlife in Renaissance England*, Chicago/London: University of Chicago Press.
Theweleit, K. (1987), *Male Fantasies: Women, Floods, Bodies, History*, trans. Stephen Conway, Cambridge: Polity Press.
Thomson, H. (2017), 'Fanny Brawne and Other Women' in M. O'Neill (ed.), *Keats in Context*, 38–46, Cambridge: Cambridge University Press.
Thormählen, M. (1993), *Rochester: The Poems in Context*, Cambridge: Cambridge University Press.
Thorslev, P. L. (1962), *The Byronic Hero: Types and Prototypes*, Minneapolis: University of Minnesota Press.
Todd, J. (1999), *The Critical Fortunes of Aphra Behn*, Rochester: Camden House.
Toulalan, S. (2007), *Imagining Sex: Pornography and Bodies in Seventeenth-Century England*, Oxford: Oxford University Press.
Turner, J. G. (2003), *Schooling Sex: Libertine Liberation and Erotic Education in Italy, France and England, 1534–1685*, Oxford: Oxford University Press.
Tracy, R. (1990), 'Loving You All Ways: Vamps, Vampires, Necrophites and Necrophiles in Nineteenth-Century Fiction' in R. Barreca (ed.), *Sex and Death in Victorian Literature*, 32–59, London: Macmillan.
Tromly, F. B. (2002), 'Grief, Authority and the Resistance to Consolation in Shakespeare' in M. Swiss and D. Kent (eds.), *Speaking Grief in English Literary Culture: Shakespeare to Milton*, 20–41, Pittsburgh: Duquesne University Press.
Vaught, J. C. (2008), *Masculinity and Emotion in Early Modern Literature*, Farnham: Ashgate.
Vanhaesebrouck, K. and P. Dehert (2012), 'Introduction: Libertine Bodies or the Politics of Baroque Corporeality', *Journal for Early Modern Cultural Studies* 12:1–11.
Wahrman, D. (2004), *The Making of the Modern Self: Identity and Culture in Eighteenth-Century England*, New Haven/London: Yale University Press.
Wallbank, A. J. (2016), 'Coleridge's "Deep Romantic Chasm": Kubla Khan, the Valley of Rocks and the Geomorphological Imagination' in B. P. Robertson (ed.), *Romantic Sustainability: Endurance and the Natural World, 1780–1830*, Lanham: Lexington Books.

Weir, D. (1994), 'A Womb of His Own: Joyce's Sexual Aesthetics', *James Joyce Quarterly* 31:207–31.

Wells, S. (2012), *Shakespeare, Sex, and Love*, Oxford: Oxford University Press.

White, L. M. (2006–07), 'The Person from Porlock in "Kubla Khan" and Later Texts: Inspiration, Agency and Interruption', *Connotations* 16:172–93.

Williams, G. (1997), *A Glossary of Shakespeare's Sexual Language*, London: Athlone.

Williams, L. R. (1993), *Sex in the Head: Visions of Femininity and Film in D. H. Lawrence*, New York/London: Harvester Wheatsheaf.

Wilson, A. N. (2003), *The Victorians*, London: Arrow Books.

Wilson, A. N. (2005), *After the Victorian Age*, London: Arrow Books.

Wilson, D. B. (1993), *The Romantic Dream: Wordsworth and the Poetics of the Unconscious*, Lincoln NE/London: University of Nebraska Press.

Wiltshire, J. (1992), *Jane Austen and the Body: 'The Picture of Health'*, Cambridge: Cambridge University Press.

Wolfson, S. (2006), *Borderlines: The Shiftings of Gender in British Romanticism*, Stanford: Stanford University Press.

Wood, J. (2001), *Passion and Pathology in Victorian Fiction*, Oxford: Oxford University Press.

Worthen, J. (2014), *Wordsworth: A Critical Biography*, Oxford: Wiley-Blackwell.

Wright, A. (2002), 'European Disruptions of the Idealized Woman: Matthew Lewis's *The Monk* and the Marquis de Sade's *La Nouvelle Justine*' in A. Horner (ed.), *European Gothic: A Spirited Exchange 1760–1960*, 39–54, Manchester: Manchester University Press.

Wu, D. (2008), *William Hazlitt: The First Modern Man*, Oxford: Oxford University Press.

Wu, D. (2015), *30 Great Myths about the Romantics*, Oxford: Wiley-Blackwell.

Wuthnow, R. (2002), 'Reassembling the Civic Church in the Changing Role of Congregation of American Civil Society' in R. Madsen (ed.), *Meaning and Modernity: Religion, Polity and Self*, 163–80, Los Angeles: University of California Press.

Zwicker, S. N. (2015), 'Lord Rochester: A Life in Gossip' in M. C. Augustine and S. N. Zwicker (eds.), *Lord Rochester in the Restoration World*, 79–98, Cambridge: Cambridge University Press.

Index

abjection 4, 11, 12, 50, 87, 92, 93, 112, 189, 192, 201, 204, 205, 208
Absurd, Theatre of the 203, 232
Addison, J. *Cato: A Tragedy* 8
Aeschylus 159
Amis, K. 236
anthropology 2–3, 66
Aretino, P. 56
Argentini, G. 239–40
Arnold, M. 139, 142
    Hebraism and Hellenism 158, 178, 179, 212, 214, 215, 233, 234
Artaud, A. 202
Ascham, R. 26
Ashbee, H. S. 169
Austen, J. 127–9

Baden-Powell, R. S. S. 221
Bakhtin, M. 52, 141, 188. *See also* carnivalesque
    grotesque body concepts 35
    leaky vessel phenomenon 12
Barnes, J. 2
Baroque culture
    continental paintings 33
    openness concept 42–3
    porousness 5, 35, 37, 40, 45–9, 73, 83, 88, 97
Barthes, R. 4, 21
    Lover's Discourse, A 1
Bate, J. 11, 36
Bataille, G. 77
Baudelaire, C. 92, 103, 171, 191–2, 212, 223
Beckett, S. 233
    Waiting for Godot 197
Begnal, M. H. 206–7
Behn, A. 58, 74–6
Benn, G. 237
Bildungsroman 133–43
Blake, W. 111, 146

blood 1, 4, 16, 20, 28, 34, 38, 43–7, 51, 53, 54, 82, 83, 92–4, 102, 110, 132, 152, 153, 155, 157, 160, 175, 176, 178–9, 185, 213, 218, 231
    blood clot 219–21
    blood-letting 84, 188
    blood-shedding 97
    blood-sucking 160–70
    haemorrhage 107
    menstrual blood 1, 5, 8, 38, 68, 186
    transfusions 165, 174
Boethius 26
Boone, J. A. 205
Boucher, F. 70
Bowen, Z. 229
Braddon, M. E. *Lady Audley's Secret* 10
Braine, J. 236
breastfeeding 33, 144, 166, 215
breasts 17, 33, 46, 49, 55, 71, 78, 88, 89, 91, 131, 157, 169, 200, 210, 214. *See also* lactation
Brienza, S. 198, 207–8
Bright, T. 31
    Treatise of Melancholy, A. 28
Bronfen, E. 154
Brontë, C. *Jane Eyre (JE)* 133–43, 150
Brooke, A. 25
Brooke, R. 184, 229
Browning, R. 95, 191
Brummell, B. 11
Budgen, F. 201
Bunyan, J. *Pilgrim's Progress, The* 131–2, 134–5
Burgess, A. 211
Burns, R. 95
Burton, R. 111
Byrne, K. 215
Byron, Lord G. G. 139, 142, 148, 159, 184, 234
    Age of Bronze, The 115

Childe Harold's s Pilgrimage (CHP) 10, 16–17, 115–20, 123, 141, 240
  Don Juan (DJ) 17, 54, 57–9, 62, 64, 79, 114–15, 117–25, 127, 147, 181, 201, 210, 228, 236, 237
  Parisina 116
  porosity personification 11–12, 17
  tidal and porous 'affairs 115–25

Cano, A. *San Bernardo y la Virgen* (Saint Bernard and the Virgin) 49–50
Canova, A. 118
Carew, T.
  To my Friend G.N. from Wrest 54
  Rapture, A 56–7
Carey, P. *Chemistry of Tears, The* 8
Carlyle, T. 95, 124, 171
carnivalesque 13, 17, 20, 35, 56, 99, 141, 182, 185–9, 191, 193–5, 198, 204, 208, 209, 212, 218, 220, 229, 235, 238, 240
Carpenter, M. W. 132
Carus, F. A. *History of Psychology* 116
Castiglione, B. *Courtyer, The* 19–20
Cavalier Poetry 54–60, 121, 200, 236
Celan, P. 16, 182
  Engführung 15
  Porenbau 17, 182
  porosity concepts 16
Chain of Being 2, 22–7, 56, 61, 63–4, 99
Chapman, G. *Revenger's Tragedy, The* 22
Chatterton, T. 95
Cleland, J. 81–4
  Memoirs of a Woman of Pleasure (Fanny Hill) 81–6, 204
Cogan, T. *Haven of Health* 53
Cohen, W. 141
Coleridge, S. T. 93, 100–3
  Dejection. An Ode 104
  effusions 93, 102
  Kubla Khan 104–5, 108, 115, 132
  Rime of the Ancient Mariner, The 120
  riotous fountains 100–7
  Notebooks 102–3, 105
Congreve, W. 58
Connor, S. 137
Correggio 164
Courbet, G. *L'origine du monde* (The Origin of the World) 121–2

Cox, J. 109
Craft, C. 167
Crashaw, R. 40, 43, 47–51, 53
  Steps to the Temple 47
  Weeper, The 47–51
  ventriloquizing female martyrs 34, 50–1
Cromwell, O. 38
Crooke, H. *Microcosmographia* 52
Csengei, I. 79
culture of reticence 127, 232
Cunard, N. 214

Dabhoiwala, F. 87
dadaism 188, 194, 196, 208, 229
dandyism 11–13, 115, 148, 150, 153, 156, 171–9, 181, 184, 219–20, 234–6
Dante 3
Dawson, G. 193
Defoe, D. 158
Delacroix, E. 93
De Quincey, T. 108
Dibdin, T. 147
Dickens, C. 141–2, 146, 147, 237
  American Notes 147
  Bleak House (BH) 143–5, 151–2
  David Copperfield (DC) 133–43, 196
  Dombey and Son (DS) 143, 146–9
  Our Mutual Friend 166
Dijkstra, B. 148–9, 168
disgust 6, 65, 67, 73, 156, 198, 208, 211, 227, 231, 240
Dixon, T. 1–2, 8
Doherty, G. 227–8
Don Juan / Donjuanism 17, 54, 59, 62, 64, 79, 127, 147, 228, 229, 236, 237
Donne, J. 6, 36–44, 47–8, 51, 59, 64, 85, 145, 229, 238
  Extasie, The 59, 229, 238
  Holy Sonnet XIV 39–40, 47
  Nocturnall upon S. Lucies Day, Being the Shortest Day, A 42
  Twickenham Garden 40, 48
  Valediction: Forbidding Mourning, A 39–40
  Valediction: Of Weeping 41
Dowland, J. 46
Dowson, E. 106
Dryden, J. 63
Duchamp, M. 188

Duncan, I. 231
Durieux, T. 204

Eagleton, T. 127
eighteenth century literature
    gender roles 80, 82, 84–5
    homme machine 85, 89, 191–2
    libertinistic texts 75–6, 78
    stoniness 10
ejaculation 7, 41, 59, 84–5, 105, 170, 209
    ejaculatio praecox 58–60
Elfenbein, A. 123
Eliot, T. S. *Waste Land, The* 3, 155, 195, 205
Elkins, J. 1
Elyot, Sir T. *Castle of Helth, The* 7, 53
Etherege, G. *Man of Mode, The* 65
Evangelical austerity 77–8, 80, 148, 155, 211–12
excrements 21, 28, 29, 52, 67, 71, 73, 101, 187–8, 227

Fallopio, G. 29
female body. *See also* breasts; gigantic female bodies; lactation; milk; tears and bodily fluids
    eighteenth century literature 81, 83–4
    negation of female body 29–30, 36, 42, 62, 74
    Rochesterian vision 66, 71, 85, 125
female genitals 9, 29, 61–4, 67, 83, 115, 121, 123–4, 170, 203, 213. *See also* genital oozings
    pseudoscientific learning 29–30
female porousness 29, 67–8, 83, 209
    discovery of pores, the 21–5, 27, 29–32, 34, 36, 39–42, 44, 46–8, 53–64, 67–8, 70
    in Romanticism era 74–8, 81–4, 86–93, 100–1, 103, 106, 109, 111–16, 120–1, 123–5
Fielding, H. 76
Fisher, R.-L. *Topography of Tears, The* 1
Flanders, J. 215, 217
Flaubert, G. 2, 202, 216, 225
Foucault, M. 154, 232
Fowles, J. *French Lieutenant's Woman, The (FLW)* 233–5
Froula, C. 207
Fulford, T. 99
Fuseli, H. 104

Galsworthy, J. *Forsyte Saga, The* 238–9
Garofalo, D. 121
Gay, P. 14
Genêt, J. 204
genital oozings 8, 114–15, 123
Géricault, T. 120
Gerôme, J.-L. *Pygmalion et Galatée* (Pygmalion and Galatea) 128–9
Gifford, D. 207
Gigante, D. 101, 108
gigantic female bodies 17, 29, 63, 71, 91, 113, 228
Gilbert, S. M. 136
Gill, S. 93
Goethe, J. W. von 10, 94, 100, 124
    Faust 91, 202
    Sorrows of Young Werther, The 2, 9, 73, 82, 94, 116
Golding, A. 4–5
Goldstein, D. B. 19
Gorgon 143–8
Gosse, E. 215
Gothic novels 8, 11, 77, 86–9, 92, 96, 165–6
Gramich, K. 227
Greuze, J. B. *La cruche cassée* (The Broken Pitcher) 74, 75
Grundy, Mrs 150–3, 156, 159, 160, 184, 202, 209, 214, 224, 226, 227, 232, 238
Grundyism 14, 154, 160, 163, 169, 171, 172, 179, 181, 186, 196, 201, 204, 230, 232
Gubar, S. 136
Guthke, K. S. 23

Hagstrum, J. 113
Haley, B. 102
Haraway, D. 99
Hardy, T. 100, 148, 150, 152, 153, 155–62, 195, 237
    Jude the Obscure (JO) 156–61
    Return of the Native, The 155
    Tess of the d'Urbervilles (T) 146, 151–6, 172, 179
Hauptmann, G. 202
Hazlitt, W. 96, 97, 118
Henke, S. 194–5, 202
Herbert, G. 47, 64
Hewitt, A. 155
Hoby, Sir T. *Courtyer, The* 19

Hochmann, B. 15
Hollander, A. 77
Holmes, R. 101
Homer 201
Hopkins, G. M. 17
Höppner, H. (Meister Fidus) 229
Hopps, G. 16–7
Horace, Satires 120
Hutchinson, S. 103, 104
humours/bodily fluids 4, 6, 20, 68, 84. *See also* blood
    black/yellow bile 4, 20
    phlegm 4, 20, 23, 41, 73
Humphries, S. 131, 132
Hunt, W. H. 100
Huysmans, J.-K. 175, 206

Ibsen, H. 146, 159, 162
Ingres, A. D. 93

Jahn, F. L. (Turnvater) 229
Jarry, A. *Ubu Roi* 193–4, 202
Jones, S. A. 239
Jonson, B.
    Bartholomew Fair 99, 157
    Poetaster, The 53
Joyce, J. 12–13, 16, 17, 41
    Dubliners 217, 222
    Portrait of the Artist as a Young Man, A 199–200
    Ulysses (U) 12–13, 41, 181–5, 187, 188, 190–9, 201, 202, 210, 212–13, 225, 228–9
Joyce, S. 205

Kafka, F. 221
Keats, J. 10, 107–14, 176
    To Autumn 83, 112–14, 123
    Lamia 109–11, 138
    Ode on a Grecian Urn 11, 108–9
    Ode to a Nightingale 107–8
Kellogg, J. H. 221
Kempe, M. 2
Khan, A. 239
Kingsley, C. 161
Kneale, D. J. 102
Kohut, H. 236
Krafft-Ebing, R. v. 130, 167, 202
Kristeva, J. 4, 51
Kuchar, G. 49

Lacan, J. 121
lactation 5, 49, 55, 144, 186, 197, 200. *See also* breastfeeding; breasts
Lamb, C. 98
Laqueur, T. 124, 133
Law, J. 143–4
Lawrence, D. H. 13–14, 182, 194–7, 200, 201, 209–27, 229, 232, 234, 235, 238, 239
    Deadly Victorians, The 182
    Lady Chatterley's Lover (LCL) 13, 182, 187, 196, 210–12, 216–29, 231, 233, 235, 236
    Medlars and Sorb Apples 211
    misogynist wrath 209–16
    Pornography and Obscenity 210, 220–1, 225
    puritanism 209–11, 214, 216, 221, 224, 229
    Sons and Lovers (SL) 212–17
    word-prudery 224–30
Leatherdale, C. 168
Le Brun, C. 97
Lee, C. 237
Lewis, M. G. *Monk, The (M)* 8, 86–9, 92–4
libertinistic texts 56–7, 76, 82, 113, 165
Lockhart, J. G. 114
Lovelace, R. 54–5, 89, 106, 200
Lutz, T. 1, 8–9, 73
Lyly, J. 26

Mackenzie, H. *Man of Feeling, The* 79
Magritte, R. *Le viol* (The Rape) 182–3
male porousness 2, 4–7, 9, 14, 20
    discovery of pores, the 22–5, 31, 36, 40, 47–8, 51, 53–4, 57–8, 63
    male Niobean fountains 43, 45, 60–2
    in Romanticism era 78, 82–5, 88–90, 106, 111, 114, 116, 119
Mallarmé, S. 15
Mann, T. 227, 228
Marcus, S. 232
Marinetti, T. 219
Marino, G. 47
Marsh, E. 211
Marsh, J. 237
Mary Magdalene 5, 10, 43, 46–50, 74, 97, 232, 238
masculinity 4–7, 14, 19, 22, 24–5, 27. *See also* male porousness

masturbation 9, 36, 56, 106–7, 114, 163
medical manuals 52–3
Medusa 91, 238, 239
Mellor, A. K. 101
Menninghaus, W. 82
menstruation 1, 8, 23, 50, 62, 152, 205, 215, 224. *See also* menstrual blood
Meredith, G. *Modern Love* 143, 145–6, 169
Metaphysical Poetry 6, 15, 35–47, 59, 231
La Mettrie, J. O. de, *homme machine* 81, 85, 89, 191
Meyer, S. 237
milk 5, 8, 23, 33, 48, 49, 55, 94, 106, 107, 153–4, 170, 185, 186, 200, 201, 213, 215, 236. *See also* lactation
Mill, J. S. 139
Miller, E. 163
Milton, J. 92, 101, 116
Mirandola, P. d. 26
Mole, T. 121
Moncrieff, T. W. 124
Morgan, S. 84, 127
Morton, T. 151
Moulton, T. *This Is the Myrrour or Glasse of Helth* 53
Mozart, W. A. 228
Muchembled, R. 227, 235
mucus 28, 148

Narcissus 12, 175, 176, 235, 236
Newton, I. *Opticks* 16
Nietzsche, F. 13, 227
Niobe/Niobean 3–6, 9–12, 19, 27, 48, 51, 67, 84, 114–18, 149, 152, 156, 174, 183, 224, 229, 231, 232, 235, 238–40. *See also* petrification
    body 7–8, 10–12, 165, 230, 234, 240
    fountains 28–35, 40, 43, 60, 62, 66–7
    grief 6, 71, 96, 101, 131, 152, 213
    porosity 6, 9, 26, 53, 88, 127
    in post-war 231–40
    sentimentalism 73–93
    stoicism 156–61
    tears 7, 21, 37, 74, 80, 108, 155, 163, 178, 189, 213
Norris, M. 225–6

O'Donnell, P. 198
Otis, L. 14
Ovid
    Amores 58
    Metamorphoses 3, 88, 137, 164, 191
    Ovide moralisé 3

Pandora 63, 65, 67, 71, 73, 238
Pater, W. 181
penis 29, 35, 56, 60, 65, 82, 84, 124, 127, 189, 207–8, 223–4
Pepys, S. 73, 103
perspiration. *See* sweat
Peterson, K. L. 23
petrification 3, 6, 10, 24, 67, 86, 99, 109, 117, 129, 133, 138, 139, 143, 148, 155, 182, 189, 195, 212, 221, 231, 238. *See also* stoniness
Pinney, A. 93
Pinter, H. 236
Poe, E. A. 166, 168
Polanski, R. 237
Pope, A. 8, 120
pornography 45–6, 55, 57–8, 63, 77–8, 81, 83–7, 89, 92, 115, 161, 165, 169, 192, 205, 210, 225–6
porousness
    Bloom and 201–9
    concept 15–16
    female 57–64, 66–71
    imaginary streams 4
    men's liquidity *vs.* female fountains 54–5, 60–2
    sentimentalism 8–10, 17
    Utopian and dystopian floods 51–7
Pound, E.
    Cantos, The 238
    Culture 193
Puritan fundamentalism 53–4
Pygmalion 12, 68, 110, 127–9, 133, 137, 143, 173, 174, 231, 238
    and Bildungsroman 133–43
    Goblin Market 127–33

Queen Victoria 193, 221, 232
Quixote Don/Quixotism 46, 65–7, 85, 158, 161, 229

Rabelais, F. 35, 71, 99, 157, 185, 188, 193–7, 211

Radcliffe, A.
  Italian, The 87
  Mysteries of Udolpho, The 94
Reni, G. *San Sebastian* (Saint Sebastian) 177–9
Restoration culture 7, 28, 37, 53, 57–8, 60, 63–6, 73–4, 76, 78, 80–2, 84, 176, 201, 206, 210
Richardson, S. *Pamela (PA)* 2, 73–4, 76–82, 86–7, 90–1, 100, 133, 154, 162–4, 182
Richgels, R. W. 135–6
Richthofen, F. von 210
Riefenstahl, L. 184
Rochester, J. W. Earl of 53
  on Enlightenment myth 63
  Imperfect Enjoyment, The 12, 58–61
  Metaphysicals' vocabulary 59–61
  modern courtier, concept 65
  Ramble in St James's Parke, A 61–3
  Satyr against Mankind 63–5
Roe, N. 109
Romanticism 11, 73–80
  male porousness 78, 82–5, 88–90, 106, 111, 114, 116, 119
  Niobean sentimentalism 73–80
Rossetti, C. *Goblin Market (GM)* 106, 127–33, 147, 153
Rossetti, D. G. 130, 181
Rossini, G. 189
Rousseau, J. J. 80, 100
Rowlandson, T. *Family on a Journey. Laying the Dust, A* 69

Sade, Marquis de 83
Sacher-Masoch, L. v. 202, 203
saliva 4, 28, 38, 148
Sartre, J. P. 108
Schiller, F. 2, 96, 137–8
Schulkins, R. 110
Sedgwick, E. K. 129, 193, 221. *See also* sphincter of the will
self-containment 35, 68, 69, 99, 118–20, 125, 128, 152, 158, 171–9, 198, 204, 212, 214, 215, 221, 239
semen 1, 36, 38, 124, 153, 209, 229
Senancour, E. P. *Obermann* 94
Senf, C. 163
sentimentalism 8, 10, 71, 76, 84–6, 99, 115–16

seventeenth century litrature
  discovery of pores 6–7
  femininity concepts 32
  medical, literary and philosophical discourses 51–2
  metaphysical convention 15, 38, 45
  metaphysical love mysticism 58–9
  mythologies and Christian narratives 51, 226
  quasi-pornography 63
Severn, J. 10
sexuality 61, 76, 82, 86, 88–9, 91, 105, 110–11
Shakespeare, W. 15, 23, 33, 35–48, 60, 67, 82, 103, 121, 152, 184, 191, 215, 237
  Antony and Cleopatra (AC) 26
  As You Like It (AYL) 218
  cultural conservatism 52
  Hamlet (H) 6, 12, 21–4, 36–7, 83, 119, 155–6, 171, 192, 213, 231
  Jacobean tragedies 21–2, 34–5, 91
  Julius Caesar (JC) 123, 151
  King Henry 5 (H5) 13, 24, 37
  King Lear (KL) 33–4, 36, 61
  Macbeth (Mac) 4, 6, 19, 33–5, 37, 89, 157–8, 193–4, 200, 203, 214, 234
  Merchant of Venice (MV) 1, 51
  Merry Wives of Windsor, The (MW) 35
  Othello (Oth) 34, 36, 62, 174
  portrayal of women 32–6, 38
  Rape of Lucrece (Luc) 45, 131
  Richard 2 (R2) 46, 100
  Richard 3 (R3) 21
  Romeo and Juliet (RJ) 22, 25–9, 39, 166, 191, 211
  Sonnets, The (Son) 31, 35, 60
  Taming of the Shrew, The (TS) 6, 32–3, 239
  Tempest, The (Tem) 120
  Titus Andronicus (Tit) 21
  Troilus and Cressida (TC) 192
  Venus and Adonis (VA) 31, 43–7, 55, 123
  Winter's Tale, The (WT) 25, 129
Sha, R. C. 124
Shaw, G. B. 138
Shelley, M. *Frankenstein* 138–9
Shelley, P. B. 146
  Adonais 114
  Cloud, The 117–8

Sheridan, R. B. 171
Showalter, E. 156
Silver, A. K. 130
Sitwell, E. 214
Slater, M. 141
slime 4, 62, 73, 140
Smollett, T. 133, 139
Song of Solomon 6, 30–1
Southey, R. 102
sphincter of the will 9, 12, 129, 131, 137, 141, 189, 193, 200, 204, 213, 221 232. *See also* Sedgwick, E. K.
Steele, R. 81
Steiner, R. 229
Stenberg, A. 239
Sterne, L. 196
stoicism 10, 13, 95, 115, 117, 150, 154–61, 182
Stoker, B. *Dracula (D)* 9, 12, 150, 161–70, 174–5, 181–2, 185, 236–7
stoniness 5, 10, 34, 39, 54, 133, 143, 147, 150, 155, 158, 213. *See also* petrification
Strachey, L. 229
Strindberg, A. 149, 202, 212
surrealism 105, 182, 196
sweat 1, 4, 8, 16, 20, 28, 37, 38, 44, 52, 78, 85, 99, 102, 144, 148, 168, 231, 234
Swift, J. 66–71, 125, 186
   Gulliver's Travels 66, 71
   Lady's Bedroom, The 226
   Strephon and Chloe 68–71
Swinburne, A. C. 162, 228

Tasso, T. 54, 56
tears and bodily fluids 1, 5, 11, 16, 17, 23, 28, 35, 40, 49, 62, 94, 98, 108, 117, 134, 146, 148, 149, 152, 154, 163, 165, 174, 218, 231. *See also* milk; vagina/vaginal fluids; vaginal eyes
   all-gender weeping 19, 20, 39, 41, 51, 73
   ban on/repressed tears 7, 8, 14, 118, 139, 148, 151, 152, 159, 236
   cathartic tears 155
   Christ's tears 38, 51
   creamy tears 34
   as cultural markers 1–18
   effeminizing tears 2, 6, 22, 26, 39, 43, 94–5, 116, 176

   excremental tears 4
   hyperbolic/torrential tears 3, 8, 38, 40, 42, 47, 48, 51, 73, 74, 79, 99, 104, 115–16, 119, 137, 142, 182, 183, 231, 232, 238
   ambivalent/deceptive tears 19–22, 27, 39, 48, 97, 127
   penitential tears 41, 54, 137, 179
   sentimental tears 73–80, 97, 208
   tears and blood 43, 45, 102
Tennyson, A. Lord 139, 142, 148, 159, 184, 234
Tennyson, F. 232
Thorslev, P. 116
Tillyard, E. M. W. 4
Tissot, S. A. 133
Tolstoy, L. N. 225
Topsell, E. *History of Four-Footed Beasts, The* 26
Toulalan, S. 81, 85

urine 1, 8, 16, 34, 37, 73, 185, 186, 205, 206

vagina/vaginal fluids 5, 8, 23, 29–31, 36, 59, 61–3, 75–6, 81, 84, 87, 89, 90, 109, 120–1, 123–4
vaginal eyes 7, 45, 77, 87, 109, 182
vampire 165, 172–4, 197
   agents of porosity 161–71
   dandyism 174–5, 178
   Darwinistic 160–1
Vaught, J. 20
Vesalius, A. 29
Victorian age 9–12, 14, 60, 79, 100, 104, 106, 110, 124–5
Vinci, L. da 29, 30

Wagner, R. 173
Waller, E. On St James's Park, As Lately Improved by His Majesty 61
Watteau, A. 70
Wedekind, F. 167
Weininger, O. *Sex and Character* 202–3
Wells, H. G. 138
Wilde, O. 11, 12, 138, 148, 167, 172, 176–9, 209, 219–20, 235, 237
   Ballad of Reading Gaol, The 178–9
   Burden of Itys, The 11
   Grave of Keats, The 176–7

Picture of Dorian Gray, The 12–13, 172–9
  porosity personification 11–12
  Sphinx, The 209
Williams, L. R. 211–12
Wolfson, S. 112, 118
Woolf, V.
  Night and Day 13
  Orlando 58
  To the Lighthouse 217
Wordsworth, W. 93–6
  anti-porous architecture 93–100
  Elegiac Verses. In Memory of My Brother, John Wordsworth 96
  epitaphs 96
  Excursion, The 99–100
  Last of the Flock, The 94–5
  London 97–8
  philosophic mind 101, 103
  Prelude, The (P) 96–8, 101, 141–2
  Resolution and Independence 95
  Ruined Cottage, The 100
  stony poetics 93, 97, 181
Worthen, J. 141
Wycherley, W. *Country Wife, The* 65

Yeats, W. B. 193

Zola, E. 167, 212

www.ingramcontent.com/pod-product-compliance
Lightning Source LLC
Chambersburg PA
CBHW062122300426
44115CB00012BA/1770